UNITED PRESS INTERNATIONAL

UPI STYLEBOOK and GUIDE TO NEWSWRITING

D1190849

UNITED PRESS INTERNATIONAL

UPI STYLEBOOK
and GUIDE TO
NEWSWRITING

FOURTH EDITION

Bruce Cook and Harold Martin
and the Editors of UPI

A UPI Book
Published by

CAPITAL BOOKS, INC.
Sterling, Virginia

Capital Books, Inc.
P.O. Box 605
Herndon, Virginia 20172-0605

Photo of Roger Bennett and his daughter Dory, page v.

ISBN 1-931868-58-1 (alk. paper)

Library of Congress Cataloging-in-Publication Data
UPI style book & guide to newswriting / Harold Martin and Bruce Cook & the editors of UPI.—4th ed.
    p. cm.
  ISBN 1-931868-58-1 (alk. paper)
  1. Journalism—Style manuals. I. Title: UPI stylebook and guide to newswriting. II. Title: United Press International stylebook & guide to newswriting III. Martin, Harold, 1938– IV. Cook, Bruce, 1939–
V. United Press International. VI. Title.
  PN4783.M47 2003
  808'.066'07—dc22

                                                              2003017094

Printed in the United States of America on acid-free paper that meets the American National Standards Institute Z39-48 Standard.

First Edition

10 9 8 7 6 5 4 3 2 1

To the late Roger Bennett, a UPI editor who demanded excellence and hounded style violators until they got it right. A typical message from Bennett on the company's internal wires in the 1990s:

> *arteriovenous* (one word) *malformation* is the same as *grand mal* when it comes to capitalization. These things are just names of medical conditions, like *coronary thrombosis* or *cirrhosis of the liver.* They're not some kind of formal title. About the only time you capitalize medical terms is when they're named after a particular person, such as *Down syndrome* or *Hodgkin's disease,* and then the second word is not capitalized. I realize this probably sounds picky and esoteric, but it's hard to expect people to take us seriously if we violate standard English usage.

CONTENTS

FOREWORD

This stylebook is designed to help UPI reporters, analysts and editors — and those who want to write like them — write clearly with uniform use of spellings, abbreviations, punctuation and syntax.

The foreword to the *UPI Stylebook* traditionally has begun with a quote from Mark Twain: "The difference between the almost-right word and the right word is . . . the difference between the lightningbug and the lightning." It also has included this slogan from International News Service, which merged with United Press Associations to form UPI in 1958: "Get it first, but first get it right."

The two concepts sum up the essence of UPI and of this book: to ensure that the words written by UPI reporters, analysts and editors clearly and accurately convey to the reader the intended information — with all of the power and nuance, strength and subtlety of meaning those words carry — to shed light on the important issues of the day.

Start with a commitment that the information be accurate and the presentation fair and balanced, with comment from all relevant sides — and then write clearly, using active voice. In general use short sentences that avoid complex clauses, but sometimes the flow of the piece will require longer sentences. Write for the ear, for how a story will sound as it's being read. It's helpful to read aloud, especially the first few paragraphs, to ensure they make sense and are clear.

Whether the writing is a news report, news analysis or commentary, the goal is for the piece to be interesting and compelling — for the reader to say, "Now I get it."

— Tobin Beck

Tobin Beck, executive editor, has been a reporter, editor and manager during his 25 years with UPI.

HISTORY OF UPI

Newspaper publisher E.W. Scripps founded the United Press in 1907 after he was denied service from the Associated Press because he was in competition with AP member newspapers. Determined that news should be available to anyone who wanted it, he combined three regional news services into the United Press Associations and set out to sell the service to anyone who would buy it.

Since that beginning, United Press and, later, United Press International have striven to provide news that is fair, balanced and accurate and to make it available to all who are willing to pay for it. In the early days this became a direct threat to the news service cartels, which divided the world into spheres of coverage, so that no agency, whether it was Havas, Wolff, Reuters or AP, would compete with another for news and clients.

To compete for foreign news, UP established two new principles in news agency operation. One was that a news organization could cover the world independently. The second was that newspapers anywhere could buy this news. Under the leadership of General Manager Roy Howard, UP became the first North American news agency to serve newspapers around the globe with its own news coverage. In addition, UP extended its reach outside the United States by establishing European bureaus to provide objective news coverage.

UP also broke new ground in news agency style and method. UP was the first service to emphasize the byline of the reporter writing the dispatch. It introduced big-name interviews and developed the feature story as an important part of the daily news report. In 1935, UP became the first news service to supply news to broadcasters. Ten years later UP started the first sports wire.

In 1952, United Press entered the newspictures field on a worldwide basis. By acquiring the Acme Newspictures photo agency from Scripps, UP became the first wire service to offer photos to go along with its stories. Thus, the news service began a tradition of excellence in photo-journalism that would result in seven Pulitzer prizes for photos. The aftermath of the Cuban revolution earned Andrew Lopez a Pulitzer in 1960, UPI's first for photography. The Vietnam War brought two more Pulitzers, for UPI photographers David Kennerly and Kyoichi Sawada.

The International News Service, founded in 1909 by media mogul William Randolph Hearst, merged with United Press to form United Press International in 1958. That year UPI began the first wire service radio network, providing radio stations with voice reports from correspondents all over the globe.

United Press and UPI have launched the careers of many who have become legends in the news industry and are proud to call themselves *Unipressers*. Well-known former Unipressers include Walter Cronkite, David Brinkley, Merriman Smith, Howard K. Smith, Eric Sevareid, Harrison Salisbury, Westbrook Pegler, Oscar Fraley, Raymond Clapper, William Shirer, Charles Collingwood and Helen Thomas.

The company has won three Pulitzers for news coverage. Russell Jones's coverage of the 1956 Hungarian Revolution won UP its first Pulitzer Prize for reporting. In 1963, UPI sent the world the first bulletin on the assassination of President John Kennedy when correspondent Merriman Smith grabbed the mobile radiophone in the motorcade's lead press car and dictated dispatches to UPI's Dallas bureau. He followed with a steady stream of reports from Parkland Hospital and later from Air Force One as Lyndon Johnson took the oath of office and flew back to Washington. Smith's coverage, which won the 1964 Pulitzer Prize for National Reporting, has been called the finest example of deadline reporting in the 20th century. UPI's 1970 series by Lucinda Franks and Tom Powers examining the life of Diana Oughton, a debutante turned radical who died in a bomb blast, won a Pulitzer in 1971.

UPI has been a consistent innovator in the news industry. The company began using newsroom computers in 1968 and developed its own portable, compact photo transmission system in the early 1970s. In 1982, the news service put into operation the industry's first method to let subscribers choose to receive copy by topic and subtopic rather than only by broad category of news. It has continued its leading role by being one of the first news agencies to adopt an international standard for coding and metadata tagging using the standards set by the International Press Telecommunications Council, as well as using the XML-based format envelope known as IPTC NewsML.

Since 2000, UPI has been owned by News World Communications Inc., a worldwide media group established by the Reverend Sun Myung Moon. Today, UPI continues its tradition of fair, accurate and balanced reporting of major news, with analysis and commentary to provide insight and understanding of the world's most pressing issues.

INTRODUCTION

U PI has been producing stylebooks for more than half a century. Hundreds of UPI editors and reporters contributed to the many revisions of the books.

Strictly speaking, stylebooks are written to ensure uniformity in spelling, abbreviations and punctuation — those matters in which writers have alternatives, but on which conformity must be reached. Over the years, stylebooks have been expanded to include rules of grammar, frequently misspelled words, misused terms, nomenclature and titles, and other entries that are not style matters at all, making the stylebook a quick all-purpose reference for reporters and editors in a hurry. Stylebooks also have been enlarged to include advice about another definition of style: the manner in which thoughts are transcribed in the written language, how the syntax flows.

In 1977, UPI and AP cooperated to produce a joint stylebook for newspapers. Bobby Ray Miller, a general news editor in New York, was UPI's lead editor on that project. In 1992, Robert McNeill, style editor in Washington, did a major revision.

The latest update is by Senior Editor Bruce Cook and has been incorporated into the company's computer system so it is available on-screen for the UPI staff. The new book includes dozens of computer and Internet terms. A special section of the book, produced and edited by Special Projects Editor Harold H. Martin, features reporting, editing, writing on various subjects and an inside look at how UPI reporters and photographers do their jobs — from sports to the White House. There are also sections on libel and codes of ethics. It is an informative, and at times amusing, look at our profession.

GUIDE TO USAGE

AUTHORITIES

This stylebook's primary reference source is *Webster's New World College Dictionary.* The main source for computer terms is *Webster's New World Computer Dictionary.*

ARRANGEMENT OF ENTRIES

Main entries and their cross-references are boldfaced:

Examples:

> **alley** Do not abbreviate. See **addresses.**
>
> **download** Transfer a file from another computer to your computer. See **upload** and **FTP.**

MAIN ENTRIES IN PARENTHESES

Some main entries are enclosed in parentheses to indicate either an incorrect spelling or that some restriction is placed on usage:

Examples:

> **(seige)** Spell it *siege.*
>
> **(Near East)** Use *Middle East* instead.

SPELLING

Some main entries are listed only for spelling or style, without further comment.

Examples:

baccalaureate
minivan

Some include comments for emphasis.
Examples:

accommodate Two *c*'s, two *m*'s.
implausible Not *implausable.*

LABELS

Part-of-speech labels are provided in parentheses for some main entries:
Example:

zero (s.), **zeros** (pl.) Not *zeroes.*

Abbreviations used: *adj.,* adjective; *v.,* verb; *adv.,* adverb; *n.,* noun; *pl.,* plural; *s.,* singular.

PUNCTUATION

Separate alphabetical entries treat many of the uses of punctuation, but there are many gray areas. For this reason, the punctuation entries are to be considered guidelines, not rules. But do not disregard the guidelines.

WORD SELECTION

In general, any word listed in *Webster's New World College Dictionary* may be used freely for the definitions given unless the dictionary or this stylebook restricts its use.

Derogatory words and profanities, obscenities, vulgarisms, etc., are to be used only if there is a compelling reason.

Words labeled *substandard, obsolete, old-fashioned, archaic, rare,* etc., should be used only if attempting to illustrate substandard speech.

Words labeled *slang* are not generally regarded as conventional, but are used, even by the best speakers, in highly informal contexts. Use them with caution.

Words labeled *colloquial* are simply informal. They are neither substandard nor illiterate and are acceptable in news stories if they fit the occasion.

PART I

The UPI Style Guide

A

AAA Although the travel service organization is no longer called the American Automobile Association, *automobile association* or *association* are acceptable on second reference. There are more than 1,000 AAA offices in the United States and Canada. Headquarters is in Heathrow, Fla.

A.A. The organization prefers *A.A.* to *AA.* See **Alcoholics Anonymous**.

AARP The official name of the organization previously known as the *American Association of Retired Persons.* The AARP, founded in 1958, is for people 50 and over. Headquarters is in Washington.

a, an Use *a* before consonant sounds: a historic event, a one-year term *(one* sounds like *won),* a united stand *(united* sounds like *yoo).*

Use *an* before vowel sounds: an energy crisis, an honorable man (the *h* is silent), an NBA record *(n* sounds like *en),* an 1890s celebration.

a- No hyphen: amoral, achromatic, atonal.

A&P Acceptable in all references for *Great Atlantic & Pacific Tea Co. Inc.* Headquarters is in Montvale, N.J.

abbreviations and acronyms A few universally recognized abbreviations are sometimes required. Others are acceptable, but in general avoid alphabet soup.

Apply the same guidelines to acronyms — pronounceable words formed from the letters in a series of words: Alcoa, NATO, radar, scuba, etc.

abbreviations and acronyms *continued*

Guidelines:

1. Use *Dr., Gov., Lt. Gov., Mr., Mrs., Rep., the Rev., Sen.,* and abbreviate certain military titles before a name outside direct quotations. In direct quotations, spell out all except *Mr., Mrs.* and *Dr.* before a name.

   Never abbreviate *president, vice president, secretary, attorney general, ambassador, chairman, professor.* See **titles**.

2. Abbreviate *junior* or *senior* after a person's name. Abbreviate *company, corporation, incorporated* and *limited* after a company name. See **company** and **academic degrees**.

3. Use *A.D., B.C., a.m., p.m., No.* and abbreviate certain months with the day of the month. See **months**.

   The abbreviations are correct only with figures: In *450 B.C.;* at *9:30 a.m.;* in room *No. 6;* on *Sept. 16.*

   > *Wrong:* Early this *a.m.* he asked for the *No.* of your room.
   > *Right:* Early this *morning* he asked for the *number* of your room.

4. Abbreviate *avenue, boulevard* and *street* in numbered addresses: He lives on Pennsylvania Avenue. He lives at 1600 Pennsylvania Ave. See **addresses**.

5. Certain states, the United States, European Union, United Kingdom, United Nations are sometimes abbreviated. See **states** and individual entries.

6. Some organizations are widely recognized by their initials: *CIA, FBI, GOP, TVA,* which are acceptable on first reference. Even then, an abbreviation is not always necessary. If it fits the occasion, use *Federal Bureau of Investigation,* for example, rather than *FBI.*

7. Do not use an abbreviation or acronym in parentheses after a full name. If the abbreviation would not be clear without this arrangement, do not use it. Do not reduce names to unfamiliar abbreviations solely to save a few words.

   At times an abbreviation or acronym requires special handling, especially if an English translation is needed.

   Examples, with suggested solution in italics:

   > The Federal Security Service, *known by its Russian initials FSB,* is a successor to the KGB.

> The Independent Moralizing Front, or *Frente Independiente Moralizador*, is headed by Fernando Olivero Vega. Six members of the *FIM* were . . .

If you must use an abbreviation or acronym but don't know the translation that fits the initials, or if it is too awkward to explain it with clarity, go ahead and put it in parentheses after the first mention of the organization. But avoid doing this if possible.

8. Acronyms need not be preceded by an article, since they are pronounceable: NASA announced Monday. But initials should be preceded by an article if the article is normally used with the spelled-out version: The EPA announced Monday.

9. Follow the listings in this book for capital letters and periods. For words not in this book, use the first-listed abbreviation in *Webster's New World College Dictionary.*

ABC Acceptable in all references for *American Broadcasting Cos.* The plural is part of the corporate name. Divisions include ABC News, ABC Radio and ABC-TV.

ABCs No apostrophe.

Abdullah King *Abdullah* of Jordan. Not *Abdallah.*

able-bodied

ABM (s.), **ABMs** (pl.) Acceptable in all references for *anti-ballistic missiles.* Avoid the redundant *ABM missiles.*

A-bomb

abortion Use *anti-abortion* to describe individuals or groups opposed to abortion: The anti-abortion group staged a peaceful demonstration.

Abortion-rights may be used for those in favor of legalized abortion, but use the term with care: Abortion-rights advocates supported the legislation.

Shun labels such as *pro-abortion, pro-choice, anti-choice.* The labels overgeneralize and are objectionable to some people, who, for instance, may favor abortion in some cases but object to it in others.

Where possible, be specific and state clearly what people propose or oppose.

Examples:

> The candidate *supported a woman's right to abortion.*

> *People opposed to the use of Medicaid funds for abortion* demonstrated outside the White House.

abortion *continued*

> *Women supporting the Supreme Court decision legalizing abortion assembled on the Capitol steps.*
>
> *Supporters of legal abortion* are backing the legislation.

(abortionist) Avoid this term, which is offensive to many and suggests illegality.

absent-minded The professor is *absent-minded*. An *absent-minded* professor.

absent without leave *AWOL* is acceptable on second reference.

Abu Sayyaf Not *Sayaff*. Islamic guerrilla group in the Philippines.

academic degrees If it is necessary to establish credentials, avoid an abbreviation. Make it: a *bachelor's degree*, a *master's* (note the apostrophe), a *doctorate* in psychology. Use *B.A., M.A., LL.D., Ph.D.,* etc., only when many listings would make the preferred form cumbersome. Use the abbreviation after a full name only (Mary Smith, Ph.D.) — never after just a last name.

  For spelling and abbreviations of academic degrees, follow the first listing in *Webster's New World College Dictionary.* See **doctor**.

academic departments Lowercase except for proper nouns or adjectives: department of history, history department, department of English, English department.

academic titles Capitalize and spell out such formal titles as *professor, dean, president, chancellor, chairman,* etc., before a name. Lowercase elsewhere.

  Lowercase such modifiers as *history* in history Professor Oscar Handlin, or *department* in department Chairman Jerome Wiesner.

academy See **military academies**.

Academy Awards Presented annually by the Academy of Motion Picture Arts and Sciences. Also: *the Oscars, the academy, the awards.*

accept, except *Accept* means *to receive; except* means *to exclude.*

accommodate Two *c*'s, two *m*'s.

according to Avoid this awkward attribution when possible. Use *said* or *announced,* etc.

accused One is accused *of,* not *with,* a crime. Avoid any suggestion that someone is being judged before a trial. Do not use: accused slayer John Jones. Make it: John Jones, accused of the slaying. See **allege, arrest** and **indict**.

Ace A trademark for an elastic bandage.

acknowledgment Not *acknowledgement.*

acoustics Usually with plural verbs and pronouns: The acoustics were not at their best. Use singular verbs and pronouns for the study: Acoustics is an exact science.

acre Equal to 43,560 square feet, or 4,840 square yards. The metric equivalent is 0.4 (two-fifths) of a hectare, or 4,047 square meters. To convert to hectares, multiply by 0.4 (5 acres × 0.4 equals 2 hectares).

acronyms See **abbreviations and acronyms**.

act Capitalize for legislation: the Taft-Hartley Act. See **act numbers**.

acting Always lowercase: acting Mayor Peter Barry.

act numbers Use Arabic numerals and capitalize: Act 1, Act 2, Scene 2. But: the first act, the second act.

actor (man), **actress** (woman)

Actors Equity Association Headquarters is in New York.

A.D. Acceptable in all references for *anno Domini:* in the year of the Lord.
Because the full phrase would read in the year of the Lord 96, place A.D. before the year: A.D. 96. Omit A.D. in: the fourth century (A.D.). If A.D. is not specified with a year, it is presumed to be A.D. See **B.C**.

adage *Old adage* is redundant.

-added The form: the *$50,000-added* sweepstakes, a *value-added* tax.

Addison's disease After Thomas Addison, an English physician who identified the disease caused by failure of the adrenal glands.

addresses Use *Ave., Blvd.* and *St.* with a numbered address: 1600 Pennsylvania Ave. Spell out without a number: Pennsylvania Avenue.
Lowercase standing alone or in plural uses: the avenue, Massachusetts and Pennsylvania avenues.
Do not abbreviate similar words, such as *alley, drive, road* and *terrace.* Capitalize as part of a formal name: Printers Alley. Lowercase standing alone or in plural uses: the alley, Broadway and Tin Pan alleys.
Use figures for an address number: 9 Morningside Circle.
Spell out and capitalize *First* through *Ninth* as street names; use figures with two letters for *10th* and above: 7 Fifth Ave., 100 21st St.
Abbreviate compass points that indicate directional ends of a street or quadrants of a city in a numbered address: 220 E. 42nd St., 600 K St. N.W. Do not abbreviate if the number is omitted: East 42nd Street, K Street Northwest.

ad-lib

administration Lowercase: the administration, the president's administration, the Eisenhower administration. If a news story clearly refers to the incumbent administration, it is not necessary to use the name of the president. See **government**.

administrative law judge A federal title formerly known as *hearing examiner.* To avoid a long title before a name, try to set if off with commas: The administrative law judge, Judy Williams, disagreed.

administrator Do not abbreviate. Capitalize as a formal title before a name.

admiral See **military titles**.

admissible Not *admissable.*

admit, admitted These words may in some contexts give the erroneous connotation of wrongdoing. A person who owns up to being old is *conceding* it or *acknowledging* it. A person who *announces* he is a homosexual may be *proclaiming* it, not admitting it. *Said* is usually sufficient.

ad nauseam To the point of disgust.

adopt Amendments, ordinances, resolutions and rules are *adopted* or *approved.* Bills are *passed.* Laws are *enacted.*

Adria Airways Slovenia's national airline. Headquarters is in Ljubljana, Slovenia.

Adventist See **Seventh-day Adventist Church**.

adverse, averse *Adverse* means *unfavorable; averse* means *reluctant* or *opposed:* He predicted adverse weather. She is averse to change.

adviser Not *advisor.* (This is an exception to *Webster's New World College Dictionary.*)

Aer Lingus Ireland's national airline. Headquarters is in Dublin. Aer Lingus is an anglicization of *Air Loingeas,* Irish for *air fleet.*

Aeroflot The Russian airline. Headquarters is in Moscow.

AeroMexico No space, capital *M.* Headquarters is in Mexico City.

aesthetic Not *esthetic.*

affect, effect *Affect,* as a verb, means *to influence:* The game will affect the standings. As a noun it is best avoided. It occasionally is used in psychology to describe an emotion, but there is no need for it in everyday language.

   Effect, as a verb, means *to cause:* He will effect many changes in the company. As a noun it means *result:* The effect was overwhelming. He miscalculated the effect of his actions. It was a law of little effect.

affidavit Not *affadavit.*

Afghan A native or inhabitant of Afghanistan. *Afghani* is the Afghan unit of currency.

afghan A crocheted blanket or shawl. But *Afghan hound.*

AFL-CIO Preferred in all references for the *American Federation of Labor and Congress of Industrial Organizations.* Headquarters is in Washington.

A-frame

African The peoples or languages of Africa. See **black** and **colored**.

African-American Always hyphenated. May be used interchangeably with *black* when referring to black Americans of African heritage. See **black**.

after- No hyphen to form a noun: aftereffect, afterthought. Hyphenate compound modifiers: after-dinner drink, after-theater snack.

afterward Not *afterwards*.

Agency for International Development *AID* is acceptable on second reference.

agenda A list. It takes singular verbs and pronouns: The agenda has run its course. The plural is *agendas*.

agent Lowercase unless a formal title before a name. In the FBI the formal title is *special agent*. Use agent John Jones, FBI agent John Jones or Special Agent John Jones as appropriate.

ages Always use figures. When the context does not require *years* or *years old*, the figure is presumed to be years. Avoid *aged* in designating age.

Hyphenate as a compound modifier before a noun or as a noun substitute. Use commas to set off the ages of individuals.

Examples: A *5-year-old* boy. The boy is *5 years old*. The *boy, 7,* has a *sister, 10*. The *woman, 26,* has a daughter *2 months old*. The law is *8 years old*. The race is for *3-year-olds*. The woman is in her *30s* (no apostrophe).

ages of history See **historical periods**.

aging Not *ageing*.

agnostic, atheist An *agnostic* believes it is impossible to know whether there is a God. An *atheist* believes there is no God.

aid, aide *Aid* is assistance; an *aide* is an assistant.

aide-de-camp (s.), **aides-de-camp** (pl.) A military officer who serves as an assistant to a superior.

AIDS Acceptable in all references for *acquired immune deficiency syndrome*. See **HIV**.

ain't A dialectical or substandard contraction. Avoid it.

air bag

air base Two words. Use *air force base* in the United States and *air base* abroad: Lackland Air Force Base, Texas; Clark Air Base, Philippines. On second reference: *the Air Force base, the air base or the base.*

Do not abbreviate, even in datelines:

LACKLAND AIR FORCE BASE, Texas, May 13 (UPI) —

CLARK AIR BASE, Philippines, May 13 (UPI) —

airbus

Air Canada Headquarters is in Montreal.

aircraft Use a hyphen to add figures to letters; no hyphen to add a letter to figures:

AC-130	FH-227	F-117A Nighthawk
B-1	F-14 Tomcat	L-1011
B-1B Lancer	F-15 Eagle	MiG-25
B-2 Spirit	F-16 Fighting	RC-135
B-52H	Falcon	Tu-144
BAC-111	F/A-18 Hornet	727-100C
C-5A	F/A-22 Raptor	747
C-130	F-86 Sabre	747B
DC-10	F-111	VC-10

An exception: Airbus A380.

For other elements of a name, follow the terminology adopted by the manufacturer or user. If in doubt, consult *Jane's All the World's Aircraft.*

Do not use quotation marks for aircraft names: Air Force One, the Spirit of St. Louis, Concorde. For plurals: DC-10s, 727s. But: 747B's. For sequence of aircraft, spacecraft and missiles, use Arabic numerals, but no hyphens: Apollo 13.

aircraft terms Use *engine,* not *motor,* for the units that propel aircraft: a twin-engine plane (not twin-engined).

Nearly all commercial and military aircraft are now jets, so the term *jet* is not routinely necessary. But when the term is used, make it *jet plane, jetliner, jet fighter, jet bomber,* etc., to describe only those aircraft driven solely by jet engines.

Do not flip-flop the adjective and noun and use *fighter jet* or *bomber jet.*

Use *turboprop* to describe an aircraft on which the jet engine is geared to a propeller. Turboprops are sometimes called *propjets.*

aircrew

airfield

air force Capitalize references to the U.S. Air Force: the U.S. Air Force, the Air Force, Air Force regulations. Do not use *USAF.*

Many nations do not use *air force* as a proper name. For consistency, lowercase all others: the Canadian air force. Exception: Capitalize *Royal Air Force* when referring to the *British air force. RAF* is acceptable on second reference.

An *air force* is a tactical unit of the U.S. Air Force, usually consisting of several divisions, each of which is composed of two or more wings. Capitalize a numbered air force: the *8th Air Force*. See **military units, military titles** and **wing**.

air force base See **air base**.

Air Force One The Air Force applies this name to whatever airplane the president of the United States happens to be using. In ordinary usage, however, Air Force One is the airplane normally reserved for the president's use.

airline (s.), **airlines** (pl.) Capitalize *airlines, air lines* or *airways* as part of a proper name. Note: Major airlines (and some smaller carriers) are listed separately.

Air France Headquarters is in Paris.

Air-India Use the hyphen. Headquarters is in Bombay.

Air Jamaica Headquarters is in Kingston.

air-launched cruise missile Also called an *ALCM,* it is carried beneath a bomber, launched in flight and guided to its target by an onboard computer.

airman See **military titles**.

Air National Guard

airport Capitalize as part of a proper name: La Guardia Airport, Newark International Airport.

The first name of a person and the word *international* may be deleted while the remainder is capitalized: John F. Kennedy International Airport, Kennedy International Airport or Kennedy Airport, as appropriate.

Do not make up proper names such as Boston Airport. The proper name is Logan International Airport. The Boston airport is acceptable.

airtight

airways The federal system of routes for airplane traffic.

aka No spaces or periods in this police term for *also known as.* (This is an exception to *Webster's New World College Dictionary,* which uses spacing.)

AK-47 A Soviet-designed rifle first produced in 1947, capable of full-automatic or semiautomatic fire. The initials stand for *automat* (automatic) *Kalashnikov* (the last name of the designer). The original design has been modified several times. For accuracy's sake, all models may be referred to as *Kalashnikovs.* Caliber is 7.62mm. See **weapons**.

Alabama Abbreviation: *Ala.* See **state(s)**

a la carte, a la king, a la mode

Alaska Do not abbreviate. See **state(s)**.

Alaska Airlines Headquarters is in Seattle.

Alaska Standard Time Used in all of Alaska, except St. Lawrence Island and the western Aleutians, which are on Hawaii-Aleutian Standard Time. There is an Alaska Daylight Time. See **time** and **Hawaii Standard Time**.

Alberta A province of western Canada. Do not abbreviate. In datelines: *EDMONTON, Alberta, May 13 (UPI)* —

albino (s.), **albinos** (pl.)

Albuquerque The city in New Mexico stands alone in datelines.

Alcoa Inc. *Alcoa* is acceptable in all references to the company formerly known as the *Aluminum Company of America.* Headquarters is in Pittsburgh.

Alcoa is also a city in Tennessee.

alcoholic Use *recovered,* not *reformed,* in referring to those previously afflicted with the disease of alcoholism.

Alcoholics Anonymous *A.A.* may be used on second reference. The organization for people recovering from alcoholism was founded in 1935. Following is the definition of A.A. appearing in its literature and cited frequently at meetings of A.A. groups:

> Alcoholics Anonymous is a fellowship of men and women who share their experience, strength and hope with each other that they may solve their common problem and help others to recover from alcoholism. The only requirement for membership is a desire to stop drinking.

alderman Do not abbreviate. See **legislative titles**.

Al Fatah A Palestinian guerrilla organization. Drop the article *Al* if preceded by an English article: the Fatah statement, a Fatah leader.

align

Alitalia Airlines Headquarters is in Rome.

all- Hyphenate: *all-around* (not *all-round), all-clear, all-out, all-star.*

all-America, all-American

allege The word must be used with great care.

Guidelines:

1. Avoid any suggestion that the writer is making an allegation.
2. Specify the source of an allegation. It should be an arrest record, an indictment or the statement of a public official connected with the case.
3. Use *alleged bribe,* etc., to make it clear that an unproved action is not being treated as fact.

4. Avoid redundant uses of *alleged.* It is proper to say: The district attorney *alleged* that she took a bribe. Or: The district attorney *accused* her of taking a bribe. But not: The district attorney *accused* her of *allegedly* taking a bribe.

5. Do not use *alleged* before an event known to have occurred when the dispute is over who participated in it. Do not say: He attended the *alleged meeting* when what you mean is: He *allegedly attended* the meeting.

6. Do not use *alleged* as a routine qualifier. Instead, use *apparent, ostensible, reputed,* etc.

See **accuse, arrest** and **indict**.

Allegheny Mountains Or simply: *the Alleghenies.*

alley Do not abbreviate. See **addresses**.

allies, allied Capitalize only when referring to the combination of the United States and its allies during World War I or World War II: The Allies defeated Germany. He was in the Allied invasion of France.

allot, allotted, allotting

all right Not *alright.* Hyphenate the slang: an all-right guy.

all-star Usually lowercase: Carter was an all-star catcher. Gretzky scored 25 points in 18 all-star games. Capitalize as part of the formal name of an event: the NHL All-Star Game.

all time, all-time An *all-time* high. But: The greatest runner of *all time.* Avoid the redundant *all-time record.*

allude, refer To *allude* to something is to speak of it without specifically mentioning it; to *refer* to something is to mention it directly.

allusion, illusion An *allusion* is an indirect reference; an *illusion* is an unreal or false impression: The allusion was to his opponent's war record. The director created the illusion of choppy seas.

alma mater

alpha test The initial test(ing) of new computer hardware or software. The second stage is *beta* testing.

al-Qaida

also-ran (n.)

altar, alter An *altar* is used in a church service; to *alter* is to change.

AltaVista An Internet search engine. See **search engine**.

alternately, alternatively *Alternately* means *one after the other; alternatively* means *one or the other.*

Altria Group Inc. Formerly *Philip Morris Companies Inc.* Holdings include the *Philip Morris* tobacco companies and *Kraft Foods.* Headquarters is in New York. (Note the single *l* in Philip Morris.)

Alzheimer's disease

AM Acceptable in all references for the *amplitude modulation* system of radio transmission.

a.m., p.m. Lowercase, with periods. Note: 10 a.m. this morning is redundant. In these designations, *m.* stands for *meridiem,* from the Latin meaning *noon.* Thus, *p.m.* means *post meridiem,* or *afternoon; a.m.* means *ante meridiem,* or *before noon.* Midday is designated by *noon,* not *12 noon* or *12 m.*

Amalgamated Transit Union Headquarters is in Washington.

ambassador Use for both men and women. Capitalize as a formal title before a name. Never abbreviate.

ambassador-at-large, ambassador extraordinary, ambassador plenipotentiary Capitalize as a formal title before a name: Ambassador-at-Large Averell Harriman, Ambassador Extraordinary John Jones.

Amber Alert A program in which news bulletins and electronic highway signs are used to alert the public in child-abduction cases. It is named for Amber Hagerman, a 9-year-old Texas girl who was abducted and killed in 1996.

amendments to the Constitution See **constitution**.

Ameriasian A person of both American and Asian descent.

American Airlines Headquarters is in Fort Worth, Texas.

American Baptist Association See **Baptist churches**.

American Baptist Churches in the U.S.A. See **Baptist churches**.

American Bar Association *ABA* is acceptable on second reference. Also: *the bar association, the association.* Headquarters is in Chicago.

American Civil Liberties Union *ACLU* is acceptable on second reference. Headquarters is in New York.

American Federation of Government Employees Use the full name on first reference to prevent confusion with other unions that represent government workers. Headquarters is in Washington.

American Federation of Musicians of the United States and Canada May be shortened to *American Federation of Musicians* on first reference. *Musicians union* is acceptable in subsequent references. Headquarters is in New York.

American Federation of State, County and Municipal Employees Use the full name on first reference to prevent confusion with other unions that represent government workers. Headquarters is in Washington.

American Federation of Teachers Use the full name on first reference to prevent confusion with other unions that represent teachers. Headquarters is in Washington.

American Federation of Television and Radio Artists *AFTRA* is acceptable on second reference. Headquarters is in New York.

American Hospital Association *AHA* is acceptable on second reference. Also: *the hospital association, the association.* Headquarters is in Chicago.

American International Group Inc. *AIG* is acceptable on second reference for the financial services and insurance company. Headquarters is in New York.

Americanisms Words and phrases that have become part of the English language as spoken in the United States are marked in *Webster's New World College Dictionary* with a star. They are acceptable in news stories if they fit the occasion.

American Legion Also: *the Legion, the Legionnaires.* A *legion* (lowercase) is a large group of soldiers, or by derivation, a large number: His friends are legion.

American Medical Association *AMA* is acceptable on second reference. Also: *the medical association, the association.* Headquarters is in Chicago.

American National Standards Institute. See **ANSI**.

(American Newspaper Publishers Association) The name was changed. See **Newspaper Association of America**.

American Petroleum Institute *API* is acceptable on second reference. Headquarters is in Washington.

American Postal Workers Union *Postal Workers union* is acceptable on second reference. This union represents clerks and similar employees who work inside post offices. Headquarters is in Washington. Use the full name on first reference to prevent confusion with the National Association of Letter Carriers.

American Press Institute *API* is acceptable on second reference. Headquarters is in Reston, Va.

American Society for the Prevention of Cruelty to Animals *ASPCA* is acceptable on second reference. Note that this organization, with *American* in its name, is limited to the five boroughs of New York. See **Society for the Prevention of Cruelty to Animals.**

American Society of Composers, Authors and Publishers *ASCAP* is acceptable on second reference.

American Standard Code for Information Interchange See **ASCII**.

American Stock Exchange In second reference: *the American Exchange, the Amex* or *the exchange.*

(American Telephone & Telegraph Co.) See **AT&T Corp.**

American Trans Air Headquarters is in Indianapolis.

America Online (AOL) The world's largest commercial online service. Headquarters is in Dulles, Va.

amid Not *amidst.*

amnesty See **pardon.**

amok Not *amuck.*

among, between Usually *between* relates two items; *among,* more than two: The money was divided among Ford, Carter and McCarthy.

But use *between* for three or more items related one pair at a time: Bargaining on the debate is under way between the network and the Ford, Carter and McCarthy committees.

ampersand (&) Use an ampersand if it is part of a company's proper name: Baltimore & Ohio Railroad, Newport News Shipbuilding & Drydock Co. Do not otherwise use the ampersand in place of *and.*

Amtrak This acronym, from *American travel by track,* is acceptable in all references to the *National Railroad Passenger Corp.* Headquarters is in Washington.

The corporation was established by Congress in 1970 to take over intercity passenger operations from railroads that wanted to drop passenger service. All except Southern Railway, Denver and Rio Grande Western Railroad, and the Chicago, Rock Island and Pacific Railroad elected to do so. See **Conrail.**

AMVETS Acceptable in all references for *American Veterans of World War II, Korea and Vietnam.* Headquarters is in Washington.

anchorman, anchorwoman Do not use *anchor* to refer to people in these jobs.

and-or, and/or Legalese that should be avoided when possible.

anemia, anemic

anesthetic

Anglican Communion The worldwide association of the 22 separate, independent national Anglican churches. Members include the Church of England, the Scottish Episcopal Church, the Anglican Church of Canada and, in the United States, the Episcopal Church. See **Episcopal Church.**

Anglo Always capitalized. Hyphenate with a capitalized suffix: Anglomania, Anglophile, Anglo-American, Anglo-Catholic, Anglo-Indian, Anglo-Saxon.

animals Do not apply a personal pronoun to an animal unless its sex has been established or the animal has a name:

The dog was scared; it barked.

Rover was scared; he barked.

The cat, which was scared, ran to *its* basket.

Susie the cat, *who* was scared, ran to *her* basket.

The bull tossed *his* horns.

Capitalize the name of a specific animal, and use Roman numerals to show sequence: **Bowser, Whirlaway II.**

For breed names, follow the spelling and capitalization in *Webster's New World College Dictionary.* For breeds not listed in the dictionary, capitalize words adopted or derived from proper nouns; use lowercase elsewhere: **Labrador retriever, basset** hound.

If a zoological name is used, capitalize the first word, the genus, but lowercase the second, the species: *Homo sapiens* (humans), *Ailuropoda malanoleuca* (giant panda).

annual meeting Lowercase in all uses.

anoint Not *annoint.*

ANSI *American National Standards Institute.* Pronounced *an'–see.* A United States technical standards organization of industry and university representatives. *ANSI* standards (in some computer programs) include those affecting graphics and color, cursor location, line-wrapping and keyboard functions.

antarctic, Antarctica, Antarctic Ocean

ante- Hyphenate with a capitalized word or to avoid a double *e:* ante-Victorian. Elsewhere, follow *Webster's New World College Dictionary,* hyphenating words not listed there.

anthems Lowercase *national anthem.* See **composition titles.**

anti- Hyphenate all except the following words

antibiotic	antiknock	antiseptic
antibody	antimatter	antiserum
anticlimax	antiparticle	antithesis
antidote	antipasto	antitoxin
antifreeze	antipathy	antitrust
antigen	antiperspirant	antitussive
antihistamine	antiphon	

Hyphenated words, many of them exceptions to *Webster's New World College Dictionary,* include:

anti-abortion	anti-inflation	anti-slavery
anti-aircraft	anti-intellectual	anti-social
anti-bias	anti-labor	anti-war

anticipate, expect *Anticipate* means *to expect and prepare for something;* *expect* does not include the notion of preparation: They expect a record crowd. They have anticipated it by adding more seats to the auditorium.

antitrust Federal laws to prevent restraint of trade and monopolies.

Antiochian Orthodox Christian Archdiocese of North America Formed in 1975 by the merger of the Antiochian Orthodox Christian Archdiocese of New York and All North America and the Antiochian Orthodox Archdiocese of Toledo, Ohio, and Dependencies in North America. It is under the jurisdiction of the patriarch of Antioch. See **Eastern Orthodox churches**.

anybody, any body, anyone, any one Use one word for an indefinite reference: Anyone can do that. Use two words to single out one element of a group: Any one of them may speak up.

any more, anymore *Any more* means *something additional:* Do you have any more money? I don't have have any more.

Anymore is an adverb meaning *now, at present* or *any longer:* He doesn't work here anymore. Don't do that anymore.

A-OK

AOL See **America Online**.

AP Acceptable on second reference for *The Associated Press.* Do not capitalize *the* when it precedes *AP.*

apostrophe (') Use an apostrophe to show possessives. See **possessives**. Elsewhere:

1. Use the apostrophe to show omitted letters or figures: I've, it's, don't, rock 'n' roll. 'Tis the season to be jolly. He is a ne'er-do-well. The class of '62. The Spirit of '76. The '20s.
2. Use the apostrophe to show the plurals of single letters, but not multiple letters: Mind your p's and q's. He learned the three R's and brought home a report card with four A's and two B's. But: She learned her ABCs. See **plurals**.

Appalachia In the broadest sense, it is the entire region along the Appalachian Mountains from Maine to northern Alabama. In a stricter sense, it refers to those sections characterized by economic depression and poverty.

Appalachian Mountains Or simply: *the Appalachians.*

apparently Avoid an ambiguous usage.

> *Ambiguous:* He apparently killed himself. (Is he dead?)
> *Better:* He died, apparently a suicide.

appeals court See **U.S. Court of Appeals**.

Apple Computer Manufacturer of the Macintosh line of computers. Headquarters is in Cupertino, Calif.

appraise, apprise *Appraise* means *to set a price or estimate value; apprise* means *to inform or notify.*

approve See **adopt.**

April See **months.**

April Fools' Day

Aqua-Lung A trademark for an underwater breathing apparatus.

Arabic names Transliteration is difficult. One basic rule: Use a hyphen after *al-* or *el-* unless another style for a particular name or place has been established: Yousef al-Ahmad, Saud al-Faisal, Sharm el-Sheik resort, al-Sujoud presidential palace, crossing the Shatt al-Arab, al-Qaida, al-Jazeera correspondents, etc.

The word *al* means *the.* It is part of a person's name when referring to tribal origins but may be dropped in many cases. For example, in the Masri family: Rabihya Masri.

The naming system is done simply: The parents give a male child one name; the second name is the name of the father; the third, of the grandfather; and so on. But when you see *al-Saud,* it refers to the Saud tribal family. The family name is the last name — and may or may not be used in the name chosen for use in English — but this is the one to use on second reference if it is available: She said al-Saud was an avid reader.

Drop titles (*king, prince, sheik,* etc.) on second reference: Saud said (not Prince Saud said).

Avoid using *the* before *al-,* because you then have *the, the.* Recast sentences to get around this problem. Remove *al-* if a double *the* is unavoidable on second reference.

Further complicating the transliteration is the way *al* is pronounced, depending on the first letter of the name. In Arabic, *al-Saud* is pronounced *as-Saud'* and *al-Shabi* is *ash-Sha'–bi.* There are a number of letters that, if appearing after the word *al,* change its pronunciation. *Al* is used in Arabic as *the* in front of other nouns: *al-baite* (the home).

When *el* is used before a name in English, it is another way of transliterating the *al* sound. Usually when a name appears that way, it is because the person has chosen that spelling in English.

Abu means *father of* and *ibn* means *son of. Abu* is either part of a nickname given to a man because of a cause or jovial greeting (for example, *Abu Jihad* means *father of the struggle*) or a nickname that

Arabic names *continued*
uses the first son. If a man has only daughters, he occasionally will be nicknamed (by friends) using the eldest daughter's name. In some more conservative Arabic cultures, the latter is not done since it is considered improper. The word *ibn* can be used as part of the tribal name. *Ibn Saud* means *son of the Saud family.*

Arabic numerals The numerical figures *1, 2, 3, 4, 5, 6, 7, 8, 9* and *0.* In general, use Arabic forms except for wars and for personal sequence for people or animals. See **numerals** and **Roman numerals**.

arbitrate, mediate These terms of labor negotiations are not interchangeable. One who *arbitrates* hears evidence from all persons concerned, then hands down a decision. One who *mediates* listens to arguments of both parties and tries by the exercise of reason or persuasion to bring them to an agreement.

arch- Hyphenate with a capitalized word: arch-Democrat. Otherwise, mostly solid: archbishop, archduke, archenemy, archfiend. Follow *Webster's New World College Dictionary,* hyphenating words not listed there.

archaeology

archaic

archbishop See **Episcopal Church** and **Roman Catholic Church**.

archbishop of Canterbury Lowercase *archbishop* unless it precedes the name of the person who holds the office.

archdiocese The diocese of an archbishop. Lowercase unless part of a proper name: the archdiocese of Chicago, the Chicago archdiocese. But: Anglican Orthodox Christian Archdiocese of North America. See entries for each denomination.

arctic, Arctic Circle, arctic fox, Arctic Ocean

are A surface measure in the metric system, equal to 100 square meters. An are is equal to about 1,076.4 square feet or 119.6 square yards.

area codes See **telephone numbers**.

argot Slang words and phrases used by people in the same occupation or way of life, sometimes with the intention to limit the meaning to those within their own ranks. See **slang, jargon**.

argument, arguments Either may be used: The court will hear arguments. Or: The court will hear argument.

Arizona Abbreviation: *Ariz.* See **state(s)**.

Arkansas Abbreviation: *Ark.* See **state(s)**.

Armenian Church of America The term encompasses two independent dioceses that cooperate in some activities: the Eastern Diocese of the

Armenian Church of America, for areas outside California, and the Western Diocese of the Armenian Church of America, which serves California. See **Eastern Orthodox churches**.

Armistice Day See **Veterans Day**.

army Capitalize references to the U.S. Army: the U.S. Army, the Army, Army regulations. Do not use the abbreviation *USA*.

Some nations do not use *army* as a proper name. For consistency, lowercase for all others: the Canadian army. Exception: Capitalize *Red Army* when referring to the Soviet army of World War II.

In the U.S. Army, a tactical *army* is composed of two or more *corps.* Two or more *armies* compose an *army group,* the largest tactical formation.

Capitalize with numerical designations: 3rd Army, 12th Army Group. Otherwise, lowercase: Patton's army, Bradley's army group. See **corps, military titles** and **military units**.

army worm

arrest To avoid any suggestion that someone is being judged before a trial, do not use arrested for killing, etc. Make it: arrested on a charge of killing. See **accuse, allege** and **indict**.

arrive It requires a preposition: He will arrive at Kennedy. Do not omit the preposition as some airline dispatchers do in: He will arrive (at) Kennedy.

art See **composition titles**.

arthroscopic surgery An operation performed with a fiber-optic instrument.

artifact

ASCII *American Standard Code for Information Interchange.* A computer character set that enables exchange of data among different computer devices. ASCII is pronounced *ass'–kee. ASCII files* are sometimes referred to as *text files* and are the opposite of *binary files.* See **binary files**.

ashcan, ashtray

Asian, Asiatic Use *Asian* or *Asians* when referring to people. Some Asians regard *Asiatic* as offensive when applied to people.

Asian flu

aspirin Formerly a trademark, now a generic term.

assassin The killer of a politically important person. See **homicide**.

assassination, date of A politically important person is shot one day and dies the next. Which day was he assassinated? The day he was shot.

assault, battery Popularly, *assault* almost always implies physical contact and sudden, intense violence. In legal terms, however, an *assault* means simply *to threaten violence,* as by pointing a pistol at someone without firing it. *Assault and battery* is the legal term for physical harm or violence.

assault rifle See **weapons**.

assembly Capitalize as the proper name of a legislative body, with or without a state name: the California Assembly, the state Assembly. Lowercase plural uses: the California and New York assemblies.

assemblyman, assemblywoman Do not abbreviate. See **legislative titles**.

assistant Do not abbreviate. Lowercase as a job description: The typist is *assistant secretary* John Jones. Capitalize as part of a formal title before a name: Assistant Secretary of State Geoff Connor.

associate Do not abbreviate. Capitalize only when part of a formal title before a name: Associate Editor Allison Smith.

Associated Press, The The capitalized article is part of the formal name of the newsgathering cooperative. *AP* or *the AP* (lowercase *the*) is acceptable on second reference. Headquarters is in New York.

association Do not abbreviate. Capitalize only as part of a proper name: The American Medical Association is a doctors' association.

astronaut It is not a formal title. Do not capitalize: astronaut John Glenn.

AstroPlay, Astroturf Trademarks for artificial grass.

AT&T Corp. Formerly known as *American Telephone & Telegraph.* Headquarters is in New York.

atheist See **agnostic, atheist**.

athlete's foot, athlete's heart

Atlanta The city in Georgia stands alone in datelines.

Atlantic Ocean

Atlantic Standard Time, Atlantic Daylight Time Used in the Maritime Provinces of Canada and in Puerto Rico. See **time**.

at large Usually two words for a person representing more than a single district: *congressman at large, councilman at large.* But it is *ambassador-at-large* for an ambassador assigned to no particular country.

ATM See **automated teller machine**.

Atomic Age It began Dec. 2, 1942, at the University of Chicago, with the creation of the first self-sustaining nuclear chain reaction.

Atomic Energy Commission See **Energy Research and Development Administration**.

at sign (@) Used in an e-mail address between the user's ID, or username, and the domain name: maryjones@wherever.com. See **domain name**.

attache Not a formal title. Always lowercase.

attorney A person legally appointed or empowered to act for another; usually, but not always, a lawyer. An *attorney at law* is a lawyer.

Do not abbreviate. Do not capitalize unless it is an officeholder's title before a name: defense attorney Perry Mason, attorney Perry Mason, District Attorney Hamilton Burger. See **lawyer**.

attorney general (s.), **attorneys general** (pl.) Do not abbreviate. Capitalize only as a title before a name: Attorney General John Jones.

augur Not *augur for.* Omit *for* in: The tea leaves augur (for) success.

August See **months**.

author Do not use as a verb.

> *Wrong:* He *authored* the book.
> *Right:* He *wrote* the book.

automaker (s.), **automakers** (pl.)

automatic See **weapons**.

automated teller machine *ATM* may be used on second reference. (It is redundant to say *ATM machine.*) Also *bank machine, cash machine.*

automobiles Capitalize brand names: Buick, Ford, MG, Maxima. Lowercase generic terms: a Volkswagen bus, a Mack truck.

autoworker (s.), **autoworkers** (pl.)

avant-garde, avant-gardism, avant-gardist

avenue See **addresses**.

average *Average* refers to the result obtained by dividing a sum by the number of quantities added together: the *average* of 7, 9, 17 is 33 divided by 3, or 11.

Mean commonly designates a figure intermediate between two extremes: the *mean* temperature of the day with a high of 56 and a low of 34 is 45.

Median is the middle number of points in a series arranged in order of size: the *median* grade in the group of 50, 55, 85, 88, 92 is 85; the *average* is 74.

Norm implies a standard of average performance for a given group: The child was below the *norm* for his age in reading comprehension.

average of It takes a plural verb in: An average of 100 jobs are lost daily.

averse See **adverse, averse**.

Avianca Headquarters of this airline is in Bogota.

aviator Use for both men and women. Do not use *aviatrix* even for those women who were commonly referred to as *aviatrixes* or *aviatrices* during their lifetimes.

avoid When an entry in this book uses the word *avoid,* it should not be considered a prohibition. It means *do not use unless you have a reason; try to find an alternate form.*

awards Capitalize them: Bronze Star, Medal of Honor, Best Actress, Song of the Year, Citizen of the Month, Most Valuable Player, etc.

awhile (adv.), **a while** (n.) He plans to stay awhile. He plans to stay for a while. A rule of thumb is to use the two-word form when preceded by a preposition.

awe-struck

ax Not *axe.* The verb forms: *ax, axed, axing.*

Axis The alliance of Germany, Italy and Japan during World War II.

Azores Not *Azore Islands.* The form in datelines: *PONTA DELGADA, Azores, March 16 (UPI) —*

Specify an individual island in the text if needed.

B

baby boomer

baby-sit, baby-sitting, baby sitter

baccalaureate

bachelor of arts, bachelor of science A *bachelor's degree* is acceptable in all references. See **academic degrees**.

backpack, backpacker

back up (v.), **backup** (n., adj.)

backward Not *backwards.*

back yard (n.), **backyard** (adj.)

bad, badly *Bad* is either an adjective or an adverb: It was a bad deal. They didn't know how bad off they were.

Badly is an adverb: I want it badly.

Use *I feel bad* if you mean your health is poor. Use *I feel badly* if you mean your sense of touch is deficient.

Baghdad The capital of Iraq stands alone in datelines.

Bahamas In datelines: *NASSAU, Bahamas, March 13 (UPI) —* In stories use *Bahamas, the Bahamas,* or *the Bahama Islands* as appropriate. Specify an individual island in the text if needed.

bail Acceptable in all references for *bail bond.*

bailout (n.), **bail out** (v.)

baker's dozen Thirteen items.

Bakery, Confectionery, Tobacco Workers and Grain Millers International Union Use *Bakery Workers union,* but explain in the story that the union also represents confectionery, tobacco and grain mill workers. Headquarters is in Washington.

balance of payments, balance of trade The *balance of payments* is the difference between the money that leaves a nation and the amount that enters it for all purposes — goods, services, travel, loans, foreign aid, etc. — during a specific period.

The *balance of trade* is the difference between the monetary value of the goods a nation imports and exports.

Example:

> The United States and its citizens might spend $20 billion abroad — $10 billion for goods, $6 billion for loans and foreign aid, $4 billion for tourism and other purposes.
>
> Other nations might spend $12 billion for U.S. goods, $4 billion for services and $2 billion for tourism and other purposes, a total of $18 billion.
>
> The United States then would have a *balance-of-payments* deficit of $2 billion, but a *balance-of-trade* surplus of $2 billion.

balance sheet A compilation of assets, liabilities and net worth showing the financial position of a company.

Balkans, Balkan States Countries on the Balkan Peninsula: Albania, Bosnia-Herzegovina, Bulgaria, Croatia, Greece, Macedonia, Romania, Slovenia, Serbia-Montenegro (formerly *Yugoslavia*) and the European part of Turkey.

ball boy, ballfield, ball game, ball joint, ballpark, ball-peen hammer, ball point pen, ballroom

baloney, bologna *Baloney* is foolish or exaggerated talk; *bologna* is sausage or luncheon meat.

Baltic states Estonia, Latvia and Lithuania — independent nations that regained their independence in 1991 after being forcibly absorbed by the Soviet Union in 1940.

Baltimore The city in Maryland stands alone in datelines.

bancassurance Lowercase and provide an explanation of this term, which refers to a combination of banking and insurance services.

Example: The chairman said bancassurance accounted for 20 percent of the bank's business. In its bancassurance program, the bank offers life insurance and other services and products usually sold by insurance companies.

Band-Aid A trademark for an adhesive bandage.

bandleader, bandstand, bandwagon

bandwidth The transmission capacity of an electronic communications channel.

Bangkok The capital of Thailand stands alone in datelines.

Bank of America Corp. Headquarters is in Charlotte, N.C.

bankruptcy Occurs when a federal court judges that a business or an individual has liabilities exceeding assets and is unable to pay debts. Law provides that the debtor's affairs be turned over to an impartial receiver or trustee who will administer and perhaps liquidate and distribute what assets remain.

   Bankruptcy may be voluntary, on petition of the debtor, or involuntary, at the behest of creditors. Voluntary bankruptcy, filed by the debtor under *Chapter 11* (business) or *Chapter 13* (individual) of the law, permits a reorganization while the debtor is protected from creditors. *Chapter 7* deals with liquidation.

baptism Always lowercase. See **sacraments**.

baptist, Baptist One who baptizes is a *baptist* (lowercase); a *Baptist* (uppercase) is a member of the Protestant denomination so named. But *John the Baptist* when referring to the apostle.

Baptist churches There are more than 20 Baptist bodies in the United States. The largest is the Southern Baptist Convention, with churches in every state, mostly in the South. The largest Northern body is American Baptist Churches USA.

   Blacks predominate in three other large Baptist bodies: the National Baptist Convention of America, the National Baptist Convention, U.S.A. Inc. and the Progressive National Baptist Convention Inc.

   Other Baptist bodies include the Baptist General Conference, the Conservative Baptist Association of America, the General Association of Regular Baptist Churches, the General Association of General Baptists and the North American Baptist General Conference.

   All members of the Baptist clergy may be referred to as *ministers*. *Pastor* may be substituted for the leader of a congregation. On first reference, use *the Rev.* before the full name of a minister. Drop the title on subsequent references.

barbiturate Not *barbituate.*

barmaid, barroom, bartender

bar mitzvah A Jewish religious ritual and family celebration marking a boy's 13th birthday, which Judaism regards as the benchmark of religious maturity. A similar ceremony for girls is the *bat mitzvah.*

baron, baroness See **nobility**.

baronet A man holding the lowest hereditary British title, below a baron but above a knight. A baronet may be addressed as *Sir.* See **honorary titles**.

barrel A standard barrel contains 31.5 gallons. In dealing with petro-leum, a barrel contains 42 gallons. See **oil**.

barrister See **lawyer**.

baseball The spelling of some common words and phrases:

backstop	double play	outfielder
ballclub	first baseman	passed ball
ballpark	foul ball	pinch-hit
ballplayer	foul line	pitchout
bullpen	ground-rule	RBI *(s., pl.)*
center field	double	shortstop
center fielder	home plate	shutout *(n., adj.)*
change-up	home run	shut out *(v.)*
(n., adj.)	left-hander	triple play
designated hitter	major league	twi-night
doubleheader	major-leaguer	doubleheader

Some sample uses of numbers: seventh-inning stretch, 10th inning, first base, one RBI, 10 RBI, the pitcher's record is 6-5, the final score was 1-0.

(-based) Avoid as an indicator of address.

> *Wrong:* George Will is a *Washington-based* columnist.
> *Right:* George Will is a *Washington* columnist.

BASIC Acronym for *Beginners All-Purpose Symbolic Instruction Code,* a computer programming language.

basketball The spelling of some common words and phrases:

backboard	free throw	jump shot
backcourt	full-court press	layup
baseline	goaltending	man-to-man
field goal	halftime	
foul line	hook shot	

Some sample uses of numbers: nine field goals, 10 field goals, the 6-foot-5 forward, the 6-10 center, he is 6 feet 10 inches tall, three-point shot.

battalion A military formation comprising two or more companies, usu-ally about 600–800 soldiers. Capitalize with a numbered battalion: the 3rd Battalion. Otherwise, lowercase: the battalion, the battalion com-mander. See **brigade** and **military units**.

battlefield, battlefront, battleground, battleship, *but* **battle station**

battery (military) In the U.S. Army, the basic unit of field artillery, comparable to an infantry company, and usually designated by a letter. Capitalize a specific battery: **C Battery.** Lowercase otherwise: **the battery, the battery commander.** See **military units.**

baud The rate of voltage or frequency change per second in a communications channel. *Baud* is often used to describe computer data transmission speed, although *bps (bits per second)* is technically more accurate. (The commonly used term *baud rate* is redundant, because baud is a rate.)

bay Capitalize only as an integral part of a proper name: **Hudson Bay, Chesapeake Bay.** But: **the bay, any bay.** Also: **San Francisco Bay** area or **the Bay area** as the popular name for the nine-county region that has San Francisco as its focal point.

bazaar, bizarre A *bazaar* is a marketplace or shopping quarter; *bizarre* means *very odd or grotesque.*

BBC Acceptable in all references for *British Broadcasting Corp.* See **British Broadcasting Corp.**

BB gun

B.C. Acceptable in all references to a calendar year in the period before Christ. Because the unabbreviated phrase would be **in the year 43 before Christ,** place B.C. after the year: **43 B.C.** See **A.D.**

bear market A time of declining stock prices.

Beijing The capital of China stands alone in datelines.

Belize Formerly *British Honduras.* In datelines: *BELMOPAN, Belize, Jan. 9 (UPI) —*

bellwether Not *bellweather.*

Belt Capitalize geographical designations: **Bible Belt, Sun Belt, Frost Belt, Corn Belt,** etc.

benefit, benefited, benefiting

Benelux Belgium, Netherlands and Luxembourg. If *Benelux* is used, explain it.

Ben-Gurion International Airport Note the hyphen. Located at Lod, Israel, near Tel Aviv.

Benzedrine A trademark for a pep pill.

Berlin Stands alone in datelines.

Berlin Wall On second reference: *the wall.*

Bermuda In datelines: *HAMILTON, Bermuda, Oct. 3 (UPI) —*

Bermuda grass, Bermuda shorts

beside, besides *Beside* means *at the side of; besides* means *in addition to.*

besiege Not *beseige.*

best-seller, best-selling

beta test See **alpha test**.

betting odds Use figures and a hyphen: The odds were 5-4. He won despite 3-2 odds against him. If *to* appears, hyphenate it in all constructions: 3-to-2 odds, odds of 3-to-2, the odds were 3-to-2.

bettor A person who bets.

between See **among, between**.

bi- Hyphenate only with a capitalized word or to avoid a double *i*.

biannual, biennial *Biannual* means *twice a year* and is a synonym for *semiannual; biennial* means *every two years*.

bibb lettuce Lowercase.

Bible Capitalize the book or its parts without quotation marks: the Bible, a Bible verse, the Old Testament, the New Testament, the Gospels. Lowercase as a non-religious term: My dictionary is my bible.

Do not abbreviate individual books of the Bible. To cite chapter and verse: Matthew 3:16, Luke 21:1-13, 1 Peter 2:1.

The books of the Old Testament, in order, are:

Genesis	2 Chronicles	Daniel
Exodus	Ezra	Hosea
Leviticus	Nehemiah	Joel
Numbers	Esther	Amos
Deuteronomy	Job	Obadiah
Joshua	Psalms	Jonah
Judges	Proverbs	Micah
Ruth	Ecclesiastes	Nahum
1 Samuel	Song of Solomon	Habakkuk
2 Samuel	Isaiah	Zephaniah
1 Kings	Jeremiah	Haggai
2 Kings	Lamentations	Zechariah
1 Chronicles	Ezekiel	Malachi

The books of the New Testament, in order, are:

Matthew	Ephesians	Hebrews
Mark	Philippians	Epistles of James
Luke	Colossians	1 Peter
John	1 Thessalonians	2 Peter
Acts	2 Thessalonians	1 John
Romans	1 Timothy	2 John
1 Corinthians	2 Timothy	3 John
2 Corinthians	Titus	Jude
Galatians	Philemon	Revelation

Bible Belt Those sections of the United States, especially in the South and Middle West, where fundamentalist religious beliefs prevail. Use with care, because in certain contexts it can give offense.

biblical Always lowercase.

big-bang theory The theory that the universe began with the explosion of a superdense primeval atom and has been expanding ever since.

The *oscillating theory,* a refinement, maintains that expansion will eventually stop, followed by contraction to a superdense atom, followed by another big bang.

The *steady-state theory,* an alternate hypothesis, maintains that the universe always has existed and that matter constantly is being created to replace matter that constantly is being destroyed.

Big Board May be used on second reference for the *New York Stock Exchange.*

big brother One's older brother is a *big brother. Big Brother* (capitalized) means *the all-seeing, omnipresent power of big government* from George Orwell's *1984,* or refers to *Big Brothers Inc.,* an organization that encourages men to spend time with boys who need guidance.

Big Three automakers General Motors Corp., Ford Motor Co., DaimlerChrysler AG.

billion A thousand million (1,000,000,000). Always expressed with figures: I billion, I0 billion. See **millions, billions**.

Bill of Rights The first 10 amendments to the Constitution.

bimonthly, semimonthly *Bimonthly* means *every other month; semimonthly* means *twice a month.*

binary files Programming files containing ones and zeros. They are the opposite of *ASCII files.* See **ASCII**.

bioterrorism

birthday Capitalize as part of the name for a holiday: Washington's Birthday. Lowercase in other uses.

bishop Capitalize only when used as a title preceding a name: Bishop Frank L. Jones, the bishop.

bit In the computer numbering system, eight bits comprise one *byte* (character). See **byte**.

biweekly, semiweekly *Biweekly* means *every other week; semiweekly* means *twice a week.*

bizarre See **bazaar, bizarre**.

black Use *black* or *African-American.* Do not use *Negro* or *colored* except in names of organizations or direct quotations. See **African-American, colored, race**.

Black Caucus

black Muslims See **Muslims**.

blackout, brownout In electrical terms, a *blackout* is a total power failure over a large area. *Rotating blackout* describes the cutting off of power to some sections on a rotating basis to assure that voltage will meet minimum standards elsewhere. A *brownout* is a small, temporary reduction, usually from 2 percent to 8 percent, to save power.

blast off (v.), **blastoff** (n., adj.)

blatant, flagrant *Blatant* means *offensively noisy, boisterous, clamorous; flagrant* means *glaringly bad, notorious or outrageous. Blatant* is frequently misused for *flagrant.*

blizzard Wind speeds of 35 mph or more with heavy snow and visibility near zero. A *severe blizzard* has wind speeds of 45 mph or more, heavy blowing snow, visibility near zero and temperatures of 10 degrees F or lower.

bloc, block A *bloc* is an alliance of people, organizations or nations with a common purpose. Lowercase as in **Eastern bloc, the farm bloc**.

Block has many definitions, including a number of persons or things regarded as a unit: **block of votes, block of tickets**.

Bloomberg L.P. Note the periods. The New York company owns *Bloomberg News, Bloomberg Television* (a financial news network) and radio and publishing operations. The news organization started as a financial news service in 1990. (Founder Michael R. Bloomberg was elected mayor of New York in 2001.)

blond, blonde Use *blond* as a noun for males and as an adjective for both sexes; use *blonde* as a noun for females. **She is a blonde. He is a blond. Both have blond hair.**

Bloody Mary Capitalize the drink made of vodka and tomato juice.

blowup (n.), **blow up** (v.)

blue-chip stock Stock in a company known nationally for its record of making money and paying dividends.

(blue-ribbon) Avoid using the adjective as a synonym for *prestigious.*

B'nai B'rith

board of aldermen See **city council**.

board of directors, board of trustees Always lowercase.

board of supervisors See **city council**.

boats, ships A *boat* is a watercraft of any size; a *ship* is a large seagoing vessel, big enough to carry smaller boats.

Boat, however, is used in some terms that apply to large craft: *ferryboat, PT boat, gunboat*. Submarines are traditionally called *boats*. Do not put the names in quotation marks: **the Delta Queen**. In datelines: *ABOARD THE DELTA QUEEN, May 31 (UPI) —*

The reference for military ships is *Jane's Fighting Ships;* for non-military ships, *Lloyd's Register of Shipping.*

Boeing Co. Formerly *Boeing Aircraft Co.* Headquarters is in Chicago.

Bogota The capital of Colombia stands alone in datelines.

bologna See **baloney, bologna**.

Bolshevik Originally a member of the *Bolsheviki,* the majority faction of the Russian Social Democratic Workers Party, forerunner of the Russian Communist Party. Capitalize in reference to Russian revolutionaries of 1917: the Bolshevik Revolution, but the revolution. Lowercase when used generically to mean *a revolutionary.*

Bombay Still used in datelines. Explain in the story that the seaport in western India was officially renamed *Mumbai.*

bona fide

bond See **loan terminology**.

bond ratings The two most popular are prepared by Moody's Investors Service Inc. and Standard & Poor's Corp.

Moody's uses nine ratings. The range, from the designation for top-quality issues to the one for those judged the greatest risk: Aaa, Aa, A, Baa, Ba, B, Caa, Ca, and C.

Standard & Poor's uses seven basic grades. The range, from top to bottom: AAA, AA, A, BBB, BB, B, and D. Occasionally it adds a plus or minus sign on grades AA through BB.

bookmark Marking the location of a Web site so the user can easily return to it later. Bookmarks are also called *favorites.*

book titles See **composition titles**.

book value The difference between a company's assets and liabilities. The book value per share of common stock is obtained by dividing the total amount of common shares into the book value of the company as a whole. While book value may have little relationship to the selling price, it may be used as an indicator of undervalued stocks and of the value of the shares in the event of liquidation.

Boolean search Derived from a branch of mathematics founded by 19th century English logician George Boole. In a *Boolean search* on the Internet, the words *AND, OR* and *NOT,* usually typed in capital letters, are used to refine the scope of the search.

borderline (n., adv.)

Bosnia-Herzegovina Acceptable on first reference for *Bosnia and Herzegovina.* The country in southeast Europe is commonly known as *Bosnia.* Until declaring its independence in 1992, it was part of the country formerly known as *Yugoslavia.* In datelines: *SARAJEVO, Bosnia-Herzegovina, July 1 (UPI)* —

Bosporus, the Not *the Bosporus Strait.*

Boston The city in Massachusetts stands alone in datelines.

boulevard See **addresses**.

boundary Not *boundry.*

bourgeoisie Note spelling.

boxing The three major sanctioning bodies for professional boxing are the World Boxing Association, the World Boxing Council and the International Boxing Federation.

Boxing terms include: *knock out* (v.), *knockout* (n., adj.), *outpointed, technical knockout* (*TKO* is acceptable on second reference), *kidney punch, rabbit punch.*

box office (n), **box-office** (adj.)

boy Applicable until 18th birthday is reached. Use *man* or *young man* afterward.

boycott, embargo A *boycott* is an organized refusal to buy a product or service, or to deal with a merchant or group of merchants. An *embargo* is a legal restriction against trade. It usually prohibits goods from entering or leaving a country.

boyfriend, girlfriend

Boy Scouts The official name of the national organization is *Boy Scouts of America.* Headquarters is in Irving, Texas.

Cub Scouting is for boys 8 through 10. Members are *Cub Scouts* or *Cubs. Boy Scouting* is for boys 11 through 17. Members are *Boy Scouts* or *Scouts. Exploring* is a separate program open to boys and girls high school age through 20. Members are *Explorers,* not *Explorer Scouts.* Members of units that stress nautical programs are *Sea Explorers.* See **Girl Scouts**.

BP Corporate brand formed by the combination of *British Petroleum* and other companies, including *Amoco Corp, Atlantic Richfield* and *Burmah Castrol.* Headquarters is in London.

bps For *bits per second.* Lowercase.

bra Acceptable in all references for *brassiere.*

Brahman, Brahmin *Brahman* applies to the priestly Hindu caste and to the breed of cattle: a Brahman bull. *Brahmin* applies to aristocracy in general: Boston Brahmin.

brand names When they are used, capitalize them. Brand names normally should be used only if they are essential to a story. Sometimes, however, the use of a brand name may not be essential but is acceptable because it lends an air of reality to a story: He fished a Camel from his shirt pocket may be preferable to the less specific *cigarette.*

When a company sponsors an event such as a golf tournament to obtain publicity, use a generic term for the event in all references. Provide the name of the sponsor in a separate paragraph that can be deleted easily. See **trademark**.

brand-new (adj.)

breakaway, breakdown, breakout, breakthrough, breakup, breakwater, *but* **break-even, break-in**

breeds See **animals**.

Bricklayers, Masons and Plasterers' International Union of America *Bricklayers union* is acceptable in all references. Headquarters is in Washington.

bride, bridegroom, bridesmaid *Bride* is appropriate in wedding stories, but use *wife* or *spouse* in other circumstances. A *bridegroom* is the husband of a *bride;* a *groom* attends horses.

brigade A U.S. Army formation of two or more battalions. Before Army regiments were eliminated as tactical units in 1963, brigades comprised two or more regiments. Capitalize with a numerical designation: 3rd Infantry Brigade. Otherwise, lowercase: the brigade, the brigade commander. See **regiment** and **military units**.

brigadier A British army rank above a colonel and below a major general. Equivalent to *brigadier general* in the U.S. Army.

brigadier general See **military titles**.

Bright's disease After Dr. Richard Bright, the London physician who first diagnosed this form of kidney disease.

Brill's disease After Nathan E. Brill, a U.S. physician. A form of epidemic typhus fever in which the disease recurs years after the original infection.

Britain Acceptable in all references for *Great Britain,* which consists of England, Scotland and Wales. See **United Kingdom**.

British, Briton(s) The people of Great Britain: the English, Scottish and Welsh. Do not use *Brits* except in direct quotations.

British Airways Headquarters is in Hounslow, England.

British Broadcasting Corp. *BBC* is acceptable in all references. The corporation's many businesses include *BBC Worldwide, Ltd., BBC Broadcast, BBC Monitoring* and *BBC International.* Headquarters is in London.

British Columbia The Canadian province bounded on the west by the Pacific Ocean. Do not abbreviate. In datelines: *VANCOUVER, British Columbia, March 14 (UPI) —* .

(British Commonwealth) See **Commonwealth, the**.

British thermal unit The amount of heat required to increase the temperature of a pound of water one degree Fahrenheit. *Btu* (the same for singular and plural) is acceptable in first reference, but explain its meaning in the story. Do not use *BTU* in all caps.

British ton See **ton**.

British Virgin Islands Do not abbreviate. In datelines: *ROAD TOWN, British Virgin Islands, Dec. 23 (UPI)* — Specify an individual island, if needed, in the text.

broadcast Present and past tense.

Broadway When applied to stage productions, *Broadway, off-Broadway* and *off-off-Broadway* refer to distinctions made by union contracts, not to the location of a theater.

Actors Equity Association and unions representing craft workers have set one set of pay scales for *Broadway* productions (generally those in New York theaters of 300 or more seats) and a lower scale for *off-Broadway* theaters (generally those for smaller theaters.)

Off-off-Broadway refers to workshop productions that may use Equity members for a limited time at substandard pay. Other unions maintain a hands-off policy to allow actors and actresses the opportunity to whet their talents in offbeat roles without losing their Equity memberships.

Bromo Seltzer A trademark for a brand of bicarbonate of soda.

Bronze Age The age characterized by the development of bronze tools and weapons, from 3500 to 1000 B.C.

brother As a religious title: Brother John Jones, the brother. As a family title, use lowercase unless it is a substitute for a name: My brother is well. But: It was Brother on the phone.

brothers Abbreviate as *Bros.* in company names that use the abbreviation: Warner Bros. For possessives: Warner Bros.' profits.

brownout See **blackout, brownout**.

browser A program that enables a computer user to navigate the Internet.

brunet, brunette Use *brunet* as an adjective for both sexes and as a masculine noun; use *brunette* as a feminine noun: He is a brunet. She is a brunette. He and she have brunet hair.

brushoff (n.), **brush off** (v.)

Brussels The capital of Belgium stands alone in datelines.

brussels sprouts Lowercase.

Buddha, Buddhism, Buddhist

Buenos Aires The capital of Argentina stands alone in datelines.

bug, tap Surreptitious listening devices: You bug a room and tap a telephone.

building Never abbreviate. Capitalize proper names. Lowercase *building* unless it is an integral part of a proper name: the Empire State Building.

build up (v.), **buildup** (n., adj.)

bullet The component of a cartridge that serves as the projectile. See **weapons**.

bull market A time of increasing market prices.

bullpen One word, for the place where baseball pitchers warm up and for a pen that holds cattle.

bulls-eye Not *bull's-eye*.

bureau Capitalize as part of the formal name for an organization or agency: the Bureau of Labor Statistics, the Newspaper Advertising Bureau Inc. Lowercase when used alone or to designate a subdivision: the bureau, the Washington bureau of United Press International.

Bureau of Immigration and Customs Enforcement *ICE* is acceptable on second reference. The bureau, with thousands of employees including customs and immigration agents, was created in 2003 under the *Department of Homeland Security*. It is responsible for investigative and enforcement functions once handled by other agencies, including the former *Immigration and Naturalization Service*.

burglary See **theft**.

burp gun Slang for World War II German 9mm submachine gun, MP-38 and MP-40, commonly called *Schmeisser*. Often applied to any submachine gun. See **weapons**.

Burma See **Myanmar**.

burro, burrow A *burro* is an ass; a *burrow* is a hole in the ground.

bus (s.), **buses** (pl.) Vehicles. The verbs: *bus, bused, busing*. See **buss**.

bushel A dry measure equal to four pecks (32 dry quarts) or about 35.2 liters. To convert to liters, multiply by 35.2 (5 × 35.2 equals 176 liters).

business names See **company**.

buss, busses Kisses. The verbs: *buss, bussed, bussing*. See **bus**.

buyout

by-election A special election held between regularly scheduled elections, most often used for special elections to the British House of Commons.

bylaws

byproduct

byte The basic unit of measurement for computer storage. A *byte* is one *character* and has eight *bits*. (Note: In the Internet community, eight-bit groups are also called *octets*.) See **kilobyte, megabyte, giga-, terabyte**.

C

C A high-level computer programming language.

Cabinet Capitalize references to a specific body of advisers for a president, king, governor, etc.: The president-elect said he has not made his Cabinet selections. See **kitchen cabinet**.

Cabinet departments Only three are abbreviated: *HUD, HHS, VA.* Do not use *DOT, DoD, USDA,* etc. See **executive departments**.

Cabinet titles Capitalize the full title before a name, lowercase elsewhere: Secretary of Defense Mary Jones or Defense Secretary Mary Jones, but James Smith, secretary of state. Do not capitalize *treasury, state, defense, interior,* etc., when used in titles that stand alone or follow the name of the titleholder.

cactus (s.), **cactuses** (pl.)

cadet See **military academies**.

Caesarean section

Cairo The capital of Egypt stands alone in datelines.

Calcutta Still used in datelines. Explain in the story that the city in northeast India was officially renamed *Kolkata.*

caliber The form: a .38-caliber pistol. See **weapons**.

California Abbreviation: *Calif.* See **state(s)**.

caller ID A telephone service that displays a caller's number, name or both when the phone rings.

call girl

call letters Use all caps. Hyphens separate the type of station from the basic call letters: WSB-AM, WSB-FM, WSB-TV.

Amateur radio stations, which transmit on different frequencies than citizens band stations and may use greater power, are assigned a combination of letters and figures: WA2UUR.

call up (v.), **call-up** (n., adj.)

Cambodia Use this name rather than *Democratic Kampuchea* (formerly the *Khmer Republic*) in datelines. When *Kampuchea* is used in the body of a story, identify it as the formal name of *Cambodia*.

camcorder Acceptable in all references to a portable videotape recorder and television camera.

Cameroon Not *Camerouns* or *Cameroun*. See **geographic names**.

campaign manager Do not treat as a formal title. Always lowercase.

Camp David The presidential retreat in the Catoctin Mountains near Thurmont, Md., 70 miles northwest of Washington. The form for datelines: *CAMP DAVID, Md., March 8 (UPI)* —

Camp Fire USA The national organization was renamed in 2001. (Its former names were *Camp Fire Girls, Camp Fire Inc.* and *Camp Fire Boys and Girls*.) Headquarters is in Kansas City, Mo.

Canada *Montreal, Ottawa, Quebec* and *Toronto* stand alone in datelines. For all other datelines, use the city name and the name of the province or territory spelled out.

The 10 provinces of Canada are Alberta, British Columbia, Manitoba, New Brunswick, Newfoundland (includes Labrador), Nova Scotia, Ontario, Prince Edward Island, Quebec and Saskatchewan.

The three territories are the Yukon, the Northwest Territories and Nunavut.

Canada goose Not *Canadian goose*.

Canadian Broadcasting Corp. *CBC* is acceptable on second reference.

canal Capitalize as an integral part of a proper name: the Suez Canal.

cancel, canceled, canceling, cancellation

canister Not *cannister*.

cannon, canon A *cannon* is a weapon. The plural is *cannons*. Form: 155mm cannon or 8-inch cannon. See **weapons**.

A *canon* is a law or rule, particularly of a church.

cannot One word.

cantor See **Jewish congregations**.

Canuck Avoid the word except in proper names (the Vancouver Canucks, a professional hockey team) or in quoted matter.

canvas, canvass *Canvas* is heavy cotton cloth; a *canvass* is a survey.

cape Capitalize as part of a proper name: Cape Cod, Cape Hatteras.

cape *continued*

Lowercase *the cape* standing alone, even though local practice may capitalize it.

Cape Canaveral, Fla. Formerly *Cape Kennedy*. See **John F. Kennedy Space Center**.

capital The city where a seat of government is located. Do not capitalize.

In a financial sense, *capital* describes money, equipment or property used in a business by a person or corporation.

capitalization Avoid unnecessary capitals. Use a capital letter only if you can justify it by one of these guidelines:

1. Capitalize proper names of a specific person, place or thing: John, Mary, America, Boston, England.
2. Capitalize common nouns such as *party, river, street* and *department* as an integral part of a proper name: Democratic Party, Mississippi River, Fleet Street, Department of Defense. Lowercase common nouns that stand alone: the party, the river, the street, the department. Lowercase common noun elements in all plural uses: the Democratic and Republican parties, the Hudson and Mississippi rivers, Main and State streets, the departments of State and Defense.

   Capitalize popular, unofficial names that serve as a proper name: the Combat Zone (a section of Boston), the Badlands (of South Dakota).
3. Capitalize words derived from a proper noun and still dependent on it for their meaning: American, Christianity, English, French, Marxism, Shakespearean.

   Lowercase words derived from a proper noun but no longer dependent on it for their meaning: french fries, herculean, manhattan (cocktail), malapropism, pasteurize, quixotic, venetian blind.
4. Capitalize the first word in every sentence. See **sentences**.

   In poetry, capital letters are often used for the first words of phrases that would not be capitalized in prose. See **poetry**.
5. Capitalize the principal words in the names of books, movies, plays, poems, etc. See **composition titles**.
6. Capitalize formal titles before a name. Lowercase mere job descriptions and formal titles standing alone or set off by commas. See **titles**.
7. Capitalize some abbreviations and acronyms. See **abbreviations and acronyms**.
8. Capitalize the interjection *O* and the pronoun *I*.

capitol Capitalize references to the national or state buildings and their sites: The meeting was on Capitol Hill in the west wing of the Capitol. Thomas Jefferson designed the Capitol of Virginia.

captain For military and police usage, see **military titles**. Lowercase elsewhere: team captain Carl Yastrzemski.

carat, caret, karat A *carat,* about 200 milligrams or 3 grains, expresses the weight of precious stones, especially diamonds. A *caret* (^) is a writers' and proofreaders' mark and a symbol, commonly on the 6 key, that is used for certain computer functions. The proportion of pure gold used with an alloy is expressed in *karats.*

cardinal Capitalize as a formal title before a name: Cardinal Timothy Manning. Not: Timothy Cardinal Manning. See **Roman Catholic Church**.

CARE Acceptable in all references for *Cooperative for American Relief Everywhere Inc.* Headquarters is in Atlanta.

Caribbean One *r,* two *b*'s.

carmaker (s.), **carmakers** (pl.)

carpal tunnel syndrome A repetitive stress injury causing pain in the wrist and hand; often linked to typing.

Carpenters union Acceptable in all references for the *United Brotherhood of Carpenters and Joiners of America.* Headquarters is in Washington.

car pool Two words.

carry-over (n., adj.)

caseload

case-sensitive A *case-sensitive* computer search distinguishes uppercase from lowercase letters. A *case-insensitive* search ignores the difference.

caseworker

cash on delivery The term *c.o.d.* is preferred in all references.

caster, castor A *caster* is a roller; *castor* is the oil and the bean from which it is derived.

catalog, cataloged, cataloger, cataloging, catalogist

(catchup, catsup) Spell it *ketchup.*

Caterpillar A trademark for earth-moving equipment. Lowercase the wormlike larva of various insects.

catholic, catholicism Lowercase in the generic sense, meaning *general* or *universal.* Capitalize in the religious sense.

Use *Roman Catholic* or *Roman Catholicism* if the context requires a distinction between Roman Catholics and members of other denominations who describe themselves as Catholic. See **Roman Catholic Church**.

(CAT scan) Use *CT scan*. See **CT scan**.

cave in (v.), **cave-in** (n., adj.)

CB See **citizens band radio**.

CBS Acceptable in all references for *CBS Inc.*, the former *Columbia Broadcasting System*. Divisions include CBS News, CBS Radio and CBS-TV. Headquarters is in New York.

CD May be used in all references for *compact disc* if the context is clear.

CDC See **Centers for Disease Control and Prevention**.

CD-ROM Acronym for *compact disc-read only memory.*

CEO Acceptable on second reference for *chief executive officer.*

cease fire (v.), **cease-fire, cease-fires** (n., adj.)

cellblock, cellmate

cellophane Formerly a trademark, now a generic term.

cell phone, cellular phone, cellular telephone

Celsius Use this metric term rather than *centigrade*. Named for Swedish astronomer Anders Celsius, who invented it. Zero is the freezing point of water and 100 the boiling point at sea level.

To convert to Fahrenheit, multiply a Celsius temperature by 9, divide by 5 and add 32 (25 × 9 equals 225 divided by 5 equals 45 plus 32 equals 77 degrees Fahrenheit).

The forms: **40 degrees Celsius**, or **40 C** (note the space and no period after the capital *C*). See **temperatures**.

cement, concrete, mortar *Cement* is a powder mixed with sand, gravel and water to make *concrete* pavement, blocks, etc. *Cement* mixed with lime, sand and water makes *mortar* that masons use to bind bricks together in walls.

censer, censor, censure A *censer* is a container in which incense is burned; to *censor* is to prohibit or restrict; to *censure* is to condemn.

Centers for Disease Control and Prevention Note the plural *Centers*. The U.S. Public Health Service's national agency for control of infectious and other preventable disease. Headquarters is in Atlanta. The normal form for first reference is *the national Centers for Disease Control*. *CDC* is acceptable on second reference.

centi- A prefix meaning *one-hundredth;* a *centimeter* is one-hundredth of a meter. See **metric system**.

centigrade See **Celsius**.

centimeter One-hundredth of a meter. There are 10 millimeters in a centimeter. A centimeter is about the width of a large paper clip.

To convert to inches, multiply by .4 (5 centimeters × .4 equals 2 inches).

Central America The strip of land between Mexico and Colombia. It encompasses Belize, Costa Rica, El Salvador, Guatemala, Honduras, Nicaragua and Panama.

Central Conference of American Rabbis See **Jewish Congregations**.

Central Europe

Central Intelligence Agency *CIA* is acceptable in all references.

The formal title for the person who heads the agency is *director of central intelligence.* The forms: CIA Director Christopher Smith or Christopher Smith, director of central intelligence.

Central Standard Time (CST), Central Daylight Time (CDT) See **time**.

cents Spell out *cents* and lowercase, using figures for amounts less than a dollar: 5 cents, 10 cents. Use the *$* sign and decimals for larger amounts: $1.01, $2.50.

century Lowercase. Spell out numbers under 10: first century, 20th century. For proper names, follow the organization's practice: 20th Century Fox, Century III Mall, Twentieth Century Limited.

Chagas' disease After Charles Chagas, a Brazilian physician who identified the chronic wasting disease caused by a parasite carried by insects.

chairman, chairwoman Capitalize as a formal title before a name: company Chairman Henry Jones, committee Chairwoman Margaret Smith. Lowercase a casual temporary position: meeting chairman Robert Wilson.

Use *chairperson* or *chair* only in quoted matter or if they are an organization's formal title for an office. See **president, chief executive officer**.

chamber of deputies See **foreign legislative bodies**.

chancellor The first minister in Germany and Austria. Capitalize before a name: Chancellor Helmut Kohl.

changeable, changeover

channel Capitalize with a figure; lowercase elsewhere: He tuned to Channel 3. No channel will broadcast the game. Also: the English Channel. On second reference, *the channel.*

(Chanukah) The Jewish Feast of Lights is *Hanukkah.*

Chapter 7, 11, 13 See **bankruptcy**.

chapters Capitalize with a figure. Use Arabic numerals: Chapter 1, Chapter 20. Lowercase standing alone: the book's best chapter.

charge d'affaires (s.), **charges d'affaires** (pl.) A diplomatic officer, ranking below an ambassador or minister, who represents his government to a foreign nation, or who temporarily takes the place of an ambassador or minister.

Charleston, Charlestown, Charles Town *Charleston* is the capital of West Virginia and a port city in South Carolina; *Charlestown* is a section of Boston; *Charles Town* is a small city in West Virginia.

chat room A service that enables computer users to "chat" (by keyboard) on the Internet.

chauffeur

chauvinism, chauvinist Unreasoning devotion to one's sex, country, etc. The terms are derived from Nicolas Chauvin, a soldier of Napoleon I, who was famous for his devotion to the lost cause.

Chechnya The people are *Chechens.* The capital is *Grozny.*

check up (v.), **checkup** (n.)

Chemical Mace A trademark, usually shortened to *Mace,* for a tear gas in an aerosol canister. It temporarily stuns its victims.

ChevronTexaco Corp. No space. Chevron and Texaco merged in 2001. The company produces oil and natural gas and sells gasoline under the Caltex, Chevron and Texaco brands. Headquarters is in San Ramon, Calif.

Chicago The city in Illinois stands alone in datelines.

Chicano (s.), **Chicanos** (pl.) Although not always derogatory, the term should be avoided as a routine description for U.S. citizens or residents of Mexican descent. *Mexican-Americans* is preferred.

    Chicano has been adopted by some social activists of Mexican descent, and may be used when people use it to describe themselves.

chief Capitalize as a formal title before a name: **He spoke to Police Chief** John Smith. Lowercase if not a formal title: union chief Jack James.

chief executive officer Capitalize before a name. *CEO* is acceptable on second reference. The same rules apply to other corporate titles.

chief justice Capitalize only as a formal title before a name: Chief Justice Sarah Smith. The officeholder is the chief justice *of the United States,* not *of the Supreme Court.*

chief petty officer See **military titles**.

chief warrant officer See **military titles**.

child care (n.), **child-care** (adj.)

Chile The nation.

chili (s.), **chilies** (pl.) The peppers; the dish: *a bowl of chili.*

chilly Moderately cold.

China When used alone, it refers to the mainland nation. Use *People's Republic of China, Communist China* or *mainland China* only when needed to distinguish the mainland and its government from Taiwan.

Restrict *Red China* to quoted matter. *Beijing* and *Shanghai* stand alone in datelines. The form for others: *KUNMING, China, Jan. 9 (UPI)* — .

For datelines on stories from the island of Taiwan: *TAIPEI, Taiwan, Jan. 9 (UPI)* —

In the body of a story, use *Taiwan.* Use *Nationalist China* only when needed to distinguish the island from the mainland. Use the formal name of the government, *Republic of China,* only when required for legal precision.

(Chinaman) A patronizing term. Confine it to quoted matter.

Chinese names Under China's official *Pinyin* transliteration system, the three names of most mainland people become two when converted to English: Ding Yihui. *Ding* is the family name. (Hyphens and apostrophes are removed from names in the Pinyin system, which was adopted by the People's Republic of China in 1979.)

In Taiwan and Hong Kong, the old system is used and most people have three names, the last two separated by a hyphen and the final one not capitalized: Wu Ching-kuo.

In Singapore and other Southeast Asia areas, most Chinese people use three names, all capitalized and not separated by a hyphen: Prime Minister Goh Chok Tong.

Chinese who also have Western names usually put them before their family names: Martin Lee Chu-ming.

The family name is always used on second reference: Ding stopped in Beijing. Wu visited the university. Goh was appointed in 1990. Lee builds computers.

Christian Church (Disciples of Christ) The parentheses and the words they surround are part of the formal name.

All members of the clergy may be referred to as *ministers. Pastor* may be substituted for those who lead a congregation.

On first reference use *the Rev.* for men or women. On second reference use only the last name.

Christian Methodist Episcopal Church See **Methodist churches**.

Christian Science Church See **Church of Christ, Scientist**.

Christmas Dec. 25. The federal legal holiday is observed on Friday if Dec. 25 falls on a Saturday, on Monday if it falls on a Sunday. Never abbreviate to *Xmas* or any other form.

church Capitalize as part of the formal name of a building, a congregation or a denomination: St. Mary's Church, the Roman Catholic Church, the Methodist Church. But lowercase these in plural uses: the Catholic and Episcopal churches.

45

church *continued*

Also lowercase generic usage: a Roman Catholic church, a church; and in an institutional sense: He believes in separation of church and state. The pope said the church opposes abortion.

Churches of Christ Thousands of independent congregations cooperate under this name. Each church is autonomous. The minister is addressed by members as *brother.* The ministers do not use clergy titles. Do not precede their names by a title. The churches do not regard themselves as a denomination. Rather, they stress a non-denominational effort to preach what they consider basic Bible teachings.

churchgoer

Church of Christ, Scientist *Christian Science Church* or *Churches of Christ, Scientist* are acceptable in all references to the denomination. *The Mother Church* in Boston is the international headquarters.

The church is composed entirely of lay members and does not have clergy in the usual sense. Either men or women may hold the three principal offices — reader, practitioner or lecturer. The preferred form is to set these titles off from a name with commas. Capitalize them only when used as a formal title before a name. Do not continue use of the title in subsequent references.

The terms *pastor* and *minister* are not applicable. Do not use *the Rev.* in any reference.

Church of England See **Anglican Communion**.

Church of Jesus Christ of Latter-day Saints Note the spelling and punctuation of *Latter-day. Mormon Church* is acceptable in all references. Headquarters is in Salt Lake City.

The only formal titles are *president, bishop* and *elder.* Capitalize them before a name on first reference. Use only the last name on second reference. The terms *minister* or *the Rev.* are not used.

Mormon is not properly applied to the Latter Day Saints churches that split from the main body. The largest is the *Reorganized Church of Jesus Christ of Latter Day Saints* (no hyphen and capitalize *Day*), with headquarters in Independence, Mo.

Church of Scientology Members are *Scientologists.* The church was founded by L. Ron Hubbard. Headquarters is in Los Angeles.

CIA Acceptable in all references for *Central Intelligence Agency.*

cigarette Not *cigaret.*

Cincinnati The city in Ohio stands alone in datelines.

CIO See **AFL-CIO**.

C.I.S. See **Commonwealth of Independent States**.

Citibank See **Citigroup**.

Citigroup Financial services company in New York. Its holdings include Citibank, Diners Club International and Travelers Life & Annuity.

citizen A *citizen* is a person who has acquired full civil rights of a nation either by birth or naturalization. Cities and states in the United States do not confer citizenship. Use *resident,* not *citizen,* in referring to inhabitants of states and cities.

Subject is used when the government is headed by a monarch or other sovereign.

National is applied to a person residing away from the country of which he is a citizen or to a person under the protection of a specified country.

Native is the term denoting that an individual was born in a given location.

citizens band No apostrophe. *CB* is acceptable on second reference. The term describes a group of shortwave radio frequencies set aside by the Federal Communications Commission for local use at low power by individuals or businesses.

city Capitalize *city* (and *town, village,* etc.) as an integral part of a proper name: Kansas City, New York City, Greenwich Village. See **datelines**.

Lowercase elsewhere: a Texas city, the city government, the city Board of Education and all *city of* phrases: the city of Boston.

Capitalize as part of a formal title before a name: City Manager Francis Jones. Lowercase when not part of the formal title: city Health Commissioner Frank Smith.

The preferred form for a section of a city is lowercase: the west end, northern Los Angeles. But capitalize widely recognized popular names: Southside (Chicago), Lower East Side (New York), the Combat Zone (Boston). If in doubt, use lowercase.

Spell out the names of cities unless in direct quotes: a trip to *Los Angeles.* But: "We're going to *LA.*"

city commission See **city council**.

city council Capitalize as part of a proper name: the Boston City Council. If the meaning is clear the city may be dropped and capitalization is retained: BOSTON, April 4 (UPI) — The City Council met.

Lowercase other uses: the council, the Boston and New York city councils, any city council.

Use the proper name if the body is not known as a city council: the Miami City Commission, the Louisville Board of Aldermen. Use *city councils* to refer to more than one: the Boston, Louisville and Miami city councils.

city editor Capitalize as a formal title before a name.

city hall Capitalize with or without the name of a city if the reference is specific: Boston City Hall, City Hall. Lowercase plural or generic uses: the Boston and New York city halls. You can't fight city hall.

city manager Capitalize as a former title before a name.

Civil War Capitalize only in reference to the U.S. war (1861–65).

clean-cut, clean-shaven, but **cleanup**

clear-cut, but **cleareyed, clearheaded, clearsighted**

clerical titles See **religion**.

Cleveland The city in Ohio stands alone in datelines.

cliches Good writers avoid them. See **journalese**.

cloak-and-dagger (adj.)

Clorox A trademark for a bleach.

closed shop, union shop, agency shop, guild shop A *closed shop* is an agreement between a union and an employer that requires workers to be members of the union before they may be employed. See **right-to-work**.

A *union shop* requires workers to join the union within a specified period after they are employed.

An *agency shop* requires that the workers who do not want to join the union pay the union a fee instead of union dues.

A *Guild shop,* a term often used when the union is The Newspaper Guild, is the same as a *union shop.*

close-up (n., adj.)

cloture Not *closure* for the parliamentary procedure for closing debate.

clue, clew A *clue* is something that helps to solve a mystery; a *clew* is the lower corner of a sail.

CNN *Cable News Network. CNN* is acceptable in all references. Headquarters is in Atlanta.

co- Hyphenate to indicate occupation or status: co-author, co-chairman, co-defendant, co-host, co-owner, co-partner, co-pilot, co-respondent (in a divorce suit), co-star, co-worker. (Several of these are exceptions to *Webster's New World College Dictionary.*) No hyphen elsewhere: coed, coeducation, coequal, coexist, coexistence, cooperate, coordinate.

Co. See **company**.

coach Capitalize only when it is used without a qualifying term before the name of the person who directs an athletic team: The Blue Devils, under Coach Mike Krzyzewski, won their first national title in 1991.

Coach is lowercased if preceded by a qualifying term: wide receivers coach Mike Nolan, pitching coach Mel Stottlemyre.

Also lowercase *coach* when standing alone or set off by commas: The coach, Flip Saunders, was charged with a technical.

coast Lowercase when referring to a physical shoreline: Atlantic coast, Pacific coast, east coast.

Capitalize when referring to regions of the United States lying along such shorelines: the Atlantic Coast states, a Gulf Coast city, the West Coast, the East Coast.

Lowercase references to smaller regions: the Virginia coast.

Capitalize *the Coast* only if the reference is to the West Coast.

Coast Guard Capitalize references to the U.S. force: the U.S. Coast Guard, the Coast Guard, Coast Guard policy. Do not use *USCG*.

Many nations do not use *coast guard* as a proper name. For consistency lowercase all others: the Canadian coast guard. See **military academies**.

Coast Guardsman Capitalize as a proper noun when referring to someone in a U.S. Coast Guard unit: He is a Coast Guardsman. Lowercase *guardsman* standing alone. See **military titles**.

COBOL Acronym for *Common Business Oriented Language,* a computer programming language designed for business applications.

Coca-Cola, Coke Trademarks for the soft drink.

cocaine Confine the slang term *coke* to quoted matter.

co-captain Lowercase before and after a name.

c.o.d. Acceptable in all references for *cash on delivery,* or *collect on delivery.* The periods and lowercase are exceptions to *Webster's New World College Dictionary.*

cohort A group or an individual. Be careful with this word, which often has a negative connotation when used in reference to a person's associates (and can suggest they are conspirators or accomplices).

cold launch A technique for popping a missile out of a silo without the engine firing. See **hot launch**.

cold war Lowercase unless referring specifically to the rivalry between the United States and the former Soviet Union.

collateral See **loan terminology**.

collective nouns Nouns that denote a unit take singular verbs and pronouns: *class, committee, crowd, family, group, herd, jury, orchestra, team:* The committee is meeting to set its agenda. A herd of cattle was sold.

Words plural in form become collective nouns and take singular verbs when the group or quantity is regarded as a unit:

A thousand bushels were created. (Individual bushels.)
A thousand bushels is a good yield. (A unit.)

collective nouns *continued*

> The data have been carefully collected. (Individual items.)
> The data is sound. (A unit.)
>
> Meat and potatoes are the two items we sell most. (Individual items.)
> Meat and potatoes is a tasty dish. (A unit.)

collectors' item Not *collector's.*

college Capitalize as part of a proper name: Dartmouth College.

collide, collision Two objects must both be in motion before they can collide. An automobile cannot collide with a utility pole.

colloquialisms The words and phrases characteristic of informal speech and writing: *bum, giveaway, phone, talk a blue streak, easy on the eyes,* etc. They are neither substandard nor illiterate and are acceptable in news stories if they fit the occasion. See **slang**.

Webster's New World College Dictionary uses *colloq.* to label colloquialisms. If the dictionary also notes that the word or phrase is *substandard,* as it does with *ain't,* avoid the usage. See **dialect**.

colon (:) The most frequent use of a colon is at the end of a sentence to introduce lists, tabulations and texts. Capitalize the first word after a colon only if it is a proper name or the start of a complete sentence: There were three considerations: expense, time and feasibility. He promised this: The company will make good all the losses.

Elsewhere, use a colon:

1. To give emphasis: He had only one hobby: eating.
2. To give elapsed time: (1:31:07.2), time of day (8:31 p.m.) and biblical and legal citations (2 Kings 2:14, Missouri Code 3:245-260).
3. In dialogue, in coverage of a trial, for example (no quotation marks around the quoted matter):

   > Bailey: What were you doing the night of the 19th?
   > Mason: I refuse to answer that.

4. For question-and-answer interviews:

   > Q: Did you strike her?
   > A: Indeed I did.

5. To introduce a direct quotation of more than one sentence. Use a comma for shorter quotations. Colons go outside quotation marks unless they are part of the quotation.

colonel See **military titles**.

colonies Capitalize only for the British dependencies that declared their independence in 1776, now known as the United States.

Colorado Abbreviation: *Colo.* See **state(s)**.

Colorado Springs The city in Colorado stands alone in datelines.

colorblind

colored In some societies, including the United States, the word is considered derogatory and should not be used. In some African countries, *colored* denotes those of mixed racial ancestry. If *colored* is used, place it in quotation marks and explain its meaning. See **race**.

(Columbia Broadcasting System) The former name of *CBS Inc.* See **CBS**.

Columbia Gazetteer of the World Online The reference source for the spelling of foreign place names not covered in this book or in *Webster's New World College Dictionary.* See **geographic names**.

Columbus Day Oct. 12. The federal legal holiday is the second Monday in October.

column numbers Use figures and lowercase: column 7, column 10.

combat, combated, combating

comedian Use for both men and women. *Comedienne* also may be used for women.

comma (,) As demanded by the structure of the sentence, use a comma:

1. After an introductory clause: When he had tired of the mad pace of New York, he moved to Dubuque.

   Omit the comma if no ambiguity would result unless it would slow comprehension: During the night he heard many noises. On the street below, the curious gathered.

2. To set off an element not essential to the meaning: We saw the 1977 winner in the Academy Award competition for best movie, "Rocky." (Only one movie won the award. The name is informative, but even without the name no other movie could be meant.)

   Omit commas if the element is essential to the meaning: We saw the award-winning movie "Rocky." (No comma, because many movies have won awards, and without the name the reader would not know which movie was meant.)

3. To separate parts of a series. Omit the final comma in a simple series: The flag is red, white and blue. Use a final comma in a complex series: I had orange juice, toast, and ham and eggs for breakfast. Also use commas, not semicolons, in such constructions as: The tour included Birmingham, Ala., Nashville, Tenn., Louisville, Ky., and South Bend, Ind. See **semicolon**.

comma *continued*

4. To separate equal adjectives. If the commas could be replaced by *and* without changing the sense, the adjectives are equal: a thoughtful, precise manner. A dark, dangerous street. Omit the comma for unequal (superposed) adjectives: A cheap fur coat. The old oaken bucket. A new blue spring bonnet.

5. To separate main clauses joined by *and, but, or, nor* or *for:* She was glad she looked, for a man was approaching the house. Omit the comma if no confusion would result: Jack went up the hill and Jill went down.

6. To set off a complete one-sentence quotation, but not a partial quotation: "Rub my shoulders," Miss Cawley suggested. Wallace said, "She spent six months in Argentina and came back speaking English with a Spanish accent." He said his victory put him "firmly on the road to a first-ballot nomination." Use a colon to introduce quotations of more than one sentence.

7. To separate a city from a state or nation: His journey will take him from Dublin, Ireland, to Fargo, N.D., and back. The Selma, Ala., group saw the governor. Use parentheses to insert a location within a proper name. The Knoxville (Tenn.) News-Sentinel.

8. To set off the year from the day of the month: He was born July 16, 1928, in Statesville, N.C.

9. To replace *of* between a name and hometown: Mary Richards, Minneapolis, and Maude Findlay, Tuckahoe, N.Y., were there. However, the *of* is preferred: Mary Richard of Minneapolis and Maude Findlay of Tuckahoe, N.Y., were there. If an age is used, set it off with commas: Maude Findlay, 48, of Tuckahoe, N.Y., participated.

10. To set off direct address or an introductory *yes* or *no:* Yes, I will be there. Mother, I will be late. No, sir, I did not do it.

11. To separate duplicated words that might be confusing: What the problem is, is not clear.

Commas always go inside quotation marks. Commas also are used in most numerals above 999: 654,321. The major exceptions are addresses (1234 Main St.), broadcast frequencies (1400 kilohertz), serial numbers (A02205689), Social Security numbers (000-00-0000) and years (1999).

For special uses see separate entries such as **dates, scores** and **party affiliations**. See also the "comma" entry under "Rules of Punctuation" in the back of *Webster's New World College Dictionary.*

commander See **military titles**.

commander in chief No hyphens. Capitalize as a formal title before a name: Commander in Chief Joe Smith.

commando (s), **commandoes** (pl.)

commercial paper See **loan terminology**.

commissioner Do not abbreviate. Capitalize as a formal title before a name.

committee Do not abbreviate. Capitalize as part of a formal name: the House Appropriations Committee. Lowercase shortened versions of long names: the Special Senate Select Committee to Investigate Improper Labor-Management Practices, for example, became the rackets committee. See **subcommittee**.

commodity In a financial sense it describes the products of mining and agriculture before they have undergone extensive processing.

Common Market See **European Union**.

common stock, preferred stock An ownership interest in a corporation. If other classes of stock are outstanding, the owners of *common stock* are the last to receive dividends and the last to receive payments if a corporation is dissolved. The company may raise or lower common stock dividends as its earnings rise or fall.

When *preferred stock* is outstanding and company earnings are sufficient, a fixed dividend is paid. If a company is liquidated, holders of preferred stock receive payments up to a set amount before any money is distributed to holders of common stock.

commonwealth See **state(s)**.

Commonwealth of Independent States Spell out as noun. Use *C.I.S.* only as an adjective. Never use in datelines.

A loose association of 12 nations that were republics in the former Union of Soviet Socialist Republics (Soviet Union):

Armenia	Kazakhstan	Tajikistan
Azerbaijan	Kyrgyzstan	Turkmenistan
Belarus	Moldova	Ukraine
Georgia	Russia	Uzbekistan

Estonia, Latvia and Lithuania chose not to join the C.I.S. after the dissolution of the Soviet Union in 1991. (Georgia initially declined C.I.S. membership but decided to join in 1993.) See **Baltic States, Russia, Soviet Union**.

Commonwealth, the Formerly the *British Commonwealth*. The members of this free association of sovereign states recognize the British

Commonwealth, the *continued*

sovereign as head of the Commonwealth. Some also recognize the sovereign as head of their states; others do not.

The members are:

Antigua and	Kiribati	Seychelles
Barbuda	Lesotho	Sierra Leone
Australia	Malawi	Singapore
Bahamas	Malaysia	Solomon Islands
Bangladesh	Maldives	South Africa
Barbados	Malta	Sri Lanka
Belize	Mauritius	Swaziland
Botswana	Mozambique	Tanzania
Cameroon	Namibia	Tonga
Canada	Nauru	Trinidad and
Cyprus	New Zealand	Tobago
Dominica	Nigeria	Tuvalu
Fiji	Pakistan	Uganda
Gambia	Papua New	United Kingdom
Ghana	Guinea	Vanuatu
Grenada	St. Kitts and	Western Samoa
Guyana	Nevis	Zambia
India	St. Lucia	Zimbabwe
Jamaica	St. Vincent and	
Kenya	the Grenadines	

Communications Workers of America *Communications Workers union* is acceptable in all references. Headquarters is in Washington.

communism, communist Always lowercase *communism*. Lowercase *communist* unless the reference clearly is to the Communist Party or its members: The communist influence is spreading. The Communists won the election. See **political parties**.

commutation See **pardon**.

compact disc *CD* may be used in all references if the context is clear.

company, companies Use *Co.* (plural: *Cos.*) at the end of a business name: Ford Motor Co., American Broadcasting Cos. But: Aluminum Company of America.

If in doubt about the proper name, consult the company or Standard & Poor's Register of Corporations.

For possessives: Ford Motor Co.'s profits, a company's profits, two companies' profits.

Spell out in theatrical usage: the Chicago Barn Dance Company.
Do not use a comma before *Inc.* or *Ltd.*

company (military) A military formation comprising two or more platoons, usually containing about 200 people. Most are designated by a letter. Spell out and capitalize to indicate a named company: B Company, Headquarters Company. Lowercase otherwise: the company, the company commander. See **military units** and **battalion**.

compare to, compare with *Compare to* means *to place in the same class,* usually to point out similarities: He compared the storm to a hurricane.

Compare with means *to examine in relation to,* usually to point out dissimilarities: Compared with a hurricane, this was not much of a storm.

compass points Hyphenate compounds: south-southeast, east-northeast. Use figures for degrees: sailed on a course of 270 degrees. See **directions**.

compatible Not *compatable.*

complacent, complaisant *Complacent* means *self-satisfied; complaisant* means *eager to please:* The student was complacent about his straight A average, saying it was nothing unusual. The waiter was very complaisant, inquiring frequently if there was anything we needed.

complement, compliment A *complement* completes or supplements; a *compliment* expresses praise or respect: The ship has a complement of 200 sailors, and the captain will compliment their behavior. The flowers complement the dress, and they were sent with our compliments.

complementary, complimentary *Complementary* means *to mutually make complete; complimentary* means in one sense *giving praise,* but in another it means *something given free:* The husband and wife have complementary careers and got complimentary tickets to a show.

compose, comprise The whole *comprises* the parts; the parts *compose* the whole. Thus the United States *comprises* 50 states; 50 states *compose* the United States, or the United States is *composed of* 50 states. *Comprise* never takes the word *of.*

composition titles In titles of books, movies, plays, poems, programs, songs, works of art, etc., capitalize the first word and all succeeding words except articles and short (four letters or less) conjunctions or prepositions. Use quotation marks for most:

"The Star-Spangled Banner"	"For Whom the Bell Tolls"
"The Rise and Fall of the Third Reich"	"Time After Time"
"Gone with the Wind"	the NBC-TV "Today" program
"Of Mice and Men"	the "CBS Evening News"

composition titles *continued*

Use no quotation marks for the titles of:

- A sacred book or its parts: the Bible, the New Testament, the Koran, the Apocrypha, the Torah, the Talmud.
- Reference works: *Jane's All the World's Aircraft, Encyclopaedia Britannica, Webster's New World College Dictionary,* the World Almanac.

Translate a foreign title into English unless it is known to Americans by its foreign name: *Rousseau's "War."* Not: *Rousseau's "La Guerre."* Also: Leonardo da Vinci's *"Mona Lisa,"* Mozart's *"The Marriage of Figaro"* and *"The Magic Flute."* But: *"Die Walkure"* and *"Gotterdammerung"* from Wagner's *"The Ring of the Nibelungen."*

compound modifiers See **hyphen**.

comprise See **compose, comprise**.

comptroller The U.S. comptroller of the currency is an appointed official in the Treasury Department responsible for the chartering, supervising and liquidation of banks organized under the National Bank Act. See **controller**.

computer See individual entries for dozens of computer and Internet terms.

computerese The jargon used by computer operators in communicating with each other. Avoid the word when possible. If you use it, explain it.

computer virus See **virus**.

concede Not *conceed.*

concrete See **cement, concrete, mortar**.

Confederate States of America The *Confederacy* is acceptable in all references for the states that seceded during the Civil War.

confess, confessed In some contexts the words may be erroneous. See **admit**.

confidant (masculine), **confidante** (feminine)

Congo Central African country formerly named *Zaire.* Official name is the *Democratic Republic of the Congo.* The capital is *Kinshasa.* In datelines: *KINSHASA, Congo, July 6 (UPI) —* In stories: *Congo* or *the Congo* as appropriate.

Note: The much smaller *Republic of the Congo* is an adjoining country to the west. Its capital is *Brazzaville.* In datelines: *BRAZZAVILLE, Republic of Congo, April 11 (UPI) —*

Congregationalist churches *Congregational* is still used by some congregations. The principal national body that used the term dropped it in 1961 when the Evangelical and Reformed Church merged with the Congregational Christian Churches to form the United Church of Christ. A small body of churches that did not enter the United Church of Christ is known as the *National Association of Congregational Churches.*

All members of the clergy may be referred to as *ministers. Pastor* may be substituted for those who lead a congregation. Use *the Rev.* before the name of a minister on first reference. Drop the title on second reference.

congress Capitalize *Congress* in references to the U.S. Senate and House. Lowercase to mean any assembly. See **foreign legislative bodies**.

congressional Lowercase, unless part of a proper name: congressional salaries, the Congressional Quarterly.

Congressional Directory The reference source for questions about the federal government not covered in this stylebook.

congressional districts See **districts**.

Congressional Record A daily publication of the proceedings of Congress, including a complete stenographic report of all remarks and debate.

congressman, congresswoman See **legislative titles**.

Congress of Racial Equality *CORE* is acceptable on second reference.

Connecticut Abbreviation: *Conn.* See **state(s)**.

connote, denote To *connote* is to imply; to *denote* is to be explicit: To some people marriage *connotes* too much restriction. Demolish *denotes* destruction.

ConocoPhillips Formed in a 2002 merger of *Conoco Inc.* and *Phillips Petroleum Co.* Its brands include *Conoco, Phillips 66* and *76* service stations and *Circle K* stores. Headquarters is in Houston.

Conrail Changed from the original *ConRail.* Acceptable in all references to the *Consolidated Rail Corp.* The private for-profit corporation was set up by Congress in 1976 to consolidate six bankrupt Northeast railroads — the Penn Central, the Erie Lackawanna, Reading, Central of New Jersey, Lehigh Valley and Lehigh & Hudson River. Conrail was purchased in 1997 by CSX Corp. and Norfolk Southern Corp. See **Amtrak**.

consensus

conservative In a political sense, lowercase unless the reference clearly is to the *Conservative Party* or its members. See **political parties**.

Conservative Judaism See **Jewish congregations**.

constable Capitalize as a formal title before a name. Lowercase otherwise: Constable Harry Jones, the constable.

constitution Capitalize all references to the U.S. Constitution: The president supports the Constitution.

Capitalize elsewhere only with the name of a state or nation: the French Constitution, the Massachusetts Constitution, but the state constitution, the Jaycees' constitution, any constitution.

Capitalize numbered amendments: First Amendment, 10th Amendment. Lowercase informal names of amendments: the presidential succession amendment. Avoid casual shortening of the Fifth Amendment, but if it fits the occasion: He took the Fifth seven times.

Lowercase the *clauses* that are frequently cited in legal documents: the due process clause, the commerce clause.

constitutional, unconstitutional Always lowercase.

consul, consul general (s.), **consuls general** (pl.) Capitalize as a formal title before a name.

consulate The office or residence of a consul in a foreign city, it handles the business affairs and personal needs of citizens of the appointing country. Capitalize with the name of a nation; lowercase without it: the French Consulate, the U.S. Consulate, the consulate. See **embassy**.

Consumer Price Index Capitalize as a title. *CPI* is acceptable on second reference. The CPI measures changes in the retail prices of a market basket of goods and services. It is issued monthly by the Bureau of Labor Statistics. Do not call it a *cost-of-living index,* because it includes neither income taxes nor Social Security taxes, nor does it reflect changes in buying patterns. But it is used to compute cost-of-living raises in many union contracts.

Contac A trademark for a decongestant.

contagious Not *contageous.*

contemptible Not *contemptable.*

continent Lowercase *continent* in all uses. From largest to smallest: Asia, Africa, North America, South America, Antarctica, Europe and Australia.

Continental Airlines Headquarters is in Houston.

Continental Divide The ridge along the Rocky Mountains that separates rivers flowing east from those that flow west.

continental drift, continental shelf, continental slope Lowercase.

Contra, Contras Nicaraguan rebels or rebel groups. The word is a short form of *contrarrevolucionario* (counterrevolutionary).

contractions Contractions (Example: *aren't* for *are not*) reflect informal speech and writing. They are acceptable in news stories if they fit the occasion. But avoid such extreme contractions as *who'd, she'd,* etc. Follow the spellings in *Webster's New World College Dictionary.*

controller In a financial sense, *controller* is commonly an officer of a business, *comptroller* of a government. Capitalize either term as a formal title before a name. Lowercase job descriptions: an air controller.

controversial An overused word. See **non-controversial**.

convention Capitalize as part of the name for a specific national or state political convention: the Democratic National Convention, the Republican State Convention. Lowercase other uses: the Republican convention, the annual convention of the American Medical Association.

convertible bond See **loan terminology**.

convict (v.) Use *of,* not *for:* He was convicted of murder.

(n.) A *prisoner,* frequently more appropriate than *inmate.*

convince, persuade You may be *convinced that* or *of;* you must be *persuaded to.*

> *Wrong:* They convinced her to fly and persuaded her that it was safe.
>
> *Right:* They persuaded her to fly and convinced her that it was safe.

cookie (s.), **cookies** (pl.) Not *cooky.*

cooperate, cooperative But *co-op,* short for *cooperative,* to distinguish it from *coop,* a cage for animals.

coordinate, coordination

cop Often a derogatory term for police officer; avoid it.

copter Short for *helicopter.*

copyright (n., v., adj.) The disclosure was made in a copyright story. Use *copyrighted* only as the past tense of the verb: He copyrighted the article.

CORE Acceptable on second reference for *Congress of Racial Equality.*

co-respondent In a divorce suit.

Corn Belt The region in the north central Midwest where much corn and cornfed livestock are raised. It extends from western Ohio to eastern Nebraska and northeastern Kansas.

Corp. See **corporation**.

corporal See **military titles**.

corporate names Copy the form of the company name except where corporations use far-fetched constructions as logos.

Guidelines:

1. Follow company usage in cases where there is a capital letter in the middle of a name: AirCal, BellSouth, PepsiCo.

corporate names *continued*

> 2. But use upper- and lowercase for all-cap names: Alltell (for ALL-TELL), Alza (for ALZA), BancTexas (for BancTEXAS), Rand Corp. (for THE RAND CORP.). See **company**.

corporation An entity treated as a person in the eyes of the law. It can own property, go in debt, sue and be sued. Use *Corp.* at the end of a name: Gulf Oil Corp. Spell out elsewhere: the Corporation for Public Broadcasting. Possessives: Gulf Oil Corp.'s profits.

corps Capitalize as part of a proper name: Marine Corps, Signal Corps, 9th Corps, U.S. Army Corps of Engineers. Lowercase elsewhere. The possessive is *corps'* for both singular and plural: one corps' location, two corps' assignments.

In the U.S. Army, a tactical *corps* comprises two or more divisions. Armies worldwide traditionally designate corps by Roman numerals: I Corps, X Corps. When used in this sense, convert the Roman numerals to Arabic numerals: 1st Corps, 10th Corps. See **army, division** and **military units**.

Corsica In datelines: *AJACCIO, Corsica, May 13 (UPI) —* .

Cortes The Spanish Parliament. See **foreign legislative bodies**.

cosmonaut Russian astronaut. Always lowercase.

cost of living The amount of money needed to pay taxes and to buy the goods and services deemed necessary for a given standard of living, taking into account changes in tastes and buying patterns. Hyphenate as an adjective: The *cost of living* went up, but we got no *cost-of-living* raise. See **inflation** and **Consumer Price Index**.

Cotton Belt The sections of the South where much cotton is grown.

council, councilor, councilman, councilwoman A meeting and those who meet. See **counsel** and **legislative titles**.

Council of Economic Advisers The economic advisers to the U.S. president who also help him prepare his annual economic report to Congress.

counsel, counseled, counseling, counselor, counselor-at-law To *counsel* is to advise. A *counselor* is one who conducts a case in court, usually, but not always, a lawyer. A *counselor-at-law* is a lawyer. See **council** and **lawyer**.

count, countess See **nobility**.

counter- Usually solid as a prefix:

counteract	counterespionage
counterattack	counterinsurgency
counterbalance	counterintelligence

counteroffensive
counterproductive
counterproposal

counterrevolution
counterspy

but **counter-Reformation, counter-terrorism.**

See *Webster's New World College Dictionary* and hyphenate compounds not listed there.

country-dance, country mile, countryside, countrywide

county Capitalize as an integral part of a proper name: Dade County, the Dade County Commission. But: the county Board of Health, the county. Lowercase all *county of* and generic and plural uses: Westchester and Rockland counties, the county of Westchester, any county.

Capitalize as part of a formal title before a name: County Manager John Smith. Lowercase when it is not part of the formal title: county Health Commissioner Frank Jones.

county court In some states, it is not a court but the administrative body of a county. In most cases, the *court* is presided over by a *county judge,* who is not a judge in the traditional sense but the chief administrative officer of the county. Explain the terms if they are not clear in the context.

Capitalize references to a specific county court. Capitalize *county judge* as a formal title before a name. Use *judge* alone before a name only in direct quotations.

Example:

> SEVIERVILLE, Tenn, Jan. 12. (UPI) — A reluctant County Court approved a school budget Monday that calls for a 10 percent tax increase for property owners.
>
> The county had been given an ultimatum by the state: Approve the budget or shut down the schools.
>
> The chief administrative officer, County Judge James Smith, said, etc.

coup d'etat *Coup* is usually sufficient.

couple In the sense of two persons, the word takes plural verbs and pronouns: The *couple were* married Saturday and left Sunday on *their* honeymoon.

To denote a unit, use a singular verb: Every *couple was* asked to give $10.

Do not omit a necessary *of* in: A couple of tomatoes were stolen.

coupon See **loan terminology**.

course numbers Use Arabic numerals and capitalize the subject with a figure: History 6, Philosophy 209.

court decisions Use figures and a hyphen: The Supreme Court ruled 5-4, a 5-4 decision. *To* is not needed, but use hyphens if it appears in quoted matter: the court ruled 5-to-4, a 5-to-4 decision.

courtesy titles In general, UPI does not use courtesy titles *(Mr., Mrs., Ms., Miss)*. Exceptions: In direct quotations and to identify husband and wife, mother and son, etc., in the same story.

courthouse Capitalize with the name of a jurisdiction: the Cook County Courthouse, the U.S. Courthouse. Lowercase other uses: the county courthouse, the courthouse, the federal courthouse.

Court House, two words, is used in the proper names of some communities: Appomattox Court House, Va.

court-martial (s.), **courts-martial** (pl.) Not *court-martials.*

court names Capitalize the full proper names of courts at all levels, with or without the name of the jurisdiction: the U.S. Supreme Court, the Supreme Court, U.S. District Court, the Massachusetts Superior Court, the state Superior Court, the court.

For courts identified by a numeral: 2nd District Court, a district court, 8th U.S. Circuit Court of Appeals, the appeals court, the court.

See **judge, judicial branch**, and separate entries under **U.S.** and the court name.

Court of St. James's Note the *'s.* The formal name for the royal court of the British sovereign.

courtroom

coverup (n., adj.), **cover up** (v.) He tried to cover up the scandal. He was prosecuted for the coverup.

crackup (n., adj.), **crack up** (v.)

crawfish Not *crayfish.* An exception to *Webster's New World College Dictionary* based on the dominant spelling in Louisiana, where the dish is a popular delicacy.

(cripple) Avoid except in direct quotations in reference to physically impaired people. Use *disabled* instead. Many people also object to being called *handicapped* or labeled by a condition or disease, such as being called an *epileptic* rather than referred to as *a person who has epilepsy.* Make such distinctions if useful.

Crisco A trademark for a vegetable shortening.

crisis (s.), **crises** (pl.)

crisscross

criterion (s.), **criteria** (pl.)

cross-country Hyphenated in general use, but no hyphen in sports stories about *cross country* events, based on the practices of U.S. and international governing bodies for the sport.

cross fire

cruise missile Lowercase. A generic name for a low-flying guided missile. The U.S. Navy's *Tomahawk* is a cruise missile.

CT scan, CT scanner, CT scanning *CT* stands for *computerized tomography.* Do not use *CAT scan.*

Cub Scouts The organization is the *Cub Scouts.* Members, ages 8 through 10, are *Cub Scouts* or *Cubs.* See **Boy Scouts**.

Cultural Revolution Chinese upheaval of the 1960s.

cup Equal to 8 fluid ounces. In metric it is about 240 milliliters or .24 liters. To convert to liters, multiply by .24 (14 cups × .24 equals about 3.36 liter, or 3,360 milliliters). See **recipes**.

currency depreciation, devaluation, revaluation A nation's money *depreciates* when its value falls in relation to the currency of other nations or in relation to its own prior value.

A nation's money is *devalued* when its government deliberately reduces its value in relation to the currency of other nations, or when the value of other currencies rise. The goods it imports tend to become more expensive. Its exports tend to become less expensive in other nations and thus more competitive.

A nation's currency is *revalued* when it arbitrarily raises the value of its currency in terms of the U.S. dollar, the unit on which most major world currencies are valued. A country is forced to revalue when its low inflation rate and high productivity rate in comparison with its trading partners gives it a competitive advantage in exports to world markets.

Nations usually are reluctant to revalue because they lose competitiveness in world markets, but since their currency is worth more, they can pay off international debts with fewer bank notes; they can buy raw materials at lower prices; their citizens can enjoy favorable exchange rates while traveling abroad.

(currently) Overused as a synonym for *now.* Avoid it.

cupful, cupfuls Not *cupsful.*

customs Capitalize *U.S. Customs Service,* or simply *the Customs Service.* Lowercase elsewhere: a customs official, a customs ruling, he went through customs.

cutback (n., adj.), **cut back** (v.) The *cutback* will require frugality. He *cut back* spending.

cutoff (n., adj.), **cut off** (v.) The *cutoff* date for applications is Monday. He *cut off* his son's allowance.

cutthroat

cybernetics, cyberpunk, cybersecurity, cybersex, cyberterror, cyberweapons

cyberspace The worldwide system of interlinked computer systems, or the virtual space created by them. See **Internet**.

cyclone A storm with strong winds rotating about a moving center of low atmospheric pressure. In the United States it often means a *tornado*. In the Indian Ocean it means a *hurricane*. Because of the ambiguity, avoid *cyclone* in favor of the more precise terms. See **hurricane** and **tornado**.

cynic, skeptic A *skeptic* is a doubter; a *cynic* is a disbeliever.

Czechoslovakia Former country in Central Europe, split into the Czech Republic and Slovakia in 1993.

Czech Republic Central European country that used to be the western part of Czechoslovakia. (In 1993, Czechoslovakia was divided into the Czech Republic and Slovakia.) The Czech Republic's capital is *Prague*. See **Slovakia**.

czar Not *tsar*. Derived from the Latin *caesar*, it means *emperor* and usually is an informal label. It was a formal title only for the ruler of Russia and some other Slavic nations: *Czar Nicholas II* was the last emperor of Russia. Acceptable in such uses as drug czar.

D

Dacron A trademark for a polyester fiber.

DaimlerChrysler AG No space or hyphen in *DaimlerChrysler.* The company has group headquarters in Stuttgart, Germany, and Auburn Hills, Mich.

Dalai Lama The traditional high priest of Lamaism, a form of Buddhism practiced in Tibet and Mongolia. The Dalai Lama is understood by Tibetan Buddhists to be a reincarnation of Avalokitesvara, the Buddha of compassion. *Dalai Lama* is a title rather than a name, but is all that is used when referring to the man and is capitalized. (The same rule applies to *Pachen Lama* and *Karmapa Lama.*)

Dallas The city in Texas stands alone in datelines.

Dalles, The A city in Oregon. In datelines: *THE DALLES, Ore., April 23 (UPI) —*

dam Capitalize as part of a proper name: Hoover Dam.

damage, damages *Damage* is destruction; *damages* are compensation for injury or loss: Authorities said *damage* from the storm would total more than $1 billion. The woman received $25,000 in *damages.*

dame The equivalent for women of a knighthood for men. If used, it must always be with a given name and capitalized: Dame Agatha Christie, Dame Agatha. See **honorary titles**.

damn it Use instead of *dammit,* but like other profanity it should be avoided unless there is a compelling reason to use it. See **obscenities**.

damsite

dangling modifiers Avoid modifiers (participles) that do not refer clearly and logically to some word in the sentence.

Dangling: Taking our seats, the game started. (*Taking* does not refer to the subject, game, or to any other word in the sentence.)

Correct: Taking our seats, we watched the opening of the game. (*Taking* refers to *we,* the subject of the sentence.)

Dardanelles, the Not *the Dardanelles Strait.*

Dark Ages The period beginning with the sack of Rome and ending with the early Renaissance (A.D. 476 to about 1450), a period in Europe characterized by intellectual stagnation, widespread ignorance and poverty.

Dark Continent

dark horse No hyphen: a dark horse candidate.

dash Indicate the dash by striking the hyphen key twice (--) Do not use the longer (underscore) dash, which is usually on the same key.

Put a space on both sides of a dash in all uses.

1. A dash is a strong punctuation mark that should not be used in lieu of a comma. Reserve the dash to denote an abrupt change in thought or an emphatic pause: We will fly to Paris in June — if I get a raise. Smith offered a plan — it was unprecedented — to raise revenues. But be wary of the damage this does to the flow of a sentence.

2. When a phrase that would otherwise be set off with commas contains a series of words that must be separated by commas, use dashes to set off the full phrase: He listed the qualities — intelligence, charm, beauty, independence — that he liked in women.

3. Use a dash before an author's name at the end of a quotation: "Who steals my purse steals trash." — Shakespeare.

4. A dash is used in datelines: NEW YORK, Nov. 1 (UPI) — The city is broke.

5. Use dashes, with spaces before and after, to introduce individual sections of a list. Capitalize the first word following the dash.

> Jones gave the following reasons:
> — He never ordered the package.
> — If he did, it didn't come.
> — If it did, he sent it back.

data A plural noun that normally takes plural verbs and pronouns. See **collective nouns** for exceptions.

database, data bits, data processing, data stream

date line Two words for the imaginary line that separates one day from another. See **international date line**.

datelines A *dateline,* one word, should tell the reader that the basic information for the story came from the dateline community.

Do not, for example, use a Washington dateline on a story written primarily from information that a newspaper reported under a Washington dateline. Use the home city of the newspaper instead.

A dateline written in capital letters contains the name of a community, often followed by a country, state or territory, the date the story was written and the UPI identifier.

> TAEGU, South Korea, Oct. 19 (UPI) —
> MIAMI, Oct. 19 (UPI) —
> BETHESDA, Md., Oct. 19 (UPI) —

Note the space before and after the dash: HILO, Hawaii, Oct. 19 (UPI) — Snow fell today.

Do not use *here, this town,* etc., to refer back to a dateline. It slows reading. If a reference must be made, repeat the name of the community.

When a story has been assembled from sources in widely separated areas, use no dateline. Instead, use *By United Press International* or a writer's byline and UPI affiliation: By AL SWANSON, United Press International; By IAN CAMPBELL, UPI Chief Economics Correspondent.

From rural areas, use the name of the nearest community.

Use a byline over a dateline only if a reporter was in the dateline community to gather the information reported.

Domestic Datelines:

The authority for spelling of domestic communities is the *National Five-Digit ZIP Code & Post Office Directory.*

These domestic cities stand alone in datelines:

ALBUQUERQUE	DALLAS	MEMPHIS
ATLANTA	DENVER	MIAMI
BALTIMORE	DETROIT	MILWAUKEE
BOSTON	HOLLYWOOD	MINNEAPOLIS
CHICAGO	HONOLULU	NASHVILLE
CINCINNATI	HOUSTON	NEW ORLEANS
CLEVELAND	INDIANAPOLIS	NEW YORK
COLORADO	LAS VEGAS	OKLAHOMA
SPRINGS	LOS ANGELES	CITY

datelines *continued*

OMAHA	ST. LOUIS	SEATTLE
PHILADELPHIA	SALT LAKE CITY	TUCSON
PHOENIX	SAN ANTONIO	WASHINGTON
PITTSBURGH	SAN DIEGO	
SACRAMENTO	SAN FRANCISCO	

Spell out *Alaska, Hawaii, Idaho, Iowa, Maine, Ohio, Texas* and *Utah*. Abbreviate others as listed in this book under the full name of each state.

In Hawaii, use *Hawaii* with all communities outside Honolulu. Specify the island in the text if needed.

Follow the same practice for communities on islands within the boundaries of other states: **EDGARTOWN, Mass.,** for example, not **EDGARTOWN, Martha's Vineyard.** If there is no community on an island, use the island name followed by the state: **Portsmouth Island, N.C.**

Datelines from U.S. possessions follow the same guidelines as those from foreign nations.

Foreign Datelines:

Use a specific foreign dateline only if the basic information in a story was obtained by a full- or part-time correspondent physically present in the dateline community.

If a radio broadcast monitored in another city was the source of information, use the dateline of the city where the monitoring took place and mention the fact in the story.

The first source for spelling foreign place names is *Webster's New World College Dictionary.* If the dictionary does not have an entry, use the first-listed spelling in the *Columbia Gazetteer of the World Online.* See **geographic names**.

These foreign locations stand alone in datelines:

BAGHDAD	CAIRO	KUWAIT CITY
BANGKOK	GIBRALTAR	LIMA
BEIJING	GUATEMALA	LONDON
BERLIN	CITY	LUXEMBOURG
BOGOTA	HAVANA	MACAO
BOMBAY	HONG KONG	MADRID
BRUSSELS	JAKARTA	MELBOURNE
BUENOS AIRES	JERUSALEM	MEXICO CITY

MONTREAL	ROME	TEHRAN
MOSCOW	SAN MARINO	TOKYO
NEW DELHI	SAO PAULO	TORONTO
OTTAWA	SEOUL	VATICAN CITY
PARIS	SHANGHAI	VIENNA
QUEBEC	SINGAPORE	
RIO DE JANEIRO	SYDNEY	

Do not, however, use a country's name if it would repeat exactly the dateline community: MONACO, for example. Not: MONACO, Monaco. But: MONTE CARLO, Monaco; PANAMA CITY, Panama.

In Canada: *Montreal, Ottawa, Quebec* and *Toronto* stand alone. All other cities are followed by the province or territory. Do not abbreviate any province or territory name.

In the Commonwealth of Independent States: *Moscow* stands alone, but all other former Soviet cities are followed by the republic: *MINSK, Belarus, Dec. 16 (UPI)* —

Stories from other foreign cities that do not stand alone in datelines should contain the name of the country or territory spelled out.

In most cases, use the conventionally accepted short name: Argentina, for example. Not: Republic of Argentina.

Note these special cases:

* Instead of *United Kingdom*, use *England, Northern Ireland, Scotland* or *Wales*.
* For divided nations, use the commonly accepted names based on geographic distinctions: *North Korea, South Korea*.
* Use an article in a country's name only with *El Salvador*. Others: *Netherlands, Philippines*.

For island nations and territories, use the general name. Specify an individual island, if needed, in the text. If there is no community on an island, use the island name, followed by the name of the territory: *British Virgin Islands, Indonesia, Philippines, Cyprus*.

Use the commonly accepted separate names for areas that have them, even though they are not independent nations:

Bermuda	Gibraltar	Puerto Rico
Canal Zone	Greenland	Sardinia
Canary Islands	Guadeloupe	Sikkim
Corsica	Guam	Sicily
Faeroe Islands	Martinique	Tibet

datelines *continued*

When a datelined story contains supplementary information obtained in another city, make that point clear. Do not put parentheses around such material, however, unless the correspondent in the dateline community was cut off from incoming communications.

Examples:

1. Material from another area with communications intact:

> LONDON, June 1 (UPI) — Prime Minister Harold Wilson submitted his resignation Monday.
>
> In Washington, a State Department spokesman said the change in government leadership would have no effect on negotiations involving the Common Market.

2. Material from another area was not available to the correspondent in the dateline city because communications from the outside world were cut off:

> PHNOM PENH, Cambodia, Oct. 19 (UPI) — Khmer Rouge troops pushed into Phnom Penh Monday, barely hours after the United States ran down the Stars and Stripes and abandoned Cambodia to the Communists.
>
> (In Washington, the State Department said Americans evacuated in a mass airlift had arrived safely aboard aircraft carriers and at bases in Thailand.)

3. If the reporter is aboard a ship, aircraft, spacecraft, etc.:

> ABOARD THE USS FORRESTAL, Oct. 19 (UPI) —

> ABOARD AIR FORCE ONE, Oct. 19 (UPI) —

> ABOARD THE SPACE SHUTTLE ENTERPRISE, Oct. 19 (UPI) —

dates Use figures without letters: April 1, not April 1st.

When a month is used with a specific date, use the abbreviations *Jan., Feb., Aug., Sept., Oct., Nov.* and *Dec.* Spell out other months.

When a phrase lists only a month and a year, do not separate with commas. When a phrase refers to a month, day and year, set off the year with commas.: January 1972 was a cold month. Jan. 2 was the coldest day of the month. Feb. 14, 1976, was the target date. His birthday is May 15.

daughter-in-law (s.), **daughters-in-law** (pl.) Not *daughter-in-laws.*

Daughters of the American Revolution *DAR* is acceptable on second reference. Headquarters is in Washington.

da Vinci See **Leonardo da Vinci.**

day care (n.), **day-care** (adj.)

daylight saving time Not *savings.* When linking the term with a time zone: Eastern Daylight Time, Pacific Daylight Time, etc. Lowercase *daylight saving time* in all uses and *daylight time* standing alone.

A federal law specifies that *daylight time* applies from 2 a.m. on the first Sunday of April until 2 a.m. on the last Sunday of October in all areas that do not specifically exempt themselves. See **time.**

daylong, daytime

days Capitalize them: *Monday, Tuesday,* etc.

Other guidelines:

1. Spell out days of the week in all stories. Do not use *today, tonight, yesterday* or *tomorrow.*

2. Avoid an unnecessary use of *last* or *next.* Past, present or future tense are an adequate indication of which day is meant.

> *Wordy:* It happened last Tuesday.
> *Better:* It happened Tuesday.

3. Do not abbreviate, except in tabular format (three letters, without periods): *Sun, Mon, Tue, Wed, Thu, Fri, Sat.*

See **time** and **release times.**

D-day June 6, 1944, the day the Allies invaded France in World War II. *D-day plus 1* means June 7, 1944, etc.

DDT Preferred in all references for the insecticide *dichloro diphenyl trichloroethane.*

de- See **foreign particles** for instructions on how to handle names such as *de Gaulle.*

DEA Acceptable on second reference for *Drug Enforcement Administration.*

deacon Capitalize as a formal title before a name. Lowercase otherwise: Deacon John Jones, the deacon.

dead end (n.), **dead-end** (adj.) A *dead-end* street has a *dead end.*

deaf-mute This term may be used, but it is preferred to say a person cannot hear or speak. Do not use *deaf and dumb.*

dean Capitalize as a formal title before a name: Dean Shane Smith, Deans Shane Smith and Susan Smith. Lowercase in other uses: Shane Smith, dean of the college; the dean.

dean's list Lowercase, no hyphen: He is on the dean's list. She is a dean's list student.

deathbed, deathrow, deathtrap

debenture See **loan terminology**.

debt service The outlay necessary to meet all interest and principal payments on outstanding debt during a given period.

debut Do not convert this noun to a verb.

decades Use figures to indicate decades of history. Use an apostrophe to indicate numerals that are left out; show plural by adding *s:* the 1890s, the '90s, the Gay '90s, the 1920s, the mid-1930s.

December See **months**.

deci- A prefix meaning *one-tenth;* a *decigram* is one-tenth of a gram, about .0035 ounces. See **metric system**.

decimal units Use a period and figures to indicate decimal amounts. Carry decimals to *two* places unless there are special circumstances, as in this example: The company's net profit was $4.644 billion, up from $4.642 billion in the same quarter last year. In this case, rounding the figure to two places would make a comparison meaningless, because it would give the same total of $4.64 billion. See **fractions**.

decimate The literal meaning is *to destroy one out of 10.* Do not use as a general term for *destruction.*

Declaration of Independence Lowercase *the declaration.*

decorations See **awards**.

Deepfreeze A trademark for a home freezer. Use two words for something postponed indefinitely: The project is in the deep freeze.

deep-six Slang for *dispose of.* Use only in quotes.

Deep South Capitalize both words when referring to the region that encompasses Alabama, Georgia, Louisiana, Mississippi and South Carolina.

default In computing, an automatic setting that will be used unless the user specifies a different one. In a financial sense, see **loan terminology**.

defendant Not *defendent.*

defense attorney Always lowercase. Never abbreviate.

definitely Overused as a vague intensifier. Avoid it.

deflation A decrease in price levels resulting from a decrease in total spending relative to the supply of available goods.

degrees See **academic degrees** and **temperatures**.

deity Lowercase. See **religion**.

deka- A prefix meaning *10;* a *dekameter* is 10 meters, one-tenth of a hectometer. A *dekagram* is 10 grams, one-tenth of a hectogram. A *dekare* is 10 ares, one-tenth of a hectare.

Use *dek-* before a vowel, as in dekare, and *deka-* before a consonant, as in dekameter. See **metric system** and **hecto-**.

Delaware Abbreviation: *Del.* See **state(s)**.

delegate The title for members of the lower houses of some legislatures. Do not abbreviate. Capitalize as a formal title before a name. Lowercase other uses: convention delegate Robert Jones.

Delmarva Peninsula Sometimes called the *Eastern Shore,* it is the peninsula between Chesapeake Bay and the Atlantic Ocean. It consists of parts of the states of Delaware, Maryland and Virginia.

Delphi In the computer industry, *Delphi* is a programming language created by Borland International Inc.

Delta Air Lines. Headquarters is in Atlanta.

demagogue, demagoguery Note the *u*.

demilitarized zone *DMZ* is acceptable on second reference.

democrat, democratic Lowercase unless the reference is to the *Democratic Party* or its members. Do not use *Democrat* as an adjective:

> *Wrong:* Democrat Sen. Lea Smith; Democrat leaders in Washington; the Democrat Party.
> *Right:* Democratic Sen. Lea Smith; Democratic leaders in Washington; the Democratic Party.

See **political parties**.

Democratic Governors' Conference Note the apostrophe.

demolish, destroy Both mean *to do away with completely.* It is redundant to say totally demolished or totally destroyed.

denote See the **connote, denote** entry.

Denver The city in Colorado stands alone in datelines.

depart It requires a preposition: He will depart from LaGuardia. She will depart at 11:30 p.m. Do not drop the preposition as some airline dispatchers do. In most cases, *leave* is a better choice.

department Do not abbreviate. Capitalize as part of a government: the Department of Defense. The *of* may be dropped and the title flip-flopped and capitalization retained: the Defense Department.

Lowercase *department* standing alone, in plural uses or as part of an internal element: *department* officials said, the Labor, Justice and Homeland Security *departments*, the *departments* of Labor, Justice and Homeland Security, the sports *department* of the Daily Planet. See **academic departments** and **Cabinet departments**.

dependent Not *dependant*.

depression Capitalize *Depression* and *Great Depression* for the world-wide economic collapse that began with the stock market collapse of Oct. 28–29, 1929. Lowercase other uses: the depression of the 1970s.

depths See **dimensions**.

deputy Capitalize as a formal title before a name. Lowercase otherwise.

derogatory terms Do not use derogatory terms such as *Kraut* except in direct quotes and when their use is an essential part of the story.

desktop publishing The use of a computer, special software and a printer to produce typeset-quality text and graphics for newsletters, brochures and other documents.

-designate Hyphenate. Capitalize only the first word as a formal title before a name: Chairman-designate Susan Smith.

designed Frequently superfluous journalese, as in: Congress passed a law designed to outlaw racial discrimination. The infinitive *to outlaw* clearly implies intent.

destroy See **demolish, destroy**.

detective Do not abbreviate, always lowercase unless it is a formal title: police detective Frank Serpico; private detective Nero Wolfe, Detective Sgt. Mary Smith.

detente

detention center See **prison, jail**.

Detroit The city in Michigan stands alone in datelines.

devil But capitalize *Satan*.

Dexedrine A trademark for an appetite depressant.

dialect There are some words and phrases in everyone's vocabulary that are typical of a particular region or group. Quoting dialect, unless used carefully, implies substandard or illiterate usage. Avoid dialect, even in quoted matter, unless it is clearly pertinent.

When there is a compelling reason to use dialect, use phonetic spellings. Apostrophes show missing letters and sounds: "Din't ya yoosta live at Toidy-Toid Street and Sekun Amya? Across from da moom pitchers?" See **quotations in the news**.

dialogue The verb forms: *dialogue, dialogued, dialoguing*.

dialup, dialup access, dialup modem.

diarrhea Two *r*'s.

Dictaphone A trademark for a dictation recorder.

dictionaries For spelling, style and usage questions not covered in this stylebook, consult *Webster's New World College Dictionary*. See **geographic names**.

Use the first spelling listed. If spellings differ in separate entries (*tee shirt and T-shirt,* for example), use the spelling that has a full definition *(T-shirt).* If each entry has a full definition (*although or though,* for example), either is acceptable.

For spelling and usage not covered in this book or in *Webster's New World College Dictionary,* consult *Webster's Third New International Dictionary,* which has more entries.

die-hard Not *diehard.*

Diet The Japanese Parliament. See **foreign legislative bodies**.

dietitian Not *dietician.*

differ To *differ from* means *to be unlike;* to *differ with* means *to disagree.*

dilemma Not synonymous with *problem.* It means a choice between two, and only two, equally distasteful alternatives.

dimensions Use figures and spell out inches, feet, yards, etc. to indicate depth, height, length and width. Hyphenate adjectival forms before nouns: He is 5 feet 6 inches tall; the 5-foot-6-inch man; the 5-foot-6 man; the 5-foot man; the basketball team signed a 7-footer; the 6-3 guard fouled out. The car is 17 feet long, 6 feet wide and 5 feet high. The rug is 9 feet by 12 feet; the 9-by-12 rug. The storm left 5 inches of snow. The trench was 3 feet deep. The building has 4,000 square feet of office space. It was a 100 square-foot storage room.

Use an apostrophe to indicate feet and quotation marks to indicate inches (5'6") only in very technical contexts.

Diners Club No apostrophe. Headquarters is in New York.

diocese The district under a bishop's jurisdiction. Lowercase unless part of a proper name: the diocese of Rochester, the Rochester diocese, the diocese. But: the Eastern Diocese of the Armenian Church of America.

See **Episcopal Church** and **Roman Catholic Church**.

directions Always lowercase compass points (*north, south, northeast, northern,* etc.) that indicate direction: He drove west. The cold front is moving east. Elsewhere:

1. Capitalize compass points that designate regions of the world or United States: The North was victorious. The South will rise again. Settlers from the East went west in search of new lives.

   Also: the Far East, the Eastern establishment, Eastern bloc nations, the Eastern Hemisphere, the Middle East, the Mideast, the Midwest, the Northeast, a Northerner, the North Woods, a Northern liberal, Southeast Asia, a Southern strategy, the South Pacific, the West, a Western businessman, Western Europe, the Western Hemisphere, the Western

directions *continued*

United States, the West Coast (the region; lowercase *west coast* for the physical coastline itself — see **coast**).

2. Capitalize compass points as part of a proper name: North America, the South Pole, North Dakota, Northern Ireland, West Virginia, the Eastern Shore.

3. Lowercase compass points with other nations except to designate a politically divided nation: northern France, eastern Canada. But: East Germany, South Korea.

4. In general, lowercase compass points to describe a section of a state or city: western Texas, south Atlanta. But capitalize them if a particular section has a widely known popular name: Southern California, Southside (Chicago), Lower East Side (New York). If in doubt, use lowercase.

director Capitalize as a formal title before a name: FBI Director J. Edgar Hoover. Lowercase as a job description: company director Barbara Warren.

director general No hyphen.

dis- No hyphen: dismember, dissemble, disservice.

disasters See **passenger lists**.

disc This spelling is generally used in non-computer references. Examples: laserdisc, disc brakes. See **disk**.

disc jockey *DJ* is acceptable on second reference in a column or other special context. Use *announcer* in other contexts.

disk See **floppy disk** and **hard disk**.

diskette May be used in all references to *floppy disk*. See **floppy disk**.

disk operating system. See **DOS** and **MS-DOS**.

discreet, discrete *Discreet* means *prudent;* *discrete* means *detached, separate:* "I'm afraid I was not very *discreet,*" she wrote. There are four *discrete* sounds in a quadraphonic system.

discus The disc thrown in track and field events.

diseases Lowercase arthritis, emphysema, leukemia, malaria, migraine, pneumonia, etc. Capitalize only when a disease bears the name of a person or group identified with it: Bright's disease, Parkinson's disease, etc.

disinterested, uninterested *Disinterested* means *unbiased* or *impartial; uninterested* means *bored* or *indifferent.*

dispel, dispelled, dispelling

dissociate Preferred to *disassociate.*

distances Use figures: We walked 3 miles.

district Do not abbreviate. Use a figure and capitalize to form a proper name: District 3, the 2nd District, the 1st Congressional District. Lower-case standing alone: the district, the congressional district.

district attorney Do not abbreviate. Capitalize as a formal title before a name: District Attorney Hamilton Burger.

district court See **court names**.

District of Columbia If used with Washington, abbreviate as *D.C.* Spell out when used alone. Use *the district,* not *D.C.,* on second reference.

dive, dived, diving Not *dove* for the past tense.

dive bomber (n.), **divebomb** (v.) A technique in which a bomb is aimed by the pilot diving a plane steeply toward a target.

dividend See **profit terminology**.

division See **organizations and institutions** and **political divisions**.

division (military) A U.S. Army formation comprising two or more brigades. In the U.S. Navy, a *division* is a subdivision of a *squadron.* In the U.S. Air Force, a *division* is composed of two or more *wings.*

Capitalize with a numerical designation: 1st Infantry Division, 4th Armored Division, 2nd Marine Division. Otherwise, lowercase: the division, the division commander.

See **military units, corps, brigade** and **wing**.

divorce Report that a person is divorced only if it is clearly pertinent. Even when relevant, it seldom belongs in the lead. Avoid stories that begin: *A 35-year-old divorcee,* etc. If relevant, report in the body of the story that someone is divorced.

Dixie cup A trademark for a paper drinking cup.

DMZ Acceptable on second reference for *demilitarized zone.*

DNA *[deoxyribonucleic acid]* A chemical structure that carries the genetic code. It is the primary genetic material in all living organisms. *DNA fingerprinting* is a study of DNA patterns and is often used as evidence in criminal cases. Also called *DNA profiling,* or *typing.* No two people (except for identical twins) have the same DNA profile.

doctor Spell out if not a title: An apple a day keeps the doctor away. Use *Dr.* (or *Drs.* in plural) as a title before the name of a physician, including direct quotations: Dr. Jonas Salk. Drop the title after first reference.

People are inclined to identify *Dr.* only with practitioners of the healing professions: physicians, dentists, veterinarians, etc. In general, confine *Dr.* to these groups, and avoid it in referring to academics and clerics.

If it is necessary to indicate that a person such as an expert witness holds a doctorate in a certain field, explain it like this: James Green,

doctor *continued*

who has a Ph.D. in chemistry from Harvard University, testified the substance was not flammable.

In cases where it is pertinent, *Dr.* may also be used with *the Rev.* in first reference to Protestant clergy who have doctor of divinity degrees: the Rev. Dr. Norman Vincent Peale.

Never use *Dr.* for those who hold only honorary doctorates. See **academic degrees**.

dollars Always lowercase. Use figures and the *$* sign in all except casual references or amounts without a figure: The book cost $4. Dad, please give me a dollar. Dollars are flowing overseas.

For amounts of more than $1 million, use the *$* and figures up to two decimal places. Do not use hyphens: He is worth $4.35 million. He is worth exactly $4,351,242. He proposed a $300 billion budget.

The form for amounts less than $1 million: $4, $6.35, $25, $500, $1,000, $650,000.

domain name In the Internet system of domains, a *domain name* most often refers to an address or URL of a Web site, or to the wording after the *at* sign in an e-mail address. For example: In UPI's Web address *(www.upi.com)* and e-mail addresses *(jdoe@upi.com),* the domain name is *upi.com.* See **URL**.

domino (s.), **dominoes** (pl.)

DOS Acronym for *disk operating system.* See **MS-DOS** and **operating system**.

dot-com A term gaining popularity as a nickname for Internet companies or their personnel.

double dipper (n.), **double dipping** (n.), **double-dipping** (adj.)

double titles Avoid them before names. Instead, set them off from a name with commas: Gen. John Johnson, chairman of the Joint Chiefs of Staff, rather than Chairman Gen. John Johnson, etc. See **titles**.

doughnut Not *donut.*

Dow Jones & Co. The company publishes *The Wall Street Journal, Barron's* and other publications. It also operates Dow Jones Newswires and compiles stock market indexes, including the Dow Jones industrial average, the Dow Jones transportation average, the Dow Jones utility average, and the Dow Jones composite average. Headquarters is in New York.

Downhold Club An organization of former Unipressers. See **Unipressers**.

Down East Use only to refer to the state of Maine.

download Transfer a file from another computer to your computer. See **upload** and **FTP**.

downriver

downstate Lowercase unless part of a proper name: downstate Illinois. But: the Downstate Medical Center.

Down syndrome Not *Down's syndrome.*

Down Under Australia, New Zealand and their surroundings.

Dr. See **doctor**.

draft beer Not *draught* beer.

drama See **composition titles**.

Dramamine A trademark for a motion sickness remedy.

draperies, drapes *Draperies* are curtains; *drapes* is a verb.

drier, driest, dryer The air is *drier,* it has been the *driest* month, etc. Use *dryer* for a machine or device that dries things: clothes dryer, hair dryer.

drive Do not abbreviate. See **addresses**.

drive-in (n., adj.)

dropout (n.), **drop out** (v.)

drowned If a person suffocates in water or other fluid, say the victim *drowned.* To say that someone *was drowned* implies that another person caused the death by holding the victim's head under the water.

Dr Pepper A trademark for a soft drink. No period.

drugs Because *drugs* is often used as a synonym for narcotics, *medicine* is often better for references to medication. *Prescription drugs* is also acceptable.

Drug Enforcement Administration Not *agency. DEA* is acceptable on second reference.

drunk, drunken Use *drunk* after the verb: He was drunk. Use *drunken* before a noun: a drunken driver. Note that some organizations erroneously use *drunk* in their titles, e.g., *Mothers Against Drunk Driving,* otherwise known as *MADD.* See **Mothers Against Drunk Driving**.

dryer See **drier, driest, dryer**.

DSL For *digital subscriber line.* See **ISDN**.

duchess See **nobility** and **royal titles**.

duel A contest between two persons. Three persons cannot duel.

duffel Not *duffle.*

duke See **nobility** and **royal titles**.

Dumpster Trademark for a large steel trash bin handled by a specially equipped truck. Use a generic term instead, *trash bin* or *garbage container,* etc.

Dunkirk Not *Dunkerque.* In datelines: *DUNKIRK, France, June 2 (UPI) — .*

duo Journalese for *two.* Avoid it.

du Pont, E.I. The U.S. industrialist born in France. Use *du Pont* to refer to the family but *DuPont* (capitalized, no space) for the company named for him, the *E.I. du Pont de Nemours Co.* of Wilmington, Del.

dust storm Visibility of one-half mile or less due to dust, wind speeds of 30 mph or more.

DVD Acceptable in all references for *digital video disk.* (Also called *digital versatile disk.*) Similar to a CD-ROM but with much greater capacity.

dyed-in-the-wool (adj.)

dyeing, dying *Dyeing* refers to changing colors. *Dying* refers to death.

E

each Takes a singular verb.

earl See **nobility**.

earth Capitalize when used as the proper name of the planet; lowercase in casual context: He is down to earth. How does that pattern apply to Mars, Jupiter, Earth, the sun and the moon? The astronauts returned to Earth. He hopes to move heaven and earth.

When referring to the planet, do not use an article before the noun. Make it Earth, not the earth. See **planets**.

earthquakes *Temblor* (not *tremblor*) is a synonym for earthquake. *Epicenter* means *the center of an earthquake.*

The two important scales in measuring earthquakes are the Richter and the Mercalli. The *Richter scale,* the more common, measures the magnitude, or inherent strength. The *Mercalli scale,* which runs from 1 to 12, gauges the intensity at a specific location.

Every increase of 1 on the Richter scale, say from magnitude 5.5 to magnitude 6.5, means the ground motion is 10 times greater. Theoretically, there is no upper limit to the scale. Readings of 8.9, the highest on record, were obtained from a quake off the coast of Ecuador in 1906 and from a quake off the coast of Japan in 1933.

The potential for damage in a populated area:

> Magnitude 3.5: The quake can cause slight damage.
> Magnitude 4: The quake can cause moderate damage.
> Magnitude 5: The quake can cause considerable damage.

earthquakes *continued*
>Magnitude 6: The quake can cause severe damage.
>
>Magnitude 7: A major earthquake, capable of widespread, heavy damage.
>
>Magnitude 8: A "great" earthquake, capable of tremendous damage.

Some notable earthquakes (in date order):

- Shensi province of China, January 1556: Killed 830,000 people, the largest number of fatalities on record from an earthquake.
- San Francisco, April 1906: Highest Richter reading later computed as 8.3. The quake and subsequent fire were blamed for about 700 deaths.
- Tokyo and Yokohama, Japan, September 1923: Highest Richter reading later computed as 8.3. The quake and subsequent fires destroyed most of both cities, killing an estimated 200,000 people.
- Guatemala, Feb. 4, 1976: Authorities said about 23,000 people were killed. Highest Richter reading 7.9.
- Hopeh province of northern China, July 28, 1976: Highest Richter reading 8.3. A government document later said 655,237 people were killed and 779,000 were injured.
- Mexico City and vicinity, Sept. 19–20, 1985: More than 8,000 killed. Highest Richter reading 8.1.
- Armenia, Dec. 7, 1988: 25,000 killed. Highest Richter reading 6.9.
- Northern Iran, June 21, 1990: 40,000 killed. Highest Richter reading 7.7.
- Kobe, Japan, Jan. 17, 1995: 5,500 killed. Highest Richter reading 7.2.
- Gujarat state, India, Jan. 26, 2001: 20,000 killed. Highest Richter reading 7.9.

east, eastern See **directions**.

Easter This religious holiday falls on the first Sunday after the first full moon that occurs on or after March 21. If the full moon falls on Sunday, Easter is the next Sunday. Thus Easter may fall between March 22 and April 25 inclusive.

Eastern Europe *Eastern* and *Western Europe* are political, not geographic, divisions.

Eastern Hemisphere The half of Earth composed primarily of Africa, Asia, Australia and Europe.

Eastern Orthodox churches The autonomous churches that constitute Eastern Orthodoxy are organized along mostly national lines. They recognize the patriarch of Constantinople (modern-day Istanbul) as their leader. They include the Greek Orthodox Church, the Romanian Orthodox Church and the Russian Orthodox Church.

In the United States, organizational lines are based on the national backgrounds of various ethnic groups. The largest churches are the Greek Orthodox Archdiocese of North and South America and the Orthodox Church in America.

The eucharistic service in Eastern Orthodox churches is called *liturgy* or *divine liturgy*. Do not refer to members as *Protestants,* though they may be called *Orthodox Christians.*

Some churches call the archbishop who leads them a *metropolitan,* others use *patriarch.* He normally heads the principal archdiocese within a nation. Working with him are other *archbishops, bishops, priests* and *deacons.*

Archbishops and bishops frequently follow a monastic tradition in which they are known only by a first name. When no last name is used, repeat the title before the first name on second reference. Some forms: Metropolitan Ireney, archbishop of New York and metropolitan of America and Canada. On second reference: Metropolitan Ireney. *Archbishop* may be replaced by *the Most Rev.* on first reference. *Bishop* may be replaced by *the Rt. Rev.* on first reference.

Use *the Rev.* before the name of a priest on first reference. Capitalize *Deacon* before a name on first reference. Use only last names, customarily available for priests and deacons, in subsequent references.

Eastern Rite churches A group of Roman Catholic churches organized along ethnic lines. Among the largest Eastern Rite churches are the Greek Catholic Church, the Melchite Church, the Syrian Catholic Church and the Ukrainian Catholic Church.

Eastern Shore A region on Chesapeake Bay, sometimes called the *Delmarva* (Delaware, Maryland, Virginia) *Peninsula. Eastern Shore* is not a synonym for *East Coast.*

Eastern Standard Time (EST), Eastern Daylight Time (EDT) See **time**.

East Germany See **Germany**.

easygoing

eBay

E. coli

ecology The study of the relationship between organisms and their surroundings. It is not synonymous with *environment.*

> *Wrong:* Even so simple an undertaking as maintaining a lawn affects ecology. (Use *the environment* instead.)
>
> *Right:* The laboratory is studying the ecology of man and the desert.

e-commerce Doing business on the Internet. Also, *e-book, e-business, e-shopping, e-trade,* etc. See **e-mail**.

economic reports Government economic reports that have formal titles should be capitalized: Consumer Price Index, Producer Price Index, Index of Leading Economic indicators, but the index.

Those that have common names should be lowercased: gross national product, but GNP on second reference.

See the individual entries for the various reports.

editor Capitalize *editor* before a name only when it is an official corporate or organizational title. Do not capitalize as a job description.

editorial, news In references to a newspaper, reserve *news* for the news department, its employees and news articles. Reserve *editorial* for the department that prepares the editorial page, its employees and articles that appear on the editorial page.

editor in chief No hyphens. Capitalize as a formal title before a name: Editor in Chief Horace Greeley.

effect See the **affect, effect** entry.

Eglin Air Force Base, Fla. Not *Elgin.*

EgyptAir No space. Headquarters is in Cairo.

El Al Israel Airlines *El Al* is acceptable in all references. Headquarters is in Tel Aviv.

elder See separate entries for each denomination.

elderly Use *elderly* or *senior citizen* sparingly. Do not use them to describe anyone under 65, and not casually for anyone beyond that age. Some general references are appropriate: concern for the elderly, a home for the elderly.

To show someone's faculties have deteriorated, cite a graphic example: His memory fades. She walks with a cane.

-elect Always hyphenate and lowercase: President-elect Bush.

Election Day Capitalize. Federal elections are the first Tuesday after the first Monday in November in even-numbered years.

election returns Use figures. Use *to,* not a hyphen, to separate totals: Martha Smith defeated Robert Jones 40,827,292 *to* 39,146,157 in 1976 (the final figure). Not: a 40,827,292-39,146,157 vote.

Use *votes* if there is any chance the figures could be confused with a ratio: Smith defeated Jones 13 votes to 11 votes in Dixville Notch. See **votes**.

Electoral College But *electoral vote(s).*

Electrical Workers union Acceptable in all references for the *United Electrical, Radio and Machine Workers of America.* Headquarters is in New York.

electrocardiogram *EKG* is acceptable on second reference.

ellipsis (...) An ellipsis is constructed with a space, three periods and another space.

1. Use an ellipsis to indicate an omission of one or more words within a quoted passage in texts or transcripts: "No man is an island ... every man is a piece of the continent, a part of the main." — John Donne.

2. When an ellipsis separates two sentences, some form of punctuation must signify the end of the first sentence. Use a period or question mark if the words form a complete sentence even though they did not constitute the complete sentence in the original.

    A period: "This is not a boycott. ... The fact is that no boycott is involved."

    Or a question mark: "Is this a boycott? ... The fact is that no boycott is involved."

3. In news writing, an ellipsis is seldom necessary at the beginning or end of a quotation.

    > *Wrong:* Kennedy said," ... ask not what your country can do for you ..."
    >
    > *Right:* Kennedy said, "And so my fellow Americans: Ask not what your country can do for you — ask what you can do for your country."
    >
    > *Also right:* Kennedy said, "Ask not what your country can do for you."

   See **sentences**.

4. When words are omitted between paragraphs, place a period, space and ellipsis (. . . .) at the end of the first paragraph.

ellipsis *continued*

5. Do not use an ellipsis to indicate an interruption, pause or hesitation in speech, or a thought that the speaker or writer does not complete. Use a *dash (—)* instead.

Wrong: "Your honor, I object on grounds ..."
"Overruled," said the judge.

Right: "Your honor, I object on grounds that — ."
"Overruled," said the judge.

6. An ellipsis may be used to separate small items in certain features, such as a people or movie column.

El Nino A warming of the Pacific Ocean off South America that disrupts the ocean-atmosphere system and affects weather around the world, altering wind patterns and storm tracks, increasing rainfall, etc. See **La Nina**.

El Paso Corp. The natural gas company. Headquarters is in Houston.

El Salvador Use the article *(El)* to help distinguish this nation from its capital, San Salvador. Use *Salvadoran(s)* in references to citizens of the nation.

e-mail Short for *electronic mail,* a system of sending and receiving messages by computer. The term is also commonly used in reference to a message or messages within the system: They communicate by e-mail. She sent him 15 e-mail messages. He sent an e-mail to the president. The professor e-mailed his students. The company is e-mailing its customers.

Although the plural is *e-mail,* not *e-mails,* the latter is permissible because of widespread use, but try to avoid it: She received 300 e-mail messages (instead of *300 e-mails*). See **e-commerce**.

embargo See **boycott, embargo**.

embarrass, embarrassment Two *r's*, two *s's*.

embassy The official residence of an ambassador in a foreign country, and the office that handles the political affairs of one nation to another. Capitalize with the name of a nation; lowercase without it: the French Embassy, the U.S. Embassy, the embassy. See **consulate**.

embedded journalist A news reporter who accompanies a military unit during wartime, going into combat with the unit and reporting from the scene, with certain limitations. The *embedded journalist* concept was introduced by the United States military in the 2003 invasion of Iraq.

emcee, emceed, emceeing *Master of ceremonies* is preferred.

em dash In typography, a dash equal to the width of the capital letter *M*.

emeritus When used, place *emeritus* after the formal title. Capitalize before a name, lowercase elsewhere: Professor Emeritus Samuel Eliot Morison. Samuel Eliot Morison, professor emeritus of history.

emigrate, immigrate One who leaves a country *emigrates* from it. One who comes into a country *immigrates.* The same principle holds for *emigrant* and *immigrant*.

Emmy, Emmys The annual awards by the National Academy of Television Arts and Sciences.

employee Not *employe.*

Employment Cost Index Quarterly report by the Labor Department that measures changes in compensation costs, including wages, salaries and benefits for workers in both the public and private sectors.

empty-handed

enact See **adopt**.

encyclopedia But use the spelling of formal names: Encyclopaedia Britannica.

Energy Research and Development Administration The Atomic Energy Commission was replaced in 1975 by this agency and the Nuclear Regulatory Commission. *ERDA* is acceptable on second reference.

enforce But *reinforce.*

engine, motor An *engine* develops its own power: *an airplane engine, an automobile engine, a jet engine, a steam engine, a turbine engine.* A *motor* gets power elsewhere: *an electric motor, a hydraulic motor.*

England London stands alone in datelines. The form for others: *HOUNSLOW, England, Dec. 23 (UPI)* — See **United Kingdom**.

English Channel, English muffin, English sparrow, English walnut, English setter

Enovid A trademark for a birth control pill.

(enquire, enquiry) The preferred words are *inquire, inquiry.*

enroll, enrolled, enrolling

en route Always two words.

ensign See **military titles**.

ensure, insure Use *ensure* to mean *guarantee; insure* for *insurance:* Steps were taken to *ensure* accuracy. The policy *insures* his life.

(enthused) Colloquial for *enthusiastic.* Avoid it.

entitled Use it to mean a right to do or to qualify for. Do not use it to mean *titled.*

entitled *continued*

> *Wrong:* The book was entitled "Gone with the Wind."
> *Right:* The book was titled "Gone with the Wind."
> *Right:* She was entitled to the promotion.

envelop, enveloping, enveloped (v.), **envelope** (n.)

environment See **ecology**.

Environmental Protection Agency *EPA* is acceptable in a lead paragraph if the full name is spelled out shortly thereafter.

envoy Not a formal title. Lowercase: envoy Joseph Grew, the envoy.

epicenter The center of an earthquake. See **earthquakes**.

Episcopal, Episcopalian *Episcopal* is the adjective form; use *Episcopalian* only as a noun referring to a member of the Episcopal Church: She is an *Episcopalian*. But: She is an *Episcopal* priest.

Episcopal Church Acceptable in all references for the *Protestant Episcopal Church,* the U.S. national church that is a member of the Anglican Communion.

The clergy consists of *bishops, priests* and *deacons.* A priest who heads a parish is described as a *rector* rather than a pastor. The term *minister* is not used.

U.S. bishops may be called *the Rt. Rev.* Use *the Most Rev.* only before the name of the archbishop of Canterbury. Elsewhere: Bishop John Jones, the bishop; Deacon John Jones, the deacon; Brother John Jones, the brother.

Always lowercase *priest* and *rector.*

equal, equaled, equaling *Equal* has no comparative forms. When people speak of a *more equal* distribution of wealth, what is meant is *more equitable* or *more nearly equal.*

Equal Employment Opportunity Commission *EEOC* is acceptable on second reference.

equally as Do not use the words together. One is sufficient.

Omit *equally* in: She was (equally) as educated as Marilyn.

Omit *as* in: She and Marilyn were equally (as) educated.

Equal Rights Amendment *ERA* is acceptable on second reference.

equator Always lowercase.

equitable See **equal**.

equity The value of property beyond what is owed on it.

ERA Acceptable on second reference for *Equal Rights Amendment.*

eras See **historical periods**.

ergonomics The science of designing computers and other workplace devices to suit the worker. An example is an ergonomic keyboard built to reduce strain on the wrists.

escalator clause A contract clause providing for increases or decreases in wages or prices based on fluctuations in the cost of living or expenses.

(escapee, escaper) The terms *escaped convict* or *fugitive* are preferred.

Eskimo (s.), **Eskimos** (pl.) Original inhabitants of that part of North America stretching from Greenland across Canada to Alaska and through the northeastern tip of Asia. *Eskimo* means *eater of raw flesh.* The term is objectionable to some who prefer the synonym *Inuit,* which means *the people.* Make the distinction if useful. See **Indians, native Americans**.

espresso The coffee is *espresso,* not *expresso.*

(esthetic) Spell it *aesthetic.*

Ethernet A widely used type of *local area network.* See **LAN**.

eucharist Lowercase.

Eurasian Of European and Asian descent.

euro (s.), **euros** (pl.) Do *not* capitalize. The common currency of 12 of the 15 members of the European Union: Austria, Belgium, Finland, France, Germany, Greece, Ireland, Italy, Luxembourg, Netherlands, Portugal and Spain. As of Jan. 1, 2003, Denmark, Sweden and the United Kingdom had not adopted the euro.

The euro was created on Jan. 1, 1999, with the goal of making it a single currency for Europe. Euro banknotes and coins were put into circulation in 2002. Member countries are part of the European Economic and Monetary Union (EMU), more commonly known as the European Monetary Union. The latter is acceptable. See **European Union**.

eurodollar A U.S. dollar on deposit in a bank or lending institution in Europe, including branches of U.S. banks. Note: Lowercase spelling is an exception to *Webster's New World College Dictionary.*

euroland, eurozone

European Community See **European Union**.

European Union *EU* (no periods) is acceptable on second reference. The union was created in 1992. It was formed out of the *European Community,* which included the *European Economic Community, the European Atomic Energy Community, and the European Coal and Steel Community.* The group was initially known as the *Common Market.*

The EU comprises Belgium, France, Germany, Italy, Luxembourg, Netherlands (the six founders), Austria, Denmark, Finland, Greece,

European Union *continued*

Ireland, Portugal, Spain, Sweden and the United Kingdom. Headquarters is in Brussels, Belgium.

The common currency of the EU is the euro. See **euro**.

Evangelical Friends Alliance See **Quakers**.

evangelism The practice of preaching for converts.

evangelist Capitalize only in references to *Matthew, Mark, Luke* and *John,* the men to whom the four Gospels are attributed: Mark was an Evangelist.

eve Capitalize a holiday: Christmas Eve. But: the eve of Christmas.

even-steven Not *even-stephen.*

every day, everyday *Every day* means *each day; everyday* means *ordinary:* He goes to work every day in his everyday shoes.

everyone, every one *Everyone* means *all, everybody; every one* means *each.*

ex- No hyphen unless it means *former:* excommunicate, expropriate, ex-convict, ex-president. It modifies the entire term: ex-New York Gov. Mario Cuomo. Not: New York ex-Gov., etc. Better: former Gov. Mario Cuomo.

exaggerate

except See **accept, except**.

excite (Small *e.*) An Internet search engine. See **search engine**.

exclamation point (!) Use it sparingly, only in very exceptional cases to express a high degree of surprise, incredulity or other strong emotion.

Do not use the exclamation mark with mild interjections, mildly exclamatory sentences or to indicate irony or humor.

Place the exclamation mark inside quotation marks if it is part of the quoted material; outside if it isn't: "Never!" she shouted. I hated reading "The Carpetbaggers"!

execute To kill in accordance with a legally imposed death sentence. Do not use in reference to a terrorist or gangland *murder.* See **homicide**.

executive branch Always lowercase.

executive departments Capitalize: the Department of State. But lowercase *department* when it stands alone: the department's monthly report. And lowercase *departments* in plural uses: the Agriculture and Interior departments, the departments of State and Defense.

Titles may be flip-flopped with standard capitalization: Commerce Department for Department of Commerce, Interior Department for Department of Interior, etc. Homeland Security may be used for Department of

Homeland Security but generally avoid bureaucratic shorthand that personifies executive departments by referring to them in third-person singular, as in Commerce reported, or Interior announced. These three are abbreviated: *HUD* for the *Department of Housing and Urban Development, HHS* for the *Department of Health and Human Services, VA for the Department of Veterans Affairs.* All others are spelled out, even in direct quotations. Never use *DOT, DoD, USDA,* etc. See **Cabinet titles.**

executive director Capitalize when used as a formal title before a name. Lowercase otherwise: Executive Director William Green. The executive director arrived.

Executive Mansion Capitalize only in reference to the *White House.*

Executive Protective Agency Not *Protection.* This agency, a part of the Secret Service, is responsible for protecting embassies in Washington.

executive secretary Capitalize before a name only if it is a formal corporate or organizational title.

executor Use for both men and women. Not a formal title. Always lowercase.

exercise, exorcise To exercise *is to exert.* To exorcise *is to drive out.*

expel, expelled, expelling

expletive See **obscenities**.

Export-Import Bank of the United States *Export-Import Bank* is acceptable in all references. Headquarters is in Washington.

(expresso) The coffee is espresso.

extol, extolled, extolling

extra- Hyphenate with a capitalized word and to avoid a double *a:* extra-alimentary, extra-Britannic, but extramarital, extraterritorial, etc. Follow *Webster's New World College Dictionary,* hyphenating words not listed there.

extrasensory perception *ESP* is acceptable on second reference.

extraterrestrial

Exxon Mobil Corp. Headquarters is in Irving, Texas. Exxon and Mobil merged in 1999.

eye, eyed, eyeing

eye to eye, eye-to-eye No hyphens when used after the verb: He looked at him *eye to eye.* But use hyphens in a compound modifier before a noun: It was an *eye-to-eye* confrontation.

eyewitness *Witness* is usually sufficient.

F

---

fact All facts are true. A false fact *is impossible;* actual fact, real fact *and* true fact *are redundant.*

fact-finding (adj.)

fade-out (n., adj.), **fade out** (v.)

Fahrenheit The temperature scale commonly used in the United States, after Gabriel Daniel Fahrenheit, a German physicist who invented it. In this scale, the freezing point of water is 32 degrees and the boiling point is 212 degrees at sea level.

The forms, if needed: **86 degrees Fahrenheit**, or **86 F** (note the space and no period after the *F*).

To convert to Celsius, subtract 32 from the Fahrenheit figure, multiply by 5 and divide by 9 (77 minus 32 equals 45 × 5 equals 225 divided by 9 equals 25). See **temperatures.**

fallout (n., adj.), **fall out** (v.)

(failed to) Avoid use in a positive sense.

> *Wrong:* The Legislature failed to approve the seat belt bill.
> *Right:* The Legislature defeated the proposed seat belt bill.

fall See **seasons.**

false titles Always lowercase.

family names Capitalize words denoting family relationships only as a part of or substitute for a person's name: I wrote to Grandfather Smith. I wrote Mother a letter. I wrote my mother a letter.

famous If the term must be used, the person probably isn't famous.

Fannie Mae See **Federal National Mortgage Association**.

FAO Schwarz Not Schwartz.

FAQ For *frequently asked questions* on Internet sites.

Far East

far-flung

far-ranging

farsighted Better vision for distant objects than near ones.

farther, further Farther *refers to distance;* further *to time or degree:* He walked *farther* into the woods. She will look *further* into the mystery.

Far West The U.S. region generally west of the Rockies.

fascism, fascist Lowercase unless the reference clearly is to the *Fascisti,* an Italian political organization under Mussolini, or to its members. See **political parties.**

fast-food

father Do not use *father* as a religious title for priests. If it appears in quoted matter, capitalize it before a name: Father Brown solved the mystery.

father-in-law (s.), **fathers-in-law** (pl.)

Father's Day The third Sunday in June.

Father Time

fatwa A decree or edict issued by an Islamic religious council or leader.

fax (n., v.) Short for *facsimile* or *facsimile machine.*

faze, phase To *faze* is to embarrass or disturb; a *phase* is an aspect or stage: The snub did not *faze* her. They will *phase* in a new system.

FBI Acceptable in all references for *Federal Bureau of Investigation.*

feather bedding, featherbedding *Feather bedding* is bedding stuffed with feathers, used as a mattress; *featherbedding* is the practice of using more workers than needed to handle a job.

February See **months**.

federal Lowercase unless part of a proper name: federal assistance, federal court, the federal government, a federal judge, federal Judge John Sirica. But: the Federal Trade Commission (the name of a federal agency), Federal Express (a private company).

Federal Aviation Administration *FAA* is acceptable on second reference.

Federal Bureau of Investigation *FBI* is acceptable in all references, and *bureau* is acceptable in later references.

Federal Communications Commission *FCC* is acceptable on second reference.

federal court Always lowercase. See **judicial branch**.

Federal Crop Insurance Corp. Do not abbreviate.

Federal Deposit Insurance Corp. *FDIC* is acceptable on second reference.

Federal Emergency Management Agency *FEMA* is acceptable on second reference.

Federal Energy Administration *FEA* is acceptable on second reference.

Federal Farm Credit Board Do not abbreviate.

Federal Highway Administration Do not abbreviate. Reserve *FHA* for the *Federal Housing Administration.*

Federal Home Loan Mortgage Corp. Do not abbreviate. Its nickname, *Freddie Mac,* may be used on second reference.

Federal Housing Administration *FHA* is acceptable on second reference.

Federal Maritime Commission Do not abbreviate.

Federal Mediation and Conciliation Service Do not abbreviate. The *Federal Mediation Service* is acceptable.

Federal National Mortgage Association Do not abbreviate. The organization is more commonly known as *Fannie Mae,* which may be used on second reference.

Federal Power Commission *FPC* is acceptable on second reference.

Federal Register This publication, issued every workday, is the legal medium for recording and communicating the rules and regulations established by the executive branch of the federal government.

Federal Reserve Board, Federal Reserve System On second reference: *the Federal Reserve, the Fed, the system, the board.* Also: *the Federal Reserve Bank of New York* (Boston, etc.), *the bank.*

Federal Trade Commission *FTC* is acceptable on second reference.

felony, misdemeanor A *felony* is a serious crime; a *misdemeanor* is a minor offense. Further distinctions vary from jurisdiction to jurisdiction.

At the federal level, a *misdemeanor* carries a potential penalty of no more than a year in jail. A *felony* carries a potential penalty of more than a year in prison. Anyone convicted of a *felony* is a *felon* even if no time is actually spent in confinement. See **prison, jail.**

Ferris wheel After George W.G. Ferris, a U.S. engineer who constructed the first one for the World's Fair in Chicago in 1893.

ferryboat

fertility rate As calculated by the federal government, it is the number of live births per 1,000 females age 15 through 44.

fewer, less Use *fewer* for individual items; use *less* for bulk or quality.

Wrong: The trend is toward more machines and less people.
(*People,* in this instance, refers to individuals.)

Right: Fewer than 10 applicants called. (Individuals.)

Right: I had less than $50 in my pocket. (An amount.) But: I had fewer than 50 $1 bills in my pockets. (Individual items.)

fiber optics Technology that uses *fiber-optic cable* to transmit data. Note the hyphen in *fiber-optic cable,* which is made from thin fibers of glass.

fiance (man), **fiancee** (woman)

fiberglass The trademark is *Fiberglas* (single *s*).

figuratively, literally *Figuratively* symbolizes: Their phone rang off the hook. The software company puts job applicants through a wringer.

Literally means *actually.* It is incorrect to say the phone literally rang off the hook *or* the company literally put its applicants through a wringer.

figure The symbol for a number: the figure 5. See **numerals.**

File Transfer Protocol See **FTP.**

filibuster To *filibuster* is to make long speeches to obstruct legislation. A legislator who uses such methods is also a *filibuster,* not a *filibusterer.*

Filipinos The people of the Philippines.

filmmaker One word.

film ratings See **movie ratings.**

finance, fund (v.) *Finance* means *to pay with money on hand or with borrowed money.* Example: He financed his car with a bank loan. *Fund* means *to pay with money accumulated through interest-bearing accounts:* He funded his daughter's education through a money market account.

fiord Not *fjord.*

fireball, firebomb, fire chief, firecracker, fire drill, fire engine, firefight, firehouse, fire escape, fireplug, fire station, firetruck, firewall, firewood, fireworks

fire department Capitalize a specific agency if the reference is clear: the Boston Fire Department, the Fire Department. Lowercase plural uses: the Boston and Worcester fire departments. See **military titles** for guidelines on titles.

firefighter, fireman Anyone who fights a fire is a *firefighter.* Reserve *fireman* for a male firefighter or anyone who tends fires in a furnace or locomotive engine.

firm A business partnership is correctly referred to as a *firm:* He joined a law firm. Careful writers don't use *firm* to refer to a corporation.

first base, firstborn, first-class, first-degree, first down, firsthand, first offender, first-person, first-string

first family Always lowercase.

first lady Not a formal title. Lowercase even when used before the name of a chief of state's wife.

fiscal, monetary *Fiscal* applies to a budget; *monetary* to currency.

fiscal year A 12-month period used for bookkeeping purposes. The federal government's fiscal year starts three months ahead of the calendar year. Fiscal 2003, for example, runs from Oct. 1, 2002, to Sept. 30, 2003.

fistfight

fitful It means *restless,* not a condition of being fit.

flack, flak *Flack* is slang for press agent; *flak* is anti-aircraft fire (*Flieger-abwehrkanone*), hence figuratively a barrage of hostile criticism.

flag-burning, flagpole, flagship, flag station, flagstone, flag stop, flag-waving

flagrant See **blatant, flagrant.**

flair, flare *Flair* is conspicuous talent or a sense of what is stylish; *flare* is an outburst of light or anger, or a part that curves outward, as a skirt.

flash flood See **flood.**

flaunt, flout To *flaunt* is to display; to *flout* is to mock or scoff: She *flaunted* her wealth. He *flouts* the law.

fleet Use figures and capitalize *fleet* in a proper name: the 6th Fleet. Otherwise, lowercase: The fleet sails at dawn.

flier, flyer A *flier* is an aviator or handbill; *flyer* is the proper name of some trains and buses: the Western Flyer.

flight Capitalize with a numbered airline flight: I have a ticket for Flight 401. Lowercase elsewhere: My flight was an hour late.

flight (military) In the U.S. Air Force, a tactical subdivision of a *squadron,* consisting of two or more airplanes. Lowercase in all usages. See **squadron.**

flimflam, flimflammed

flip-flop, flip-flopped

flood, floodwater(s) It is always pertinent to say where floodwater comes from and where it runs off. Stories about floods usually tell how high the water is and where it is expected to crest, but make sure it also gives flood stage and how high the water is above, or below, flood stage.

> *Incomplete:* The river is expected to crest at 39 feet.
> *Better:* The river is expected to crest at 39 feet, 12 feet above flood stage.

A *flash flood* is a sudden, violent flood, as after a heavy rain or the melting of heavy snow. A *flash flood watch* alerts the public that flash flooding is possible. A *flash flood warning* notifies that flash flooding is imminent or in progress. See **passenger lists** for the forms in providing a list of victims.

floppy disk A removable computer disk for storing data. *Diskette* is an acceptable substitute in all uses.

floor leader Treat it as a job description, lowercase, rather than a formal title: Republican floor leader David Brown. See **legislative titles**.

Florida Abbreviation: *Fla.* See **state(s)**.

Florida Keys A chain of small islands extending southwest from the southern tip of the Florida peninsula. Key West, the southernmost point, is a seaport on the island of the same name.

The form for datelines: *KEY WEST, Fla., Dec. 23 (UPI)* — If there is no community on an island, use the island name instead.

flounder, founder A *flounder* is a fish; to *flounder* is to move clumsily or jerkily, like a fish on land; to *founder* is to bog down or sink.

fluid ounce Equal to 1.8 cubic inches, two tablespoons or six teaspoons. In metric it is about 30 milliliters. To convert to milliliters, multiply by 30 (3 ounces × 30 equals 90 milliliters).

fluorescent, fluoride, fluorine, fluorite Note the *uo* spelling.

flush To become red in the face. See **livid**.

flyer See **flier, flyer**.

FM Acceptable in all references for radio's *frequency modulation.*

f.o.b Acceptable in all references for *free on board*. Explain this term if using it in a story: *A seller agrees to pay a product's shipping costs to a specific destination, beyond which the buyer takes responsibility.*

-fold Spell out numbers when used in a compound: ten-fold, two-fold, etc.

follow-up (n., adj.), **follow up** (v.)

food Most food names are lowercase: apples, cheese, peanut butter. But capitalize brand names and trademarks: Accent, Roquefort cheese, Tabasco sauce, Smithfield ham.

Many words derived from proper names are capitalized: eggs Benedict, Bloody Mary, Salisbury steak. Many are lowercase: french fries, graham crackers, pasteurized milk. There is no acceptable standard to apply in all cases.

If a question arises, see the separate entries in this book. If there is no entry, follow *Webster's New World College Dictionary,* using lowercase if it is one of the options listed. See **recipes**.

Food and Agriculture Organization Not *Agricultural*. *FAO* is acceptable on second reference to this U.N. agency.

Food and Drug Administration *FDA* is acceptable on second reference.

foot The basic unit of length commonly used in the United States. A foot is exactly 30.48 centimeters. For most conversions, multiply by 30 (5 feet × 30 equals 150 centimeters). To be more exact, multiply by 30.48 (5 × 30.48 equals 152.4 centimeters). To convert to meters, multiply by .3 (5 feet × .3 equals about 1.5 meters). To be more exact, multiply by .3048.

foot-and-mouth disease Note hyphens. A highly contagious, degenerative viral disease affecting cattle, sheep and other animals with cloven hooves. Also known as *hoof-and-mouth disease*.

football The spelling of some common words and phrases:

ball carrier	goal line	playoff *(n.)*
ballclub	goal-line stand	play off *(v.)*
end zone	goal post	quarterback
halfback	kickoff *(n.)*	running back
halftime	kick off *(v.)*	tight end
field goal	linebacker	wide receiver
fullback	line of scrimmage	

Use figures for yardage: the 5-yard line, a 7-yard pass. But: a fourth-and-two play. Elsewhere: the score was 21-14, the team's record is 4-5-1.

Foot Locker Inc. Name of the company that once was *Woolworth Corp.* and later the *Venator Group*. The company operates *Foot Locker* shoe stores and *Champ Sports*.

footrace

forbear, forebear *Forbear* means *to refrain from;* a *forebear* is an ancestor.

forbid The past tense is *forbade*.

forcible rape A redundancy to be avoided. But it may be used in stories dealing with both rape and statutory rape, which does not necessarily involve the use of force.

Ford Motor Co. Use *Ford,* not *FMC,* on second reference. Headquarters is in Dearborn, Mich.

fore- Hyphenate to avoid a double *e:* fore-edge, fore-elder. Certain nautical terms also take a hyphen: fore-chains, fore-topgallant, fore-topmast, fore-topsail. Usually no hyphen elsewhere: forearm, forecast, forecourt, foreshock. If in doubt for others, follow *Webster's New World College Dictionary*, hyphenating words not listed there.

forecast The same in present and past tense.

forego, forgo *Forego* means *to precede; forgo* means *to do without.*

foreign governmental bodies Capitalize the name of a specific foreign governmental agency: the French Foreign Ministry, or simply: the Foreign Ministry. But: the ministry.

foreign legislative bodies Capitalize the proper name of a foreign legislative body: Diet (in Japan), Knesset (in Israel), Parliament (in Britain), etc. Capitalize also if an English equivalent is used in a clear and specific reference:

> TOKYO, Aug. 3 (UPI) — Leaders of Parliament met Monday.

But lowercase an English equivalent supplied as a translation:

> TOKYO, Aug. 3 (UPI) — Leaders of the Diet, Japan's parliament, met Monday.

Lowercase plural uses: the British and French parliaments.

Parliament is the English equivalent of the Diet, the Cortes in Spain and the Knesset in Israel. It is also the name in Australia, Canada, Denmark, Finland, France, India, Iran, Ireland, Italy, New Zealand, Norway, Poland and the United Kingdom.

The name is *national assembly* in many countries, including Bulgaria, Egypt, Hungary, Nepal, Pakistan, Portugal, Tunisia, Uganda and Zambia. Lowercase *assembly* standing alone.

foreign money Generally, amounts of foreign money should be converted to U.S. dollars. If it is pertinent to mention the foreign amount, insert it in parentheses and spell out the currency name: He gave the Pakistani driver $12.50 (724 rupees).

If the foreign amount must be mentioned first: The sign in the window said the price was 3,500 yen ($30).

Standard international abbreviations (listed below) may be used for dollar-to-dollar conversions (Australian dollar to U.S. dollar, etc.). Use this form: "We estimate a deficit of $800 million (USD460 million)," the Singapore official said. She spent $93 (HKD725) in Hong Kong. "I sold my car in Buffalo for $5,000 (CAD7,408)," the Canadian said.

In stories where all foreign amounts are converted to U.S. dollars, put a note of explanation in parentheses at the bottom: (All money is in U.S. dollars.)

It is not necessary to always use the forms shown above. In some stories — features, for instance — it may be preferable to make comparisons in this manner: He gave the Pakistani driver $12.50, about 724

foreign money *continued*

rupees. He spent 5,000 yen, a little over $42. The $10 given each child equaled almost $15 in Canadian money, the tour guide explained.

The foreign monetary units are listed in *Webster's New World College Dicationary* under *Monetary Units*. To convert foreign units to dollars, use the official exchange rates, which change daily, on the world markets.

Abbreviations for dollar countries include:

Australia, AUD	Fiji, FJD
Bahamas, BSD	Hong Kong, HKD
Bermuda, BMD	Jamaica, JMD
Brunei, BND	New Zealand, NZD
Canada, CAD	Singapore, SGD
East Caribbean (Antigua	Trinidad and Tobago, TTD
and Barbuda), XCD	United States, USD

foreign particles Lowercase particles *(de, la, von,* etc.) as part of a given name: Charles de Gaulle, General de Gaulle, Baron Manfred von Richthofen. Capitalize only at the start of a sentence: De Gaulle spoke of von Richthofen.

foreign spelling Change *Labour* Party to *Labor* Party, Ministry of *Defence* to Ministry of *Defense,* etc.

foreign words Many words and abbreviations with foreign origins, such as *bon voyage* and *etc.,* are widely accepted in English and may be used without explanation if they are clear in the context.

Words and phrases not widely accepted in English — they appear in *Webster's New World College Dictionary* in boldface italic type — may be used if they are placed in quotation marks and an explanation is provided: "ad astra per aspera," a Latin phrase meaning "to the stars through difficulties."

foreman Seldom a formal title. Lowercase.

(for free, for real) Slang.

forgo See **forego, forgo.**

former Always lowercase: former President Bush. Do not use *former* before a title to denote the action of a person when he previously held the title.

> *Wrong:* In 1968 former Gov. Nelson Rockefeller ran for president. (He was the governor of New York at the time.)
> *Right:* In 1968 Gov. Nelson Rockefeller ran for president.

Formica A trademark for a laminated plastic.

Formosa See **Taiwan**.

Formosa Strait Not *the Straits of Taiwan*.

formula (s.), **formulas** (pl.) Use figures: 5 feet × 30 equals 150 centimeters.

forsake, forsook, forsaken, forsaking Not *fore-*, etc.

fort Do not abbreviate for cities or for military installations:

> FORT LAUDERDALE, Fla., Feb. 12 (UPI) — City officials met Monday.

> FORT BRAGG, N.C., Feb. 12 (UPI) — Military leaders met Monday.

fortnight Two weeks.

FORTRAN Short for *formula translator,* a computer programming language.

fortuneteller, fortunetelling

forty, forty-niner *'49er* is also acceptable.

foul, fowl A *fowl* is a bird; a *foul* is an infraction of rules or anything offensive or disgusting: foul ball, foul language.

founder See **flounder, founder**.

4-H Not *Four-H*. The youth organization, sponsored by the U.S. Department of Agriculture, was founded in 1902. It teaches "life skills" in agriculture, citizenship, cooking, computers, the environment, leadership, etc. Members belong to *4-H clubs* and are called *4-H'ers*. The *h's* stand for *head, heart, hands* and *health*. National 4-H headquarters is in Washington.

Fourth Estate Journalism or journalists. The term is attributed to Edmund Burke, who is reported to have called the reporters' gallery in Parliament *"a Fourth Estate."* The other three were the clergy, the nobility and the bourgeoisie.

Fourth of July, July Fourth The federal legal holiday is observed on Friday if July 4 falls on a Saturday, on Monday if it falls on a Sunday.

four-wheel-drive A vehicle with four wheels connected to the drive train. Hyphenated as a compound modifier: four-wheel-drive truck. Not 4×4 truck. See **jeep, Land-Rover**.

401(k) Small *k* in parentheses; no space: He said 401(k) plans must be protected. The plural has no apostrophe: "These are tough times for 401(k)s," she said.

Fox, Fox Broadcasting Co., Fox Entertainment Group, Fox Television, Fox News Channel, Fox Sports, etc. Fox properties are part of *The News Corporation Ltd.* Headquarters is in Los Angeles.

fractions Whenever practical, convert fractions to decimals. See **decimal units** and **numerals**. Fractions are preferred in certain stories involving measurements (recipes, lumber, etc).

When writing fractional characters, use ½, ¾, etc. For mixed numbers, use *1 ½, 2 ¼*, etc., with a space between the whole number and the fraction.

If fractions must be spelled out, hyphenate them: two-thirds, three-fourths, twenty-seven-hundredths.

fragmented, fragmentary *Fragmented* means *broken into pieces; fragmentary* means *disconnected* or *incomplete:* The vase fell on the floor and was fragmented. Early returns were fragmentary.

frame-up (n.), **frame up** (v.)

frankfurter They were first called *hot dogs* in 1906 when a cartoonist, T.A. "Tad" Dorgan, showed a dachshund inside an elongated bun.

Freddie Mac See **Federal Home Loan Mortgage Corp.**

freedom of the press Freedom to publish any opinions in newspapers, magazines, books, etc., without government interference or censorship.

free-for-all

freehand

free lance (n.), **free-lance** (adj.)

free on board See **f.o.b.**

freeware Copyrighted computer programs that are available without charge. It is illegal to resell the programs. See **shareware**.

freewheeling

free world An imprecise description. Use only in quoted matter.

freeze A surface temperature below 32 degrees Fahrenheit. *Severe freeze* or *hard freeze* are used if a cold spell exceeding two days is expected. See **subfreezing**.

freezing drizzle, freezing rain See **ice storm**.

french bread, french cuff, french dressing, french fries, french toast Lowercase.

French Canadian (s.), **French Canadians** (pl.) Without a hyphen.

French Foreign Legion Also: *the Foreign Legion.* Lowercase *the legion* and *legionnaires.*

fresh water (n.), **freshwater** (adj.)

Friday See **days**.

Friends General Conference, Friends United Meeting See **Quakers**.

Frigidaire A trademark for a refrigerator.

Frisbee A trademark for a toy disc.

front line (n.), **front-line** (adj.) The battalion was sent to the front line. The front-line troops suffered heavy casualties.

front page (n.), **front-page** (adj.) The story on the *front page* is a *front-page* story.

front-runner (n.), **front-running** (adj.) Smith is the front-runner. Smith is the front-running candidate.

frost The formation of thin ice crystals, which might develop under conditions similar to dew except for the minimum temperatures involved.

Frost Belt See **Sun Belt**.

frostbite

FTP For *file transfer protocol,* a method of exchanging files on the Internet.

full faith and credit bond See **loan terminology**.

fulfill, fulfilled, fulfilling

full- Hyphenate only to form compound modifiers before a noun: a full-dress review, a full-length dress. But: the dress was full length.

full time, full-time She works full time. She has a full-time job.

fulsome It means *disgustingly excessive.* Do not use it to mean *lavish* or *profuse.*

fund See **finance, fund**.

fundamentalist As a religious designation, use the word with care. It can suggest a closed mentality rather than a theological position.

fundraising, fundraiser Solid in all uses: He attended the fundraising dinner. Fundraising is hard work. The candidate organized a fundraiser.

funeral A *funeral* is a ceremony; a *funeral service* is redundant.

funnel cloud A violent, rotating column of air that does not touch the ground. See **tornado**.

further Indicates degree, not distance. See **farther, further**.

fuselage An *e* and one *l*.

fusillade An *i* and two *l*'s.

FYI *For your information.* Do not use it in news copy.

G

G The *general audience* rating. See **movie ratings**.

Gadhafi, Moammar There are several transliterations of the name of the Libyan leader. This is the spelling used by UPI.

gage, gauge A *gage* secures or pledges; a *gauge* measures. See **gauge**.

gaiety

gale Sustained winds of 39 to 54 mph (34 to 47 knots).

gallbladder

gallon Equal to 128 fluid ounces. In metric it is about 3.8 liters. To convert to liters, multiply by 3.8 (3 gallons × 3.8 equals 11.4 liters).

Gallup Poll See **polls**.

gantlet, gauntlet You run a *gantlet* and pick up a *gauntlet*. A *gantlet* was an old form of military punishment in which a person ran between two rows of tormentors who clubbed him as he passed. *Gauntlet* is a glove, such as one thrown to the ground to challenge an adversary. *Gauntlet* is frequently used for *gantlet*, but not by careful writers.

garnish, garnishee To *garnish* is to adorn; to *garnishee* is to attach legally: steak garnished with parsley; wages garnisheed by court order.

gauge Use to designate the caliber of a shotgun. The form: a 12-gauge shotgun, 20-gauge shotgun. No decimal except in the case of *the .410 shotgun,* which is expressed in thousandths of an inch and is properly called a *.410 bore.* See **gage, gauge** and **weapons**.

gay Acceptable as a synonym for homosexuals of both sexes. It is generally associated with males; *lesbian* is commonly used for females. See **lesbian**.

Gaza, Gaza Strip Gaza is a city in the Gaza Strip, which adjoins Israel and Egypt. In datelines: *GAZA, Nov. 27 (UPI)* —

GBU-27 A laser-guided bomb. The initials stand for *Guided Bomb Unit.*

GED Trademark for *General Educational Development,* formal name of the high school equivalency testing program. The initials are acceptable in all references, but explain in the story that a person who passes the tests earns the equivalent of a high school diploma. (The tests measure knowledge in reading, writing, science, social studies and mathematics.)

general See **military titles**.

General Accounting Office This federal agency, the investigative arm of Congress, may be referred to as *the GAO* in second reference.

general assembly Lowercase a non-governmental body: the general assembly of the World Council of Churches. Lowercase *assembly* alone in all cases. Capitalize the U.N. body or a state legislature if the specific reference is clear: the U.N. General Assembly, the Virginia General Assembly. Or:

UNITED NATIONS, Sept. 3 (UPI) — The General Assembly adjourned Monday.

RICHMOND, Va., Sept. 3 (UPI) — The General Assembly convened Monday.

general court The proper name (although rarely used in news stories) for the legislatures in Massachusetts and New Hampshire. Capitalize if a specific reference is clear: the Massachusetts General Court. But: the Massachusetts and New Hampshire general courts. If the name is used, explain it: General Court is the formal name of the Massachusetts Legislature.

General Electric Co. *GE* is acceptable on second reference. Headquarters is in Fairfield, Conn.

general manager Capitalize before a name: General Manager Chuck LaMar. Lowercase elsewhere.

General Motors Corp. *GM* is acceptable on second reference. Headquarters is in Detroit.

general obligation bond See **loan terminology**.

General Services Administration *GSA* is acceptable on second reference.

Generation X The generation of people born in the 1960s and 1970s.

gentile Generally, any person not a Jew; often specifically a Christian. But to Mormons it is anyone not a Mormon.

gentleman Do not use as a synonym for *man.*

geographic names The authority for spelling place names in the U.S. states and territories is the *National Five-Digit ZIP Code & Post Office Directory.* Do not use the postal abbreviations for state names (see separate entries). Abbreviate *saint* as *St.* and *sainte* as *Ste.* in U.S. names.

   The first source for the spelling of all foreign place names is *Webster's New World College Dictionary.* Use the first-listed spelling if an entry gives more than one. If the dictionary provides different spellings in separate entries, use the spelling that is followed by a full description of the location.

   If the dictionary does not have an entry, use the first-listed spelling in the *Columbia Gazetteer of the World Online.*

   Follow the styles adopted by the United Nations and the U.S. Board of Geographic Names on new cities, new independent nations and nations that change their names.

   Capitalize common nouns as an integral part of a proper name, but lowercase them standing alone: Pennsylvania Avenue, the avenue; the Philippine Islands, the islands; the Mississippi River, the river; the Gulf of Mexico, the gulf.

   Lowercase all common nouns that are not part of a specific proper name: the Pacific islands, the Swiss mountains, Chikiang province.

Georgia Abbreviation: *Ga.* See **state(s).**

German measles Also known as *rubella.*

Germany Berlin stands alone in datelines. Use *East Germany* or *West Germany* as applicable when referring to the divisions of the formerly divided nation. See **Berlin.**

getaway, get-out, get-together, get-up, get-up-and-go

ghetto (s.), **ghettos** (pl.) The section of a city to which minorities or the poor are restricted by economic pressure or social discrimination. Avoid the term in favor of a popular place name: Harlem, Watts.

GI (s.), **GIs** (pl.) Also: *GI'd, GI'ing.* Slang term *(government issue)* for a U.S. Army enlisted man that originated during World War II. Not applicable to personnel in any other branch of service.

gibe, jibe To *gibe* is to taunt or sneer; to *jibe* is to shift direction or, colloquially, to agree: They gibed him about his mistakes. They jibed the ship into the wind. Their stories didn't jibe.

Gibraltar The British colony stands alone in datelines.

giga- A prefix meaning *1 billion;* a *gigabyte* of disk or memory capacity is 1,073,741,824 *bytes* or 1,000 *megabytes.* A *gigaton* is the explosive force of 1 billion tons of TNT. See **metric system** and **byte, kilobyte, megabyte, terabyte.**

girl Applicable until 18th birthday. Use *woman* or *young woman* afterward.

girlfriend, boyfriend

Girl Scouts The organization is the *Girl Scouts of the United States of America.* Headquarters is in New York. Levels of scouts include *Brownies,* ages 6–8; *Juniors,* ages 9–11; *Cadettes,* ages 12–14, and *Seniors,* ages 15–17. See **Boy Scouts.**

gizmo Not *gismo.*

gladiolus (s.), **gladioluses** (pl.) Not *gladioli.*

glamour One of the few *-our* endings still used in American writing. But the adjective is *glamorous.*

globe-trotter, globe-trotting But the proper name of the basketball team is the *Harlem Globetrotters,* with no hyphen.

GMT For *Greenwich Mean Time.* The modern equivalent of GMT is *Coordinated Universal time, UTC,* also known as *Zulu Time.*

Note in the following table that GMT/UTC time is four hours ahead of Eastern Daylight time and five hours ahead of Eastern Standard Time:

GMT (UTC)	EDT	EST	GMT (UTC)	EDT	EST
0000	8 p.m.	7 p.m.	1200	8 a.m.	7 a.m.
0100	9 p.m.	8 p.m.	1300	9 a.m.	8 a.m.
0200	10 p.m.	9 p.m.	1400	10 a.m.	9 a.m.
0300	11 p.m.	10 p.m.	1500	11 a.m.	10 a.m.
0400	Midnight	11 p.m.	1600	Noon	11 a.m.
0500	1 a.m.	Midnight	1700	1 p.m.	Noon
0600	2 a.m.	1 a.m.	1800	2 p.m.	1 p.m.
0700	3 a.m.	2 a.m.	1900	3 p.m.	2 p.m.
0800	4 a.m.	3 a.m.	2000	4 p.m.	3 p.m.
0900	5 a.m.	4 a.m.	2100	5 p.m.	4 p.m.
1000	6 a.m.	5 a.m.	2200	6 p.m.	5 p.m.
1100	7 a.m.	6 a.m.	2300	7 p.m.	6 p.m.

See **UTC** and **time.**

gobbledygook Pompous, wordy, involved language.

godchild, goddamned, goddaughter, godfather, God-fearing, godforsaken, God-given, godhead, godhood, godless, godliness, godmother, godparent, God's acre, godsend, godson, godspeed

gods, goddesses See **religion**.

golf Some frequently used terms:

birdie	fairway	tee
bogey	hole high	tee off
caddie	hole in one	
chip shot	pin high	

Some sample uses of numbers:
- Use figures for handicaps: He has a 3 handicap; a 3-handicap golfer; a handicap of 3 strokes.
- Use figures for par listings: She had a par 5 to finish 2-up for the round; a par 4 hole, a 7-under-par 65, the par-3 seventh hole.
- Use figures for club ratings: a 5-iron, a 7-iron shot, a 4-wood.
- Also: The second hole, the 10th hole, the back nine, the third round, he won 3 and 2.

good Not generally acceptable as an adverb.

> *Substandard:* He reads good. He works good.
> *Standard:* He reads well. He works well. He does good work.

Use *I feel good* if you mean you are in good health. Use *I feel well* if you mean your sense of touch is proficient.

Also: It is good for you. He is as good as dead. All this is to the good.

goodbye Not *goodby* or *good-bye.*

Good Friday The Friday before Easter.

good will (n.), **goodwill** (adj.) She showed good will. A goodwill attitude.

Google An Internet search engine. See **search engine**.

GOP See **Grand Old Party**.

gorilla An ape. See **guerrilla**.

gospel Lowercase unless referring to the first four books of the New Testament: a famous gospel singer, the Gospel of St. John, the Gospels.

gourmand, gourmet A *gourmand* likes good food and tends to eat to excess; a glutton. A *gourmet* likes and is an excellent judge of fine food and drink.

Gov. (s.), **Govs.** (pl.) See **governor**.

government Always lowercase. Never abbreviate. A *government* is an established system of political administration: the U.S. government.

A *junta* is a group or council that often rules after a coup: A military junta controls the country. A junta becomes a government after it establishes a system of political administration.

Regime is a synonym for *political system:* a democratic regime, an authoritarian regime. Do not use it to mean *government* or *junta.* For example, use Franco government in referring to the government of Spain under Francisco Franco. Not: Franco regime. But: The Franco government was an authoritarian regime.

An *administration* consists of the officials who make up the executive branch of government: the Roosevelt administration.

governmental bodies Capitalize the full proper names of governmental agencies, departments and offices: the U.S. Department of State, the Georgia Department of Human Resources, the Boston City Council, the Chicago Fire Department. Retain capitals if the specific meaning is clear without the jurisdiction: the Department of State, the Department of Human Resources, the state Department of Human Resources, the City Council, the Fire Department, the city Fire Department. Elsewhere:

1. Capitalize names flip-flopped to delete *of:* the State Department, the Human Resources Department.
2. Capitalize widely used popular names: Walpole State Prison (the proper name is *Massachusetts Correctional Institution-Walpole*).
3. Lowercase when the reference is not specific: Nebraska has no state senate.
4. Lowercase generic terms standing alone or in plural uses: the Boston and Chicago city councils, the department.

See **foreign governmental bodies** and **foreign legislative bodies**.

governor Use *Gov.* (plural: *Govs.*) as a formal title before a name on first reference in regular text. Drop the title on second reference. Capitalize and spell out as a formal title before a name in direct quotations. Lowercase and spell out in all other uses.

governor general (s.), **governors general** (pl.) The formal title for the British sovereign's representatives in Canada and elsewhere. Never abbreviate.

graduate (v.) A person may *graduate from* a school. It is correct, but unnecessary, to say he *was graduated.* But do not drop *from* in: John Adams graduated from Harvard.

graham A finely ground whole-wheat flour used in baking. Named for Sylvester Graham, a U.S. dietary reformer. Lowercase: *graham crackers.*

grain The smallest unit in the system of weights commonly used in the United States. It was originally defined as the weight of one grain of wheat. There are 437.5 grains in an ounce.

gram The basic unit of weight in the metric system, equal to about one-twenty-eighth of an ounce. To convert to ounces, multiply by 0.035 (86 grams × 0.035 equals 3 ounces). See **metric system**.

grammar, grammarian, grammar school, grammatical

Grammy Award, or statuette, given by the National Academy of Recording Arts & Sciences for achievement in the recording industry. The plural is *Grammys,* not *Grammies.*

granddad, granddaughter, grandfather, grandmother, grandson

grand jury Always lowercase: a Los Angeles County grand jury, the grand jury.

Grand Old Party *GOP* is acceptable as a second-reference synonym for *Republican Party* without first spelling out *Grand Old Party.*

grant-in-aid (s.), **grants-in-aid** (pl.) Not *grant-in-aids.*

gray Not *grey.* But: greyhound, Greyhound bus.

great- Hyphenate for relatives: great-grandfather, great-great-grandmother, etc. Drop the hyphens only if the intended meaning is to designate someone as distinguished.

Great Britain *Britain* is acceptable in all references. See **United Kingdom**.

Great Depression See **Depression**.

greater Capitalize when used to define a community and its surrounding region: Greater Knoxville.

Great Lakes The five, from the largest to the smallest: Lake Superior, Lake Huron, Lake Michigan, Lake Erie, Lake Ontario.

Great Plains The U.S. prairie lands that extend from North Dakota to Texas and from the Missouri River to the Rocky Mountains. Also: *the Plains.* Lowercase words that refer to a portion of the region: northern Plains.

Greek Catholic Church See **Eastern Rite churches**.

Greek Orthodox Archdiocese of North and South America See **Eastern Orthodox churches**.

Greek Orthodox Church See **Eastern Orthodox churches**.

Greenwich Mean Time (GMT) See **GMT** for conversion table. Also see **UTC** and **time**.

(grey) The correct spelling is *gray.*

(gringo) Avoid this contemptuous term for an American or Briton.

grisly, grizzly *Grisly* means *horrifying, repugnant; grizzly* is short for *grizzly bear.*

grits Ground hominy. Normally with plural verbs: Grits are to country ham what Yorkshire pudding is to roast beef, but alone they taste like soap. See **collective nouns**.

gross domestic product Lowercase. *GDP* is acceptable on second reference. The value of all goods and services produced within a country's borders, excluding the foreign output. The U.S. GDP is calculated quarterly by the Department of Commerce.

gross national product Lowercase. *GNP* is acceptable on second reference. It is the total retail value of a nation's output of goods and services in a specified period. The U.S. GNP, calculated quarterly by the Department of Commerce, is considered the broadest available measure of the nation's economic activity.

gross profit, gross revenue See **loan terminology**.

groundbreaker, groundbreaking

Groundhog Day Feb. 2. According to an old tradition, the groundhog comes out of hibernation on this date; if it is sunny and he sees his shadow, he supposedly returns to his hole for six more weeks of winter weather.

Ground Zero Capitalize when referring to the site of the Sept. 11, 2001, terrorist attacks on the World Trade Center in New York.

group Usually takes singular verbs and pronouns: The group is reviewing its position. But use plural verbs and pronouns when the emphasis is on individual action: The group waved their flags.

group (military) A U.S. Air Force formation consisting of two or more squadrons. Capitalize with a numbered unit: 4th Fighter-Interceptor Group. Otherwise, lowercase: the group, the group commander. See **military units, squadron** and **wing**.

G7, G8 No hyphen in the abbreviated references to the *Group of Seven* (United States, Britain, France, Germany, Italy, Japan, Canada) or the *Group of Eight* (those countries and Russia).

Guadalupe (Mexico), **Guadeloupe** (West Indies) Note different spellings.

Guam An unincorporated U.S. territory in the Western Pacific. In datelines: *AGANA, Guam, Dec. 23 (UPI)* —

guard A job description, lowercase.

guardsman See **National Guard** and **Coast Guardsman**.

Guatemala City The capital of Guatemala stands alone in datelines.

gubernatorial

guerrilla Irregular soldiers or their tactics. See **gorilla**.

Guild, the See **Newspaper Guild, The**.

guillotine Two *l*'s, one *t*.

Gulf Coast Capitalize references to the region along the Gulf of Mexico, but lowercase references to the physical shoreline.

(Gulf of Iran) Use *Persian Gulf*, the long-established name, unless quoting the government of Iran. When *Gulf of Iran* is used, explain in the

(Gulf of Iran) *continued*

text that this body of water off the southern coast of Iran is more commonly known as the *Persian Gulf.*

Gulf of Mexico On second reference: *the gulf.*

Gulf Oil Formerly *Gulf Oil Corp.,* it is now known as the *Gulf Oil Limited Partnership. Gulf Oil* may be used on first reference. Headquarters is in Chelsea, Mass.

Gulf Stream But the racetrack is *Gulfstream Park.*

Gulf War A 1991 war in which an international military coalition led by the United States drove Iraqi forces from Kuwait. Also called the *Persian Gulf War.*

Gulf War syndrome Small *s.*

gun Acceptable term for any firearm. See **weapons**.

gunbattle, gunfight, gunmaker, gunpowder, gunrunner

gypsy (s.), **gypsies** (pl.) Lowercase unless it clearly is a direct reference to the tribes of itinerant dark-skinned people believed to have come from India in the 14th or 15th century: She learned the dance around the campfire of a Gypsy caravan. But: Oilmen are gypsies of the prairie. Also: gypsy bonnet, gypsy cab, gypsylike, gypsy moth, gypsyweed, gypsy winch.

H

Ha'aretz Note the apostrophe in reference to the Israeli newspaper.

habeas corpus A petition requiring those detaining someone to justify it. If the term is used, define it.

hacker A skilled amateur computer enthusiast. The term is now mostly used to describe a person who has unlawfully penetrated private computer systems or committed other illegal acts on the Internet.

Hades Capitalize, but lowercase *hell.*

Hague, The In datelines: *THE HAGUE, Netherlands, May 31 (UPI)* —

halfback, half-baked, half brother, half dollar, halfhearted, half-hour, half-moon, half pint, halfway. Hyphenate if not listed in *Webster's New World College Dictionary.*

half-mast, half-staff On ships and at naval stations ashore, flags are flown at *half-mast.* Ashore, flags are flown at *half-staff.*

hallelujah

Halley's comet After Edmund Halley, an English astronomer who predicted the comet's appearance about every 75 years. It was seen most recently in 1986 and 1910.

Halloween No apostrophe.

halo (s.), **halos** (pl.)

Hamas Militant Palestinian organization formed in 1987. *Hamas* is an Arabic acronym for *Harakat al-Muqawama al-lslamiya* (Islamic Resistance Movement).

handcrafted, handgun, handmade, handpicked, handset, handshake, handshaking, hands-off, hand-to-hand

hang, hanged, hung One *hangs* a picture, a criminal or oneself. Use *hanged* (past tense or passive) to refer to executions or suicides, *hung* for other actions.

hangar, hanger A *hangar* is a building; a *hanger* is for clothes.

Hanukkah The Jewish Feast of Lights, an eight-day commemoration of the rededication of the Temple by the Maccabees after their victory over the Syrians. It usually occurs in December, but sometimes falls in late November. This spelling is an exception to *Webster's New World College Dictionary.*

harass, harasser, harassment Only one *r.*

hard disk, hard drive A computer storage system with several rigid disks. See **floppy disk**.

hard-line (adj.), **hard-liner** (n.)

hardware In reference to computers, *hardware* consists of the boards, electronic components and other equipment that make up a computer. *Software* tells the computer what to do. See **software**.

(harebrained, harelip) Do not use these terms. Use *cleft lip* instead of *harelip.*

Harris Survey See **polls**.

has-been (n.)

Havana The capital of Cuba stands alone in datelines.

Hawaii Do not abbreviate. The state comprises 132 islands. Collectively: *the Hawaiian Islands.* See **state(s)**.

   The largest island is Hawaii. Honolulu and Pearl Harbor are on Oahu, where 80 percent of the state's residents live. Honolulu stands alone in datelines. The form for others: *PEARL HARBOR, Hawaii Dec. 7 (UPI)* —

   Residents of Hawaii are generally called *Hawaiians,* but in Hawaii, the term is generally restricted to descendants of the original Polynesian settlers of the islands. Any other inhabitant is usually called an *islander* or *Hawaiian resident,* or is described as *someone who lives in Hawaii.* Make the distinction if it is useful.

Hawaii Standard Time The time zone in Hawaii. The state has no daylight-saving time. See **time** and **Alaska Standard Time**.

Hawaiian Airlines Headquarters is in Honolulu.

hazmat Lowercase this abbreviation for *hazardous materials:* "We're sending in a hazmat team," the mayor said.

H-bomb

he, him, his Lowercase personal pronouns referring to the deity.

head-on (adj., adv.)

headquarters Use either a singular or plural verb with *headquarters,* whichever fits the occasion Avoid awkward uses of this plural noun. Do not use *headquarter, headquartered.*

> *Wrong:* The company will headquarter in the town. The troops headquartered in a mountain cave.

> *Right:* The company set up headquarters on the south side. The company has its headquarters in Dallas. Company headquarters has approved the new contract. The company's headquarters are in Chicago. Headquarters is in Detroit.

healthcare, health farm, health food, health spa

health maintenance organization. See **HMO.**

hearing examiner See **administrative law judge.**

heaven Always lowercase.

heavenly bodies Capitalize the proper names of planets, stars, etc.: Mars, Arcturus, the Big Dipper, Aries, Halley's comet. See **earth** and **planets.**

Lowercase *sun* and *moon,* but if their Greek names are used, capitalize them: *Helios* and *Luna.* Lowercase nouns and adjectives derived from the proper names of planets and other heavenly bodies: earthling, jovian, lunar, martian, solar, venusian.

heavy-handed (adj.)

hecto- A prefix meaning *100;* the form before a vowel is *hect-.* A *hectare* is a metric surface measure equal to 100 ares, 10,000 square meters, 2.47 acres, 107,639.1 square feet or 11,959.9 square yards. To convert to acres, multiply by 2.47 (5 hectares × 2.47 equals 12.35 acres). See **metric system.**

heights See **dimensions.**

heir apparent The heir whose right to a certain property or title cannot be denied if he outlives the ancestor.

hell But capitalize *Hades.*

helter-skelter

hemisphere Capitalize Northern Hemisphere, Western Hemisphere, etc. Lowercase standing alone or in plural uses: the hemisphere, the Eastern and Southern hemispheres.

hemorrhage, hemorrhoid Two *r*'s.

her Do not use this pronoun to refer to nations or ships, except in quoted matter. Use *it* instead.

herculean Lowercase *herculean* unless you are referring to a feat performed by Hercules himself.

(here) Do not use *here* to refer to the dateline community of a story. If a reference must be made, repeat the name of the community.

Her Majesty Use it only in direct quotations.

heroics, heroism *Heroics* means *melodramatic, pretentious, extravagant behavior or language; heroism* means *bravery, the action of a hero.*

heroin The narcotic, originally a trademark.

hertz Do not abbreviate. The international unit of frequency, or one cycle per second, is the same in singular and plural. If its meaning is not clear, explain it in parentheses: 15,400 hertz (cycles per second).

Herzegovina See **Bosnia-Herzegovina**.

Hezbollah Militant Shiite movement in Lebanon. The name means *Party of God.*

Hewlett-Packard Co. *HP* is acceptable in second reference. Headquarters is in Palo Alto, Calif. Note: HP acquired Compaq Computer Corp. in 2002.

HHS Acceptable on second reference for the *Department of Health and Human Services.*

highhanded (adj., adv.)

high-rise (n., adj.)

high-tech

highways Do not abbreviate. The forms, as appropriate: U.S. Highway 1, U.S. Route 1, U.S. 1, Route 1, Illinois 34, Illinois Route 34, state Route 34, Route 34, Interstate Highway 495, Interstate 495.

Hyphenate if a figure follows a letter; no hyphen if a letter follows a figure: I-495, Route 1A.

highway patrol Capitalize the agency if a specific reference is clear: the Kansas Highway Patrol. Or: TOPEKA, Kan., April 1 (UPI) — Leaders of the Highway Patrol said, etc. Lowercase *the patrol* and *highway patrolman.*

hike Journalese. Overused for *increase, raise,* etc.

Hiroshima A Japanese seaport largely destroyed Aug. 6, 1945, by a U.S. atomic bomb, the first ever used in warfare. The explosion had the force of 20,000 tons (20 kilotons) of TNT. It destroyed more than 4 square miles and killed or injured 160,000 people.

his, her Do not presume maleness in stories, but avoid the constructions *he or she* and *his or hers* in an effort to include both sexes. Use masculine pronouns to refer to a word that may be either male or female: A reporter attempts to protect his sources. (Not *his or her sources.* But: *reporter,* not *newsman.*) Or recast the sentence: Reporters attempt to protect their sources.

His Majesty Use it only in direct quotations.

Hispanic

Hispaniola West Indies island between Cuba and Puerto Rico.

historic, historical A *historic* event is important. It stands out in history. Any occurrence in the past is a *historical* event. The article before *historic* and *historical* is *a,* not *an.*

historical periods Capitalize proper nouns and adjectives in describing periods of history: ancient Greece, classical Rome, the Victorian era.

Elsewhere, some cultural and historical periods and events are capitalized: the Atomic Age, the Pliocene Epoch, Prohibition, the Reign of Terror, the Stone Age, the Middle Ages, the Boston Tea Party, the Exodus (of the Israelites from Egypt).

Some are not: antiquity, the neolithic period, the fall of Rome, the gold rush, the ice age, the industrial revolution, the westward movement.

See separate entries in this book. If this book has no entry, follow the capitalization in *Webster's New World College Dictionary,* using lowercase if it is one of the options listed. If there is no listing in *Webster's New World,* use lowercase except for proper nouns and adjectives.

history Avoid the redundant *past history.*

hit-and-run (n., adj.), **hit and run** (v.) The coach told him to hit and run. He scored on a hit-and-run. She was injured in a hit-and-run accident.

hitchhike, hitchhiker Note the double *h.*

Hitler, Adolf Not *Adolph.*

hit list, hit man

HIV Acceptable on second reference for *human immunodeficiency virus,* the cause of AIDS. See **AIDS**.

HMO Acceptable in all references to *health maintenance organization.* The plural is *HMOs* (no apostrophe).

hockey The spelling of some common words and phrases:

blue line	goaltender	slapshot
faceoff *(n., adj.)*	hat trick	shorthanded
face off *(v.)*	power play	two-on-one
goal post	power-play goal	break
goal line	red line	

A *hat trick* is the scoring of three goals in one game by one player. A team is on a *power play* when the opposing team is *shorthanded* because of penalties.

hocus pocus

hodgepodge

Hodgkin's disease After Dr. Thomas Hodgkin, the English physician who first described the disease of the lymph nodes.

ho-hum

holding company A holding company's main assets are the securities it owns in companies that actually provide goods and services. Its usual purpose is to control several companies by holding a majority of their stock.

hold up (v.), **holdup** (n., adj.)

holidays and holy days Capitalize special calendar events: New Year's Eve, New Year's Day, Groundhog Day, Washington's Birthday, Easter Sunday, Memorial Day, Independence Day, etc.

Hollywood Stands alone in datelines when used instead of *Los Angeles* on stories about films and the film industry.

Holocaine A trademark for a local anesthetic.

holy communion, holy eucharist Lowercase.

Holy Land

Holy See The Roman headquarters of the Roman Catholic Church.

home builder, home building (n.), **home-building** (adj.), **home buyer, home-grown, homemade, homemaker, homemaking, homeowner, home page, hometown**

Home Depot Inc. Headquarters is in Atlanta.

homicide The killing of one human by another.

Murder is malicious or premeditated homicide. Do not say a victim was *murdered* until someone is convicted of murder. Instead, use *killed* or *slain*. Do not describe someone as a *murderer* until he or she is convicted of the charge in court.

Manslaughter is homicide without malice or premeditation.

A *killer* is anyone who kills with a motive of any kind.

An *assassin* is a killer of a politically important person.

To *execute* is to kill in accordance with a legally imposed sentence. See **execute**.

homograph, homonym *Homographs* are words that are spelled alike but have different meanings: bow of a ship and a bow from the waist. *Homonyms* are words that are pronounced the same but have different meanings: bow and bough.

homosexual. See **gay**.

Hong Kong Stands alone in datelines.

(honky) A term of abuse directed toward whites by blacks. Avoid it.

Honolulu The city in Hawaii stands alone in datelines.

honorary degrees Do not use *Dr.* for those whose only doctorate is honorary.

honorary titles Disregard such titles as those bestowed by British honors lists (Sir Charlie Chaplin, Dame Margo Fonteyn) unless clearly pertinent to a story. See **nobility**.

hoof-and-mouth disease Note hyphens. See **foot-and-mouth disease**.

hooky Not *hookey.*

hookup (n.) No hyphen.

hopefully In its proper context, something must be *filled with hope.* Do not use for *it is to be hoped.*

> *Wrong:* Hopefully, the storm will pass. (*The storm* cannot be filled with hope.)
> *Right:* Hopefully, we waited for the storm to pass. (*We* are filled with hope that the storm will pass.)

horses Capitalize proper names of horses and races: Secretariat, Kentucky Derby, the Preakness. See **animals**.

(host) Do not turn this noun into a verb. See **noun**.

HotBot An Internet search engine. See **search engine**.

hot dog See **frankfurter**.

hot dog! Exclamation.

hotdog A showoff.

hotel Capitalize in the name of a specific hotel: the Waldorf-Astoria Hotel. Lowercase an indefinite reference: The city has a Sheraton hotel.

Hotel and Restaurant Employees and Bartenders International Union *Hotel and Restaurant Employees union* or *Bartenders union* is acceptable in all references. Headquarters is in Cincinnati.

hot launch Conventional means of lifting a missile out of its silo by the rocket propulsion system. See **cold launch**.

hot line Lowercase, including the circuit linking the United States and the former Soviet Union.

hourlong As in the hourlong meeting.

house Lowercase most non-governmental uses: a fraternity house, a house of worship, the house of Tudor, bring down the house, like a house on fire.

Capitalize proper names of organizations and institutions: the House of Delegates of the American Medical Association, the House of Bishops of the Episcopal Church.

Capitalize a reference to a specific legislative body: the U.S. House of Representatives, the Massachusetts House, the Virginia House of Delegates,

house *continued*

the House of Commons, the House of Lords, the House of Burgesses. Or: BOSTON, Nov. 29 (UPI) — The House adjourned for the year.

Lowercase plural uses: the Massachusetts and Rhode Island houses.

housecleaning

house guest

Houston The city in Texas stands alone in datelines.

Hovercraft A trademark for a vehicle that travels on a cushion of air.

howitzer A short-barreled cannon that fires shells on a high trajectory. The form: 105mm howitzer. See **weapons**.

HTML For *HyperText Markup Language.* It is the programming language used to create most Web pages.

HTTP For *HyperText Transfer Protocol,* the Internet standard for exchanging information.

HTTPS For *HyperText Transfer Protocol Secure,* a variation of HTTP that is used to access a *secure* Web server.

HUD Acceptable on second reference for *Department of Urban Development.*

Hula Hoop A trademark.

human, human being Either is acceptable.

Hungarian Reformed Church in America

hurley-burley

hush-hush

Hussein, Saddam *Saddam* on second reference.

hurricanes Capitalize as part of the name assigned to a storm: Hurricane Hugo. Do not use the presence of a feminine name as an excuse to invoke sexist images.

Wrong: Fickle Gloria teased the Virginia coast.

Hurricane stories should include the latitude and longitude of the storm center as well as its location in relation to recognizable landmarks.

A *hurricane* is a rotating wind system with a minimum sustained surface wind speed of 74 mph or more. Hurricanes are formed east of the international dateline. *Typhoons,* which have the same criteria, develop west of the line. When a hurricane's winds drop below 74 mph, it becomes a *tropical storm.*

A *hurricane eye* is the relatively calm area in the center of the storm.

The *hurricane season* is the part of the year with a relatively high number of hurricanes, June through November.

A *hurricane warning* advises that a hurricane or its dangerous effects, dangerously high water, perhaps with exceptionally high waves, are expected in a coastal area within 24 hours. A *hurricane watch* alerts a specific area that a hurricane may pose a threat.

The *National Hurricane Center* in Miami provides information about hurricanes in the Atlantic, Caribbean and Gulf of Mexico. The *Eastern Pacific Hurricane Center* is in San Francisco; the *Central Pacific Hurricane Center* is in Honolulu.

The term *packing winds* is low-grade journalese. Avoid it.

husband, widower Use *husband,* not *widower,* in referring to the spouse of a woman who dies. See **(widow, widower)**.

hyper- This prefix is generally solid: hyperactive, hyperphysical, hypertension.

hyphens There are no rules that can cover all cases of hyphenation. Many hyphenated words are listed in these pages, but it is not within the scope of this book to provide individual entries for all hyphenated words a reporter is likely to use. See *Webster's New World College Dictionary* for words not listed here.

General guidelines:

1. Compounds not listed separately in the dictionary usually take a hyphen before a noun, but no hyphen after it: A first-quarter touchdown, a touchdown in the first quarter. But never use a hyphen when the compound includes *very* or an adverb ending in *-ly:* a very good time, an easily remembered rule.

2. Use a hyphen whenever ambiguity would result if it were omitted: She will speak to small-business men. (The normal spelling is *businessmen,* but *small businessmen* is unclear.) Also: He recovered his health. He re-covered the leaky roof.

3. Use a hyphen if a compound modifier — two or more words that express a single concept — is listed separately as an adjective with hyphens in *Webster's New World College Dictionary.* (Example: *well-known*), the compound is always hyphenated: She is a well-known woman. She is well-known. Also: The child is soft-spoken. The censor is self-appointed. The children are quick-witted.

4. Some prefixes and suffixes are hyphenated. See **prefixes** and **suffixes**.

5. Some numerals, odds, ratios, etc., are hyphenated. See **numerals**.

6. Suspensive hyphenation: the 5- and 6-year-olds attend morning sessions.

7. Do not hyphenate common phrases unless they are used as compound modifiers before a noun.

hyphens *continued*

> *Wrong:* They confronted each other face-to-face.
> *Right:* They confronted each other face to face.
> *Right:* It was a face-to-face confrontation.

Some frequently used compounds:

aftereffect
anti-war
backup
biweekly
breakaway *(n, adj.)*,
   break away *(v.)*
breakup *(n.)*, break up *(v.)*
break-in *(n.)*, break in *(v.)*
breakout *(n.)*, break out *(v.)*
buildup *(n.)*, build up *(v.)*
byproduct
call-up *(n., adj.)*, call up *(v.)*
cave-in *(n.)*, cave in *(v.)*
checkup *(n.)*, check up *(v.)*
cleanup *(n.)*, clean up *(v.)*
close-up *(n., adj.)*, close up *(v.)*
counterattack
counterespionage
counterintelligence
counterrevolution
counter-terrorism
coverup *(n.)*, cover up *(v.)*
cutback *(n.)*, cut back *(v.)*
cutoff *(n., adj.)*, cut off *(v.)*
die-hard
front-line *(adj.)*, front line *(n.)*
front-page *(adj.)*, front page *(n.)*
front-runner, front-running
full-time *(adj.)*, full time *(v.)*
fundraiser, fundraising *(n., adj.)*
hard-line *(adj.)*, hardliner
lineup *(n.)*, line up *(v.)*
long-term *(adj.)*

longtime *(adj.)*, long time *(n.)*
long-shot *(adj.)*, long shot *(n.)*
makeup *(n., adj.)*, make up *(v.)*
midafternoon, midair,
   midmorning
multimillion, multinational
part-time *(adj.)*, part time *(v.)*
peacekeeper, peacekeeping,
   peacemaker
postwar, post-World War II
pre-dawn *(adj.)*, pretrial, prewar
pullback *(n., adj.)*, pull back *(v.)*
pushup *(n., adj.)*, push up *(v.)*
re-elect
rule-making
runoff, runnerup, running mate
rush-hour *(adj.)*, rush hour *(n.)*
self-defense
semifinal
shake-up *(n.)*, shake up *(v.)*
short-term *(adj.)*, short term *(n.)*
speechmaker, speechmaking
   (adj.), speechwriter
speedup *(n.)*, speed up *(v.)*
stand-in *(n.)*, stand in *(v.)*
standout *(n.)*, stand out *(v.)*
takeoff *(n.)*, take off *(v.)*
takeover *(n.)*, take over *(v.)*
trade-in *(n.)*, trade in *(v.)*
well-being, well-known,
   well-to-do
whistle-blower
workout *(n.)*, work out *(v.)*

Iberia Airlines

IBM Acceptable on first reference for *International Business Machines.* Headquarters is in Armonk, N.Y.

ICBM See **intercontinental ballistic missile(s)**.

ice age Any of a series of cold periods marked by substantial glaciation.

iceberg, icebound, icebox, icebreaker, icecap, icehouse, but **ice cream, ice floe, ice pack, ice pick, ice skate, ice tea, ice water**

Iceland Air Headquarters is in Reykjavik.

ice storm The freezing of rain or drizzle on objects as it strikes them. An *ice storm warning* is reserved for occasions when significant, and possibly damaging, accumulations of ice are expected.

ID For *identification.* No periods: Each member wore an ID badge. They carried IDs. "We were ID'd by the police."

Idaho Do not abbreviate. See **state(s)**.

(if and when) A pretentious redundancy. Avoid it.

illegal Use it only to mean a violation of the law. Be especially careful in labor-management disputes, where one side will often call an action by the other side *illegal.* Usually it is a charge that a contract or rule, not a law, has been violated.

Illinois Abbreviation: *Ill.* See **state(s)**.

illusion See **allusion, illusion**.

imam Lowercase for the leader of a prayer in a Muslim mosque. Capitalize as a formal title before the name of a Muslim leader or ruler. See **religion**.

immigrate See **emigrate, immigrate**.

(Immigration and Naturalization Service) The service that was known as the *INS* was abolished in 2003. Its functions were transferred to other agencies within the *Department of Homeland Security*. See **Bureau of Immigration and Customs Enforcement**.

(impact) Avoid using as a verb in sentences like these: The judge said the court's ruling will impact the community. Scientists said the meteorite impacted the planet. The new rule impacts on the campus.

impanel Not *empanel*.

impassable, impassible, impassive Something *impassable* cannot be passed: an impassable bridge. Someone *impassible* cannot feel pain. Someone *impassive* shows no emotion.

impel, impelled, impelling

imperial gallon The standard British gallon, 277.42 cubic inches or about 1.2 U.S. gallons. In metric it is about 4.5 liters.

imperial quart One-fourth of an imperial gallon.

implausible Not *implausable*.

imply, infer Writers or speakers *imply* in the words they use. Listeners or readers *infer* from the words others use.

impostor Not *imposter*.

impromptu Without preparation or advance thought. Do not use it to refer to an event that is merely informal or held without advance notice.

in- Generally solid to indicate *not*: inadmissible, incapable, invisible, etc. Frequently solid elsewhere: inboard, inbounds, incoming, infield, infighting, inland, inlet, inshore. But occasionally hyphenated: in-depth, in-house, in-law, in-service.

-in Hyphenated as a suffix: break-in, cave-in, sit-in, shoo-in, walk-in, write-in.

in, into *In* indicates location within: He was *in* the room. *Into* indicates motion to a location within: She walked *into* the room.

inasmuch as

Inauguration Day Capitalize only when referring to the total collection of events that include the inauguration of a U.S. president; lowercase in other uses: Inauguration Day is Jan. 20. The inauguration day for the change has not been set.

Inc. Not set off with commas when used at the end of a title. See **incorporated**.

inch Equal to one-twelfth of a foot and exactly 2.54 centimeters. To convert to centimeters, multiply by 2.54 (6 inches × 2.54 equals 15.24 centimeters).

include Use *include* for an incomplete list, *comprise* for a whole list: The zoo comprises 100 animals, and includes a lion and tiger. See **compose, comprise**.

income, income before taxes See **profit terminology**.

income statement Indicates how much a business earns or loses over a specific period, typically a year or quarter. Also known as an *earnings report*.

incorporated Use *Inc.* at the end of a formal corporate name. It usually is not needed but, if used, do not set off with commas: Volkswagen of America Inc.

incredible, incredulous *Incredible* means *not believable; incredulous* means *unable to believe:* The story was incredible. The audience was incredulous.

incumbent Avoid redundant use before the title of an officeholder.

> *Wrong:* Incumbent Mayor John Jones said today.
> *Right:* Mayor John Jones said today.

incur, incurred, incurring

Independence Day *July Fourth* or *Fourth of July* are acceptable. The federal legal holiday is on Friday if July 4 falls on a Saturday, on Monday if it falls on Sunday.

index (s.), **indexes** (pl.) Not *indices*.

Index of Leading Economic Indicators Capitalized as a title. A composite of 12 economic measurements developed to help forecast likely shifts in the whole economy, compiled monthly by the Department of Commerce.

Indiana Abbreviation: *Ind.* See **state(s)**.

Indianapolis The city in Indiana stands alone in datelines.

Indian Ocean See **oceans**.

Indians Avoid disparaging words: *wampum, warpath, powwow*, etc. American Indians are native Americans, but so is everyone else born in the United States. See **native Americans**.

indict To avoid any suggestion that someone is being judged before a trial, do not use *indicted for* killing, etc. Use *indicted on a charge of* killing. See **accuse, allege** and **arrest**.

indiscreet, indiscrete *Indiscreet* means *lacking prudence,* and its noun form is *indiscretion; indiscrete* means *not separated into distinct parts,* and its noun form is *indiscreteness.*

indiscriminate, indiscriminately

indispensable Not *indispensible.*

individual Do not use as a general synonym for *person.*

> *Wrong:* Police questioned an individual fitting the description.
> *Right:* Police questioned a person fitting the description.
> *Right:* Individuals and corporations were liable under the law.

Indochina The large peninsula south of China that comprises Myanmar (formerly Burma), Thailand, Cambodia, Laos, Malaysia and Vietnam. The former French colony of Indochina was composed of Cambodia, Laos and Vietnam.

Indonesia Republic in the Malay Archipelago comprising Celebes, Java, Sumatra, West Irian, most of Borneo, and many smaller islands. *Jakarta* stands alone in datelines. The form for others: *SURABAYA, Indonesia, Dec. 2 (UPI)* — Specify an individual island, if needed, in the text.

indoor (adj.), **indoors** (adv.) She went indoors to play indoor tennis.

infant Applicable to children through 12 months old.

(infantile paralysis) The preferred term is *polio.*

inflation A sustained increase in prices causing a decrease in the purchasing power of money. There are two basic types:

Cost-push inflation occurs when rising costs are the chief reason for the increased prices.

Demand-pull inflation occurs when the amount of money available exceeds the amount of goods and services available for sale.

InfoSeek An Internet search engine. See **search engine**.

infra- Hyphenate to avoid a double *a:* infra-angelic, but usually no hyphen: infrared, infrasonic. Follow *Webster's New World College Dictionary,* hyphenating words not listed there.

initials Use periods and no space: H.L. Mencken. For middle initials, if used: John Q. Public. Exception: Use no periods when referring to presidents by three initials: FDR, JFK, LBJ.

injuries They are *suffered* or *sustained,* not *received.*

in-law

inmate A person living with others in the same building. Properly used for non-criminals, such as the mentally ill, who are confined against their will. But more frequently used euphemistically for *convict* or *prisoner* when referring to felons. Use it advisedly.

innocent Use *innocent,* rather than *not guilty,* to describe a defendant's plea or a jury's verdict, to guard against *not* being dropped.

innocuous, innuendo Two *n*'s.

inoculate One *n.*

inquire, inquiry Not *enquire, enquiry.*

INS Acceptable on second reference for *Immigration and Naturalization Service.*

insignia Singular and plural.

insolvency An individual or business is *insolvent* when unable to pay debts when due. Even though a company's assets may exceed its liabilities, it could be insolvent if those assets could not be converted into sufficient cash to meet current obligations.

inspector general Do not abbreviate.

in spite of *Despite* means the same thing and is shorter.

insure See **ensure, insure**.

Intel Manufacturer of microprocessors and other semiconductors. Intel central processing units *(CPUs)* are widely used around the world. Headquarters is in Santa Clara, Calif.

Intelsat Acceptable in all references for *International Telecommunications Satellite Organization* (originally *Consortium* instead of *Organization*). Headquarters is in Washington.

inter- Hyphenate with a capitalized word: inter-American. Elsewhere, follow *Webster's New World College Dictionary,* hyphenating words not listed there.

intercontinental ballistic missile(s) *ICBM(s)* is acceptable on second reference.

(interface) Computerese. Avoid to mean *interact* or *connect with.*

intermediate range ballistic missile(s) *IRBM(s)* is acceptable on second reference.

Internal Revenue Service *IRS* is acceptable on second reference.

International Brotherhood of Electrical Workers *IBEW* is acceptable on second reference. Headquarters is in Washington. Do not call this union the *Electrical Workers union,* a term reserved for the United Electrical, Radio and Machine Workers of America.

International Business Machines See **IBM**.

International Court of Justice The principal judicial organ of the United Nations, established at The Hague in 1945. On second reference: *international court* or *world court* in lowercase. See **world court**.

international date line The imaginary line drawn north and south through the Pacific Ocean, largely along the 180th meridian. By international agreement, when it is 12:01 a.m. Sunday just west of the line, it is 12:01 a.m. Saturday just east of it. See **time**.

International Labor Organization *ILO* is acceptable on second reference. Headquarters is in Geneva.

International Ladies Garment Workers Union See **Union of Needle-trades, Industrial and Textile Employees**.

International Longshore and Warehouse Union *ILWU* is acceptable on second reference. Headquarters is in San Francisco.

International Longshoremen's Association *Longshoremen's union* is acceptable in all references. *ILA* is acceptable after the full name has been used. Headquarters is in New York.

International Monetary Fund *IMF* is acceptable on second reference. Headquarters is in Washington.

Internet A worldwide system of linked computer networks. The *Net* is acceptable on second reference. See **World Wide Web**, which is part of the Internet.

Internet address See **IP address** and **URL (URLs)**.

Interpol Acceptable in all references for *International Criminal Police Organization.* Headquarters is in Paris.

Interstate Commerce Commission *ICC* is acceptable on second reference.

intifada An uprising, specifically the revolt started in 1987 by Palestinian Arabs to protest Israel's occupation of the Gaza Strip and West Bank. Always lowercase.

intra- Hyphenate with a capitalized word or to avoid a double *a:* intra-European, intra-atomic. Elsewhere, follow *Webster's New World College Dictionary,* hyphenating words not listed there. Also: Intracoastal Waterway.

intranet Lowercase. A computer network for a single company or organization.

intrauterine device *IUD* is acceptable on second reference.

invasion of privacy See **libel**.

IOU (s.), **IOUs** (pl.)

Iowa Do not abbreviate. See **state(s)**.

IP address A unique address for each computer connected to the Internet. Example: 120.101.27.6. *IP address* is synonymous with *Internet address.* See **URL (URLs)**.

IPTC International Press Telecommunications Council.

IQ Acceptable in all references for *intelligence quotient.*

Iran The nation formerly called *Persia.* It is not an Arab country; do not call its citizens *Arabs.* The people are properly called *Iranians,* though they are sometimes called *Persians* or *Irani.* Iranians call their language *Farsi,* but outside Iran it is more commonly called *Persian.*

Iraq The Arab nation, coinciding more or less with ancient *Mesopotamia.* Its people are *Iraqi(s).* The dialect of Arabic is *Iraqi.*

Ireland Usually acceptable for the *Irish Republic.* But use the full name if needed to differentiate it from *Northern Ireland,* a part of the United Kingdom.

Irish Republican Army. *IRA* is acceptable on second reference.

Iron Curtain Term used by Winston Churchill in 1946 to describe the Soviet-imposed barrier between Eastern and Western Europe: *"From Stettin in the Baltic to Trieste in the Adriatic an iron curtain has descended across the continent."*

(irregardless) The correct word is *regardless.*

Islam The Muslim religion. Its deity is Allah. Mohammed is its founder and prophet. The adjective is *Islamic.* See **Muslim**.

islands Capitalize *island* or *islands* as an integral part of a proper name: Prince Edward Island, the Hawaiian Islands. Lowercase elsewhere, including all *island of* constructions: an island, a Mississippi island, the Pacific islands, the island of Nantucket. See **datelines**.

ISDN For *Integrated Services Digital Network.* An *ISDN* line is a digital telephone line that can transfer information at faster speeds than conventional lines. An even faster digital service is a *DSL* line (Digital Subscriber Line). Both types of service are offered by telephone companies in many cities. See **DSL.**

ISP For *Internet service provider,* a company that provides Internet access.

it Use this pronoun, not *she* or *her,* to refer to countries and ships.

it's, its *It's* is a contraction for *it is* or *it has:* It's up to you. It's been a long time. *Its* is possessive: The company lost its assets.

IV Acceptable on second reference to the intravenous procedure or apparatus.

Ivy League Brown, Columbia, Cornell, Dartmouth, Harvard, Princeton, Yale and the University of Pennsylvania.

J

Jacuzzi Trademark for a therapy pool.

jail See **prison, jail**.

Jakarta The capital of Indonesia stands alone in datelines.

Jamaica rum Not *Jamaican rum*.

Jane's All the World's Aircraft, Jane's Fighting Ships The reference sources for questions about aircraft and military ships not covered in this book. The reference for non-military ships is *Lloyd's Register of Shipping.*

January See **months**.

Japan Air Lines *JAL* is acceptable on second reference. Headquarters is in Tokyo.

Japanese names The family name is last and is used on second reference: Sumie Koba studied in Vienna. Koba is a soprano.

jargon The special vocabulary of a particular class or occupational group. If jargon is used, explain it. See **argot, slang**.

Java A computer programming language.

Jaycees Members of the United States Junior Chamber. Headquarters is in Tulsa, Okla.

J.C. Penney Co. Inc. Headquarters is in Plano, Texas, a suburb of Dallas.

JDAM A satellite-guided bomb. The initials stand for *Joint Direct Attack Munitions.*

jeep, Jeep Lowercase the military vehicle. Capitalize in reference to the civilian vehicle so trademarked and now manufactured by Chrysler. See **four-wheel-drive**.

Jehovah's Witnesses *Witnesses* do most of their work through three corporations: the Watch Tower and Tract Society of Pennsylvania, the Watchtower Bible and Tract Society of New York Inc., and, in England, the International Bible Students Association. There are no formal titles.

Jell-O A trademark for a gelatin dessert.

jerry-built Made quickly, cheaply. Often confused with *jury-rigged.* See **jury-rigged**.

Jerusalem Stands alone in datelines.

Jesus The central figure of Christianity may also be called *Jesus Christ.* Personal pronouns referring to him are lowercase.

jet, jetliner, jet plane, jet fighter, jet bomber Do not transpose to *fighter jet* or *bomber jet.* See **aircraft**.

JetBlue Airways No space in *JetBlue.* Headquarters is at JFK Airport in New York.

Jew Use for men and women. Do not use *Jewess.*

Jewish congregations A Jewish congregation is autonomous. No synods, assemblies or hierarchies control the activities of an individual synagogue.

   In the United States, there are three basic expressions of Judaism:

   1. *Orthodox Judaism.* Its congregations are represented nationally by the Union of Orthodox Jewish Congregations of America. Most of its rabbis are members of the Rabbinical Council of America.

   2. *Reform Judaism.* Its national representatives are the Union of American Hebrew Congregations and the Central Conference of American Rabbis.

   3. *Conservative Judaism.* Its national representatives are the United Synagogue of America and the Rabbinical Assembly.

   These groups compose the *Synagogue Council of America,* with headquarters in New York, which represents all three expressions.

   The spiritual leader of a congregation is a *rabbi;* the leader of prayer and song is a *cantor.* Capitalize the titles if used before a name. See **Zionism**.

jibe See **gibe, jibe**.

jihad Holy war or spiritual struggle. Lowercase except when written as *Islamic Jihad.*

job descriptions Always lowercase. See **titles**.

John F. Kennedy Space Center *Kennedy Space Center* is acceptable in all references. Located at Cape Canaveral, Fla., it is the National Aeronautics and Space Administration's principal launch site for manned spacecraft. In datelines: *CAPE CANAVERAL, Fla., Nov. 2 (UPI)* — See **Lyndon B. Johnson Space Center**.

Johns Hopkins University No apostrophes.

Johnson Space Center Acceptable in all references for the space center near Houston. See **Lyndon B. Johnson Space Center**.

Joint Chiefs of Staff Also: *the Joint Chiefs*. But lowercase *chiefs of staff* or *the chiefs*.

journalese Newswriters' jargon; words and phrases habitually used in news reports but seldom seen elsewhere in the same context. Avoid it.

Some examples:

hammered out an agreement	chilling effect
in the wake of	wily veteran
took center stage	slugfest
blue-ribbon panel	court of public opinion
marathon negotiations	facelift
sifted through the rubble	ratcheted up
the campaign trail	laid the groundwork
rushed to the hospital	packing winds of
claimed the life of	the mercury plunged
wreaked havoc	drug lord
bullet-riddled	duo, trio, quartet
die-hard fans	axed
blinding speed	split the uprights

Also:

blasted for *criticized:* The president *blasted* the report.

blaze for *fire:* The hotel *blaze* killed 50 people.

closed-door for *private:* The committee met behind *closed doors*.

first-ever for *first:* It was their *first-ever* championship.

grilled for *questioned:* Police *grilled* the suspect.

gunned down for *shot:* He *gunned down* his best friend.

hiked for *increased:* Congress *hiked* taxes 5 percent.

hosted for *held:* Mrs. Reagan *hosted* a reception.

huddled for *met:* The committee *huddled*.

hurled for *made:* The charges were *hurled* by the suspect's lawyer.

launched for *started:* He *launched* an investigation.

lauded for *praised:* She *lauded* the chairman's work.

leveled for *presented:* The charges were *leveled* in an indictment.

kicked off for *began:* He *kicked off* his campaign Monday.

price tag for *cost:* The program's *price tag* is $1 million.

probe for *investigation:* The *probe* lasted three weeks.

sprawling for *large:* The *sprawling* air base in Texas.
sweeping for *encompassing:* The *sweeping* law affects all.
triggered for *set off:* His speech *triggered* the riot.
unveiled for *announced:* He *unveiled* his plan Monday.
whopping for *large:* A *whopping* 10 percent increase.

Jr. Not set off with commas. See **junior, senior**.

judge Capitalize a formal title before the name of a public official who presides in a court of law. Drop the title on second reference. Lowercase *judge* as a job description: contest judge James Jones.

   Do not use *court* as part of a title unless ambiguity would result without it: U.S. District Judge John Williams, District Judge John Williams, federal Judge John Williams, Judge John Williams. But: Juvenile Court Judge Henry Jones, Criminal Court Judge Henry Jones, Superior Court Judge Henry Jones, state Supreme Court Judge Henry Jones.

judge advocate (s.), **judge advocates** (pl.), **judge advocate general** (s.), **judge advocates general** (pl.) Capitalize as a formal title before a name.

judgment Not *judgement.*

judicial branch Always lowercase. The federal court system is composed of the Supreme Court of the United States, the U.S. Court of Appeals, U.S. District Courts, the U.S. Court of Claims, the U.S. Court of Customs and Patent Appeals and the U.S. Customs Court.

   The U.S. Tax Court and the U.S. Court of Military Appeals are not part of the judicial branch as such.

jukebox

July See **months**.

June See **months**.

junk bond See **loan terminology**.

junior, senior Spell out for a class or its members: She is a junior in college. He is a high school senior.

   Use *Jr.* and *Sr.* to designate a son or father only when used with a full name. Do not set off by a comma: Henry Smith Jr. Some people may also use *II* or *2nd,* although these designations are generally given to grandchildren or nephews.

junk food, junk mail, junkman, junkyard

junta See **government**.

juror, jurist A *juror* is a member of a jury; a *jurist* is a judge or expert in the field of law.

jury Always lowercase. It takes singular verbs and pronouns: The jury has been sequestered until it reaches a verdict. Avoid awkward phrases such as seven-man, five-woman jury. Make it a jury of seven men and five women.

jury-rigged Not *jerry-rigged.* Rigged or fixed in a makeshift manner for temporary or emergency use. Often confused with *jerry-built.* See **jerry-built**.

justice Capitalize before a name if it is the formal title for a jurist. It is the formal title for members of the U.S. Supreme Court and for some state courts. In such cases, do not call the jurist a *judge* in any reference.

justice of the peace Do not abbreviate. Capitalize before a name.

juvenile delinquent In addition to violations of the law, juveniles may be declared *delinquents* in many states for anti-social behavior. Some states prohibit publishing or broadcasting the name of a juvenile delinquent.

Follow the local practice unless there is a compelling reason to the contrary. Consult your supervisor if you believe such an exception is warranted.

K

Kabylia Not *Kabylie*. A region in northeast Algeria. *Kabyles* are a tribal people concentrated in the *Kabylia region*. They speak *Kabyle*, a Berber dialect.

Kansas Abbreviation: *Kan.* See **state(s)**.

Kansas City Use *Kansas City, Kan.,* or *Kansas City, Mo.,* in datelines to avoid confusion between the two.

karat See **carat, caret, karat**.

Karmapa Lama See **Dalai Lama**.

Katmandu Not *Kathmandu.* The capital of Nepal.

Kazakhstan Not *Kazakstan.*

Kelvin scale A scale of temperature based on, but different from, the Celsius scale. It is used primarily in science to record very high and very low temperatures. The Kelvin scale starts at zero and indicates the total absence of heat (absolute zero).

On the Kelvin scale, the freezing point of water is 273.16 degrees; the boiling point 373.16 degrees.

Zero on the Kelvin scale is equal to minus 273.16 degrees Celsius and minus 459.67 degrees Fahrenheit. See **temperatures**.

Kennedy Space Center See **John F. Kennedy Space Center**.

Kentucky Abbreviation: *Ky.* Strictly speaking, it's a commonwealth, not a state. See **state(s)**.

Kentucky Derby On second reference: *the Derby.*

ketchup Not *catchup* or *catsup.*

keynote speech (or *address*) Always lowercase.

Keystone Kops Not *Cops.*

KGB Acceptable on first reference, but the story should identify it as the former Soviet intelligence agency. In Russian, the initials stand for *Committee for State Security.*

kidnap, kidnapped, kidnapping, kidnapper Not *kidnaped,* etc.

killer See **homicide.**

kilo- A prefix meaning *1,000;* a *kilogram* is 1,000 grams. See **metric system.**

kilobyte Although *kilo* means 1,000, a *kilobyte* of computer disk or memory capacity actually equals 1,024 *bytes.* See **byte, megabyte, giga-, terabyte.**

(kilocycles) The correct term is now *kilohertz.*

kilogram Equals 1,000 grams, about 2.2 pounds or 35 ounces. To convert to pounds, multiply by 2.2 (9 kilograms × 2.2 equals 19.8 pounds). Use the abbreviation *kg* only in tabular matter.

kilohertz Equals 1,000 hertz (cycles per second), replacing *kilocycles* as the correct term in such applications as broadcast frequencies. The official abbreviation, *kHz,* is acceptable on second reference if clear in the context.

kilometer Equals 1,000 meters, about 3,281 feet, or five-eighths (0.62) of a mile. To convert to miles, multiply by 0.62 (5 kilometers × 0.62 equals 3.1 miles). Use the abbreviation *km* only in tabular matter and for certain sports events.

kiloton The explosive force of 1,000 tons of TNT. The atomic bomb dropped Aug. 6, 1945, on Hiroshima, Japan, was the first use of the bomb as a weapon and had an explosive force of about 20 kilotons.

kilowatt-hour The amount of electrical energy consumed when 1,000 watts are used for one hour or the equivalent, such as 500 watts for two hours. The abbreviation *kwh* is acceptable on second reference.

kindergarten Not *kindergarden.*

king See **royal titles.**

Kitchen Cabinet Capitalize for a group of unofficial advisers to a head of government.

klavern See **Ku Klux Klan.**

Kleenex A trademark for a facial tissue.

KLM Royal Dutch Airlines *KLM* is acceptable on first reference. Headquarters is in Amsterdam, Netherlands.

Kmart Headquarters is in Troy, Mich.

kneecap, knee-deep, knee-high, knee-jerk, kneepad

Knesset The Israeli Parliament. See **foreign legislative bodies.**

knight A man who for some achievement is given honorary, non-hereditary rank next below a baronet, and he may be called *Sir.* See **honorary titles**.

Knights of Columbus *K. of C.* may be used on second reference.

knot A knot is one nautical mile (6,076.10 feet) per hour; *knots per hour* is redundant. To convert knots into approximate statute miles per hour, multiply knots by 1.15 (25 knots × 1.15 equals 28.75 mph). Always use figures: Winds were at 7 to 9 knots; a 10-knot wind.

know-how

Kodak A trademark for cameras and other photographic products made by Eastman Kodak Co. of Rochester, N.Y.

Koran The sacred book of Muslims.

Korean Air Headquarters is in Seoul.

Korean names Note the style differences in South and North Korean names:

South Korean — Generally capitalize the first two words and put a hyphen between the second and third: Kim Dae-jung, Suh Young-hoon.

North Korean — Each word is capitalized and there are no hyphens: So Si Pong, Kim Yong Dae.

In all Korean names, the family name comes first (Kim, Suh, So, etc.) and is used on second reference.

Koreans who live in the United States or other English-speaking countries may transliterate their names in different ways. Follow the style they have adopted.

Korean War But: Korean conflict, the war in Korea.

kosher Always lowercase.

Kosovo A southern Serbia province under U.N. administration and considered an international protectorate. Kosovo's population is largely ethnic Albanian.

Kris Kringle Not *Kriss,* an exception to *Webster's New World College Dictionary.*

Kroger Co., The The grocery retailer operates *Kroger, Ralph's, Dillon's, Pay Less Supermarkets, Smith's Food & Drug Stores, King Soopers* and other stores. Headquarters is in Cincinnati.

kudos Credit or praise for an achievement, always with a plural verb (there is no singular *kudo)*: Kudos go to Jane Jones.

Ku Klux Klan There are many separate organizations known in America as the *Klan.* Some of them do not use the full name *Ku Klux Klan,* but each may be called that, and the *KKK* initials may be used for any of them on second reference. A local chapter may be called a *Klan* or

Ku Klux Klan *continued*

klavern (lowercase). Capitalize formal titles before a name: Imperial Wizard James Smith, Grand Dragon John Jones. Members are *Klansmen* or *Klanswomen.*

Kuomintang The former Chinese Nationalist political party. But not: *Kuomintang party,* as *tang* means *party.*

Kurdistan Southwest Asia plateau and mountain region inhabited by the Kurdish people, or *Kurds.* The region encompasses parts of Turkey, Iran and Iraq with smaller sections in Armenia and Syria. The Kurds are mostly Sunni Muslim people.

Kuril Islands Not *Kurile.* The form for datelines: *BEREZOVKA, Kuril Islands, Nov. 1 (UPI)* —

Kuwait City Stands alone in datelines.

L

Labor Day The first Monday in September.

Laborers' union Acceptable in all references for the Laborers' International Union of North America. Headquarters is in Washington.

Labor Party Not *Labour,* even if British.

Labrador The mainland portion of the Canadian province of Newfoundland. The form for datelines: *GOOSE BAY, Newfoundland, Feb. 25 (UPI) —*

Specify in the text that the community is in Labrador.

Ladies' Home Journal With an apostrophe.

lady Do not use as a synonym for *woman.* See **nobility**.

Lafayette Square The park across Pennsylvania Avenue from the White House. If *Lafayette park* is used in a direct quote, lowercase *park.*

lake Capitalize as part of a proper name: Lake Erie. Lowercase plural uses: lakes Erie and Ontario.

LAN A *local area network* on which computers are linked by cable so that users can share information and access data stored on a computer called a *file server.*

landing craft, landing field, landing gear, landing strip

landlocked, landmark, landowner, landslide, landward, *but* **land mine**

Land-Rover With a hyphen. A trademark for a four-wheel-drive vehicle. See **four-wheel-drive**.

languages Capitalize the proper names of languages and dialects: Aramaic, Cajun, English, Gullah, Persian, Serbo-Croatian, Yiddish, etc.

La Nina A cooling of the Pacific Ocean off South America that affects weather in many parts of the world. See **El Nino**.

larceny See **theft**.

(last) Avoid the use of *last* as a synonym for *latest* if it might imply finality. The last time it rained, I forgot my umbrella is acceptable. But the last announcement was made at noon today may leave the reader wondering whether others are to follow.

And avoid the unnecessary use of the word. Omit *last* in: It happened (last) Wednesday. Past tense is sufficient to show which Wednesday is meant.

Last Supper Capitalize the sacrament.

late Do not use it to describe someone's actions while alive. Omit *late* in: Only the (late) senator opposed this bill. He was not dead at the time.

latex A milky liquid used to make rubber, adhesives and paints.

Latin America In general, the area of the Americas south of the United States.

latitudes The imaginary lines parallel to the equator. See **longitude**.

Laundromat Service mark for a coin-operated laundry.

Law Enforcement Assistance Administration *LEAA* is acceptable on second reference.

lawman Journalese for *policeman, officer,* etc. Avoid it.

laws Capitalize legislative acts but not bills: the Taft-Hartley Act, the Kennedy bill.

lawyer A general term for a person trained in the law. Do not use *lawyer* as a formal title.

An *attorney* is a person legally appointed or empowered to act for another, usually, but not always, a lawyer. An *attorney at law* (no hyphens) is a lawyer.

A *barrister* is an English lawyer, specially trained, who appears exclusively as a trial lawyer in higher courts. He is retained by a *solicitor,* not directly by the client. There is no equivalent in the United States.

A *counselor* is one who conducts a case in court, usually, but not always, a lawyer. A *counselor-at-law* (hyphenated) is a lawyer. *Counsel* is frequently used collectively for a group of counselors.

A *solicitor* in England is a lawyer who performs legal services for the public and appears in lower courts but does not have the right to appear in higher courts, which is reserved to barristers.

A *solicitor* in the United States is a lawyer employed by a governmental body. It is generally a job description, but in some agencies it may be a formal title.

Solicitor general is the formal title for a chief law officer (where there is no attorney general) or for the chief assistant to the law officer (when there is an attorney general). Capitalize when used before a name.

lay, lie To *lie* is to recline; to *lay* is to cause to recline.

> *Wrong:* He will lay down on the bed. He lie down the book.
> *Right:* He will lie down on the bed. He lay down the book.

Other forms of *lie:* He lay down on the bed (past tense). He has lain down on the bed (past participle). He is lying down on the bed (present participle).

Other forms of *lay:* He laid down the book (past tense). He has laid down the book (past participle). He is laying down the book (present participle).

Leaning Tower of Pisa Capitalize.

leatherneck Lowercase this nickname for a member of the U.S. Marine Corps. It is derived from the leather lining that was formerly part of the collar on the Marine uniform.

lectern A speaker stands behind a lectern, on a podium or rostrum, or in a pulpit.

lecturer A formal title in the Christian Science Church. A job description in other uses. See **religion**.

leery Not *leary.*

left-handed, left-hander

leftist In general, use a more precise description of someone's philosophy. As popularly used today, particularly abroad, *leftist* often applies to someone who is merely liberal or believes in a form of democratic socialism.

Ultra-leftist suggests one holding that liberal or social change cannot come within the present form of government. See **radical**.

leftover

left wing, left-winger

legalese Avoid the special vocabulary of lawyers and courts in news stories in favor of more common words. If legalese must be used, define it.

legerdemain Not **ledgerdemain**.

Legionnaires' disease Apostrophe after the *s.*

legislative titles Capitalize formal titles before names; lowercase elsewhere. Use *Rep., Reps., Sen.* and *Sens.* before names in regular text, but spell them out in direct quotations. See **party affiliation**.

Spell out other legislative titles (*assemblyman, assemblywoman, city councilor, delegate,* etc.) in all uses.

legislative titles *continued*

Other guidelines:

1. Use *U.S.* or *state* before a title only if necessary to avoid confusion: U.S. Sen. John Jones spoke with state Sen. Robert Smith.

2. The use of a title such as *Rep.* or *Sen.* in first reference is normal in most stories. It is not mandatory, however, provided the title is given later in the story: Robert Dole endorsed the bill Monday. The Kansas senator predicted quick passage.

3. Do not use legislative titles before a name on second reference unless they are part of a direct quotation.

4. Use *Congressman* and *Congresswoman* as capitalized formal titles before a name only in direct quotation.

5. Capitalize formal, organizational titles before a name: *Speaker, Majority Leader, Minority Leader, Democratic Whip, President Pro Tem.*

6. UPI style is to use job descriptions, *Senate Republican leader, House Democratic leader,* rather than the formal titles for these four leadership posts. In these constructions, *leader* is lowercased.

legislature Capitalize with or without a state name if a specific reference is clear: the Kansas Legislature. Or: TOPEKA, Kan., April 30 (UPI) — The state Legislature adjourned today.

Legislature is not part of the proper name in many states, but it is acceptable in any: the Virginia Legislature (the proper name is *General Assembly*).

Lowercase *legislature* in all generic and plural references: No legislature has approved the amendment; the Arkansas and Colorado legislatures.

In 47 states the separate bodies are a *senate* and a *house.* In California and New York, the separate bodies are a *senate* and an *assembly.* The Nebraska Legislature is a unicameral body.

lend (v.), **loan** (n.) Banks *lend* money to borrowers, who must pay off the *loans.*

Lent, Lenten The period of 40 weekdays from Ash Wednesday through Holy Saturday, the day before Easter.

Leonardo da Vinci Use *Leonardo da Vinci* on first reference and *Leonardo* on second. (Never *da Vinci* alone. It means *from* the town of *Vinci.*)

lesbian, lesbianism Lowercase in references to homosexual women, except in names of organizations. See **gay**.

less See **fewer, less**.

Letter Carriers union Acceptable in all references for the *National Association of Letter Carriers.* Headquarters is in Washington.

leveled, leveling, leveler

Levi's A trademark for bluejeans.

liaison Not *liason.*

liberal, liberalism Lowercase unless the reference clearly is to the *Liberal Party* or its members. See **political parties**.

lie See the **lay, lie** entry.

lie in state Formally, only those who are entitled to a state funeral may *lie in state,* which in this country occurs in the rotunda in the Capitol. In a less formal sense, say the body will be on public view or will be displayed publicly.

Those entitled to a state funeral are a president, a former president, a president-elect, or any other person specifically designated by the president.

Members of Congress also may lie in state, and a number have done so. The decision is either house's to make, although the formal process usually begins with a request from the president.

Those entitled to an official funeral, but not to lie in state, are the vice president, the chief justice, Cabinet members and other government officials when specifically designated by the president.

lieutenant See **military titles**.

lieutenant general See **military titles**.

lieutenant governor Capitalize as a formal title before names. Abbreviate as *Lt. Gov.* or *Lt. Govs.* in regular text, but spell out in direct quotations. Lowercase and spell out in all other cases. Drop the title on second reference.

Life Saver, Life Savers Trademarks for a brand of roll candy.

lifesaver Lowercase, one word.

lifestyle

light, lighted, lighting Do not use *lit* in past tense.

lightning Not *lightening* for the electrical discharge.

light-rail

light-year The distance that light travels in one year at the rate of 186,282 miles per second. It works out to about 5.88 trillion miles.

likable Not *likeable.*

like Acceptable to mean *as* or *as if:* It was just like you said. It looks like he is late.

-like No hyphen, except to avoid a triple *l:* businesslike, lifelike, bill-like, shell-like.

Lima The capital of Peru stands alone in datelines.

limited Abbreviate as *Ltd.* and capitalize as part of a formal corporate name. Do not set it off with commas.

limousine Not *limosine.*

linage, lineage *Linage* is the number of lines; *lineage* is ancestry or descent.

Lincoln's Birthday Capitalize *birthday* in references to the holiday. Lincoln was born Feb. 12 (in 1809). It is not a federal legal holiday.

line numbers Use figures and lowercase: line 1, line 9. But: the first line, the 10th line.

Line of Control The unofficial line separating India and Pakistan in the Kashmir region. Do not use the initials *LOC* except in direct quotations.

lineup (n.), **line up** (v.)

linoleum Formerly a trademark, now a generic term.

Linotype A trademark for a typesetting machine.

Linux A type of Unix operating system. See **Unix** and **operating system**.

lion's share From an Aesop fable in which the lion took all the spoils of a joint hunt. As used popularly, it also may mean *the biggest portion.*

(lit) Use *lighted* as past tense of *light.*

liter The basic unit of volume in the metric system, equal to about 34 fluid ounces, 1.06 liquid quarts or .91 dry quarts. The metric system makes no distinction between dry volume and liquid volume.

- To convert to *liquid quarts,* multiply by 1.06 (4 liters × 1.06 equals 4.24 liquid quarts).
- To convert to *dry quarts,* multiply by .91 (4 liters × .91 equals 3.64 dry quarts).
- To convert to *liquid gallons,* multiply by .26 (8 liters × .26 equals 2.08 gallons).

See **metric system**.

literally See **figuratively, literally**.

literature See **composition titles**.

liturgy The prescribed form or ritual for public worship in various religions or churches. See **Eastern Orthodox churches**.

livable Not *liveable.*

livid It is not a synonym for *fiery, bright, crimson, red* or *flaming.* If you turn *livid with rage,* your face becomes ashen or pale.

Lloyd's (insurance), **Lloyds** (bankers)

Lloyd's Register of Shipping The reference source for questions about non-military ships not covered in this book.

-load armload, truckload, workload.

loan terminology Note the meanings:

bond — An interest-bearing certificate issued by a business or government promising to pay the holder a specified sum on a specified date, usually issued for more than seven years.

collateral — Anything, such as stocks, bonds or property, that a borrower must turn over to a lender if unable to pay a loan.

commercial paper — The short-term promissory notes of banks and quality corporations issued to investors.

convertible bond — A bond that can be exchanged for a specific amount of stock in the company that issued it.

coupon — Attached to a bond, it specifies the interest due at a given time. Each coupon is returned to the issuer for payment of the interest due.

debenture — A certificate acknowledging that a debt is owed by the signer, but with no pledge of collateral.

default — The failure to meet the terms for repayment of a loan.

full faith and credit bond — Same as a general obligation bond.

general obligation bond — A government bond formally approved by either the voters or their legislature.

junk bond — A high-risk, high-yield bond primarily used to finance corporate takeovers, but also to raise money for corporate needs.

maturity — The date on which a bond, note, etc., must be repaid.

moral obligation bond — A government bond that has not had the formal approval of either the voters or their legislature and is therefore backed only by the government's "moral obligation" to repay the principal and interest on time.

municipal bond — A general obligation bond issued by a state, county, city, town, village, possession or territory; or a bond issued by an agency or authority set up by one of these governmental units. In general, interest paid on municipal bonds is exempt from federal taxes. It is usually exempt also from state and local income taxes if held by someone living within the state of issue.

note — A certificate promising to pay the holder a specified sum on a specified date, usually for less than seven years. The shorter interval for repayment is the principal difference between a note and a bond.

revenue bond — A bond backed only by the revenue of the airport, turnpike or other facility that was built using the money it raised.

loan terminology *continued*

> *treasury bill* — A certificate representing a loan to the federal government that matures in three, six or 12 months. A *treasury bond* matures in seven years or more; a *treasury note* matures in one to 10 years.

local area network See **LAN**.

local Avoid its irrelevant use. Omit *local* in: The injured were taken to a (local) hospital.

local of a union Use a figure and capitalize: Local 222 of The Newspaper Guild. Lowercase standing alone or in plural uses: The local will vote Tuesday. He spoke to locals 2, 4 and 10.

(located) Often not needed. Omit *located* in: It is (located) in Houston. The Empire State Building is (located) in New York City.

Lockheed Martin Corp. Formed by a 1995 merger of Lockheed and Martin Marietta. Headquarters is in Bethesda, Md.

logotype It separates a dateline from the body of a story: WALLA WALLA, Wash., Nov. I (UPI) — It is cold.

London The city in England stands alone in datelines.

-long daylong, hourlong, monthlong, weeklong, yearlong, but block-long, decade-long, century-long, foot-long, yard-long. Some are exceptions to *Webster's New World College Dictionary*. Hyphenate others not listed in the dictionary.

long-distance Hyphenate in reference to telephone calls. In other uses, hyphenate only when it is a compound modifier: He made a long-distance trip. He drove a long distance.

longitude The imaginary lines perpendicular to the equator.

long term (n.), **long-term** (adj.) In the *long term*, it will pay off. The company made a *long-term* commitment.

long time (n.), **longtime** (adj.) They have been married a *long time*. She is a *longtime* friend.

long titles They should follow a name. See **titles**.

long ton See **ton**.

long shot

longstanding (adj.), **long standing** (n.)

look-alike (n.), **look-alikes** (pl.)

Loran Capitalize. Acronym for *long range navigation,* a system used worldwide in which a ship or airplane determines its position by time intervals of radio signals received from two or more stations.

lord See **nobility**.

Lord's Prayer, Lord's Supper

Los Angeles The city in California stands alone in datelines. Confine *LA* (no periods) to quoted matter.

LOT Polish Airlines Headquarters is in Warsaw.

Lotus I-2-3 A computer spreadsheet program.

Lou Gehrig's disease *[amyotrophic lateral disease]* Named for the baseball player who died of the disease in 1941.

Louisiana Abbreviation: *La.* See **state(s)**.

Low Countries Belgium, Luxembourg and Netherlands.

lowercase One word (n., adj., v.) when referring to the absence of capital letters.

LSD Acceptable in all references for *lysergic acid diethylamide.*

Ltd. See **limited**.

Lt. Gov. See **lieutenant governor**.

Lucite A trademark for an acrylic plastic.

Lufthansa German Airlines *Lufthansa* is acceptable on first reference. Headquarters is in Cologne.

Luftwaffe The German air force. See **air force**.

lukewarm

Lutheran Churches: A 1988 merger of three Lutheran bodies — the Lutheran Church in America, the American Lutheran Church and the Association of Evangelical Lutheran Churches — created the Evangelical Lutheran Church in America. It is the largest Lutheran body in the United States, with headquarters in Chicago. The second largest Lutheran group is the Lutheran Church-Missouri Synod. It has headquarters in St. Louis.

Members of the clergy are known as *ministers. Pastor* applies to a minister who leads a congregation. Other titles include *bishop, elder, deacon* and *trustee.*

On first reference use *Bishop, Elder, Deacon, Trustee* or *the Rev.,* as appropriate. Drop the title on second reference.

Luxembourg Stands alone in datelines.

Lycos An Internet search engine. See **search engine**.

Lyndon B. Johnson Space Center *Johnson Space Center* is acceptable in all references. Formerly the *Manned Spacecraft Center.* Near Houston, it is the National Aeronautics and Space Administration's principal control and training center for manned spaceflight. In datelines: *SPACE CENTER, Houston, Dec. 3 (UPI)* — See **John F. Kennedy Space Center**.

M

Macao Stands alone in datelines.

Mace A trademark, shortened from *Chemical Mace,* for a tear gas that is in an aerosol canister and temporarily stuns its victims.

MADD See **Mothers Against Drunk Driving**.

Madrid The capital of Spain stands alone in datelines.

machine gun (n.), **machine-gun** (adj., v.), **machine-gunner** See **weapons**.

machine pistol European term for *submachine gun.* See **submachine gun** and **weapons**.

Machinists union Acceptable in all references for *International Machinists and Aerospace Workers.* Headquarters is in Washington.

Mach number Named for Ernst Mach, an Austrian physicist, the figure represents a multiple of the speed of sound. A body traveling at Mach 1 would be traveling at the speed of sound. Mach 2 would equal twice the speed of sound.

macroeconomics One word.

Mafia The secret society of criminals that originated in Sicily. Its members are *Mafiosi.* The term *mafia* (lowercase) is often used as a synonym for organized crime, as in the Russian mafia.

magazine names Capitalize, without quotation marks. Lowercase *magazine* unless it is part of the publication's formal title: Harper's Magazine, Newsweek magazine, Time magazine. Check the masthead if in doubt.

Magna Carta Not *Magna Charta.*

Mailgram A trademark for a telegram sent to a post office near the recipient's address, then delivered by letter carrier.

(mailman) *Letter carrier* is preferred, because many women hold this job.

Maine Do not abbreviate. See **state(s)**.

mainland China See **China**.

major See **military titles**.

major general See **military titles**.

Majorca Not *Mallorca*. The form in datelines: *PALMA, Majorca, Aug. 4 (UPI) —*

majority, plurality *Majority* means *more than half of a certain number*. If candidate A gets 100,000 votes, candidate B, 200,000, and candidate C, 350,000, then C has a majority of 50,000 votes.

Plurality means *more than the next highest number*. If candidate A gets 65,000 votes, candidate B gets 40,000 and candidate C gets 35,000, then A has a plurality of 25,000, but does not have a majority.

When *majority* and *plurality* are used alone, they take singular verbs and pronouns: The majority has made its decision.

With an *of* construction they take either a singular or plural verb, whichever fits the occasion: A majority of two votes is not adequate to control the committee. The majority of the houses on the block were destroyed.

majority leader Capitalize as a formal title before a name: Majority Leader Barbara Jones. Lowercase elsewhere. See **legislative titles**.

makeup

Malaysia Airlines Headquarters is in Kuala Lumpur.

Mall of America The mall, in Bloomington, Minn., opened in 1992. It has more than 520 stores and an amusement park called *Camp Snoopy*.

man, mankind Acceptable to mean *all human beings* or *the human race*. Avoid their use when they could give sexist connotations, favoring an alternate such as *people* or *humanity*. Avoid *humankind*. See **women**.

manageable Not *managable*.

manager Capitalize when used as a formal title before a name: Manager Joe Torre, General Manager Craig Patrick. Lowercase elsewhere: equipment manager Joe Smith.

Manitoba A province of central Canada. The form in datelines: *WINNIPEG, Manitoba, June 15 (UPI) —*

manslaughter See **homicide**.

mantel, mantle A *mantel* is a shelf; a *mantle* is a cloak.

Maoism, Maoist The communist philosophy and policies of Mao Zedong.

Mao Zedong Not *Mao Tse-tung*.

Marathon Oil Corp. Formerly *USX Corp.,* which in 2001 was renamed and divided into two independent companies, Marathon and U.S. Steel. Marathon has headquarters in Houston; U.S. Steel in Pittsburgh. See **U.S. Steel.**

March See **months.**

marchioness See **nobility.**

Mardi Gras Literally "fat Tuesday," a day of merrymaking on the Tuesday before Ash Wednesday, which marks the start of Lent.

margin The difference between two sums. In a 100-50 vote, the margin is 50. The ratio is 2-to-1. See **ratio.**

marijuana Not *marihuana.*

marines Capitalize references to U.S. forces: the U.S. Marines, the Marines, the Marine Corps, Marine regulations. Do not use *USMC.*

Many nations do not use *marines* as a proper name. For consistency, use lowercase for all others: the Canadian marines.

Maritime Provinces The Canadian provinces of Nova Scotia, New Brunswick and Prince Edward Island. Do not abbreviate.

marketbasket, marketplace One word.

marquis See **nobility.**

marshal, Marshall *Marshal* is both the verb and noun: Marilyn will marshal her forces. Stan Anderson is a fire marshal. Erwin Rommel was a field marshal. The other forms: *marshaled, marshaling. Marshall* is a proper name: George C. Marshall.

Marshall Islands A U.S. trust territory named for John Marshall, a British explorer. The form in datelines: *MAJURO, Marshall Islands, Jan. 15 (UPI)* — Specify the name of an individual island, if needed, in the text.

Martin Luther King Jr. Day A federal holiday observed on the third Monday in January.

MARV For *maneuvering re-entry vehicle,* in which each warhead can be steered after it separates from the main missile.

Marxism, Marxist A political system conceived by Karl Marx and Friedrich Engels.

Maryland Abbreviation: *Md.* See **state(s).**

Mason-Dixon Line The boundary line between Pennsylvania and Maryland, generally regarded as separating the North from the South.

Masonite Trademark for a brand of hardboard.

mass It is *celebrated, said* or *sung.* Lowercase in all uses: high mass, low mass, requiem mass. In Eastern Orthodox churches, the term is *liturgy* or *divine liturgy.*

Massachusetts Abbreviation: *Mass.* Specifically, a commonwealth, not a state. See **state(s)**.

masterful, masterly *Masterful* means *domineering, overbearing; masterly* means *skillful. Masterful* is frequently used for *masterly,* but not by careful writers.

master of arts, master of science A *master's degree* or a *master's* is acceptable in any reference. See **academic degrees**.

maximum-security (adj.) The inmate will be transferred to a *maximum-security* prison.

May See **months**.

May Day, mayday *May Day* is May 1, often a festive or political holiday; *mayday* is an international distress signal.

mayor Capitalize as a formal title before names: Mayor Willie Brown Jr., Mayors H. Brent Coles of Boise, Idaho, and Bill Campbell of Atlanta. Drop the title after first reference and lowercase in other uses: The mayor presented his tax plan. Sixteen mayors met in New Orleans.

mayors' conference See **U.S. Conference of Mayors**.

MBFR For *mutual and balanced force reduction.*

McDonnell Douglas Corp. No hyphen. Headquarters is in St. Louis.

M.D. *Physician* or *surgeon* is preferred. See **doctor**.

mean See **average**.

Medal of Freedom See **Presidential Medal of Freedom**.

Medal of Honor Not *Congressional Medal of Honor,* although the nation's highest military honor is given by Congress for risk of life in combat beyond the call of duty.

media Usually plural: Radio and television are the electronic media. But as a collective noun to refer to a unit: The news media is resisting attempts to limit its freedom.

median See **average**.

mediate See **arbitrate, mediate**.

Medicaid A federal-state program that helps pay for healthcare for the needy, aged, blind and disabled, and for low-income families with children.

Medicare The federal healthcare insurance program for people 65 and over, and for the disabled. In Canada, *Medicare* refers to the national health insurance program.

medicine See **drugs**.

medieval Not *midevil, midieval* or *mideval.*

mega- A prefix meaning *1 million;* a *megaton* is the explosive force of 1 million tons of TNT. The form before a vowel is *meg-:* megare. See **metric system**.

megabyte A measurement of disk or storage capacity equal to about 1 million bytes (actually 1,048,576 bytes). See **byte, giga-, kilobyte, terabyte**.

Melbourne The city in Australia stands alone in datelines.

Melchite Church See **Eastern Rite churches**.

meltdown See **nuclear terminology**.

memento (s.), **mementos** (pl.) Not *momento*.

memorandum (s.), **memorandums** (pl.) Not *memoranda*.

Memorial Day Formerly May 30. The federal legal holiday is the last Monday in May.

Memphis The city in Tennessee stands alone in datelines.

menage a trois

menswear Not *men's wear.*

Mercalli scale See **earthquakes**.

Mercurochrome A trademark for an antiseptic.

merry-go-round

messiah Capitalize in religious uses. Lowercase to mean *a liberator.*

meter The basic unit of length in the metric system. It is about 39.37 inches. There are 100 centimeters in a meter, 1,000 meters in a kilometer.

To convert to inches, multiply by 39.37 (5 meters × 39.37 equals 196.85 inches). To convert to yards, multiply by 1.1 (5 meters × 1.1 equals 5.5 yards). See **metric system**.

Methodist churches The principal Methodist body in the United States is the United Methodist Church, formed in 1968 by the merger of the Methodist Church and the Evangelical United Brethren Church.

There are three major black denominations: the African Methodist Episcopal Church, the African Methodist Episcopal Zion Church and the Christian Methodist Episcopal Church.

Those ordained are known as *bishops* and *ministers. Pastor* applies if a minister leads a congregation. For first reference to bishops: **Bishop Kenneth Goodson**. The designations *Most Rev.* or *Rt. Rev.* do not apply. For first reference to ministers, use *the Rev.*

metric system A decimal system of weights and measures. The basic units are the *gram,* the *meter* and the *liter.* Larger and smaller units are defined by prefixes, such as *kilo.* Thus, a *kilogram* is 1,000 grams.

Larger units include *deka-* (10), *hecto-* (100), *kilo-* (1,000), *mega-* (1 million), *giga-* (1 billion) and *tera-* (1 trillion).

Smaller units include *deci-* (one-tenth), *centi-* (one-hundredth), *milli-* (one thousandth), *micro-* (one-millionth), and *pico-* (one-trillionth).

Separate entries under **gram, meter** and **liter** provide examples of how to convert them to ordinary equivalents.

Do not abbreviate metric terms in news copy, except for certain cameras, films and weapons: an 8mm film, a 105mm cannon.

See the conversion table below. See also the tables of weights and measures in the back of *Webster's New World College Dictionary.*

A conversion table for frequently used terms (approximations):

Converting into metric

When you know	*multiply by*	*to find*
Length		
inches	2.54	centimeters
feet	30.0	centimeters
yards	0.91	meters
miles	1.6	kilometers
Area		
sq. inches	6.5	sq. centimeters
sq. feet	0.09	sq. meters
sq. yards	0.08	sq. meters
sq. miles	2.6	sq. kilometers
acres	0.4	hectares
Weight		
ounces	28.0	grams
pounds	0.45	kilograms
tons	0.9	metric tons
Volume		
teaspoons	5.0	milliliters
tablespoons	15.0	milliliters
fluid ounces	30.0	milliliters
cups	0.24	liters
pints	0.47	liters
quarts	0.95	liters
gallons	3.78	liters
cubic feet	0.03	cubic meters
cubic yards	0.76	cubic meters

metric system *continued*

Converting out of metric

When you know	*multiply by*	*to find*
Length		
millimeters	0.04	inches
centimeters	0.4	inches
meters	3.3	feet
meters	1.1	yards
kilometers	0.6	miles
Area		
sq. centimeters	0.16	sq. inches
sq. meters	1.2	sq. yards
sq. kilometers	0.4	sq. miles
hectares	2.5	acres
Weight		
grams	0.035	ounces
kilograms	2.2	pounds
metric tons	1.1	tons
Volume		
milliliters	0.03	fluid ounces
liters	2.1	pints
liters	1.06	quarts
liters	0.26	gallons
cubic meters	35.0	cubic feet
cubic meters	1.3	cubic yards

Temperature conversions

- Fahrenheit to Celsius: Fahrenheit minus 32 × $5/9$ths equals Celsius
- Celsius to Fahrenheit: Celsius × $9/5$ths plus 32 equals Fahrenheit

metric ton See **ton.**

Metro-Goldwyn-Mayer Inc. Note the hyphens. *MGM* is acceptable in all references. Headquarters is in Santa Monica, Calif.

metropolitan See **Eastern Orthodox churches.**

Mexico City The capital of Mexico stands alone in datelines.

M-14 The 7.62mm rifle adopted by U.S. forces after the Korean War. Capable of semiautomatic or full-automatic fire. Many are still used in ceremonial events. See **weapons**.

Miami The city in Florida stands alone in datelines.

MIA Acceptable on second reference for *missing in action.*

Michigan Abbreviation: *Mich.* See **state(s)**.

micro- A prefix meaning *one-millionth;* a *microgram* is one-millionth of a gram.

microprocessor A chip that serves as the central processing unit (CPU) of computers.

Microsoft Corp. *Microsoft* is acceptable in all references. The company, founded in 1975, produces software, operating systems and other products for personal and business computing. Products include the Microsoft Windows family of operating systems: Windows 98, Windows 2000, Windows NT, Windows XP, etc. Headquarters is in Redmond, Wash.

mid- No hyphen unless followed by a capitalized word: midafternoon, midair, midday, midlife, midnight, midpoint, midsection, midweek, midyear, but mid-America, mid-Atlantic. Follow *Webster's New World College Dictionary,* hyphenating words not listed there.

Middle Ages A.D. 476 to about A.D. 1450.

Middle Atlantic states As defined by the U.S. Census Bureau, they are New Jersey, New York and Pennsylvania. Less formal references often consider Delaware and Maryland as part of the group. See **Northeast region**.

middle class (n.), **middle-class** (adj.)

Middle East The term applies to southwest Asia west of Pakistan, northeastern Africa and the island of Cyprus. Avoid *Near East,* an outdated term that once designated part of the region. *Mideast* is also acceptable, but *Middle East* is preferred.

middleman

Middle states Those Eastern states between New England and the South: New York, New Jersey, Pennsylvania, Delaware and Maryland.

midnight Do not put a *12* in front of it. It is part of the day that is ending, not the one that is beginning.

midshipman See **military academies**.

Midwest, Midwesterner A region and its inhabitants in the north central United States between the Rocky Mountains and the eastern border of Ohio. Also: *the Middle West.* See **directions**.

MiG The *i* in this designation for a type of jet fighter plane is lowercase because it is Russian for *and*. The initials are from the last names of the designers, Arten Mikoyan and Mikhail Gurevich. The forms: MiG-19, MiG-21s.

(milch cow) Spell it **milk** in all uses.

mile Equal to 5,280 feet, or about 1.6 kilometers. To convert to kilometers, multiply by 1.6 (5 miles × 1.6 equals 8 kilometers).

Use figures in all cases for dimensions, distances, formulas and speeds: The farm measures 5 miles by 4 miles. The car idles at 7 mph. The new model gets 4 miles per gallon. He drove 4 miles.

miles per gallon *mpg* is acceptable on second reference.

miles per hour *mph* is acceptable in all references.

military academies Capitalize Air Force Academy, Coast Guard Academy, Military Academy, Naval Academy. Lowercase standing alone or in plural uses: the academy, the Army, Navy and Air Force academies.

Cadet is the proper title on first reference for men and women enrolled at the Army and Air Force academies. *Midshipman* is the proper title for men and women enrolled at the Navy and Coast Guard academies.

military titles Capitalize a military rank as a formal title before a name on first reference. Lowercase elsewhere. Drop the title on subsequent references.

Do not abbreviate any title standing alone or in a direct quotation.

In some cases it is pertinent to explain a title: Army Sgt. Maj. John Jones, who holds the Army's highest rank for enlisted men, said the attack was unprovoked.

Do not capitalize or abbreviate job descriptions, such as machinist, radarman, torpedoman, yeoman, etc.

To form plurals of the abbreviations, add *s* to the principal element in the title: Maj. Gens., Lt. Cols., Majs., Lts. j.g., Sgts. Maj., Spcs., Lance Cpls., Pfcs., Pvts.

The first-reference usage before a name:

Rank	*Usage Before a Name*
ARMY	
Commissioned Officers	
general	Gen.
lieutenant general	Lt. Gen.
major general	Maj. Gen.
brigadier general	Brig. Gen.

Rank	Usage Before a Name
colonel	Col.
lieutenant colonel	Lt. Col.
major	Maj.
captain	Capt.
first lieutenant	1st Lt.
second lieutenant	2nd Lt.

Warrant Officers
chief warrant officer	Chief Warrant Officer
warrant officer	Warrant Officer

Enlisted Personnel
sergeant major of the Army	Army Sgt. Maj.
command sergeant major	Command Sgt. Maj.
sergeant major	Sgt. Maj.
first sergeant	1st Sgt.
master sergeant	Master Sgt.
platoon sergeant	Platoon Sgt.
sergeant first class	Sgt. 1st Class
staff sergeant	Staff Sgt.
sergeant	Sgt.
corporal	Cpl.
specialist	Spc.
private first class	Pfc.
private	Pvt.

NAVY, COAST GUARD
Commissioned Officers
admiral	Adm.
vice admiral	Vice Adm.
rear admiral (upper and lower)	Rear Adm.
captain	Capt.
commander	Cmdr.
lieutenant commander	Lt. Cmdr.
lieutenant	Lt.
lieutenant junior grade	Lt. j.g.
ensign	Ensign
commissioned warrant officer	Commissioned Warrant Officer

military titles *continued*

Rank	Usage Before a Name

NAVY, COAST GUARD *continued*
Warrant Officers

chief warrant officer	Chief Warrant Officer
warrant officer	Warrant Officer

Enlisted Personnel

master chief petty officer	Master Chief Petty Officer
senior chief petty officer	Senior Chief Petty Officer
chief petty officer	Chief Petty Officer
petty officer first class	Petty Officer 1st Class
petty officer second class	Petty Officer 2nd Class
petty officer third class	Petty Officer 3rd Class
seaman	Seaman
seaman apprentice	Seaman Apprentice
seaman recruit	Seaman Recruit

MARINE CORPS

Ranks and abbreviations for commissioned officers are the same as those in the Army. Warrant officers are abbreviated the same as the Navy. There are no specialist ratings.

Others

sergeant major of the Marine Corps	Sgt. Maj. of the Marine Corps
sergeant major	Sgt. Maj.
master gunnery sergeant	Master Gunnery Sgt.
master sergeant	Master Sgt.
first sergeant	1st Sgt.
gunnery sergeant	Gunnery Sgt.
staff sergeant	Staff Sgt.
sergeant	Sgt.
corporal	Cpl.
lance corporal	Lance Cpl.
private first class	Pfc.
private	Pvt.

Rank	*Usage Before a Name*

AIR FORCE

Ranks and abbreviations for commissioned officers are the same as those in the Army.

Enlisted Designations

chief master sergeant of the Air Force	Chief Master Sgt.of the Air Force
chief master sergeant	Chief Master Sgt.
senior master sergeant	Senior Master Sgt.
master sergeant	Master Sgt.
technical sergeant	Tech. Sgt.
staff sergeant	Staff Sgt.
sergeant	Sgt.
airman first class	Airman 1st Class
airman	Airman
airman basic	Airman

RETIRED OFFICERS

A military rank may be used in first reference before the name of an officer who has retired if it is relevant to a story. Do not, however, used the military abbreviation *Ret.* Instead, use *retired* just as *former* would be used before the title of a civilian: They invited retired Army Gen. James Jones.

FIREFIGHTERS, POLICE OFFICERS

Use the abbreviations listed here when a military-style title appears before the name of a police officer or firefighter outside a direct quotation. Add *police* or *fire* before the title if necessary in the context: police Sgt. William Smith, fire Capt. David Jones.

Spell out titles such as *detective* that are not used in the armed forces.

military units Use figures and capitalize the key words when linked with the figures: 1st Infantry Division (or the 1st Division), 5th Battalion, 395th Field Artillery Battalion, 7th Fleet. But: the division, the battalion, the artillery, the fleet.

milli- A prefix meaning *one-thousandth;* a *milligram* is one-thousandth of a gram. See **metric system**.

milligram One thousandth of a gram; about one-twenty-eight-thousandth of an ounce. To convert to ounces, multiply by 0.000035 (140 milligrams × 0.000035 equals 0.0049 ounces).

milliliter One-thousandth of a liter; about one-fifth of a teaspoon, one-thirtieth of a fluid ounce. To convert to teaspoons, multiply by .2 (5 milliliters × .2 equals 1 teaspoon).

millimeter One-thousandth of a meter. There are 10 millimeters in a centimeter. To convert to inches, multiply by .04 (5 millimeters × .04 equals .2 of an inch). Abbreviate as *mm* with a numeral to refer to film or weapons: 35mm film, 105mm cannon.

millions, billions Use figures with *million* or *billion* in all except casual uses: I'd like to make a billion dollars. But: The nation has 1 million citizens. I need $7 billion.

Do not go beyond two decimals: 7.51 million people, $2.56 billion, 7,542,500 people, $2,565,750,000. Decimals are preferred where practical: 1.5 million. Not: 1½ million.

Do not mix millions and billions in the same numeral: 2.6 billion. Not: 2 billion 600 million.

Do not drop the word *million* or *billion* in the first figure of a range: He is worth from $2 million to $4 million. Not: $2 to $4 million, unless you really mean $2.

Do not use a hyphen to join figures with *million* or *billion:* The president submitted a $300 billion budget. Not: $300-billion budget.

milquetoast Not *milk toast,* for a shrinking, apologetic person, after Caspar Milquetoast, a character in a comic strip by Harold T. Webster.

Milwaukee The city in Wisconsin stands alone in datelines.

mimeograph Formerly a trademark, now a generic term.

mini- Hyphenate with a capitalized word or to avoid a double *i:* mini-industry, a mini-Watergate scandal. Elsewhere, follow *Webster's New World College Dictionary,* hyphenating words not listed there. Avoid as a general nonce word.

minimum-security (adj.) He was warden of a *minimum-security* prison.

(miniscule) Spell it *minuscule.*

minister Always lowercase as a religious title. Capitalize before the name of a public official who holds the title: Minister of Justice Jose Gonzalez, the minister.

ministry See **foreign governmental bodies.**

minivan

Minneapolis The city in Minnesota stands alone in datelines.

Minnesota Abbreviation: *Minn.* See **state(s).**

minority leader Capitalize as a formal title before a name. See **legislative titles**.

minuscule Frequently misspelled *miniscule.*

minus sign Use a hyphen, not a dash, in tabular material. Spell out any reference in news stories: 12 below zero.

MIRV (s.), **MIRVs** (pl.) Acceptable on first reference for *multiple independently targetable re-entry vehicle(s).* But explain in the text that it is a missile with several warheads and each can be directed to a different target.

misdemeanor See **felony, misdemeanor**.

mishap A minor misfortune. People are not killed in *mishaps.*

mispronunciations Correct malapropisms in direct quotations. See **quotations in the news**.

Miss See **courtesy titles**.

missile Use figures and capitalize the proper name: Titan 2 missile. No hyphen.

Mississippi Abbreviation: *Miss.* See **state(s)**.

Missouri Abbreviation: *Mo.* See **state(s)**.

mix-up (n.), **mixed-up** (adj.), **mix up** (v.)

(Mobil Corp). Now called *Exxon Mobil Corp.* Headquarters is in Irving, Texas. See **Exxon Mobil Corp**.

model designations In general, hyphenate with initials: B-29 bomber; omit hyphens with words: Pershing 2 missile. Don't use Roman numerals.

model numbers See **serial numbers**.

modem A device that enables computers to communicate over telephone lines.

Mohammed The founder of the Muslim religion.

Monaco After the Vatican, the world's smallest sovereign state. The town of Monaco stands alone in datelines. The form for others: *MONTE CARLO, Monaco, April 15 (UPI) —*

Monday See **days**.

M-1 The .30-caliber semiautomatic rifle used by U.S. forces in World War II and the Korean War. Some are still used in ceremonial events. See **weapons**.

money See **cents, dollars** and **foreign money**.

moneymaker

money market fund An open-end investment company *(mutual fund)* that invests shareholder money in safe, liquid short-term debt such as Treasury bills and other government securities, commercial paper and bankers' acceptances.

monsignor See **Roman Catholic Church**.

Montana Abbreviation: *Mont.* See **state(s)**.

Montessori (*method* or *system*) After Maria Montessori, a system of training young children that emphasizes the training of senses and guidance to encourage self-education.

monthlong

months Capitalize the names of months in all uses. Use the abbreviations *Jan., Feb., Aug., Sept., Oct., Nov.* and *Dec.* with a specific date. Do not abbreviate any month standing alone or with a year alone.

In tabular material, use three letters without a period: *Jan, Feb, Mar, Apr, May, Jun, Jul, Aug, Sep, Oct, Nov, Dec.* See **dates** for punctuation guidelines.

Montreal The city in Canada stands alone in datelines.

monuments Capitalize the popular names of monuments and similar public attractions: Lincoln Memorial, Statue of Liberty, Washington Monument, Leaning Tower of Pisa, etc.

moon Always lowercase.

(Moonies) Do not use this pejorative term in reference to members of the Unification Church. See **Unification Church**.

mop-up (n., adj.), **mop up** (v.)

moral obligation bond See **loan terminology**.

Mormon Church Acceptable in all references for the *Church of Jesus Christ of Latter-day Saints.* See the entry under the full name.

mortician Avoid this euphemism for *undertaker* or *funeral director.*

Moscow The capital of Russia stands alone in datelines.

(Moslem) The preferred term for adherents of Islam is *Muslim(s).* See **Muslim(s)**.

mosquito (s.), **mosquitoes** (pl.) Not *mosquitos.*

most-favored-nation (adj.) Lowercase and hyphenate this compound when referring to *most-favored-nation trade status.*

mother-in-law (s.), **mothers-in-law** (pl.) Not *mother-in-laws.*

Mother Nature

Mothers Against Drunk Driving *MADD* is acceptable on second reference. The organization was established in California in 1980 by a group of women led by Candy Lightner, whose daughter was killed by a drunken driver. See **drunk, drunken**.

Mother's Day The second Sunday in May.

motor See **engine, motor**.

Motorola Headquarters is in Schaumburg, Ill.

Mount Spell out in all uses, including the names of communities and of mountains: Mount Clemens, Mich.; Mount Everest.

mountains Capitalize as part of a proper name: Appalachian Mountains, Ozark Mountains, Rocky Mountains. Or simply: the Appalachians, the Ozarks, the Rockies.

Mountain Standard Time (MST), Mountain Daylight time (MDT) See **time**.

Mountain states As defined by the U.S. Census Bureau, the eight are Arizona, Colorado, Idaho, Montana, Nevada, New Mexico, Utah and Wyoming. See **West**.

moviegoer, moviemaker

movie ratings The ratings used by the Motion Picture Association of America:

G	General Audiences. All ages admitted.
PG	Parental guidance suggested. Some material may not be suitable for children.
PG-13	Parents strongly cautioned. Some material may be inappropriate for children under 13.
R	Restricted. Under 17 requires accompanying parent or adult guardian.
NC-17	No one under 17 admitted.

Capitalize: The movie has a G rating. Hyphenate adjectival forms: It is a G-rated movie.

movie titles See **composition titles**.

mph Acceptable in all references for *miles per hour* or *miles an hour.*

Mr. (s.), **Messrs.** (pl.), **Mrs.** (s.), **Mmes.** (pl.) Do not spell out these courtesy titles, even in direct quotation. See **courtesy titles**.

MRV For *multiple re-entry system,* in which several unguided warheads hit a preset pattern.

Ms. A title, not an abbreviation, free of reference to marital status. See **courtesy titles**.

MS-DOS Operating system created by IBM.

MSNBC TV A joint venture of Microsoft and NBC. Headquarters is in Redmond, Wash.

M-16 U.S. armed forces rifle. Caliber is 5.56mm. See **weapons**.

mujahedin Islamic guerrillas.

multi- Most are solid: multifamily, multimillion, multipurpose, multiracial, multistoried. But hyphenate with a capitalized word or to avoid a

multi- *continued*
> double *i*. Follow *Webster's New World College Dictionary*, hyphenating words not listed there.

multimedia In computing, a combination of mediums such as text, graphics and sound.

municipal bond funds See **loan terminology**.

murder, murderer See **execution** and **homicide**.

Murphy's law *If something can go wrong, it will.*

music See **composition titles** for basic guidelines. Some particulars:
> 1. Capitalize, but do not use quotation marks, on descriptive titles for orchestral works: Bach's Suite No. I for Orchestra; Beethoven's Serenade for Flute, Violin and Viola. If the instrumentation is not part of the title but is added for explanatory purposes, the names of the instruments are lowercased: Mozart's Sinfonia Concertante in E flat major (the common title) for violin and viola. If in doubt, lowercase the names of the instruments.
> 2. Use quotation marks for non-musical terms in a title: Beethoven's "Eroica" Symphony. If the work has a special full title, all of it is quoted: "Symphonie Fantastique," "Rhapsody in Blue."
> 3. In subsequent references, lowercase symphony, concerto, etc.

Musicians union See **American Federation of Musicians of the United States and Canada**.

Muslims The preferred term to describe adherents of Islam. Note: Members of a sect known as the *Black Muslims* in the United States call themselves *Muslims,* not *Black Muslims.*

Mutual Broadcasting System Inc. *Mutual Radio* is acceptable in all references to the former broadcasting network. Use *Mutual,* not *MBS,* in subsequent references. Headquarters was in Arlington, Va.

Muzak A trademark for recorded background music.

Myanmar Official name of country formerly known as *Burma* on the Indonesian Peninsula in Southeast Asia. Capital is *Yangon* (formerly *Rangoon*).

NAACP Acceptable in all references for *National Association for the Advancement of Colored People.* The organization was founded in New York on Feb. 12, 1909, the 100th anniversary of President Abraham Lincoln's birth. Headquarters is in Baltimore.

NAFTA See **North American Free Trade Agreement**.

naive *a* before *i.*

names In general, people are entitled to be known however they want to be known, as long as their identities are clear. When someone changes personal names, such as Cassius Clay's transition to Muhammad Ali, provide both names in stories until the new name is widely known. After that, use only the new name unless there is a specific reason for including the earlier identification. See **nicknames** and **sex changes**.

nano- A prefix meaning *one-billionth;* a *nanosecond* is one-billionth of a second. See **metric system**.

narrow-minded He is narrow-minded.

NASCAR Acceptable in all references for *National Association for Stock Car Auto Racing.*

Nasdaq National Association of Securities Dealers Automated Quotations. *Nasdaq Stock Market Inc., Nasdaq composite index. (Nasdaq* is an exception to *Webster's New World College Dictionary,* which uses the all-caps version of the acronym.)

National Aeronautics and Space Administration *The space agency* or *NASA* are acceptable on first reference. But the full name must be spelled out below.

National Aeronautics and Space Administration *continued*

Some NASA terminology:

apogee — The high point of a satellite's orbit. See **perigee**.

blastoff (n.), *blast off* (v.)

booster — On the space shuttle, it is one of two solid-fueled rockets used to help boost the ship toward space. A booster also can be the first stage of an unmanned rocket.

cosmonaut — A Russian astronaut.

engine — A rocket propulsion system fueled by liquid propellants.

ESA — Acceptable on second reference to *European Space Agency.*

liftoff (n.), *lift off* (v.)

military titles — Do not use unless it is a military spaceflight.

missile-satellite nomenclature — Use arabic numbers. No hyphens: Intelsat 5A, Apollo 11, Saturn 5.

perigee — The low point of a satellite's orbit. See **apogee**.

rollout (n.), *roll out* (v.) — Refers to the shuttle's trip from the Vehicle Assembly Building to the launch pad 3.5 miles away.

shuttle — Always lowercase. Only the name of the spaceship is capitalized. The shuttles are: *Discovery, Atlantis* and *Endeavour.* See **space shuttle**.

solid rocket motor — Solid-propellant rockets are *motors.* Liquid-fueled rockets are *engines.*

spacecraft — This can refer both to manned and unmanned craft, including small satellites of various types. It generally, however, refers to manned ships and larger, more complex unmanned craft.

Spacelab — Refers to European-built *Spacelab* module occasionally carried in shuttle's payload bay. Not related to the old Skylab space station.

spaceport — The Kennedy Space Center.

spaceship

spacewalk

titles — NASA refers to crew members as: *commander, pilot, mission specialist* and *payload specialist.* Do not use any military titles unless it is a military flight. Refer to the *pilot* as *co-pilot.*

Wrong: Navy Capt. Heather James.
Right: shuttle commander Heather James, co-pilot Frank Johnson.

Do not use *mission specialist,* which would require an explanation. All mission specialists are full-time NASA *astronauts.* We also do not use *payload specialist.* These are non-NASA, non-astronaut crew members assigned to flights, usually on a one-time basis, to operate experiments, etc. Say so.

> *Wrong:* Astronaut Lodewijk van den Berg.
> *Right:* Civilian scientist Lodewijk van den Berg.

national anthem Lowercase. But: "The Star-Spangled Banner."

national assembly See **foreign legislative bodies**.

National Association for the Advancement of Colored People. See **NAACP**.

National Association of Letter Carriers. *Letters Carriers union* may be used in all references. Headquarters is in Washington.

National Council of Churches Acceptable in all references for *National Council of Churches of Christ in the U.S.A.* Headquarters is in New York. See **World Council of Churches**.

National Education Association *NEA* is acceptable on second reference. Headquarters is in Washington.

National Governors' Association Note the apostrophe. Represents the governors of the 50 states and four territories. Its offices are in Washington.

National Guard Capitalize references to U.S. or state forces: the National Guard, the Guard, the Iowa National Guard, Iowa's National Guard, National Guard troops. Use lowercase for the forces of other nations.

National Guardsman Capitalize as a proper noun when referring to an individual in a federal or state National Guard unit: He is a National Guardsman. Lowercase *guardsman* standing alone. See **military titles**.

nationalist Lowercase unless the reference clearly is to the *National Party* or its members. See **political parties**.

Nationalist China See **China**.

nationalities Capitalize the proper names of nationalities, peoples, races, tribes, etc: Arab, Arabic, African, Afro-American, American, Caucasian, Cherokee, Chinese, Eskimo, French Canadian, Gypsy, Japanese, Jew, Jewish, Latin, Negro, Nordic, Oriental, Sioux, Swede, etc.

Lowercase descriptive words: black, white, yellow, etc.

Lowercase such derogatory terms as honky, nigger, etc. Use them only in direct quotations when essential to the story. See **race**.

National Labor Relations Board *NLRB* is acceptable on second reference.

National League of Cities Headquarters is in Washington. Do not confuse this organization with the U.S. Conference of Mayors.

National Oceanic and Atmospheric Administration *NOAA* is acceptable on second reference. The National Weather Service and satellite, oceanographic, fisheries and other agencies are part of NOAA, which was created within the U.S. Department of Commerce in 1970. Headquarters is in Washington. See **National Weather Service**.

National Organization for Women Not *of*. *NOW* is acceptable on second reference. Headquarters is in Washington.

National Rifle Association *NRA* is acceptable on second reference. Headquarters is in Washington.

National Science Foundation *NSF* is acceptable on second reference. An independent agency of the U.S. government. Headquarters is in Washington.

National Weather Service (No longer the *U.S. Weather Bureau.*) The *weather service* or *NWS* may be used on second reference. Headquarters is in Silver Spring, Md. See **National Oceanic and Atmospheric Administration**.

nationwide One word, no hyphen.

native See **citizen**.

native American All people born in this country are *native Americans*. Avoid as a reference to races that preceded the white man to this continent. See **Indians**.

Nativity

NATO Acceptable in all references for the *North Atlantic Treaty Organization.* Headquarters is in Brussels.

Naugahyde A trademark for a simulated leather.

nautical mile It equals 6,076.11549 feet, 1,852 meters or about 1.15 statute miles. To convert to statute miles (5,280 feet), multiply by 1.15. See **knot**.

naval, navel *Naval* pertains to a navy; a *navel* is a bellybutton.

naval station Capitalize only as part of a proper name: Norfolk Naval Station.

navy Capitalize when referring to U.S. forces: the U.S. Navy, the Navy, Navy policy. Do not use *USN*.

Many nations do not use *navy* as a proper name. For consistency, use lowercase for all others: the Canadian navy. Exception: Capitalize *Royal Navy* when referring to the *British navy*. See **military academies** and **military titles**.

navy bean, navy blue, navy yard

Nazi, Nazism After the *National Socialist German Workers' Party,* the political party founded in 1919 and abolished in 1945. Under Adolf Hitler, it seized control of Germany in 1933. See **political parties**.

NBC Acceptable in all references for the *National Broadcasting Co.,* a subsidiary of General Electric Co. Divisions include NBC-TV, NBC News, NBC Entertainment, NBC Sports, CNBC and MSNBC TV, the latter a joint venture of Microsoft Corp. and NBC. Headquarters is in New York. See **MSNBC TV**.

NCAA Acceptable in all references for the *National Collegiate Athletic Association.*

NCR Corp. Formerly *National Cash Register Co.* Headquarters is in Dayton, Ohio.

(Near East) Use *Middle East* instead.

(nearby) Avoid its irrelevant use. Omit *nearby* in: He was taken to a (nearby) hospital.

nearsighted Having better vision for near objects than distant ones.

Nebraska Abbreviation: *Neb.* See **state(s)**.

negligee Two *e'*s.

Neiman Marcus No hyphen.

neo-Nazi

nerve-racking Not *nerve-wracking.*

Net Capitalize in reference to the Internet.

net earnings, net income See **profit terminology**.

Netscape A company that makes Internet software, including the *Netscape Navigator* browser. The company's official name is *Netscape Communications Corp.* Headquarters is in Mountain View, Calif.

Netherlands The form for datelines: *AMSTERDAM, Netherlands, Feb. 12 (UPI) —* In stories: *Netherlands* or *the Netherlands,* as appropriate.

Netherlands Antilles Do not abbreviate. The form for datelines: *WILLEMSTAD, Netherlands Antilles, July 5 (UPI) —* Specify an individual island, if needed, in the text.

neutron weapon A small nuclear warhead that can be placed on missiles or in artillery shells. Frequently miscalled *neutron bomb.*

Nevada Abbreviation: *Nev.* See **state(s)**.

New Brunswick One of the three Maritime Provinces of Canada. Do not abbreviate. The form for datelines: *FREDERICTON, New Brunswick, June 1 (UPI) —*

New Delhi The capital of India stands alone in datelines. (The old part of the city is known as *Delhi.*)

New England It encompasses Connecticut, Maine, Massachusetts, New Hampshire, Rhode Island and Vermont. See **Northeast region**.

Newfoundland This Canadian province encompasses the island of Newfoundland and the mainland section known as Labrador. Do not abbreviate. The form for datelines: *GOOSE BAY, Newfoundland, Jan. 4 (UPI)* — Specify in the text whether the community is on the island or in Labrador.

New Hampshire Abbreviation: *N.H.* See **state(s)**.

New Jersey Abbreviation: *N.J.* See **state(s)**.

New Mexico Abbreviation: *N.M.* See **state(s)**.

New Orleans The Louisiana city stands alone in datelines.

news conference Use instead of *press conference.*

newsgroup An Internet forum or bulletin board devoted to a specific topic: *video games, kindergarten teachers, seniors, ice fishing, prostate cancer*, etc. There are tens of thousands of newsgroups. See **Usenet**.

(newsman) Use *reporter, editor, journalist,* etc., instead.

Newspaper Association of America. Formerly the *American Newspaper Publishers Association (ANPA). NAA* or *the association* or *newspaper association* may be used in later references. Headquarters is in Reston, Va.

New South The era that began in the South in the 1960s with a thriving economy and the election of officials who advocated the abolition of racial segregation. *Old South* applies to the South before the Civil War.

Newspaper Guild, The Formerly the *American Newspaper Guild,* it is a union for newspaper and news service employees, generally those in the news and business departments. On second reference: *the Guild.* Headquarters is in Washington.

newspapers Capitalize *the* in a newspaper's full name if that is the way a publication prefers to be known: *The New York Times.* But lowercase *the* in a shortened name: *the Times.*

Where location is needed but is not part of the official name, use parentheses: *The Knoxville (Tenn.) News-Sentinel.*

Consult the *International Year Book* published by Editor & Publisher to determine whether a two-name combination is hyphenated.

Call them *newspapers,* not *papers.* Do not describe a group of newspapers as a *chain.*

newsroom

news service

newsstand One word. Two *s*'s.

newswire, newswriter, newswriting Exceptions to *Webster's New World College Dictionary.*

New Testament See **Bible**.

New World The Western Hemisphere.

New Year's, New Year's Day, New Year's Eve But: What will the new year bring? The federal legal holiday is observed on Friday if Jan. 1 falls on a Saturday, on Monday if it falls on a Sunday.

New York Abbreviation: *N.Y.* See **state(s)**.

New York City In datelines: *NEW YORK, Oct. 4 (UPI)* — Identify the borough or individual community in the body of the story if pertinent. Do not use *Brooklyn,* a New York borough, in a dateline.

New York Stock Exchange *NYSE* is acceptable on second reference.

(next) Avoid its unnecessary use. Omit *next* in: It is set for (next) Tuesday. Future tense is sufficient to indicate which Tuesday is meant.

nicknames Use a derivative of a proper name only when it is the way the individual prefers to be known: Jimmy Carter.

A descriptive nickname, if used, takes quotation marks, not parentheses: James "Ace" Jackson. Also: Jackson is known as "Ace."

In sports stories and sports columns, widely used nicknames are acceptable without quotation marks: Chipper Jones, Penny Hardaway, Bear Bryant. But if the given name is used, and in all news stories: the late Paul "Bear" Bryant.

Capitalize other nicknames without quotation marks: Sunshine State, the Old Dominion, Motown, the Magic City, Old Hickory, Old Glory.

Nielsen Ratings

nighttime

nitpicking

nitty-gritty

No. Use this abbreviation for number with a figure to indicate position or rank: No. 1 man, No. 3 choice.

Do not use in street addresses, with this exception: No. 10 Downing St., the residence of Britain's prime minister.

Do not use *No.* in the names of schools: Public School 19.

NOAA See **National Oceanic and Atmospheric Administration**.

Nobel Prize (s.), **Nobel Prizes** (pl.) The five, established under terms of the will of Alfred Nobel, are: Nobel Peace Prize, Nobel Prize in Chemistry, Nobel Prize in Literature, Nobel Prize in Physics, Nobel Prize in Physiology or Medicine.

The Nobel Memorial Prize in Economic Science is not a Nobel Prize in the same sense. The Central Bank of Sweden established it in

Nobel Prize *continued*

1968 as a memorial to Alfred Nobel. References to this prize should include the word *memorial* to make this distinction. Explain the difference if needed.

nobility As with all other titles, capitalize titles of nobility before a name; lowercase standing alone or set off with commas. See **titles** and **royal titles**.

The British titles of nobility for men (women's equivalent in parentheses) are, in descending order of rank, *duke (duchess), marquis (marchioness), earl (countess), viscount (viscountess)* and *baron (baroness)*.

In some European countries, *count* is the equivalent of an *earl*, and *prince* is the English equivalent of various titles of nobility in other countries.

Lady and *lord* are sometimes used as titles of respect.

nobody, no one

no-fly zone

noisome, noisy *Noisome* means *offensive, noxious; noisy* means *clamorous*.

nolo contendere Literally, *"I do not wish to contend." A no-contest plea* or *he pleaded no contest* are preferred in all usage.

In using the plea, a defendant declares he will not make a defense but does not admit guilt. He is open to the same punishment as someone convicted, but he retains the option of denying the same charge in another legal proceeding.

no man's land No hyphen.

non- Hyphenate all except: *nonchalance, nonchalant, noncommittal, nonsense, nonsensical, nondescript, nonentity*.

non-aligned nations A political rather than economic or geographic term. While non-aligned nations do not belong either to Western or Eastern military alliances or blocs, they profess not to be neutral, as Switzerland does, but activist alternatives.

Do not confuse the term with *Third World,* though many Third World countries belong to the non-aligned group. See **Third World**.

(non-controversial) All *issues* are controversial. A *non-controversial issue* is impossible. A *controversial issue* is redundant.

none Either singular or plural, but make sure the verbs and pronouns agree.

> *Right:* None are so blind as those who will not see.
> *Right:* None is so blind as he who will not see.

noon Do not put a *12* in front of it.

no one

Nordstrom. Not *Nordstrom's.* Headquarters is in Seattle.

nor'easter Lowercase.

norm See **average**.

north, northern, northeast, northwest See **directions**.

North America Canada, Mexico, the United States and the Danish territory of Greenland. When the term is used in more than its continental sense, it may also include the islands of the Caribbean.

North American Free Trade Agreement *NAFTA* may be used on second reference for the agreement to establish a free-trade zone in North America. It was signed by the United States, Canada and Mexico and took effect in 1994.

North Carolina Abbreviation: *N.C.* See **state(s)**.

North Central region As defined by the U.S. Census Bureau, the 12-state region is broken into eastern and western divisions. Its common name is the *Middle West* or *Midwest.*

The five *East North Central* states are Indiana, Illinois, Michigan, Ohio and Wisconsin.

The seven *West North Central* states are Iowa, Kansas, Minnesota, Missouri, Nebraska, North Dakota and South Dakota.

See **Northeast region, South** and **West** for the bureau's other regional breakdowns.

North Dakota Abbreviation: *N.D.* See **state(s)**.

Northeast region As defined by the U.S. Census Bureau, the nine-state region is broken into two divisions — the New England states and the Middle Atlantic states.

New Jersey, New York and Pennsylvania are classified as the *Middle Atlantic states.*

Connecticut, Maine, Massachusetts, New Hampshire, Rhode Island and Vermont are in *New England.*

See **North Central region, South** and **West** for the bureau's other regional breakdowns.

Northern Ireland See **United Kingdom** and **datelines**.

Northrop Grumman Corp. Headquarters is in Los Angeles.

North Slope The portion of Alaska north of Brooks Range, a string of mountains extending across the northern part of the state.

Northwest Airlines Headquarters is in Eagan, Minn.

Northwest Territories A territorial section of Canada. Do not abbreviate. See **Canada**. In datelines: *YELLOWKNIFE, Northwest Territories, Dec. 23 (UPI)* —

noun Turn a noun into a verb with the same enthusiasm you would apply in seeking a cut in salary. However, any noun may be turned into an adjective.

It is sometimes said that one should not use a noun as an adjective if an adjective form of the noun is available. For instance, one should not say *freak weather* but rather *freakish weather.* The advice is correct provided the two words produce the desired meaning. But often they do not. A *musical critic* is not the same thing as a *music critic.* An *educational loan* is not the same thing as an *education loan.* A *psychological teacher* is not the same thing as a *psychology teacher.* A *social editor* is not the same thing as a *society editor.*

Nova Scotia One of the three Maritime Provinces of Canada. Do not abbreviate. In datelines: *HALIFAX, Nova Scotia, Dec. 1 (UPI) —*

Novell Inc. Developer of operating systems including *NetWare.* Headquarters is in Provo, Utah.

November See **months**.

Novocain A trademark for a local anesthetic.

Nuclear Regulatory Commission The Atomic Energy Commission was replaced in 1975 by this agency and by the Energy Research and Development Administration. *NRC* is acceptable on second reference.

nuclear terminology Stories involving atomic energy or nuclear accidents pose special problems of translating technical jargon into everyday terms. Certain words, such as *explosion,* must be avoided or used with extreme care in atomic accident stories to avoid needless scares.

Some guidelines:

1. *rem* — A unit of radiation measure used to describe the amount of radiation in a given location whether or not people are present. Stands for *roentgen equivalent man.* Because one rem is relatively large, radiation levels often are described in *millirem.* One rem equals 1,000 millirem. Do not abbreviate the *rem* or *millirem.* For sake of comparison, the Food and Drug Administration says an average dental X-ray equals about 10 millirem; a chest X-ray equals about 30 millirem; federal officials say a lethal human dose is considered 500 to 600 rem.

2. *person-rem* — Based on the rem, the *person-rem* is used to describe the collective potential exposure to a large number of people, such as a city's total population. The amount of radiation each person might receive is multiplied by the number of people potentially exposed. Thus, 10,000 person-rem is the potential

exposure of 5,000 people to an average dose of 2 rem each, or of 10,000 people to an average dose of 1 rem each.

3. *rad* — Used to describe the actual exposure received by an individual. Stands for *roentgen absorbed dose.* Technically defined as the amount of radiation required to deliver 100 *ergs* of energy to 1 gram of substance. Often used interchangeably with *rem* by nuclear officials, but not really the same in that *rad* refers to the exact exposure an individual has received and *rem* refers to the level of radiation in a place whether or not people are there. One rad equals 1,000 *millirads.*

4. *explosion* — It's virtually impossible for nuclear power reactors to explode like nuclear bombs. But it is possible for a reactor to incur a steam explosion, like a kitchen pressure cooker blowing up because of too much pressure. A steam explosion could widely scatter radioactive debris, but it would not have the deadly shock, heat and radiation of a bomb explosion. Use *explosion* with care.

5. *meltdown* — The melting of the uranium fuel elements that compose the core of the reactor. *Total meltdown* is the worst type of nuclear accident. Much less serious are *partial meltdown* accidents, in which only a bit of the reactor core melts. Partial meltdowns have posed serious problems, but have not resulted in the kind of radiation release catastrophe that could result from a total meltdown, in which the molten core burns its way through the bottom of the reactor containment chamber. Use care with *meltdown.* Officials sometimes use the word loosely to refer to either a partial or a total meltdown.

6. *China syndrome* — If the core of a nuclear reactor melted, there is theoretically no substance that could contain it and it would keep boring into the earth as if headed for China, until it cooled and stopped. Some nuclear physicists call this *the China syndrome,* and the term was used as the title of a 1979 movie.

number Takes a plural verb in such constructions as: A number of plans have been scrapped. But make every effort to obtain precise figures. See **No.**

numerals A numeral is a figure, letter, word or group of words expressing a number.

Roman numerals use the letters *I, V, X, L, C, D* and *M.* Use Roman numerals for wars and to show personal sequence for animals and people: World War II, Native Dancer II, King George VI, Pope John XXIII.

numerals *continued*

See **Roman numerals**. See also **fractions** and **decimal units**.

Guidelines:

1. The general rule (exceptions listed below) is to spell out numbers under 10 and use figures for those above nine: The election is three weeks from today. She visited for 10 months. Their 13-day vacation included a six-day cruise. A two-bedroom apartment; a seven-story hotel; the farmer had 14 cows, 11 horses and five pigs.

2. Figures are normally used for large numbers (3,000 voters, 700 to 800 soldiers, etc.), but when they must be spelled out, use a hyphen to connect a word ending in *y* to another word. Do not use commas between other words that are part of one number: twenty, thirty, twenty-one, thirty-one, one hundred forty-three, one thousand one hundred fifty-five, one million two hundred seventy-six thousand five hundred eighty-seven.

3. Follow an organization's practice in proper names: 20th Century Fox, Twentieth Century Fund, Big Ten.

4. Figures may be used for numbers under 10 in charts, lists, etc.

5. Always use figures for:

   addresses: 1400 Main St. N.W., P.O. Box 1. (But 100 First St.)
   ages: no matter if it is a person, place or thing
   betting odds: 3-1 (both n. and adj. hyphenated)
   broadcast channels: TV Channel 9, 630 megahertz
   caliber and gauge: .30 caliber, 9mm, 12 gauge
   dates: April 1 (not April 1st, but the 1st day of April)
   dimensions: inches, feet, yards, millimeters, etc.
   distances: miles, kilometers, etc.
   fractions and whole numbers: 1½ (but one-half if used alone)
   governmental jurisdictions: 1st Congressional District, 4th Circuit Court
   map coordinates: 45 degrees north latitude
   millions: 1 million, 9 billion
   military units: 1st Division, 7th Fleet, 8th Air Force
   money: 2 cents, $1.50, 4 pounds, 10 marks
   nomenclature: M-16 rifle, MiG-23, Title 9
   percentages: 1 percent (not 1.0 percent, but 0.1 percent)
   position or rank: No. 2 man in the department
   proportions: 1 part resin to 2 parts hardener
   ratios: 3-to-1 (n.), 3-1 (adj.)
   roads: U.S. 1, Interstate 95

rooms: Room 2 in the Rayburn Building

scores: 14-7 victory; the Redskins won 14-7

sizes: a size 9 dress; a size 10 shoe

speeds and rates: 4 mph, 7 knots, 8 miles per gallon

temperatures: 30 degrees F (but zero degrees F)

times: 9:45 a.m. (but nine-and-under rule for elapsed time: nine hours, 10 minutes)

volume: 5 cubic yards

votes: Jones defeated Smith 100-75; Jones defeated Smith 1,123 to 1,023. (Use preposition but no hyphens with units containing four or more digits.)

weights: 4 pounds, 10 ounces

6. Always spell out:

casual expressions: a thousand times no, thanks a million, an eleventh-hour decision

Fourth of July: July the Fourth, the Fourth of July

sentence openers: Spell out all numbers in the first word of a sentence except years: 2004 will be a better year than 2003, we hope.

Nunavut A territorial section of northern Canada. Nunavut, formerly part of the Northwest Territories, became a territory in 1999. Do not abbreviate. See **Canada**. In datelines: *IQALUIT, Nunavut, March 14 (UPI)* —

nuns See **sister**.

Nuremberg Not *Nuernberg*.

NWS See **National Weather Service**.

nylon Not a trademark.

O

OAS See **Organization of American States**.

oasis (s.), **oases** (pl.)

obscenities Do not use obscenities, profanity, vulgarities, etc., in stories unless they are part of direct quotations and there is a compelling reason for them.

Confine the offending language to a separate paragraph that can be easily deleted by editors who do not want it.

In reporting profanity that normally would use the words *damn* or *god,* lowercase *god* and use the following forms: **damn, damn it, goddamn it.** Do not, however, change the offending words to euphemisms. Do not, for example, change *damn it* to *darn it.*

If a full quote that contains offensive language cannot be dropped but there is no compelling reason for the offensive language, replace it with *expletive* in parentheses: "My opponent is a (expletive) liar," the candidate said. Do not use the term *expletive deleted.*

Occident, Occidental Capitalize when referring to Europe, the Western Hemisphere or an inhabitant of these regions.

Occidental Petroleum Corp Headquarters is in Los Angeles.

Occupational Safety and Health Administration *OSHA* is acceptable on second reference.

occur, occurred, occurring, occurrence

oceangoing

oceans The five, from the largest to the smallest: Pacific Ocean, Atlantic Ocean, Indian Ocean, Antarctic Ocean, Arctic Ocean. Lowercase *ocean* standing alone or in plural uses: **the ocean, the Atlantic and Pacific oceans.**

octet In computing, a unit of data equal to eight bits. See **byte**.

October See **months**.

odds See **betting odds**.

odd- Hyphenate as a prefix: odd-appearing, odd-couple, odd-numbered, but oddsmaker.

off- Hyphenate as a prefix if not listed otherwise in *Webster's New World College Dictionary:* off-color, off-season, off-track, off-Broadway, off-off-Broadway, but offhand, offbeat, offshore.

-off Hyphenate if not listed in *Webster's New World College Dictionary:* send-off, tip-off, but blastoff, takeoff.

office Capitalize as an agency's formal name: Office of Management and Budget. Lowercase elsewhere: the office of the attorney general, the U.S. attorney's office.

officeholder

(officials) Do not use *officials* to characterize company spokesmen or high-ranking employees. Call them *officers* or *executives*.

(off of) The *of* is unnecessary. Omit *of* in: He fell off (of) the bed.

Ohio Do not abbreviate. See **state(s)**.

oil In shipping, oil and oil products are normally measured by the ton. In news stories, these tonnage figures should be converted to gallons.

There are 42 gallons to each barrel of oil. The number of barrels per ton varies, depending on the type of oil product.

To convert, first determine the type of oil and how many tons are involved. Consult the following table to determine barrels per ton for that product. Multiply the barrels per ton by the number of tons involved to get number of barrels involved. Multiply the number of barrels involved by 42 to get gallons.

For example, a tanker spills 20,000 metric tons of foreign crude petroleum. The table shows 6.998 barrels of foreign crude petroleum per metric ton. Multiplying 6.998 × 20,000 equals 139,960 barrels. Multiplying 139,960 × 42 equals 5,877,320 gallons.

Type of Oil	*Barrels/* *Short Ton* *2,000 pounds*	*Barrels/* *Metric Ton* *2,204 pounds*	*Barrels/* *Long Ton* *2,240 pounds*
crude petroleum (foreign)	6.349	6.998	7.111
crude petroleum (domestic)	6.770	7.463	7.582
gasoline, naphtha	7.721	8.511	8.648

oil *continued*

Type of Oil	Barrels/ Short Ton 2,000 pounds	Barrels/ Metric Ton 2,204 pounds	Barrels/ Long Ton 2,240 pounds
kerosene	7.053	7.775	7.900
distillate fuel oil	6.580	7.253	7.369
residual fuel oil	6.041	6.660	6.766
lubricating oil	6.349	6.998	7.111
lubricating grease	6.665	7.346	7.464
wax (refined and unrefined)	7.134	7.864	7.990
asphalt	5.540	6.106	6.205
coke	4.990	5.500	5.589
road oil	5.900	6.503	6.608
petroleum jelly, petrolatum	6.665	7.346	7.464
liquefied petroleum gas	10.526	11.603	11.789
Gilsonite	5.515	6.080	6.177

The table is based on figures supplied by the American Petroleum Institute.

To determine the theoretical impact on consumers of a change in crude oil prices, divide the amount of the drop or increase by 42 to get the change per gallon. The rule of thumb is that each $1 a barrel change up or down in crude prices translates into 2.3 cents per gallon at the pump and on home heating oil — if fully passed through to the consumer.

oil field, oilman, oilskin, oil rig, oil slick

OK (s.), **OKs** (pl.), **OK'd, OK'ing** Do not use *okay.*

Oklahoma Abbreviation: *Okla.* See **state(s)**.

Oklahoma City The city in Oklahoma stands alone in datelines.

-old Avoid such a phrase as a 12-year-old murder when what is meant is a murder 12 years ago.

Old City The walled part of Jerusalem.

Old Man River Nickname of the Mississippi River.

Old South The South before the Civil War. See **New South**.

Old Testament See **Bible**.

old-timer, old times

Old West The American West as it was being settled in the 19th century.

Old World The Eastern Hemisphere: Asia, Europe, Africa.

Olympic Airways Headquarters is in Athens, Greece.

olympics Capitalize all references to the international athletic contests: the Olympics, the Winter Olympics, Winter Games, the Games. Lowercase all other uses: a beer-drinking olympics, an olympic-sized pool.

Omaha The city in Nebraska stands alone in datelines.

on Do not put *on* before a day (or date), except to avoid confusion or awkwardness: The chief justice said Monday (not *on Monday*); the boat sank in a storm Tuesday (not *on Tuesday*); the trial starts Feb. 12 (not *on Feb. 12*), etc.

Occasionally, use of *on* is appropriate: The judge sentenced John Thomas on Monday (rather than *John Thomas Monday*); Smith met Albert on Friday (rather than *Albert Friday*). Also: On Thursday, the students threw a party.

once-over

one- Hyphenate in fractions: one-half, one-third, one-fourth. Use a half, a third, etc., if precision is not intended.

one person, one vote (n.), **one-person, one-vote** (adj.) He supports the principle of one person, one vote. The districts conform to the one-person, one-vote rule. (U.S. Supreme Court rulings use *one person* instead of *one man.*)

one time, one-time He won *one time* so is a *one-time winner*. She is a *one-time* (former) friend.

(ongoing) Use this bureaucratic term only in direct quotations.

online No hyphen.

on-screen

Ontario Do not abbreviate. In datelines from this Canadian province, *Toronto* and *Ottawa* stand alone. The form for others: *LONDON, Ontario, March 6 (UPI)* —

OPEC See **Organization of Petroleum Exporting Countries**.

operating system A system that controls a computer's operations and files.

ophthalmologist, ophthalmology Don't forget the first *h* or the first *l*.

opinion polls See **polls**.

opossum The only native North American marsupial. But no apostrophe is needed to indicate missing letters in such uses as *playing possum*.

oral, verbal Use *oral* to refer to spoken words: He gave an oral promise. Use *written* to refer to words committed to paper: We had a written agreement.

oral, verbal *continued*

Verbal refers to all words, either written or spoken. Do not use it as a synonym for *oral*. Use *verbal* to compare word usage, either written or spoken, with some form of communication that does not use words, such as a gesture: Her eyes said more than her poor verbal skills could ever express.

Oregon Abbreviation: *Ore.* See **state(s)**.

Oreo A trademark for a brand of chocolate sandwich cookies held together by a white filling.

Organization of American States *OAS* is acceptable on second reference. Headquarters is in Washington.

Organization of Petroleum Exporting Countries *OPEC* is acceptable on first reference, but use the full name in the story. The OPEC members: Algeria, Indonesia, Iran, Iraq, Kuwait, Libya, Nigeria, Qatar, Saudi Arabia, United Arab Emirates, Venezuela. Headquarters is in Vienna.

organizations and institutions Capitalize the full names of organizations and institutions: the American Medical Association, First Presbyterian Church, General Motors Corp., Harvard University. Or simply: General Motors, Harvard.

Capitalize major divisions: the Pontiac Motor Division of General Motors.

Lowercase others with widely used generic names: the board of directors of General Motors, the board of trustees of Columbia University, the history department of Harvard University, the sports department of the Daily Citizen-Leader.

Capitalize those without widely used generic names: the General Assembly of the World Council of Churches, the House of Delegates of the American Medical Association, House of Bishops and House of Deputies of the Episcopal Church.

Capitalize flip-flopped names that delete *of:* College of the Holy Cross, Holy Cross College; Harvard School of Dental Medicine, Harvard Dental School. But do not flip-flop a title unless it is common usage: Massachusetts Institute of Technology. Not: Massachusetts Technology Institute.

See **abbreviations and acronyms**.

Orient, Oriental The region and its inhabitants. Also: an Oriental rug.

orthodox Lowercase unless the reference is to a religious organization with that name, or to one of its members: an Orthodox Jew, an orthodox procedure.

Orthodox Church in America See **Eastern Orthodox churches**.

Oscar, Oscars See **Academy Awards**.

oscillating theory See **big-bang theory**.

Ottawa The capital of Canada stands alone in datelines.

ounce (dry) Dry volume is not usually carried to this level. See **pint (dry)**.

ounce (liquid) See **fluid ounce**.

ounce (weight) It is defined as 437.5 grains, or about 28 grams. To convert to grams, multiply by 28 (5 ounces × 28 equals 140 grams).

outback

Oval Office The White House office of the president.

over- Solid in almost all cases: overfly, overlap, overpay, overreach, oversee, overshadow, overwrite. Follow *Webster's New World College Dictionary,* hyphenating words not listed there.

-over Mostly solid: crossover, flyover, holdover, takeover, walkover, but carry-over, make-over, sleep-over, switch-over. Follow *Webster's New World College Dictionary,* hyphenating words not listed there.

owner Always lowercase: Team owner John Smith.

Oyez Not *oyes.* The cry of court and public officials to command silence. Pronounced *oh'–yay.*

Ozark Mountains Or simply: *the Ozarks.*

P

Pablum A trademark for a soft, bland food. In lowercase, it means *any oversimplified or tasteless writing or idea.*

PAC Acceptable on second reference for *Political Action Committee.*

pacemaker Formerly a trademark, now a generic term for a device that electronically maintains a steady heartbeat.

Pachen Lama See **Dalai Lama**.

(pachyderm) Overused for *elephant.* A *pachyderm* is any of certain large, thick-skinned hoofed animals: elephant, rhinoceros, hippopotamus.

Pacific Ocean See **oceans**.

Pacific Northwest The region of the United States and Canada, usually including Oregon, Washington and British Columbia.

Pacific Standard Time (PST), Pacific Daylight Time (PDT) See **time**.

page numbers. Use figures and lowercase *page,* but capitalize, without a hyphen, any letter appended to the figure: page 2, page 10, page 20A, a page 1 story.

paintings See **composition titles**.

palate, palette, pallet *Palate* is the roof of the mouth; a *palette* is an artist's paint board; a *pallet* is a bed.

Palestine Liberation Organization Not *Palestinian. PLO* is acceptable on second reference.

Panama City Use *Panama City, Fla.,* or *Panama City, Panama,* in datelines to avoid confusion between the two.

pantsuit Not *pants suit.*

pantyhose One word.

Paper, Allied-Industrial, Chemical and Energy Workers International Union Called the *PACE International Union,* it was formed in a 1999 merger of the United Paperworkers International Union and the Oil, Chemical and Atomic Workers International Union. Use the shortened version of the name on first reference, but explain in the story that the union represents paper, chemical and energy workers. Headquarters is in Nashville.

paperwork

Pap test (or **smear**) After George Papanicolaou, the U.S. anatomist who developed this test for cervical cancer.

parallel, paralleled, paralleling

parameters Certain computer settings.

pardon A *pardon* forgives and releases a person from further punishment. It is granted by a chief of state or a governor. By itself, it does not expunge a record of conviction, if one exists, and it does not by itself restore civil rights. *Amnesty* is a general pardon, usually for political offenses.

Parole is the release of a prisoner before the sentence has expired, on condition of good behavior. It is granted by a *parole board,* part of the executive branch of government, and can be revoked only by the board.

Probation is the suspension of sentence for a person convicted, but not yet imprisoned, on condition of good behavior. It is imposed or revoked only by a judge.

parentheses ( ) Parentheses are jarring to the reader. Use them in sentences only if no other arrangement will work. There are occasions when parentheses are the only effective means of inserting necessary background or reference information.

Guidelines:

1. Place a period outside a closing parenthesis if the material inside is not a sentence (such as this fragment).

   (An independent parenthetical sentence such as this one takes a period before the closing parenthesis.)

   When a phrase placed in parentheses (this one is an example) might normally qualify as a complete sentence but is dependent on the surrounding material, do not capitalize the first word or end with a period.

2. Use parentheses if a location is inserted in a proper name: The Huntsville (Ala.) Times. But use commas if no proper name is involved: The Selma, Ala., group saw the governor.

parentheses *continued*

    3. Parentheses are sometimes used around information inserted in a story when communications have been cut off from the dateline city. See **datelines**.

    4. Parentheses are a part of the UPI logotype: *(UPI)*. See **logotype**.

    5. Use quotation marks, not parentheses, around a nickname. See **nicknames**.

    6. Use commas, not parentheses, to set off a political figure's party affiliation. See **party affiliation**.

Paris The capital of France stands alone in datelines.

parish Capitalize as part of a formal name of a religious or governmental jurisdiction: St. John's Parish, Jefferson Parish, La.

    Lowercase standing alone or in plural uses: the parish, St. John's and St. Mary's parishes, Jefferson and Plaquemines parishes.

Parkinson's disease After James Parkinson, the English physician who first described this degenerative disease of later life.

Parkinson's law After C. Northcott Parkinson, the British economist who came to the satirical conclusion that work expands to fill the time allotted to it.

parliament See **foreign legislative bodies**.

parliamentary Always lowercase.

parole See **pardon**.

parse To break down into components.

partial quotes See **quotation marks**.

particles See **foreign particles**.

part time (n.), **part-time** (adj.) He works *part time*. He is a *part-time* worker.

party Capitalize as part of a proper name: the Republican Party. See **political parties**.

party affiliation Party affiliation and home state are pointless in some stories, such as an account of a governor accepting a button from a poster child. But when it is pertinent, use any of these approaches as it fits the occasion and the flow of the story:

- *Republican* Sen. John Jones of Kansas said, etc.
- Sen. John Jones, *R-Kan.,* said, etc.
- Sen. John Jones also spoke. The *Kansas Republican* said, etc.
- Rep. Mary Smith *of Washington,* the *House Democratic leader,* etc. Not Rep. Mary Smith, *D-Wash.,* the *House Democratic leader,* etc.

In stories about party meetings, such as a report on the Republican National Convention, no specific reference to party affiliation is necessary unless an individual is not a member of the party in question.

For short forms, use the abbreviations listed for each state under the state name. (No abbreviations for Alaska, Hawaii, Idaho, Iowa, Maine, Ohio, Texas and Utah.) Use *R-* for Republicans, *D-* for Democrats, and *three-letter combinations* for other affiliations: Sen. James Johnson, Con-N.Y., spoke with Sen. John Doe, Ind-Va. Use commas, not parentheses, to set off the short forms. See **legislative titles**.

par value The nominal face value, or dollar amount, that appears on a stock certificate or bond instrument. In the case of common stock, it is a figure set by the company and bears no relation to market value. Par for bonds and preferred stock often represents the dollar value upon which interest and dividends are based and may be closer to market value.

pass See **adopt**.

passenger lists Provide a list of victims in a disaster as soon as it is available. Use a separate paragraph for each name and begin the paragraph with a number. List the last name first and include street addresses if available.

1. Jones, Joseph, 260 Town St., Sample, N.Y.
2. Williams, Susan, 780 Main St., Example, N.J.

The use of the number is designed to make it easier to identify the paragraph to be updated in the event additional information becomes available.

passenger-mile One passenger carried 1 mile, or its equivalent, such as two passengers carried one-half mile.

passerby (s.), **passersby** (pl.)

Passover The weeklong Jewish holiday commemorating the deliverance of the ancient Hebrews from slavery in Egypt. Occurs in March or April.

pasteurize Lowercase.

pastor A minister who leads a congregation. Capitalize only if a particular denomination recognizes it as a formal title rather than a job description. See separate entries for each denomination.

patriarch Always lowercase to identify anyone of great age and dignity. Capitalize as a formal title before a name in some religious uses. See **Eastern Orthodox churches** and **Roman Catholic Church**.

patrol, patrolled, patrolling

patrolman, patrolwoman Usually a job description, lowercase, rather than a formal title.

payload

PBS See **Public Broadcasting Service**.

PC Abbreviation for *personal computer.*

PDA A small hand-held computer. The initials stand for *personal digital assistant.*

peacekeeper, peacemaker, peacetime

peacock It applies only to the male. The female is a *peahen.* Both are *peafowl.*

peck A dry measure equal to eight dry quarts or one-fourth of a bushel. In metric it is about 8.8 liters. To convert to liters, multiply by 8.8 (5 pecks × 8.8 equals 44 liters).

pedal, peddle You *pedal* a bicycle to ride it; you *peddle* it to sell it.

pejorative Not *perjorative.*

(Peking) No longer acceptable for the name of the capital of China. Use *Beijing.*

pell-mell He rushed *pell-mell* through the woods.

peninsula Capitalize only as an integral part of a proper name: the Upper Peninsula (a section of Michigan), Peninsula Point (in Indonesia). Lowercase elsewhere: He lived on the Florida peninsula.

penitentiary See **prison, jail**.

Pennsylvania Abbreviation: *Pa.* Legally a commonwealth, not a state. See **state(s)**.

Pennsylvania Dutch They are of German descent. The word *Dutch,* in this context, is a corruption of *Deutsch,* the German word for *German.*

penny-wise Also: *pound-foolish.* See **-wise**.

Pentium A family of central processing units (CPUs), including Pentium, Pentium II, Pentium Pro, Pentium III, made by Intel. Previous Intel CPUs had names in an '86 series, including 286, 386 and 486. Intel began using the Pentium name in 1993.

people, persons *People* is preferable to *persons,* especially when speaking of a large or uncounted number of individuals: Thousands of people attended the fair. Some rich people pay no taxes. What will people say? Do not use *persons* in this sense.

Persons is usually used for a relatively small number of people who can be counted, but *people* often can be substituted.

> *Right:* There were 20 persons in the room.
> *Right:* There were 20 people in the room.

People is also a collective noun that requires a plural verb and is used to refer to a single race or nation: The American people are united.

In this sense, the plural form is *peoples:* The peoples of Africa speak many languages and dialects.

people's The possessive form: the People's Republic of China, the people's right to know.

Pepsi, Pepsi-Cola Trademarks for a cola drink.

PepsiCo Inc. Formerly the *Pepsi-Cola Co.* Headquarters is in Purchase, N.Y.

percent One word. It takes a singular verb when standing alone or when a singular word follows an *of* construction: The teachers said 60 percent was a failing grade. He said 50 percent of the membership was there. It takes a plural verb when a plural word follows an *of* construction: He said 50 percent of the members were there.

Repeat *percent* with each individual figure: He said 10 percent to 30 percent of the electorate may not vote.

percentage Use figures and decimals rather than fractions: 1 percent, 2.5 percent, 10 percent. For amounts less than 1 percent, use a zero and decimals: 0.5 percent, 0.03 percent.

percentage point Not the same as *percentage.* An increase from 10 percent to 11 percent is an increase of 10 percent, but an increase of 1 percentage point.

period (.) Use a period at the end of a declarative sentence, an indirect question, a polite request phrased as a question and most imperative sentences: The book is finished. He asked what the score was. Why don't we go. Shut the door. Elsewhere:

1. Use a period in some abbreviations. See **abbreviations and acronyms**.
2. Use three periods to construct an ellipsis mark. See **ellipsis**.
3. Use a period in initials in a name: John F. Kennedy, T.S. Eliot (no space between *T.* and *S.*). Use no period if initials are used instead of a name: JFK, LBJ. See **initials**.
4. Use a period to indicate order of enumeration: 1. Wash the car. 2. Clean the basement. Or: A. Punctuate properly. B. Write simply.
5. Periods always go inside quotation marks. See **quotation marks**.

perk Short for *perquisite,* often used by legislators to describe fringe benefits. In New York state, legislators also use *lulu* to describe the benefits they receive *in lieu of* pay. If either term is used, define it.

permissible Not *permissable.*

Persian Gulf Use this long-established name unless directly quoting the Iranian government, which calls it *the Gulf of Iran.* When *Gulf of Iran* is used, explain that it is more commonly known as *the Persian Gulf.*

Persian Gulf War See **Gulf War**.

personifications Capitalize personifications: Cupid, Father Time, Grim Reaper, Jack Frost, Mother Nature, Old Man Winter, Sol, etc.

(persons) See **people, persons**.

-persons Do not initiate usages such as chairperson or spokesperson. They may be used in direct quotations or when they are an organization's formal title for an office. Other words as listed in *Webster's New World College Dictionary,* however, are acceptable: salesperson.

In general, use chairwoman, spokeswoman, etc., to refer to a woman; chairman, spokesman, etc., to refer to a man. Or use a neutral term, such as leader or representative.

persuade See **convince, persuade**.

Peter Principle *Each employee is promoted until he reaches his level of incompetence,* from the book by Lawrence J. Peter.

petty officer See **military titles**.

PG The *parental guidance* rating. See **movie ratings**.

phase See **faze, phase**.

Ph.D. See **doctor** and **academic degrees**.

phenomenon (s.), **phenomena** (pl.) Not *phenomenons.*

Philadelphia The city in Pennsylvania stands alone in datelines.

Philip Morris See **Altria Group Inc.**

Philippine Airlines *PAL* is acceptable on second reference. Headquarters is in Makati City, Philippines.

Philippines The form for datelines: *MANILA, Philippines, Jan 12 (UPI) —* In stories: *the Philippines, the Philippine Islands.* The people are *Filipinos.* Specify the name of an individual island, if needed, in the text.

Phillips Petroleum Co. See **ConocoPhillips**.

Phoenix This city in Arizona stands alone in datelines.

phony Not *phoney.*

piano (s.), **pianos** (pl.)

pica A measure in printing. There are 12 points to the pica, 6 picas to the inch.

picket, pickets, picketed, picket line *Picket* is both the verb and the noun. Do not use *picketer.*

Pick's disease After Arnold Pick, a Czech physician. A condition characterized by progressive deterioration of the brain.

picnic, picnicked, picnicking, picnicker Note the *k.*

pico- A prefix meaning *one-trillionth;* a *picosecond* is one-trillionth of a second. See **metric system**.

pigeon, pidgin *Pigeon* is a bird; *pidgin* is a mixed language usually evolved from commerce with primitive people.

Pikes Peak No apostrophe. After Zebulon Montgomery Pike, a U.S. general and explorer. The peak, 14,110 feet high, is in the Rockies in central Colorado.

pill Usually lowercase. But it may be capitalized as *the Pill* in the popular name of a birth control pill in: Does she take the Pill?

pilot Not a formal title. Lowercase.

pileup (n., adj.), **pile up** (v.)

Ping Pong Table tennis. A trademark name for *table tennis.*

pint (dry) Equal to 33.6 cubic inches, or one-half of a dry quart. In metric it is about .55 liters. To convert to liters, multiply by .55 (5 dry pints × .55 equals 2.75 liters).

pint (liquid) Equal to 16 fluid ounces or two cups. In metric it is about 470 milliliters or .47 liters. To convert to liters, multiply by .47 (4 pints × .47 equals 1.88 liters).

Pinyin See **Chinese names**.

pipeline

pistol A pistol can be either a semiautomatic or a revolver, but *semiautomatic* and *revolver* are not synonymous. See **weapons**.

Pittsburgh The city in Pennsylvania stands alone in datelines.

plains See **Great Plains**.

planets Capitalize the names of planets: *Earth, Jupiter, Mars, Mercury, Neptune, Pluto, Saturn, Uranus, Venus.*

Capitalize *Earth* when used as the proper name of our planet: The astronauts returned to Earth. Not *the Earth.* Lowercase elsewhere: What on earth do you mean?

Lowercase words derived from the planets and other heavenly bodies: earthling, martian, jovian, lunar, solar, venusian.

planning Avoid the redundant *future planning.*

plants Lowercase, except for proper nouns or adjectives that occur in a name: tree, fir, white fir, Douglas fir, Dutch elm, Scotch pine, clover, white clover, white Dutch clover.

If a botanical name is used, capitalize the first word, lowercase others: *Pinus* (pine), *Juniperus virginiana* (red cedar), *Callicarpa americana* (blue azalea), *Gymnocladus dioica* (Kentucky coffee tree).

Plastic Wood A trademark for a wood-filler compound.

platoon A military formation composed of two or more squads, usually containing 30–40 people. Capitalize a named platoon: 1st Platoon,

platoon *continued*

Intelligence and Reconnaissance Platoon. Otherwise, lowercase: the platoon, the platoon leader. See **military units** and **company**.

playoff, playoffs (n., adj.), **play off** (v.)

play titles See **composition titles**.

PLC British abbreviation for *publicly limited company.*

plead The past tense is *pleaded,* not *pled.*

plexiglass The trademark is *Plexiglas* (single *s*).

PLO Palestine Liberation Organization. Not *Palestinian.*

plow Not *plough.*

plurality See **majority, plurality**.

plurals Separate, alphabetical listings give guidelines on forming and using some troublesome words. See also **collective nouns** and **possessives**. Some problem areas:

1. Use *'s* to form the plural of single letters: Mind your p's and q's.
2. Add *s* to form the plural of multiple letters: She knows her ABCs.
3. Add *s* to form the plural of figures: The custom began in the 1920s. Temperatures will be in the low 20s. There are five size 7s. No apostrophes.
4. Do not use *'s* for words used in a special sense, as a word: His speech had too many ifs, ands and buts.
5. Some words are plural in form, singular in meaning. Some take singular verbs: *measles, mumps, news.* Others take plural verbs: *grits, scissors, trousers.*

For questions not covered by this book, follow the first-listed plural in *Webster's New World College Dictionary.* See also the guidelines the dictionary provides under its alphabetical entry *plural.*

p.m., a.m. Lowercase with periods. Avoid the redundant 10 p.m. tonight. In these designations, *m.* stands for *meridiem,* from the Latin meaning *noon.* Thus, *p.m.* means *post meridiem* or *afternoon; a.m.* means *ante meridiem* or *before noon. Midday* is designated by *noon,* not *12 noon.* See **a.m.**

pocket-size Not *pocket-sized.*

pocket veto Occurs only when Congress has adjourned. If Congress is in session, a bill that remains on the president's desk for 10 days becomes law without his signature. If Congress adjourns, however, a bill that fails to get his signature within 10 days is automatically vetoed.

Many states have similar procedures, but the precise requirements vary greatly.

podium See **lectern**.

poetic license It is valid for poetry, not news or feature stories.

poetry Capitalize the first word in a line of poetry, unless the author has deliberately used lowercase for a special effect. Do not, however, capitalize the first word on a line created simply because the writer's line is too long for the available printing width. See **composition titles**.

poinsettia Note the *ia*.

point Do not abbreviate. Capitalize as part of a proper name: Point Pleasant.

point (printing) In printing there are 72 points in an inch; 12 points in a pica. See **pica**.

point blank (n.), **point-blank** (adj.) At such close range the curve of the bullet's trajectory need not be considered by the shooter.

Polaroid Trademark for a brand of polarized sunglasses and a line of cameras that produce instant pictures.

police department Capitalize a specific reference with or without the name of the community: the Los Angeles Police Department, the Police Department. Lowercase *department* alone or in plural uses: the Los Angeles and San Francisco police departments.

police titles See **military titles**.

policyholder, policymaker, policymaking

polio The preferred term for *poliomyelitis* and *infantile paralysis.*

Politburo Acceptable in all references for the *Political Bureau of the Communist Party.*

political divisions Use figures and capitalize the accompanying word when used with the figure: Ist Ward, I0th Ward, 3rd Precinct, 22nd Precinct, the ward, the precinct.

political language The forms of some frequently used political terms:

bagman	fence-mending	grassroots
bandwagon	*(adj.)*	groundswell
bellwether	front-runner *(n.)*	gut-fighter
canvass	front-running	hard line *(n.)*
cliff-hanger	*(adj.)*	hard-line *(adj.)*
consensus	fundraiser *(n.)*	hard-liner *(n.)*
dark horse	fundraising	horse race
demagogue	*(n., adj.)*	hustings
egghead	gaffe	keynote
fat cat	ghostwriter	keynoter

political language *continued*

lame duck	shoo-in	superpatriot
landslide	speechmaker	underdog
lightweight	speechmaking	vote-getter
mainstream	speechwriter	war chest
maverick	steamroller	war horse
re-elect	stem-winder	ward heeler
runner(s)-up	stem-winding	whistlestop
running mate	straw man	

political parties Most political parties have names that also indicate a general philosophy or belief. A *democrat,* for instance, is one who believes in and upholds government by the people, an advocate of majority rule. There are similar uses of *communist, conservative, liberal, national, republican, socialist* and others.

Capitalize such words if the reference clearly is to the proper name of a political party or to its members. Capitalize also *party* as an integral part of a proper name: The liberal Republican senator and his Conservative Party colleague said democracy and communism are incompatible.

Always lowercase a usage such as *communist regime. Regime* designates a type of political system, not the name of a specific government. See **government** for a comparison of the meanings of similar words.

Capitalize a philosophy derived from a proper name: Marxism, Nazism. But lowercase all philosophies not derived from proper names: communism, democracy, socialism, etc.

See **party affiliation** for the forms to designate someone's political party.

politicking Note the *k.*

politics Usually it takes a plural verb: My politics are my own business. As a study or science, it takes a singular verb: Politics is a demanding occupation.

polls Consider the following questions before using a story about a canvass of public opinion:

1. Who did the poll?
2. Who paid for it?
3. When was the poll taken? (Most pollsters concede that rapid last-minute changes in voter sentiment can take place.)
4. How were the interviews obtained? (Some pollsters think people are less candid on the telephone than in person.)

5. How were the questions worded? (They can be loaded to achieve a desired result. Even the sequence of questions should be considered.)
6. How were the people chosen? (At random or by some other procedure?)
7. How many people responded, and what is the margin of error? (The larger the number of responses, the smaller the margin of error in projecting the results.)
8. How big was any smaller group on which conclusions were based? (A nationwide survey of 1,500 people might show one set of figures on overall attitudes about abortion, while also reporting on the attitude of Catholics toward abortion. It's important, in such a poll, to ask how many Catholics were interviewed.)

pom-pom, pompom A *pom-pom* is an automatic cannon; a *pompom* (no hyphen) is an ornamental ball or tuft of wool, feathers, etc., usually waved in pairs by cheerleaders. (Sometimes spelled *pompon,* but *pom-pom* is preferred.)

pontiff Not a formal title. Always lowercase. See **pope**.

pope Capitalize as a formal title before a name; lowercase in all other uses: Pope Paul V, Pope Paul, Pope John Paul II. But: The pope speaks eight languages. See **Roman Catholic Church.**

pooh-pooh

Popsicle A trademark for flavored ice on a stick.

pore, pour To *pore* is to gaze steadily or intently; to *pour* is to cause to flow: I'll pour the coffee if you'll pore over the tax forms.

port, starboard *Port* is a nautical term for *left; starboard* is a nautical term for *right.* Use *right* and *left* unless the nautical terms are pertinent.

possessives Use an apostrophe to indicate possessive, except for personal pronouns.

1. Add an apostrophe and an *s* if the ending, either singular or plural, is not an *s* or *z* sound: the church's needs, the ship's route, today's problems, death's call, your money's worth, a month's pay, anybody's room, women's rights, the two deer's tracks.
2. Add only the apostrophe if the plural ends in an *s* or *z* sound: the churches' needs, the ships' wake, girls' toys, the horses' food, states' rights, the VIPs' entrance, two weeks' vacation, the Joneses' boy.
3. If the singular ends in an *s* or *z* sound, add the apostrophe and an *s* for words of one syllable. Add only the apostrophe for words of more than one syllable unless you expect the pronunciation of the second *s* or *z* sound: the bus's schedule, anyone else's attitude,

possessives *continued*

the press's error, the fox's den, the justice's verdict, Marx's theories, the prince's life; for goodness' sake, Jesus' life, Moses' law, Tennessee Williams' play; the princess's beau, the hostess's invitation, Xerox's profits.

4. Compounds or joint possession show the possessive in the last word only. But if there is separate possession, each noun takes the possessive: the attorney general's request, my brother-in-law's house, Joe and Susan's apartment (joint possession), Joe's and Susan's clothes (separate possession).

5. Follow the user's practice for proper names: Actors Equity, Diners Club, the Ladies' Home Journal, the National Governors' Conference.

6. Do not use the apostrophe for personal pronouns: his, hers, its, mine, ours, theirs, whose, yours.

post- Mostly solid: postcard, postdate, postgraduate, posthaste, postmeridian, postnatal, postwar, but post-bellum, post-free, post-mortem, post office, post-season, post-World War II. Follow *Webster's New World College Dictionary,* hyphenating words not listed there.

post office It may be used, but it is no longer capitalized, because the agency is now the *U.S. Postal Service:* I went to the post office.

potato (s.), **potatoes** (pl.)

pound (monetary) The English pound sterling sign (£) is not used. Convert the figures to dollars in most cases. Use a figure and spell out *pounds* if the actual figure is relevant: Today, 2 pounds is the equivalent of about $3.30.

pound (weight) Equal to 16 ounces. In metric it is about 454 grams, or .45 kilograms. To convert to kilograms, multiply by .45 (20 pounds × .45 equals 9 kilograms). Use the abbreviation *lb.* only in tabular matter.

pour See **pore, pour.**

poverty level An income level judged inadequate to provide a family or individual with the essentials of life. The figure is regularly adjusted to reflect changes in the Consumer Price Index.

practitioner See **Church of Christ, Scientist.**

pre- Hyphenate with a capitalized word or to avoid a double *e:* pre-Columbian, pre-empt, pre-exist. Solid in most other forms: prearrange, preconceive, predate, predispose, preflight, prehistoric, prejudge, preschool, preset, pretrial, prewar. Follow *Webster's New World College Dictionary,* hyphenating words not listed there.

preacher A job description. always lowercase.

precincts See **political divisions**.

preferred stock See **common stock, preferred stock**.

prefixes Three rules are constant, although they yield some exceptions to listings in *Webster's New World College Dictionary:*

1. Hyphenate with a capitalized word: trans-Atlantic.
2. Hyphenate to avoid a duplicated vowel or tripled consonant: pre-exist, shell-like.
3. Use a hyphen to join doubled prefixes: sub-subparagraph.

In addition, most words beginning with *anti-* and *non-* are hyphenated. See **anti-** and **non-** and separate entries for some of the commonly used prefixes. For prefixes not listed in this book, follow *Webster's New World College Dictionary.* Hyphenate words not listed there.

premier See **prime minister, premier**.

premiere A first performance.

Presbyterian churches Presbyterian Church (U.S.A) was organized in 1983 from the reunion of the Presbyterian Church in the United States (Southern Presbyterian Church) and the United Presbyterian Church in the United States of America (Northern Presbyterian Church), healing a rift that dates back to the Civil War. It is the largest Presbyterian body. Headquarters is in Louisville, Ky.

The denomination's chief executive officer is the *stated clerk.* The church's highest elected official is the *moderator.* Both titles should be capitalized before a name.

Any Presbyterian clergyman may be called a *minister.* A *pastor* is a minister who leads a congregation. Use *the Rev.* before a name on first reference. Drop the title on second reference. For lay leaders, capitalize *elder* or *deacon* before a name.

preschool

(presently) Avoid this adverb, which means *soon* or *in a little while.* See **currently**.

presidency Lowercase.

president Capitalize as a formal title before a name: President John F. Kennedy, President Kennedy, Presidents Kennedy and Johnson, President John Smith of Acme Corp. Drop the title after the first reference.

Lowercase in all other uses: The president left today. He is running for president. Lincoln was president during the Civil War.

Use of the first name of a present or former U.S. president is optional. Either President Bush or President George W. Bush is acceptable on first reference. Traditionally, the first name has not been used in

president *continued*

most cases. The first name should be used in a story about multiple heads of state and may be preferable in feature or personality stories. Also use a first name if needed to avoid confusing one with another: President Andrew Johnson, President Lyndon Johnson.

Use the full name on first reference to presidents of other nations.

presidential Lowercase: a presidential prerogative.

Presidential Medal of Freedom The nation's highest civilian honor. It is given by the president on the recommendation of the Distinguished Civilian Service Awards Board for "exceptionally meritorious contribution to the security or national interests of the United States, to world peace or to cultural or other significant public or private endeavors." Until 1963 it was known as the *Medal of Freedom*.

presiding officer Lowercase: They were led by presiding officer William Adams.

(press conference) Use news conference *unless part of a direct quotation.*

press secretary Seldom a formal title. For consistency, always use lowercase, even before a name. The formal title for the presidential aide is *assistant to the president for press relations.*

preventive Use *preventative* only in direct quotations.

price-earnings ratio The price of a share of stock divided by earnings per share for a 12-month period. A stock selling for $60 a share and earning $6 a share has a price-earnings ratio of 10-to-1, or a *PE* of 10.

PricewaterhouseCoopers Small *w*, no spaces.

priest Not a formal title, always lowercase. See **Episcopal Church** and **Roman Catholic Church**.

prima facie At first sight. *Prima facie evidence* is evidence adequate to establish a fact or raise a presumption of fact unless refuted.

primary Always lowercase: the New Hampshire primary, the Democratic primary, the primary, primary day.

prime minister, premier *Prime minister* is preferred as the English equivalent of various titles identifying the first minister in a national government that has a council of ministers or similar group. *Premier* is acceptable in some cases. Follow the practice of a country. Capitalize before names: Prime Minister Tony Blair, Premier John Smith. Drop the title after first reference and lowercase in other uses: The prime minister plans to visit the United States. The premier was on a fishing trip.

Use premier for the leaders of provinces in Australia and Canada. Use *chancellor* in Austria and Germany.

prime rate The interest rate expressed in *percent* that commercial banks charge on loans to their borrowers with the best credit ratings: The prime rate fell to 7 percent.

prime time

prince, princess See **nobility** and **royal titles**.

Prince Edward Island One of the three Maritime Provinces of Canada. Do not abbreviate. The form for datelines: *CHARLOTTETOWN, Prince Edward Island, Nov 5 (UPI) —*

principal, principle *Principal* means *main* or *chief:* She is the school principal. Money is the principal problem.

A *principle* is a rule: They fought for the principle of self-determination.

Memory aid: It is princip*al* for m*ain* and princip*le* for ru*le*.

prior to Overused. *Before* is less stilted.

prison, jail In general, a *prison* is any place of confinement: His back yard was his prison. As a place where criminals are confined:

- A *prison* or *penitentiary* is for those convicted of serious crimes carrying a penalty of more than a year.
- A *jail* is for those convicted of relatively minor offenses carrying a penalty of less than a year, for civil offenses such as non-payment of alimony, and for those awaiting trial or sentencing.
- A *reformatory* or *reform school* is for young offenders convicted of lesser crimes, sent for training and discipline intended to reform rather than punish.

Several euphemisms — *correctional institution, correctional center, detention center* — are widely used in proper names.

Capitalize a proper name or a widely used popular name: Massachusetts Correctional Institution-Walpole (the proper name), Walpole State Prison (a widely used popular name).

Lowercase plural or generic uses: the Colorado and Kansas state penitentiaries, the federal prison, the state prison, the prison, the county jail, a federal detention center.

prisoner of war *POW* is acceptable on second reference. Hyphenate as a compound modifier before a noun: a prisoner-of-war trial.

private See **military titles**.

privilege, privileged Not *priviledge*.

pro- Hyphenate with a capitalized word or to avoid a double *o:* pro-American. Elsewhere, follow *Webster's New World College Dictionary*, hyphenating words not listed there.

probation See **pardon**.

probability Use hyphens: His chances of winning were 1-in-4 (n.). He had a 1-in-4 chance of winning (adj.). See **betting odds.**

Procter & Gamble Co. *P&G* is acceptable on second reference. Headquarters is in Cincinnati.

Producer Price Index Measurement of changes in the average price for goods that businesses pay for a selected group of industrial commodities, farm products, processed foods and feed for animals. Capitalize when referring to the U.S. index issued monthly by the Bureau of Labor Statistics, an agency of the Labor Department.

profanity See **obscenities.**

profession A vocation requiring advanced education or training: engineering, medicine, law, etc. Ranching is an *occupation;* teaching animal husbandry at a university is a *profession.*

professor Do not abbreviate. See **academic titles.**

profit-sharing (n., adj.) The hyphen for the noun is an exception to *Webster's New World College Dictionary.*

profit terminology Note the meanings of these terms in reporting a company's financial status. Be careful to specify to what period the figures given apply — quarterly results, the first half or the fiscal year, for example. Include per-share earnings and always give year-ago comparative figures and comparison with the previous quarter if it is notable. Always include extraordinary items and an explanation.

The terms, listed in the order in which they might occur in analyzing a company's financial condition:

> *revenue* — The amount of money a company took in, including interest earned and receipts from sales, services provided, rents and royalties. The figure also may include excise taxes and sales taxes collected for the government. If it does, the fact should be noted in any report on revenue. The terms *gross earnings* and *gross income* are seldom-used synonyms for *revenue.*
>
> *sales* — The money a company receives for goods and services it sells. In some cases the figure includes receipts from rents and royalties. In others, particularly when rents and royalties make up a large portion of a company's income, these figures are listed separately.
>
> *gross profit* — The difference between the sales price of an item or service and the expenses directly attributed to it, such as the cost of raw materials, labor and overhead linked to the production effort.

income before taxes — Gross profits minus companywide expenses not directly attributed to specific products or services. These expenses typically include interest costs, advertising and sales costs, and general administrative overhead.

net income, profit, earnings, net loss — The amount left after taxes have been paid. A portion of profit may be committed to pay preferred dividends. Some of what remains may be paid in dividends to holders of common stocks. The rest may be invested to obtain interest revenue or spent to acquire new buildings or equipment designed to increase the company's ability to make future profits. *Net operating income or loss* excludes profit or loss from sources other than regular activities and certain income deductions for non-operating expenses. To avoid confusion, do not use the word *income* alone — always be specific. The terms *profit* and *earnings* are commonly interpreted as meaning *the amount left after taxes.* The terms *net profit* and *net earnings* are acceptable synonyms.

earnings per share — The figure obtained by dividing the number of outstanding shares of common stock into the amount of net income left after dividends have been paid on any preferred stock. As a rule, use primary earnings per share rather than fully diluted if both figures are given.

dividend — The amount distributed to stockholders, usually in cash or stock. Payments generally, but not necessarily, are made in quarterly installments. The dividend usually is a portion of the earnings per share. However, if a company shows no profit during a given period, it may be able to use earnings retained from profitable periods to pay its dividend on schedule.

return on investment — A percentage figure obtained by dividing the company's assets into its net income.

retained earnings — That share of a company's net profit that is not paid out to shareholders, a major source of money for expansion.

extraordinary loss, extraordinary income — An expense or source of income that does not occur on a regular basis, such as a loss due to a major fire or the revenue from the sale of a subsidiary. Extraordinary items should be identified in any report on the company's financial status to avoid creating the false impression that its overall profit trend has suddenly plunged or soared.

Prohibition Capitalize the period, 1920 to 1933, when the 18th Amendment to the Constitution prohibited the manufacture, sale or transportation of alcoholic liquors. Lowercase elsewhere: The prohibition on televising football games has ended.

prone In a face-down position. See **supine**.

propeller

prophecy (n.), **prophesy** (v.)

proportions Always use figures: 2 parts powder to 6 parts water.

proposition Do not abbreviate. Capitalize with a figure for a ballot question: He is uncommitted on Proposition 15.

proprietary A term widely used in the computer industry in reference to privately owned or developed technology, software, etc.

prosecutor A job description, always lowercase. But capitalize the formal title of a prosecutor before a name: District Attorney Hamilton Burger.

prosecutor general No hyphen.

prostate gland Not *prostrate.*

Protestant In general, it applies to any Christian not belonging to the Roman Catholic or Orthodox Eastern churches. Mormons, however, do not accept the designation *protestant.*

Protestant Episcopal Church See **Episcopal Church.**

protester Not protestor.

prove, proved, proven, proving Use *proven* only as an adjective: a proven remedy.

provinces Names of the provinces of foreign nations are punctuated in text the same way as the names of U.S. states. Do not abbreviate the names of provinces. See **Canada.**

Do not capitalize *province:* They visited the province of Nova Scotia. The earthquake struck Shensi province.

proviso (s.), **provisos** (pl.)

provost marshal (s.), **provost marshals** (pl.)

PTA Acceptable in all references for *parent-teacher association.*

Public Broadcasting Service It is not a network, but an association of public television stations organized to buy and distribute programs selected by a vote of the members. *PBS* is acceptable on first reference, but provide the full name in the story.

public schools For schools known by a numeral, use a figure: Public School 3, Public School 10. With a commemorative name: Benjamin Franklin School.

publisher Capitalize as a formal title before a name: Publisher John Jones.

Puerto Rico Do not abbreviate. In datelines: *SAN JUAN, Puerto Rico, Nov. 5 (UPI)* —

Pulitzer Prizes These yearly awards for outstanding work in journalism and the arts were endowed by Joseph Pulitzer, publisher of the old *New York World,* and first given in 1917. They are awarded by the trustees of Columbia University on recommendation of an advisory board.

Awards in the *journalism category* are for public service, national reporting, international reporting, general local reporting, special local reporting, editorial writing, editorial cartooning, spot news photography, feature photography, and criticism or commentary.

Awards in the *arts category* are for biography, drama, fiction, general non-fiction, history, music, poetry.

Capitalize *Pulitzer Prize,* but lowercase the categories: Pulitzer Prize for public service, Pulitzer Prize for fiction, etc. Also: a Pulitzer Prize winner, a Pulitzer Prize-winning author.

pullout, pullback

pulpit See **lectern**.

pushup

punctuation Think of it as a courtesy to your readers, meant to help them understand a story. There are many gray areas. For this reason, all the punctuation entries in this book are guidelines rather than rules. But don't disregard them or treat them lightly.

See separate entries: **colon, comma, dash, ellipsis, exclamation mark, hyphen, parentheses, period, question mark, quotation mark, semicolon**.

pupil, student Children in kindergarten through the eighth grade are *pupils;* those in higher grades are *students*.

Purim The Jewish Feast of Lots, commemorating Esther's deliverance of the Jews in Persia from a massacre plotted by Haman. Occurs in February or March.

Pyrex A trademark for an oven glassware.

Q

Q-and-A format See **question mark**.

Qantas Airways Headquarters is in Sydney, Australia.

Qatar

QE2 Acceptable on second reference for the ocean liner *Queen Elizabeth 2.*

Q-Tips A trademark for cotton swabs.

Quaalude A trademark for *methaqualone.*

Quakers Acceptable in all references to members of the *Religious Society of Friends.*

Quakers use the term *meeting* for many of their organizations. Capitalize the full name of a specific meeting: the Yearly Meeting of the Philadelphia Society of Friends. Lowercase elsewhere: the yearly meeting.

Associations include the French United Meeting, the Evangelical Friends Alliance and the Friends General Conference.

There is no recognized ranking of clergy over lay people. Unordained officers are called *elders* or *ministers.* Some Quaker ministers, particularly in the Midwest, use *the Rev.* before their names or describe themselves as *pastors.* Always lowercase *pastor* and *minister.* Capitalize *elder* before a name. Use *the Rev.* on first reference if it is a minister's practice. Drop the title on second reference.

quakes See **earthquakes**.

quart (dry) A volume of 67.2 cubic inches. In metric it is about 1.1 liters. To convert to liters, multiply by 1.1 (5 dry quarts × 1.1 equals 5.5 liters).

quart (liquid) A volume of 57.75 cubic inches, or 32 fluid ounces. In metric it is about 950 milliliters or .95 liters. To convert to liters, multiply by .95 (4 quarts × .95 equals 3.8 liters).

(quartet) Journalese for *a group of four.* Avoid it.

quasar Acceptable in all references for *quasi-stellar radio source.* Most astronomers consider quasars the most distant objects observable in the heavens.

Quebec The city in Canada stands alone in datelines. Use *Quebec City* in the body of a story if needed to distinguish the city from the province. Do not abbreviate any reference to the province or city.

queen, queen consort, queen dowager, queen mother See **royal titles**.

question mark (?) Use a question mark at the end of a direct question.: "Who started the riot?" he asked. (Note that a comma is not used after the question mark.) Did he ask who started the riot? Elsewhere:

1. Use a question mark at the end of a full sentence that asks a multiple question: Did you hear him say, "What right have you to ask about the riot?"

2. In a series, use a question mark after each item if you wish to emphasize each element. If no emphasis is intended, use a comma.

> *Right:* Did he plan the riot? Employ assistants? Give the signal to begin?
>
> *Right:* Did he plan the riot, employ assistants and give the signal to begin?

3. Do not use a question mark at the end of an indirect question: He asked who started the riot.

4. Do not use a question mark in parentheses to express doubt about a word, fact or number, or to indicate humor or irony.

5. In a Q-and-A format, use question marks but no quotation marks, and paragraph each speaker's words:

> Q. Where did you keep it?
> A. In a little tin box.

6. Place a question mark inside quotation marks if it applies to the quoted material; outside if they apply to the whole sentence:

> Who wrote "Gone with the Wind"?
>
> He asked, "How long will it take?"

questionnaire Two *n*'s.

(quintet) Journalese for *a group of five.* Avoid it.

quotation marks Use quotation marks to set off direct quotations, some titles, nicknames and words used in a special sense.

Guidelines:

1. Use quotation marks to surround the exact words of a speaker or writer when reported in a story:

   "I have no intention of staying," he replied.

   "I do not object," he said, "to the tenor of the report."

   Franklin said, "A penny saved is a penny earned."

   A speculator said the practice is "too conservative for inflationary times."

2. Full-sentence quotations are set off with a comma, started with a capital letter and ended with some form of punctuation. See **sentence**.

   If words must be added to a full-sentence quote to clarify the meaning, put them in parentheses, or recast the sentence as a partial quote.

   Wrong: The senator said, "I am against the motion to reconsider" the bill.
   Right: The senator said, "I am against the motion to reconsider (the bill)."
   Right: The senator said he was "against the motion to reconsider" the bill.

3. In direct quotations of two or more paragraphs, the quotation marks come before each paragraph and at the end of the last; they do not come at the end of intermediate paragraphs unless the quoted matter is an incomplete sentence.

   He said, "I am shocked and horrified by the incident.
   "I am so horrified, in fact, that I will ask for the death penalty."

   But:

   He said he was "shocked and horrified by the incident."
   "I am so horrified, in fact, that I will ask for the death penalty," he said.

4. In dialogue or conversation, place each person's words, no matter how brief, in a separate paragraph:

> "Will you go?"
> "Yes."
> "When?"
> "Thursday."

5. Quotation marks are not required in a question-and-answer format or in full texts or textual excerpts. See **ellipsis** and **question marks**.

6. Use quotation marks for some nicknames and book titles, movie titles, etc. See **composition titles** and **nicknames**.

7. Put quotation marks around words used in a special sense or being introduced to the reader:

> The "debate" soon turned into a free-for-all.
>
> Broadcast frequencies are now measured in units called "kilohertz."

Do not use quotation marks around such words after first reference. See **foreign words**.

8. Do not use quotation marks to emphasize ordinary words. Omit the quotation marks in: The senator said he would "go home to Michigan" if he lost the election.

9. When a partial quote is used, do not put quotation marks around words that the speaker could not have used.

> *Wrong:* The accused man said he "was not in the habit of setting fires."
> *What he must have said was:* "I am not in the habit of setting fires."

10. Grammar in partial quotes must conform to the grammar of the sentence as a whole.

> *Wrong:* The victim said he "did my best to defend myself."

The subject, *victim,* disagrees with the possessive *my.* Recast with the full quote:

> *Right:* The victim said, "I did my best to defend myself."

quotation marks *continued*

Or paraphrase:

Right: The victim said he did his best to defend himself.

11. For quotes within quotes, alternate between double quotation marks *("or")* and single marks *('or'):*

> She said, "I quote from the letter, 'I agree with Kipling that "the female of the species is more deadly than the male," but the phenomenon is not an unchangeable law of nature,' a remark he did not explain."

But note the damage such a complicated structure does to comprehension.

Use three marks together if two quoted elements end at the same time: She said, "He told me, 'I love you.'"

12. The period and the comma always go within the quotation marks. The dash, the semicolon, the question mark and the exclamation point go within quotation marks when they apply to the quoted matter only. They go outside when they apply to the whole sentence.

13. Standard rules of punctuation prevail in all direct quotations. Avoid the tendency to write run-on sentences (comma splice) in direct quotes. Commas should not be substituted for periods in quoted dialogue.

> *Wrong:* "It is wrong, I won't do it."
> *Right:* "It is wrong. I won't do it."

14. UPI style prevails in direct quotations. This includes the use of figures and abbreviations in *most* cases. Exception: All titles are spelled out in direct quotations except *Mr., Mrs.* and *Dr.* See **texts, transcripts.**

quotations in the news Remember that you can misquote someone by giving a startling remark without its modifying passage or qualifiers. The manner of delivery sometimes is part of the context. Reporting a facial expression or gesture may be as important as the words themselves. Also:

1. Quotations should be corrected to eliminate embarrassing solecisms and malapropisms made by a speaker.

2. Do not routinely use such phonetic spellings as *gonna* and *gotta* to convey regional dialects or sloppy diction. Such phonetic

spellings are appropriate, however, when they are relevant to the facts of the story, or when they help convey a desired touch in a feature. See **dialect**.

3. Avoid fragmentary quotes when possible. If a speaker's words are clear and concise, favor the full quote. Paraphrase cumbersome language, reserving quotation marks for particularly sensitive or controversial passages that must be identified specifically as coming from the speaker. See **obscenities**.

4. Be especially selective about one-word quotes. Do not use them for trivial words. Reserve them for introduction of obscure terms, words used in a special sense, and for rare, bizarre or outrageous words that would only be appropriate coming from the mouth of the subject.

R

R The *restricted* rating. See **movie ratings**.

rabbi Capitalize as a formal title before a name, lowercase otherwise: Rabbi David Small, the rabbi. See **Jewish congregations**.

Rabbinical Council of America See **Jewish congregations**.

race Use a racial identification only if it is clearly pertinent, such as:

- In biographical and announcement stories, particularly when they involve a feat or appointment that has not been routinely associated with members of a particular race.
- When it provides the reader with a substantial insight into conflicting emotions known or likely to be involved in a demonstration or similar event.
- When describing a person sought in a manhunt.

In some stories that involve a conflict, it is equally important to specify that an issue cuts across racial lines. If, for example, a demonstration by supporters of busing to achieve racial balance in schools includes a substantial number of whites, that fact should be noted.

Do not use racially derogatory terms unless they are part of a quotation that is essential to the story. See **nationalities**.

rack, wrack The noun *rack* applies to various types of framework; the verb *rack* means *to arrange on a rack, to torture, trouble or torment:* He was placed in the rack. She racked her brain.

The noun *wrack* means *ruin* or *destruction,* and is generally confined to the phrase *wrack and ruin.*

radar Lowercase acronym for *radio detection and ranging.*

radical In general, avoid this term in favor of a more precise description of an individual's political views. See **leftist** and **rightist**.

When used, it suggests that an individual believes change must be made by tearing up the roots or foundation of the present order.

Although it is often applied to individuals who hold strong socialist or communist views, it also is applied at times to individuals who believe an existing form of government must be replaced by a more authoritarian or militaristic one.

radiation See **nuclear terminology**.

radio Capitalize and use before the name to indicate an official voice of the government: Radio Moscow.

Lowercase and use after the name when indicating merely that the information was obtained from broadcasts in the city: Havana radio, for example, to refer to reports that are broadcast on one or more of several stations operating in Cuba.

radio station The call letters alone are frequently adequate, but if needed, lowercase: radio station WJTN. See **call letters**.

railroads Capitalize a proper name: the Illinois Central Gulf Railroad.

Railroad companies vary the spellings of their names, using *Railroad, Rail Road, Railway,* etc. Consult the *Official Railway Guide-Freight Service* and the *Official Railway Guide-Passenger Service* for official spellings.

Lowercase *railroad* standing alone or in plural uses: the railroad, the Penn Central and Santa Fe railroads. See **Amtrak** and **Conrail**.

RAM Acronym for *random-access memory,* a computer's main working memory; sometimes called *read/write memory* to distinguish it from *read-only memory (ROM).* See **ROM**.

range The form: $12 million to $14 million. Not: $12 to $14 million.

rank and file (n.), **rank-and-file** (adj.) The rank and file will vote Monday. Rank-and-file members will vote Monday.

rarely It means *seldom. Rarely ever* is redundant, but *rarely if ever* is often appropriate.

ratio Use figures and a hyphen: the ratio was 2-to-1, a ratio of 2-to-1. Omit *to* if the figures come first: a 2-1 ratio. The word *ratio* is essential to avoid any chance the figures might be misleading. See **margin**.

ravage, ravish To *ravage* is to wreak great destruction or devastation: Union troops ravaged Atlanta. To *ravish* is to abduct, rape or carry away with emotion: Soldiers ravished the women. Although both words

ravage, ravish *continued*

connote an element of violence, they are not interchangeable. Buildings and towns cannot be *ravished.* (Be very careful with *ravish,* a word often misused.)

rayon Not a trademark.

re- Hyphenate with a capitalized word: re-Christianization.

Hyphenate to avoid a double *e:* re-edit, re-elect, re-entry.

Hyphenate a double prefix: re-recover.

Hyphenate a word coined and used for a single or particular occasion: re-dictate, re-urge.

Use a hyphen any time its omission could cause confusion with another word with a different meaning (homograph): reform (to correct), re-form (form again); resign (quit), re-sign (sign again), etc.

Elsewhere, follow *Webster's New World College Dictionary,* hyphenating words not listed there.

reader See **Church of Christ, Scientist.**

Realtor Use *Realtor* only if there is a specific reason to indicate that a real estate agent is a member of the National Association of Real Estate Boards. See **service marks.**

rebut, refute *Rebut* means *to argue to the contrary:* He rebutted his opponent's statement. *Refute* connotes success in argument and almost always implies an editorial judgment. Instead, use *deny, dispute, rebut* or *respond to.*

receivership A form of bankruptcy in which a business is operated during reorganization by a court-appointed trustee called a *receiver,* who seeks to solve the company's financial problems while it is being protected from creditors.

recipes Always use figures, and use fractions rather than decimals. Do not abbreviate measurements, such as *tablespoon, teaspoon,* etc.

reconnaissance Two *n*'s, two *s*'s.

reconstruction Capitalize only if the reference is to the process of reorganizing the Southern states after the Civil War.

record Avoid the unnecessary *new record.*

rector Always lowercase. See **Episcopal Church.**

recur, recurred, recurring Not *reoccur.*

(Red China) Avoid this term. See **China.**

red haired, redhead, redheaded All are acceptable for a person with red hair.

red-handed

redneck From the characteristic sunburned neck acquired in the fields by farm laborers. It refers to poor, white rural residents of the South and is often a derogatory term.

re-elect, re-election, re-entry

refer See **allude, refer.**

reference works Capitalize proper names. Do not use quotation marks around the names of books that are primarily reference material, such as almanacs, catalogs, directories, dictionaries, encyclopedias, gazetteers, handbooks: *Congressional Directory, Webster's New World College Dictionary, the UPI Stylebook.*

But: "The Careful Writer" and "Modern American Usage."

referendum (s.), **referendums** (pl.) Not *referenda.*

reformatory See **prison, jail.**

Reform Judaism See **Jewish congregations.**

refute See **rebut, refute.**

regime See **government.**

regiment A military formation composed of two or more battalions, but since 1963 no longer a tactical unit in the U.S. Army. Capitalize numbered regiments and those with proper names: the 501st Airborne Infantry Regiment, the 5th Marine Regiment, Blackwatch Regiment. Otherwise, lowercase: the regiment, the regimental commander. See **military units** and **brigade.**

regions See **directions.**

reign, rein The leather strap for a horse is a *rein,* hence figuratively: seize the reins, give free rein to, put a check rein on. *Reign* is the period a ruler is on the throne: The king began his reign.

religion Lowercase *religion* in all uses: the Christian religion, humanism as a religion, make a religion of fighting.

Other guidelines:

1. Lowercase all titles that merely describe a job: *minister, pastor, pontiff, priest, shaman,* etc. See **Rev.**

   Capitalize a formal title before a name on first reference, lowercase standing alone or set off by commas: Bishop John Jones, the bishop; Deacon Susan Smith, the deacon; Pope Paul VI, Pope Paul, the pope; Rabbi David Small, the rabbi. Drop the title in subsequent references. If a title appears in quoted matter with a name: Rabbi Small.

   Use *Sister* or *Mother* in all references before the name of a nun. If a nun uses no surname: Sister Agnes Rita in all references.

religion *continued*

If a nun uses a surname: Sister Clare Regina Torpy on first reference, Sister Torpy on second. But lowercase *the sister* or *the mother* without a name.

2. Capitalize references to religious orders or their members: He is member of the Society of Jesus. He is a Jesuit.

3. Capitalize proper nouns referring to a monotheistic deity: God, Allah, Jehovah, the Father, the Son, Jesus Christ, the Holy Spirit, etc. Lowercase words derived from God and all pronouns referring to the deity:

god-awful	godson	who
goddaughter	godspeed	whose
godfather	he	thy
godless	him	thine
godlike	his	*etc.*
godliness	thee	
godsend	thou	

4. Lowercase *god* in references to a deity of a polytheistic religion, but capitalize names of gods and goddesses: Aphrodite, Baal, Bacchus, Janus, Venus.

5. Capitalize alternate names for Mary, the mother of Jesus: Holy Mother, Virgin Mary. But: *virgin birth.*

6. Capitalize *Last Supper* and *Lord's Supper,* but lowercase other rites, celebrations, sacraments or services: baptism, bar mitzvah, confirmation, eucharist, holy communion, liturgy *(divine liturgy),* mass *(high mass, low mass, requiem mass, etc.),* matrimony, penance, vesper service, worship service, etc.

7. Lowercase angel, cherub, devil, heaven, hell, satanic, etc., but capitalize proper names: Hades, Satan, Gabriel.

Religious Society of Friends See Quakers.

reluctant, reticent *Reluctant* is unwilling to act; *reticent* is unwilling to speak: He is reluctant to enter the primary. The candidate's husband is reticent.

reportedly Avoid the word in favor of saying who reported. If the word must be used, avoid an awkward placement.

Awkward: He reportedly died in the crash. (Is he dead? Was he in the crash?)
Better: He died, reportedly, in the crash. Or: He was in the crash and it was reported that he died.

representative, Rep. See **legislative titles and party affiliation**.

republic Capitalize *republic* when used as part of a nation's full, formal name: the Republic of Argentina. The full name usually is not needed, however. See **datelines**.

republican, republicanism Lowercase unless it is a reference to the *Republican Party* or its members. See **political parties**.

Republican Governors' Association

resident See **citizen**.

resistible Not *resistable.*

resolution Capitalize a specific resolution: U.N. Security Council Resolution 1441 (do not abbreviate as *Res.*). Lowercase elsewhere: The vote on the resolution, etc.

restaurant

restaurateur Not *restauranteur* (no *n.*)

restroom

retail sales The sales of retail stores, including merchandise sold and receipts for repairs and similar services. A business is considered a *retail store* if it is primarily engaged in selling merchandise for personal, household or farm consumption.

retired Do not abbreviate. See **military titles**.

Reuters British news agency founded in 1851 by Paul Julius Reuter. It is referred to as *Reuters.* When it is used as an adjective, the *s* is dropped: a Reuter correspondent, a Reuter story.

revenue See **profit terminology**.

revenue bond See **loan terminology**.

Rev. Use *the Rev.,* not *Rev.* alone, because the abbreviation stands for an adjective, not a noun. But this title of respect does not apply in many denominations. See separate entries for each.

   Use it only on first reference and with a full name: the Rev. John Jones. Or, if appropriate, for a Protestant clergyman with a doctor of divinity degree: the Rev. Dr. Norman Vincent Peale. See **Dr.**

   Do not combine *the Rev.* with other titles, however. If an individual also has a secular title, such as *Rep.,* use whichever is appropriate to the context, but not both.

Revolution Capitalize when part of a name for a specific historical event: the American Revolution, the Bolshevik Revolution, the French Revolution.

   Use *Revolution* alone, capitalized, only to refer to the *American Revolution:* the Revolutionary War. Lowercase plural uses: the American and French revolutions.

revolutions per minute The abbreviation *rpm* is acceptable on first reference, but use the full term in the body of the story.

revolver A revolver is a pistol that employs a revolving cylinder to hold its cartridges. The term *service revolver* is meaningless, because a policeman's revolver is no different from any other, and it may or may not be provided by the police department.

revolving credit An account on which payment is any amount less than the total balance, with interest being charged on the balance carried forward.

Rh factor, Rh negative, Rh positive

rhetoric A pejorative term in many uses. Use with care.

Rhode Island Abbreviation: *R.I.* The smallest U.S. state has the longest official name: *the state of Rhode Island and Providence Plantations.* See **state(s)**.

Richter scale See **earthquakes**.

rifle, riffle To *rifle* is to plunder or steal; to *riffle* is to leaf rapidly through a book or pile of papers.

rifle A long-barreled weapon with a rifled bore that is fired from the shoulder. See **weapons**.

right hand, right-hand The glove is on the *right hand*. He is my *right-hand* man. Also: *right-hander, right-handed.*

rightist In general, use a more precise description of someone's political philosophy. As popularly used today, particularly abroad, *rightist* often applies to someone who is conservative or opposed to socialism. It also often indicates a person who supports an authoritarian government that is militantly anti-communist or anti-socialist.

The term *ultra-rightist* suggests a person who subscribes to rigid interpretations of a conservative doctrine or in forms of fascism that stress authoritarian, often militaristic, views. See **radical**.

right of way (s.), **rights of way** (pl.)

right-to-work (adj.) A *right-to-work law* prohibits a labor contract that would require workers covered by the contract to be union members. There is no federal right-to-work law, but Section 14B of the Taft-Hartley Act allows states to pass such a law if they wish. Many have done so.

The repeal of Section 14B would have the effect of voiding all right-to-work laws. By itself, the repeal would not require workers to be union members. But in states that now have right-to-work laws it would open the way to contracts requiring union membership. See

closed shop for definitions of various agreements that require union membership.

right wing (n.), **right-wing** (adj.), **right-winger** (n.)

Ringling Brothers and Barnum & Bailey Circus Note that both *and* and the single ampersand (&) are used.

Rio De Janeiro The city in Brazil stands alone in datelines.

Rio Grande Not *Rio Grande River. (Rio* means *river.)*

rip-off (n., adj.) Slang for *theft* or *fraud.* Confine to quotations or informal writing.

river Capitalize as part of a proper name: the Mississippi River, the River Thames. Lowercase in other uses: the river, the Mississippi and Missouri rivers.

riverbed

road Do not abbreviate. See **addresses.**

Roaring '20s See **decades.**

robbery See **theft.**

rock 'n' roll Note the two apostrophes used to replace missing letters.

Rocky Mountains Or simply: *the Rockies.*

roll call (n.), **roll-call** (adj.)

Rolls-Royce A trademark for an automobile.

ROM Acronym for *read-only memory,* the portion of computer memory that contains essential system programs that cannot be altered or erased by the user. *ROM* is not lost when the power is switched off. See **RAM.**

Roman Catholic Church The pope heads the church. Ranks below the pope are, in descending order: *cardinal, archbishop, bishop, monsignor, priest* and *deacon.* In religious orders, some men who are not priests have the title *brother.*

Capitalize *pope* as a title before a name: Pope Paul VI, Pope Paul, Pope John Paul II. Lowercase in all other uses: The pope traveled.

Do not use titles after first reference. In first reference, use these forms:

cardinals — Cardinal Timothy Manning. Not: Timothy Cardinal Manning, a practice now considered archaic except in formal church documents.

archbishops — Archbishop Joseph L. Bernardin. Or: the Most Rev. Joseph L. Bernardin, archbishop of Cincinnati.

bishops — Bishop Bernard J. Flanagan. Or: the Most Rev. Bernard J. Flanagan, bishop of Rochester.

Roman Catholic Church *continued*

> *monsignors* — Monsignor Joseph E. Vogt. Do not use *Msgr.* Do not use *the Rt. Rev.* or *the Very Rev.;* this distinction between types of monsignors is no longer made.

> *priests* — the Rev. John J. Paret. Use *father* only in direct quotations. When necessary: Father Paret.

> *deacons* — Deacon Mark Smith.

> *brothers* — Brother Thomas Garvey.

> *nuns* — See **sister**.

Romania Not *Rumania.*

Romanian Orthodox Church See **Eastern Orthodox churches**. The Romanian Orthodox Church in America is an autonomous archdiocese of the Romanian Orthodox Church. The Romanian Orthodox Episcopate of America is an autonomous archdiocese within the Orthodox Church in America.

Roman numerals Letters (*I, X,* etc.) used to express numbers:

I	=	1	C	=	100
V	=	5	D	=	500
X	=	10	M	=	1,000
L	=	50			

Use Roman numerals for wars and to establish personal sequence for people and animals: World War I, Native Dancer II, King George V, Pope John XXIII, John Jones II. See **junior, senior**.

Use Arabic numerals elsewhere. See **numerals**.

Rome The capital of Italy stands alone in datelines.

rooms Capitalize the names of specially designated rooms: Blue Room, Lincoln Room, Oval Office, Persian Room. For room numbers, use figures and capitalize: Room 2, Room 211.

rosary It is *recited* or *said,* never *read.* Always lowercase.

Rosh Hashana The Jewish New Year. Occurs in September or October.

rostrum See **lectern**.

ROTC Acceptable in all references for *Reserve Officers' Training Corps.* (Note the apostrophe.) When the service is specified, use *Army ROTC, Navy ROTC* or *Air Force ROTC.* Not: *AROTC, NROTC* or *AFROTC.*

round trip (n.), **round-trip** (adj.)

route Do not abbreviate. See **addresses** and **highways**.

Royal Air Force The British air force. *RAF* is acceptable on second reference.

Royal Dutch-Shell Group of Companies This holding company, based in London and The Hague, owns substantial portions of the stock in numerous corporations that specialize in petroleum and related products. Most have *Shell* in their names. Among them is Shell Oil Co., a U.S. corporation.

royal titles As with all other titles, capitalize royal titles before a name; lowercase standing alone or set off by commas. See **titles** and **nobility**.

Some examples:

Queen Elizabeth II of England; Queen Elizabeth; Elizabeth, queen of England; the queen of England; the queen.

Prince Rainier of Monaco; Prince Rainier; Rainier, prince of Monaco; the prince of Monaco; the prince; a prince rules Monaco.

the duke of Windsor; the duchess of Windsor .

Prince Charles; Charles, prince of Wales; the prince of Wales; the prince; Charles, heir apparent to the British throne.

Princess Caroline of Monaco; Princess Caroline, the princess.

Rt. Rev. See **monsignor**.

rubella Also known as *German measles.*

rule-making

runaround

runner-up, runners-up

running mate

runoff

run-of-the-mill

rush hour (n.), **rush-hour** (adj.) rush-hour traffic; caught in the rush hour.

Russian Orthodox Church See **Eastern Orthodox churches**.

Russia, Soviet Union *Russia* is no longer acceptable as the popular name for the former *Union of Soviet Socialist Republics (Soviet Union.)* In all cases, a clear distinction must be made between Russia, the largest of the republics that composed the old Soviet federation, and the Soviet Union. See **Commonwealth of Independent States** and **Soviet Union**.

Sabbath Capitalize religious uses; lowercase to mean any period of rest.

Sabena See **SN Brussels Airlines**.

Sacramento The city in California stands alone in datelines.

sacraments See **religion**.

sacrilegious It comes from *sacrilege*, not from *religion*.

Safeway Stores Inc. Headquarters is in Pleasanton, Calif.

Sahara Not *Sahara Desert*. (*Sahara* means *desert* in Arabic.)

saint (masculine), **sainte** (feminine) Abbreviate *saint* as *St.* and *sainte* as *Ste.:* Saulte Ste. Marie, Mich.; St. Jude; St. Paul, Minn.; St. John's, Newfoundland; St. Lawrence Seaway.

Saint John The spelling for the city in New Brunswick. To distinguish it from *St. John's* in Newfoundland.

salable Not *saleable*.

sales See **profit terminology**.

Sallie Mae See **Student Loan Marketing Association**.

SALT For *Strategic Arms Limitation Talks.* Though somewhat redundant, *SALT talks* is often needed for clarity. It is acceptable on first reference, but use the full term in the story. Use Arabic numerals: *SALT 2.* See **START**.

Salt Lake City The city in Utah stands alone in datelines.

salt water (n.), **saltwater** (adj.)

SAM See **surface-to-air missile(s)**.

San Antonio The city in Texas stands alone in datelines.

sandbag, sandbagged, sandbagging, sandbagger

San Diego The city in California stands alone in datelines.

sandstorm Visibility of one-half mile or less due to sand with wind speeds of 30 mph or more.

San Francisco The city in California stands alone in datelines.

sanitarium (s.), **sanitariums** (pl.)

San Marino Use alone in datelines on stories from the Republic of San Marino.

Santa Ana A hot wind that blows from the east-northeast desert regions into Southern California.

Santa Claus

Sao Paulo The city in Brazil stands alone in datelines.

Sardinia The form in datelines: *CAGLIARI, Sardinia, Nov. 9 (UPI)* —

SARS Acceptable in a lead paragraph if the full name, *severe acute respiratory syndrome,* is spelled out shortly thereafter

SAS See **Scandinavian Airlines System**.

Saskatchewan A province of Canada north of Montana and North Dakota. Do not abbreviate. The form in datelines: *SASKATOON, Saskatchewan, Nov. 9 (UPI)* —

Satan But lowercase *devil* and *satanic.*

satellite In telecommunications, a relay station placed in orbit around Earth. See **NASA**.

Saturday See **days**.

Saturday night special The popular name for a cheap pistol used for many impulsive crimes, often committed on Saturday nights.

Saudi Arabian Oil Co. Formerly *Arabian American Oil Co. Saudi Aramco* may be used on second reference. Headquarters is in Dhahran, Saudi Arabia.

Sault Ste. Marie, Mich., Sault Ste. Marie, Ontario The abbreviation *Ste.* is for *Sainte.*

savings and loan association Not a bank. Use *the association* on second reference.

savior Not *saviour.*

sawed-off shotgun A shotgun becomes *sawed-off,* and thus illegal, when the barrel is made shorter than 18 inches. See **shotgun** and **weapons**.

scanner A device that digitizes pictures for various computer applications, such as inserting photographs into page layouts.

Scandinavian Airlines System *SAS* is acceptable on first reference. Headquarters is in Stockholm.

scene numbers Use Arabic numerals and capitalize *scene* when used with a figure: Scene 2; Act 2, Scene 4. But: the second scene, the third scene.

scheme Do not use as a synonym for a *plan* or a *project*.

Scientology See **Church of Scientology**.

schizophrenia

school Capitalize when part of a proper name: Public School 2, Madison Elementary School, Doherty Junior High School, Crocker High School.

school age, school bus, school day, school district, school guard, school year, *but* **schoolboy, schoolbook, schoolchildren, schoolgirl, schoolhouse, schoolmate, schoolroom, schoolteacher, schoolwork, schoolyard**

scissors The word takes plural verbs and pronouns: The scissors are on the table. Leave them there.

scores Use numerals exclusively: The Twins defeated the Yankees 5-4; she won the match 6-0, 4-6, 6-2; he had a 7 on the first hole but finished at 2 under par. Use a comma in this format: Los Angeles 3, San Francisco 2.

Scot, scotch, Scottish A native of Scotland is a *Scot.* The people are *the Scots,* not *the Scotch.* Somebody or something is *Scottish.*

    The whiskey is *Scotch.*

    Also: *scotch plaid, scotch pine.* Write: *scot-free, Scottish terrier* (or *Scotty*).

    To *scotch* is to stamp out, put an end to.

Scotch tape A trademark for a brand of transparent tape.

Scotland See **datelines** and **United Kingdom**.

Scripture, Scriptures Capitalize when referring to the religious writing in the Bible. See **Bible**.

scuba Lowercase acronym for *self-contained underwater breathing apparatus.*

Scud missile

sculptor Use for both men and women.

scurrilous

sea bass, sea bird, sea biscuit, sea breeze, sea captain, sea cow, sea fight, sea gull, sea horse, sea lane, sea level, sea lion, sea power, *but* **seaborne, seacoast, seafarer, seafood, seafowl, seafront, seagoing, sealift, seaman, seaplane, seaport, seascape, seashell, seashore, seasick, seaside, seaway, seaweed, seaworthy**

Sea Islands A chain of islands off the coast of South Carolina, Georgia and Florida. One of those in the chain is *Sea Island,* and a resort community on that island is called *Sea Island.*

seaman See **military titles**.

search engine A program that helps computer users search for information on the Internet, or in any database. There are dozens of search engines, including *AltaVista, excite, Google, HotBot, InfoSeek, Jayde, Lycos, Magellan, MSN, WebCrawler, Yahoo!*.

Sears, Roebuck and Co. Headquarters is in Hoffman Estates, Ill.

seasons Lowercase *spring, summer, fall, winter* and derivatives such as *springtime* unless part of a name: Dartmouth Winter Carnival, Winter Olympics, Summer Olympics.

Seattle The city in Washington stands alone in datelines.

second guess (n.), **second-guess** (v.)

second hand (n.), **secondhand** (adj., adv.) In her *secondhand* clothes was a watch with a *second hand* that she bought *secondhand*.

second-rate

Second Vatican Council, Vatican 2 The assembly, 1962 to 1965, of Roman Catholic bishops. *Vatican 1* was in 1869–70.

secretary Capitalize before a name only if it is an official corporate or organizational title. Do not abbreviate. See **Cabinet titles**.

secretary-general With a hyphen. Capitalize as a formal title before a name: Secretary-General John Jones.

secretary-treasurer With a hyphen. Capitalize as a formal title before a name: Secretary-Treasurer John Hancock.

Secret Service The federal agency administered by the Treasury Department.

section Capitalize when used with a figure to identify part of a law or bill: Section 14B of the Taft-Hartley Act.

Securities and Exchange Commission *SEC* is acceptable on second reference. The related legislation is the *Securities Exchange Act*.

Security Council (U.N.) *Security Council* is acceptable in first reference with a dateline from the United Nations. Use *U.N. Security Council* in other first references.

Seder A Passover ceremony.

Seeing Eye A trademark for guide dogs.

seesaw

(seige) Spell it *siege*.

self- Hyphenate all except *selfheal, selfhood, selfish, selfless, selfsame, selfward*.

sellout (n.), **sell out** (v.)

semi- No hyphen unless a double *i* would result: semiannual, semiarid, semifinal, semi-intoxicated, semi-invalid, semiofficial, semitropical, semiweekly.

semiannual Twice a year; a synonym for *biannual.* Do not confuse it with *biennial,* which means *every two years.*

semicolon (;) In general, the semicolon is used to indicate a greater separation of thought and information than a comma can convey, but less than the separation that a period implies.

Guidelines:

1. Use semicolons to separate elements of a series when the individual segments contain material that must also be set off by commas: The nominees for best actor are: Jack Nicholson, "One Flew Over the Cuckoo's Nest"; Walter Matthau, "The Sunshine Boys"; Al Pacino, "Dog Day Afternoon"; Maximillian Schell, "The Man in the Glass Booth"; and James Whitmore, "Give 'Em Hell, Harry."

2. Use a semicolon when a coordinating conjunction such as *and, but* or *for* is not present: The package was due last week; it arrived today.

   If a coordinating conjunction is present, use a semicolon before it only if extensive punctuation is also required in one or more of the individual clauses: They pulled their boats from the water, sandbagged the retaining walls, and boarded up the windows; but even with these precautions, the island was hard-hit by the hurricane.

3. Semicolons are placed outside quotation marks, as illustrated in the example listing Oscar nominees.

4. Use commas, not semicolons, for simple items in a series: The grants went to Jacksonville, Fla., Birmingham, Ala., Stockton, Calif., Boise, Idaho, and Austin, Texas. The winners were Joe Jones, 13, Mary Smith, 14, and Henry Brown, 15.

senate Capitalize in references to a specific governmental legislative body: the U.S. Senate, the Senate; the Virginia Senate, the state Senate; the Senate.

Lowercase plural uses: the Virginia and North Carolina senates.

Lowercase references to non-governmental bodies: the student senate at Yale.

senator, Sen. See **legislative titles** and **party affiliation**.

senatorial Always lowercase.

send-off (n.), **send off** (v.)

senior See **junior, senior**.

senior citizen Considered by many to be a patronizing term. See **elderly**.

sentences Capitalize the first letter of every sentence, including quoted statements and direct questions: Patrick Henry said, "I know not what course others may take, but as for me, give me liberty or give me death."

Capitalize the first word of a quoted statement if it constitutes a sentence, even if it was part of a larger sentence in the original: Patrick Henry said, "Give me liberty or give me death." Or: "As for me," said Patrick Henry, "give me liberty or give me death."

Do not use an ellipsis (. . .) in such constructions to indicate the omitted words at the beginning and end of the quoted passage.

Capitalize direct questions, even without quotation marks: The story answers the question, Where does true happiness really lie?

See **ellipsis** and **quotations**.

Seoul The capital of South Korea stands alone in datelines.

Sept. 11 Use the standard abbreviation in references to the 2001 terrorist attacks in the United States. Use *9/11* only in headlines and direct quotations. See **dates** and **months**.

September See **months**.

Serbia-Montenegro Acceptable on first reference for *Serbia and Montenegro*, the country in southeast Europe formerly known as *Yugoslavia*. The name change became official on Feb. 4, 2003. A hyphen is used in the name in datelines: *BELGRADE, Serbia-Montenegro, Feb. 4 (UPI)* — .

sergeant See **military titles**.

serial numbers Use figures and capital letters in solid form (no hyphens or spaces unless the source indicates they are an integral part of the code): A1234567.

serviceable

service clubs See **fraternal organizations** and **service clubs**.

serviceman, servicewoman

service marks A brand, symbol or word, registered by a supplier of services: Realtor (a member of the National Association of Realtors). Use a generic term unless the service mark is essential to a story. If it is used, capitalize it. See **brand names** and **trademarks**.

sesqui- No hyphen: sesquicentennial (every 150 years), sesquipedalian (every foot and a half).

setup (n., adj.), **set up** (v.)

Seven Deadly Sins Anger, covetousness, envy, gluttony, lust, pride and sloth.

Seven Dwarfs Bashful, Doc, Dopey, Grumpy, Happy, Sleepy, Sneezy.

7-Eleven Chain of convenience stores licensed and operated by Southland Corp. or its affiliates. Headquarters is in Dallas.

Seven Seas Arabian Sea, Atlantic Ocean, Bay of Bengal, Mediterranean Sea, Persian Gulf, Red Sea, South China Sea.

Seven Sisters Barnard, Bryn Mawr, Mount Holyoke, Radcliffe, Smith, Vassar and Wellesley.

Seventh-day Adventist Church The head of the General Conference holds the formal title of *president.* The formal titles for ministers are *pastor* or *elder.* Capitalize them before a name; *the Rev.* is not used.

Seven-Up, 7-Up Trademarks for a soft drink.

Seven Wonders of the World The Egyptian pyramids, the hanging gardens of Babylon, the Mausoleum at Halicarnassus, the temple of Artemis at Ephesus, the Colossus of Rhodes, the statue of Zeus by Phidias at Olympia and the Pharos or lighthouse at Alexandria.

severe blizzard See **blizzard**.

severe freeze See **freeze**.

sewage, sewerage *Sewage* is waste matter; *sewerage* is the drainage system.

sex changes Follow these guidelines in using proper names or personal pronouns when referring to an individual who has undergone a sex-change operation:

- If the reference is to an action *before* the operation, use the proper name and gender of the individual at that time.
- If the reference is to an action *after* the operation, use the new proper name and gender.

For example:

> Dr. Richard Raskind was a first-rate amateur tennis player. He won several tournaments. Ten years later, when Dr. Renee Richards applied to play in tournaments, many women players objected on the grounds that she had become a woman as the result of a sex-change operation. Richards said she was entitled to compete as a woman.

sexism See **women**.

(Shabuoth) See **Shavuot**.

shah Capitalize as a royal title before a name; lowercase elsewhere: Shah Mohammed Reza Pahlavi of Iran, the shah of Iran.

shake-up (n., adj.), **shake up** (v.)

shall, will Use *shall* to express determination: We shall overcome. You and he shall stay. Otherwise, use *will:* We will hold a meeting. Will he be allowed to go? He will. I will stay. See **should, would**.

Shanghai The seaport in Jiangsu province in eastern China stands alone in datelines.

shape-up (n., adj.), **shape up** (v.)

shareware Copyrighted programs that may be used without charge on a trial basis. See **freeware**.

Shariah The legal code of Islam. It is roughly comparable to the Talmudic tradition in Judaism.

Shavuot The Jewish Feast of Weeks, commemorating the receiving of the Ten Commandments. Occurs in May or June.

she Do not use this pronoun in references to ships or nations. Use *it* instead.

Sheetmetal Workers International Association *Sheetmetal Workers union* is acceptable in all references. Headquarters is in Washington.

Sheetrock A trademark for a gypsum wallboard.

sheik, sheikdom Not *sheikh, sheikhdom*.

Shell Oil Co. Headquarters is in Houston. See **Royal Dutch-Shell Group of Companies**.

sheriff Capitalize when used as a formal title before a name.

Shiite, Shiites The Muslim sect and its members.

ships See **boats, ships**.

shootout

shortfall

short term (n.), **short-term** (adj.)

short ton See **ton**.

shotgun A smoothbore that fires shot pellets, buckshot and slugs. Principally used in hunting and clay target sports, but also by law enforcement officers. Form: 12-gauge shotgun, sawed-off shotgun. See **weapons**.

(shotgun blast) Journalese. Avoid the term. People are not *killed* or *wounded* by blasts from a shotgun. Shotguns fire *pellets, buckshot* and *slugs,* all of which cause injuries and deaths.

shoulder-to-shoulder (adj.), **shoulder to shoulder** (adv.) The policemen stood shoulder to shoulder. The policemen were aligned in a shoulder-to-shoulder formation.

showoff (n., adj.), **show off** (v.)

shrapnel Lethal metal fragments produced by explosions of artillery shells and other military ordnance. Named for Henry Shrapnel, a British general who designed the first shells filled with small steel balls in the early 19th century. Use only in connection with military weapons. Fragments produced by accidental industrial explosions, for instance, are not *shrapnel*. See **weapons**.

shutdown (n.), **shut down** (v.)

shutout (n., adj.), **shut out** (v.)

shuttle See **space shuttle** and **National Aeronautics and Space Administration**.

sic Do not use *sic* unless it is in the original matter being quoted.

SIDS Acceptable on second reference for *sudden infant death syndrome*.

Sicily In datelines: *PALERMO, Sicily, Nov 8(UPI)* — .

sickout One word in reference to protesting employees who call in sick.

side-by-side (adj.), **side by side** (adv.) They stood side by side. They were posted in side-by-side columns.

siege Not *seige*.

Sierra Leone Country in West Africa next to Guinea and Liberia. The form for datelines: *FREETOWN, Sierra Leone, Sept. 10 (UPI)* — .

Sierra Nevada Not *Sierra Nevada Mountains. (Sierra means range of mountains; Nevada means snowy.)*

(sieze) Spell it *seize.*

sightsee, sightseer, sightseeing

Simoniz A trademark for a car wax.

Silicon Alley An area of high-tech activities in New York.

Silicon Valley An area of high-tech activities in the Santa Clara Valley southeast of San Francisco.

Sinai Not *the Sinai.* But: *the Sinai Desert, the Sinai peninsula.*

Singapore Stands alone in datelines.

single-handed

sir It may be used before the given name of a knight or baronet: Sir Winston Churchill, Sir Winston. See **honorary titles**.

sister Capitalize in all references before the names of nuns. Lowercase *sister* or *nun* standing alone.

If no surname is given, the name is the same in all references: Sister Agnes Rita. If a surname is used in first reference, drop the given name on second reference: Sister Clare Regina Torpy on first reference, Sister Torpy in second.

Handle *mother* the same way when referring to a woman who heads a group of nuns. See **religious titles**.

sister-in-law (s.), **sisters-in-law** (pl.)

sit-in (n., adj.)

Six Day War The Arab-Israeli war of 1967.

sizable Not *sizeable.*

sizes Use figures: a size 9 dress, size 40 long, 10½ B shoes, a 34½ sleeve.

skeptic See **cynic, skeptic**.

ski (s.), **skis** (pl.), **skier, skied, skiing** Also: **ski jump, ski jumping**.

skid row The term originated as *skid road* in the Pacific Northwest to indicate a trail along which newly cut logs were skidded; then was applied to the section of town where loggers gathered in taverns, inns, etc. In time, the term spread to other cities as a description for sections, such as the Bowery in New York, that were havens for derelicts. In the process, *row* replaced *road* in most instances.

skin diving (n.), **skin-diving** (adj.), **skin-dive** (v.)

slander See **libel**.

slang Slang generally is considered substandard usage, unlike colloquial usage, which is merely informal. Use slang (Examples: *short snort* for a drink of liquor, *bash* for a party) only if the occasion demands it. If used, do not self-consciously enclose it in quotation marks unless it is a direct quotation. See **argot** and **jargon**.

slaying See **homicide**.

sleet Ice pellets formed from frozen raindrops or refrozen melted snowflakes. Sleet, like small hail, usually bounces when it hits a hard surface.

-slide *Landslide,* but *mud slide, rock slide, earth slide.*

Slovakia Country in Central Europe (formerly the eastern part of Czechoslovakia). In 1993, Czechoslovakia was divided into Slovakia and the Czech Republic. The capital of Slovakia is *Bratislava.* See **Czech Republic.**

slumlord

slush fund

small arms In military usage, generally refers to rifles and machine guns. See **weapons.**

small-arms fire

small-business man Owner of a small business.

smashup (n., adj.), **smash up** (v.)

Smithsonian Institution Not *Smithsonian Institute.*

Smokey Or *Smokey Bear.* Not *Smokey the Bear.* But: *a smoky room.*

smolder Not *smoulder.*

snafu Lowercase acronym for the euphemistic *situation normal all fouled up.*

SN Brussels Airlines Replaced *Sabena Belgian World Airlines,* which declared bankruptcy in 2001. SN flies to cities in Europe and Africa. Headquarters is in Brussels.

(snuck) A dialect variant of *sneaked.* Avoid it.

SNOBOL Acronym for *String-Oriented Symbolic Language,* a high-level programming language.

so-called Redundant when used to modify a noun in quotes.

soccer Some frequently used terms:

attacker	corner kick	red card
back	free kick	striker
breakaway	goalkeeper	throw-in
center circle	header	volley
chest trap	midfielder	yellow card
chip pass	offsides	

The international championship every four years is the *World Cup.*

socialist, socialism Lowercase unless the reference clearly is to the Socialist Party or its members. See **political parties**.

Social Security Capitalize references to the U.S. system. Hyphenate the figures: *000-00-0000.*

Society for the Prevention of Cruelty to Animals *SPCA* is acceptable on second reference.

The *American Society for the Prevention of Cruelty to Animals* is limited to the five boroughs of New York City. The autonomous chapters in other cities ordinarily precede the organization by the name of the city. On first reference: the Philadelphia Society for the Prevention of Cruelty to Animals. On second reference: the Philadelphia SPCA.

In Britain it is the *Royal Society for the Prevention of Cruelty to Animals.*

Society of Friends See Quakers.

soft drink, softhearted, softgoods, soft landing, soft-shell, soft-shoe, soft-spoken

software Programs (or a program) that tell computers what to do. The term *software program* is redundant. Capitalize such titles as *WordPerfect* or *MacPaint,* but use quotation marks for computer games: *"Minesweeper."* See **hardware**.

solicitor See **lawyer**.

soliloquy (s.), **soliloquies** (pl.)

Solid South Those Southern states once regarded as unfailing supporters of the Democratic Party.

somebody, someone, someday, something, somehow, someplace, sometime, somewhat, somewhere

sonar Lowercase acronym for *sound navigation and ranging,* a system by which surface vessels find submerged submarines by transmitting high frequency sound waves through water and registering their reflections.

song titles See **composition titles**.

son-in-law, sons-in-law

SOS The distress signal. The trademark for the soap pad is *S.O.S* (no final period).

sound barrier The speed of sound — no longer a barrier, because it has been exceeded. See **Mach number.**

South As defined by the U.S. Census Bureau, the 16-state region is broken into three divisions.

- The four *East South Central* states are Alabama, Kentucky, Mississippi and Tennessee.
- The eight *South Atlantic* states are Delaware, Florida, Georgia, Maryland, North Carolina, South Carolina, Virginia and West Virginia.
- The four *West South Central* states are Arkansas, Louisiana, Oklahoma and Texas.

See **North Central region, Northeast region** and **West** for the bureau's other breakdowns. Also see **directions.**

South America

South Carolina Abbreviation: *S.C.* See **state(s).**

South Dakota Abbreviation: *S.D.* See **state(s).**

Southeast Asia Treaty Organization *SEATO* is acceptable on second reference.

Southwest Airlines Headquarters is at Love Field, Dallas.

Soviet Union Acceptable in all references in the body of a story for the former *Union of Soviet Socialist Republics (U.S.S.R.).* See **Commonwealth of Independent States** and **Russia.**

Space Age It began Oct. 4, 1957, with the launching of Sputnik 1.

space agency See **National Aeronautics and Space Administration.**

space centers See **John F. Kennedy Space Center** and **Lyndon B. Johnson Space Center.**

spacecraft The plural also is *spacecraft.* Use Arabic figures and capitalize the proper name: Gemini 7, Apollo 11. See **NASA.**

space shuttle A winged spacecraft designed to transport people and equipment between Earth and an orbiting space station.

Lowercase *space shuttle,* but capitalize, without quotation marks, any proper name: the Enterprise. See **NASA.** In datelines: *ABOARD THE SPACE SHUTTLE ENTERPRISE, May 3 (UPI) —*

Spam A trademark for a kind of canned luncheon meat.

spam Lowercase in reference to unsolicited advertising and junk e-mail on the Internet. If the word is used in quoted matter, or elsewhere, it should be explained. (The term apparently came from a television comedy skit.)

231

Spanish names In general, Spanish names consist of one or more given names followed by the father's family name and then the mother's family name. For example, **Xavier Perez Suarez** is the son of **Eduardo** *Perez* Santiago and Juanita *Suarez* Lopez. The short form, which is common, uses just the father's family name: **Xavier Perez.** On second reference, use only the father's family name (**Perez**) unless an individual has another preference, such as compounding family names: **Perez-Santiago.**

   People often have two first names: **Luis Jose Martínez Sanchez.** On second reference: **Martínez.**

   Women in Spain do not give up their family names when they marry, so Juanita Suarez Lopez always has that name. But in some Latin American countries a wife legally takes her husband's name, often using *de* between them: **Juanita Suarez Lopez de Perez.** On second reference, **Perez.**

speaker Capitalize as a formal title before a name. Generally, it is a formal title only for the speaker of a legislative body: **Speaker John Williams.**

special agent Capitalize before a name: **FBI Special Agent Heather James.** Lowercase elsewhere: **She is an FBI special agent.**

species Same in singular and plural. Use singular or plural verbs and pronouns depending on the sense: **The species has been unable to maintain itself. Both species are extinct.**

speeches Capitalize and use quotation marks for their formal titles, as described in **composition titles.**

speechmaker, speechmaking, speechwriter

speed of sound See **Mach number.**

speeds Use figures: **The car coasted at 7 mph, winds of 5 to 10 mph, winds of 7 to 9 knots, 10-knot wind, a 5 mph wind.**

speedup (n., adj.), **speed up** (v.)

spelling For words not in this stylebook, consult *Webster's New World College Dictionary.* See **dictionaries** and **geographic names.**

spill, spilled, spilling Not *spilt* in the past tense.

spinoff

split infinitive See **verbs.**

spokesman, spokeswoman Not *spokesperson.* Use *a representative* if you do not know the gender of the person.

sportscaster

sportswriter

sport utility vehicle No hyphen. *SUV* is acceptable on second reference. See **four-wheel-drive.**

spot-check

spot market A market for buying or selling commodities for cash and immediate delivery.

spreadsheet, spreadsheet program A program that organizes numerical data into rows and columns on a computer screen, simulating an accountant's worksheet.

spring, springtime See **seasons**.

sputnik Lowercase unless used with a figure as part of a proper name: Sputnik 1.

squad The basic unit of infantry in the U.S. Army and Marine Corps, usually containing about a dozen men. Two or more squads compose a *platoon*. Lowercase in all usage. See **military units** and **platoon**.

squadron A group of warships comprising two or more divisions; a unit of armored cavalry consisting of two or more troops; a military flight formation composed of about a dozen fighters or bombers, the basic U.S. Air Force tactical unit. Capitalize numbered units: 34th Fighter Squadron, 3rd Reconnaissance Squadron. Otherwise lowercase: the squadron, squadron commander. See **military units, troops,** and **group**.

square Do not abbreviate. Capitalize as part of a proper name: Washington Square.

square feet Do not abbreviate. See **dimensions**.

squinting modifier Avoid a misplaced adverb that can be interpreted as modifying either of two words: Those who lie often are found out.

Sr. See **junior, senior**.

Sri Lanka Formerly *Ceylon*. An island country off the southeast tip of India. The people are *Sri Lankans* or *Ceylonese*. In datelines: *COLOMBO, Sri Lanka, Nov. 9 (UPI) —*

S.S. Kresge Co. Now *Kmart*. Headquarters is in Troy, Mich.

SST Acceptable in all references for a supersonic transport.

stadium (s.), **stadiums** (pl.) Capitalize only when part of a proper name: Yankee Stadium.

stairsteps

stakeout

Stalin, Josef Not Joseph.

Standard & Poor's Register of Corporations The source for determining the formal name of a business. The register is published by Standard & Poor's Corp. of New York. See **company**.

standard-bearer Hyphenated.

standard time Capitalize *Eastern Standard Time, Pacific Standard Time,* etc., but lowercase *standard time* when standing alone. See **time**.

233

stand-in (n.), **stand in** (v.)

standoff (n., adj.), **stand off** (v.)

standout (n.), **stand out** (v.)

starboard See **port**.

"The Star-Spangled Banner" But lowercase: *the national anthem.*

START Acronym for *Strategic Arms Reduction Treaty* (or *Talks*). *START treaty* (or *talks*) is technically redundant, but like *SALT talks,* it is usually necessary for clarity. See **SALT.**

"Star Wars" Uppercase in quotes. High up, refer to *Strategic Defense Initiative,* abbreviating it *SDI.*

state(s) Usually lowercase: New York state, the state of Washington. Also: state Rep. William Smith, the state Transportation Department, state funds, state church, state bank, state of mind, state of the art. See **lie in state.**

Capitalize as part of a proper name: the U.S. Department of State, Washington State University.

Four states — Kentucky, Massachusetts, Pennsylvania and Virginia — are legally known as *commonwealths* rather than states. Make the distinction only in formal uses: The commonwealth of Kentucky filed a suit. Elsewhere: Tobacco is grown in the state of Kentucky.

Always spell out the names of the 50 U.S. states standing alone.

With the name of a community, some states are abbreviated in stories, datelines or with party affiliation. See **datelines** and **party affiliations.**

Rule of thumb: Spell out *Alaska* and *Hawaii* and each of the 48 contiguous states with five or fewer letters.

Ala.	Ind.	Neb.	S.C.
Alaska	Iowa	Nev.	S.D.
Ariz.	Kan.	N.H.	Tenn.
Ark.	Ky.	N.J.	Texas
Calif.	La.	N.M.	Utah
Colo.	Md.	N.Y.	Va.
Conn.	Maine	N.C.	Vt.
Del.	Mass.	N.D.	Wash.
Fla.	Mich.	Ohio	W.Va.
Ga.	Minn.	Okla.	Wis.
Hawaii	Miss.	Ore.	Wyo.
Idaho	Mo.	Pa.	
Ill.	Mont.	R.I.	

Postal abbreviations: Do not use postal abbreviations unless a story includes a mailing address, in which case the postal code would be used as part of the address: 100 Main St., Anywhere, PA 12345.

These are the postal abbreviations:

Alabama (AL)	Montana (MT)
Alaska (AK)	Nebraska (NE)
Arizona (AZ)	Nevada (NV)
Arkansas (AR)	New Hampshire (NH)
California (CA)	New Jersey (NJ)
Colorado (CO)	New Mexico (NM)
Connecticut (CT)	New York (NY)
Delaware (DE)	North Carolina (NC)
District of Columbia (DC)	North Dakota (ND)
Florida (FL)	Ohio (OH)
Georgia (GA)	Oklahoma (OK)
Hawaii (HI)	Oregon (OR)
Idaho (ID)	Pennsylvania (PA)
Illinois (IL)	Rhode Island (RI)
Indiana (IN)	South Carolina (SC)
Iowa (IA)	South Dakota (SD)
Kansas (KS)	Tennessee (TN)
Kentucky (KY)	Texas (TX)
Louisiana (LA)	Utah (UT)
Maine (ME)	Virginia (VA)
Maryland (MD)	Vermont (VT)
Massachusetts (MA)	Washington (WA)
Michigan (MI)	West Virginia (WV)
Minnesota (MN)	Wisconsin (WI)
Mississippi (MS)	Wyoming (WY)
Missouri (MO)	

statehouse Capitalize the name of a specific building: She saw the *Massachusetts Statehouse*. She saw the *Statehouse*.

Lowercase generic or plural uses: It has *no statehouse*. The *Massachusetts and Rhode Island statehouses*.

state of the art, state-of-the-art (adj.) Technically sophisticated; representing the highest level of achievement.

State of the Union Lowercase unless the reference is to the president's annual address: "The state of the union is good," the president said in his State of the Union address.

state police Capitalize with a state name, lowercase without it: the Virginia State Police, the state police.

states' rights

statewide

stationary, stationery To stand still is to be *stationary;* writing paper is *stationery.*

statute mile Equal to 5,280 feet or 1.6 kilometers.

(stay) Avoid this legal term, even in court stories. Use a clearer word, such as *postpone* or *delay.*

steady-state theory See **big-bang theory**.

stealth bomber, stealth fighter Lowercase.

steelmaker, steelworker

stem cell (n.), **stem-cell** (adj.)

stepbrother, stepfather, stepmother, stepsister

steppingstone

stere One cubic meter.

St. John's The city in Newfoundland. Not to be confused with *Saint John,* New Brunswick.

St. Louis The city in Missouri stands alone in datelines.

stockbroker

storyteller

strait Capitalize as part of a proper name: Bering Strait, Strait of Gibraltar.

straitjacket Not straightjacket.

Strategic Air Command *SAC* is acceptable on second reference.

street See **addresses**.

strikebreaker

strip mine, strip mining

student See **pupil**.

Student Loan Marketing Association Its nickname, *Sallie Mae,* may be used on second reference.

Styrofoam A trademark for a brand of plastic foam.

sub- Hyphenate with a capitalized word: sub-Mycenaean. Elsewhere, follow *Webster's New World College Dictionary,* hyphenating words not listed there.

subcommittee Capitalize the formal names of subcommittees: the Subcommittee on Energy and Power, or the Armed Services Committee's Investigations Subcommittee. Lowercase *subcommittee* when used only with the name of the parent committee: a Ways and Means subcommittee.

subcontinent Lowercase in all uses.

(subfreezing) *Freezing* means the same thing and is shorter. See **freeze**.

236

subject See **citizen**.

subjunctive mood Use this verb form to express desire, hypothesis, possibility and contingency, conditions contrary to fact:

His supporters wish he *were* better qualified.
If the election were over, he *would* resign.
He *would have* won if he *were* not so lazy.
Should he decide to run again, it *would* be a tragedy.
Were he a younger man, he *would* be able to try again.

submachine gun (n.), **submachine-gun** (adj.), **submachine-gunner** See **weapons, machine gun**.

subpoena, subpoenaed, subpoenaing Not *subpena*.

(succoth) See **sukkot**.

sudden infant death syndrome Lowercase. *SIDS* is acceptable on second reference.

suffixes See separate listings for commonly used suffixes.

Follow *Webster's New World College Dictionary* for words not covered in this book. If a word combination is not listed in *Webster's New World,* use two words for the verb form; hyphenate any noun or adjective forms.

suit, suite You can have a *suit of armor,* a *suit of clothes,* follow *suit* in cards, *bring suit* in court, *suit yourself* if you wish or *suit up* in uniform.

There are *suites* of music, rooms and furniture.

sukkot The Jewish Feast of Tabernacle, celebrating the fall harvest and commemorating the desert wandering of the Jews during the Exodus. Occurs in September or October.

summer, summertime See **seasons**.

sun Always lowercase.

sunbathe, sunbathed, sunbather (n.), **sunbathing** (v.)

Sun Belt Generally those states in the South and West, ranging from Florida and Georgia through the Gulf States and including California.

Sunday See **days**.

Sunday school Lowercase *school.*

Sun Microsystems Manufacturer of Unix-based workstations. Headquarters is in Mountain View, Calif.

Sunni, Sunnites The Muslim sect and its members.

super- Hyphenate with a capitalized word: super-Republican. Elsewhere, follow *Webster's New World College Dictionary,* hyphenating words not listed there.

Super Bowl The annual professional football championship game. Roman numerals are used in the formal name: Super Bowl XXXVII.

superintendent Do not abbreviate. Capitalize as a formal title before a name.

superpower

supersede

supersonic See **Mach number**.

supersonic transport *SST* is acceptable in all references.

supine Lying on the back, face upward. See **prone**.

supra- Hyphenate with a capitalized word or to avoid a double *a:* supra-auditory. Elsewhere, follow *Webster's New World College Dictionary,* hyphenating words not listed there.

Supreme Court of the United States Also: the *U.S. Supreme Court, the Supreme Court.* The chief justice is properly the *chief justice of the United States,* not *of the Supreme Court.* The other eight members are *associate justices.* They are addressed as either *justice* or *associate justice.*

supreme courts of the states Capitalize with a state name, or without it if the state is understood: the New Jersey Supreme Court, the state Supreme Court, the Supreme Court.

    If a court with this name is not a state's highest tribunal, the fact should be noted. In New York state, for example, the Supreme Court is a trial court. The state's highest court is the Court of Appeals.

Supreme Soviet The principal legislative body of the former Soviet Union.

surface-to-air missile(s) *SAM(s)* is acceptable on second reference. Avoid the redundant *SAM missiles.*

suspensive hyphenation The form: The 5- *and* 6-year-olds attend morning classes.

SUV Acceptable on second reference for *sport utility vehicle.*

swear in (v.), **swearing-in** (adj.)

sweat shirt

swim (present tense), **swam** (past tense), **swum** (past participle)

Swissair Headquarters is in Zurich.

Sybase Inc. Publisher of database management systems. Headquarters is in Emeryville, Calif.

Sydney The city in Australia stands alone in datelines.

syllabus (s.), **syllabuses** (pl.)

Symantec Publisher of software that includes Norton Utilities. Headquarters is in Cupertino, Calif.

synagogue Capitalize only when part of a formal name.

Synagogue Council of America See **Jewish congregations**.

synod A council of churches. Lowercase unless part of a proper name. See entries for each denomination.

Syrian Catholic Church See **Eastern Rite churches**.

system administrator Person responsible for running a computer system.

T

Tabasco A trademark for a hot pepper sauce.

tablespoon, tablespoonful, tablespoonfuls Not *tablespoonsful.* Do not abbreviate. Equal to three teaspoons or one-half a fluid ounce. In metric it is about 15 milliliters. See **recipes**.

table tennis See **Ping Pong**.

tabular matter Normal style rules for abbreviations do not apply to tabular matter. Use whatever abbreviations are necessary to make tabular matter fit, with or without periods or capital letters. But make the abbreviations as clear as possible.

tail coat, tail end, tail fin, tail wind, but **tailgate, taillamp, taillight, tailpipe, tailrace, tailspin**

Taiwan Use *Taiwan,* not *Formosa,* in references to the Nationalist government on Taiwan and to the island itself. See **China**.

take- Usually solid: takedown, takeoff, takeout, takeover, takeup, but take-home pay.

Taliban Fundamentalist Islamic movement in Afghanistan. *Taliban* is the plural of *Talib* (student or seeker of religious knowledge): The Taliban were in power; the Taliban are seeking, etc.

Talmud The collection of writings constituting the Jewish civil and religious law.

Tammany, Tammany Hall, Tammany Society

tanks *M1 Abrams, M1A1 (M1A2) Abrams* (named for the late Gen. General Creighton W. Abrams), *M-80, M-60.* Plural: *M1A1s, M-80s,* etc.

tape recording (n.), **tape-record** (v.)

taps Lowercase, no quotation marks. A signal, not a song title.

targeted An overused vogue verb for *selected* or *chosen*. Use it carefully.

Tass Acceptable in all references to the Russian government's news agency. Its official name is *ITAR-Tass. ITAR* is an acronym for *Information Telegraph Agency of Russia.*

task force

teachers college No apostrophe.

teammate

Teamsters union Acceptable in all references to the *International Brotherhood of Teamsters, Chauffeurs, Warehousemen and Helpers of America.* Headquarters is in Washington.

teamwork

tear gas Two words.

teaspoon, teaspoonful, teaspoonfuls Not *teaspoonsful.* Equal to one-sixth of a fluid ounce, or one-third of a tablespoon. In metric it is about 5 milliliters. See **recipes.**

Technicolor A trademark for a process of making color motion pictures.

teen, teenager (n.), **teenage** (adj.) Do not use *teenaged.* Restrict use to those 13 through 17 years old, treating those 18 and over as adults.

(tee shirt) Spell it *T-shirt.*

Teflon A trademark for a brand of non-stick coating.

Tehran Not *Teheran.* The capital of Iran.

telecast (n.), **televise** (v.)

telecommuting Performing work from home (or elsewhere outside the office) via a computer link to the office.

telephone numbers Use figures. The forms: (212) 682-0400, 682-0400. If extension numbers are given: extension 2, extension 364.

TelePrompTer Note capital letters. A trademark for a type of cuing device.

Teletype A trademark for a brand of teleprinter or teletypewriter.

television *TV* is acceptable in any informal reference to television if it fits the occasion. Also: *a TV dinner, cable TV.*

Resist the temptation to write: Her speech will be on national television when it will also be on radio. Better: Her speech will be broadcast nationally on radio and television.

The call letters alone are often adequate to refer to an individual station. But when needed use lowercase: television station WTEV. If needed for clarity: WSB-AM, WSB-FM, WSB-TV.

Capitalize a channel with a figure, lowercase elsewhere: He tuned to Channel 3. No channel will broadcast the game.

television *continued*

For television shows, use quotation marks for both the series and for individual episodes: "The Trouble with Tribbles" was a popular episode of "Star Trek." See **composition titles**.

telex, Telex (n.) Short for *Teletypewriter Exchange*. A communications system or a message sent through the system. Capitalize only if referring to a specific company. Do not use as a verb.

temblor See **earthquakes**.

temperatures Use figures for all except *zero*. In stories, use a word, not a minus sign, to indicate temperatures below zero.

> *Wrong:* The temperature was -10.
> *Right:* The low was minus 10. The low was 10 below zero. The temperature rose to zero by noon. The high was expected to be 9 or 10.
> *Also:* 5-degree temperatures, temperatures fell 5 degrees, temperatures in the 30s (no apostrophe).

The minus sign is acceptable for below-zero temperatures in tabular material.

Temperatures get *higher or lower,* not *warmer or cooler.*

> *Wrong:* Temperatures are expected to warm up in the area Friday.
> *Right:* Temperatures are expected to rise in the area Friday.

See **Fahrenheit** and **Celsius**.

To convert Fahrenheit to Celsius subtract 32 degrees and multiply by 5, divide by 9. To convert Celsius to Fahrenheit, multiply by 9, divide by 5 and add 32 degrees. Some typical conversions:

F	C	F	C	F	C
-40	-40	34	1	86	30
-30	-34	40	4	90	32
-20	-29	50	10	95	35
-10	-23	60	16	98	37
0	-18	68	20	100	38
10	-12	70	21	104	40
20	7	75	24	110	43
30	1	80	27	120	49
32	0	85	29		

Ten Commandments Do not abbreviate or use figures.

Ten Most Wanted Acceptable on first reference for *Ten Most Wanted Fugitives* (the FBI list). Do not use the figure *10*.

Tennessee Abbreviation: *Tenn.* See **state(s)**.

tera- A prefix meaning *1 trillion;* a *terahertz* is 1,000 billion hertz. See **metric system**.

terabyte A trillion bytes (actually 1,099,511,627,776). Equal to 1,000 gigabytes. See **byte, kilobyte, megabyte, giga-**.

terrorism, terrorist *Terrorism*, or an act of terror, is the use or threat of violence — particularly against civilians — to demoralize, intimidate or subjugate, especially to further a political or ideological goal. Be careful about using the term *terrorist* to describe specific people, and in general avoid it in favor of more specific descriptive terms: *the bomber, shooter,* etc. Also, in general avoid applying the term to an organization when another term such as *paramilitary group* is more appropriate. While al-Qaida openly embraces terrorism and may be called a terrorist organization, other groups are seen as terrorists by some but not others — and in those cases, attribute the label: Hamas, which the United States and European Union have labeled as a terrorist group. Avoid using *terrorists* as a synonym for militants or protesters.

terrace Do not abbreviate. See **addresses**.

Texaco Inc. Headquarters is in White Plains, N.Y.

Texas Do not abbreviate. See **state(s)**.

Textile Workers union See **Union of Needletrades, Industrial and Textile Employees**.

texts, transcripts Make texts and transcripts conform to UPI style guidelines for spelling, capitalization and abbreviations.

Use quotation marks only for words that were quoted in the text or by the speaker.

See **colon** for style on dialogue and Q-and-A forms. Use an ellipsis to mark an omission of one or more words within a quoted passage. See **ellipsis**.

Thai A native, or the language of Thailand. Use *Siamese* for the cat.

Thanksgiving, Thanksgiving Day The fourth Thursday in November.

that, which Use *who* and *whom,* not *that* or *which,* to refer to people or to animals with a name: Jones was the man who helped me. See **who, whom**.

Use the pronouns *that* and *which* to refer to inanimate objects and to animals without a name.

that, which *continued*

Use *which* to introduce a parenthetical clause. Set the clause off with commas: The books, which have no salvage value, will be destroyed. (All the books will be destroyed. The parenthetical clause could be dropped from the sentence without changing its meaning.)

Use *that* to introduce a clause essential to a sentence. Do not set the clause off with commas: The books that have no salvage value will be destroyed. (Only those books with no salvage value will be destroyed. The clause is essential to the sentence.)

A rule of thumb: If *that* will fit comfortably, use it, and do not set the clause off with commas.

theater Spelled with *-er* unless the theater spells its proper name with *-re.*

theft *Theft* is the general term and *larceny* the legal term for stealing.

Burglary implies entering a building (not necessarily by breaking in) with the intention of committing a crime.

Robbery, in a legal sense, implies violence or intimidation in committing a theft. In its popular sense, it means *to steal in any way or to deprive someone of something:* The accident robbed him of his health.

Remember, too, that you *rob* a person, bank, or house, but you *steal* the money or the jewels.

then Do not use *then* before a title to denote the action of a person who formerly held the title.

> *Wrong:* In 2000 then-Gov. George W. Bush ran for president.
> *Right:* In 2000 Gov. George W. Bush ran for president.

thermos Formerly a trademark, now a generic term for any vacuum bottle, although one manufacturer still uses the word as a brand name. Lowercase *thermos* to mean any vacuum bottle; use *Thermos* to refer to the specific brand.

think tank

Third World The economically developing nations of Africa, Asia and Latin America. Not to be confused with *non-aligned nations,* a political term. See **non-aligned nations.**

(this) Do not use *this* to refer back to a dateline community. If a distinction must be made, repeat the name of the community.

(three-D) *3-D* is preferred.

three R's Reading, 'riting and 'rithmetic.

Thursday See **days.**

Tidewater The coastal section of Virginia.

tie (s.), **ties** (pl.), **tied, tying**

till, ('til) *Till* is a synonym for *until;* *'til* is a superfluous substandard contraction; don't use it.

time Specify the time in a story if it is pertinent: a wreck at 3 a.m. Tuesday gives a clearer picture than simply a wreck Tuesday.

Time zones usually are not needed: a wreck at 3 a.m. is clear without the time zone.

In the continental United States use the time in the dateline community. Outside the continental United States provide a conversion to Eastern time, if pertinent: The kidnappers set a 9 a.m. (3 a.m. EDT) deadline. The forms:

1. Use figures except for *noon* and *midnight.* Use a colon to separate hours from minutes: 11 a.m. EST, 1 p.m. today, 3:30 p.m. Monday. Avoid redundancies such as 10 a.m. this morning. Also, if clear: 4 o'clock.

2. For sequences, use figures, colons and periods: 2:30:21.6 (hours, minutes, seconds, tenths).

3. The time zones in the United States may be abbreviated as *EST, PDT,* etc., if linked with a clock reading: noon EDT, 9 a.m. MST. Do not abbreviate if there is no clock reading. Do not abbreviate other time zones outside the United States.

4. Capitalize each word of the proper name: Chicago observes Central Daylight Time in the summer. But: Denver is in the Mountain time zone.

5. Do not abbreviate time zones outside the United States. Exception: *Greenwich Mean Time* may be abbreviated as *GMT* on second reference if used with a clock reading. See **daylight-saving time**.

TimeWarner (No space.) Its companies include *America Online; Turner Broadcasting (CNN, TBS, TNT, Atlanta Braves, Hawks, Thrashers); Time Inc. (Time Magazine, Fortune, People, Sports Illustrated); HBO and Warner Bros.* Headquarters is in New York.

Timor-Leste Note the hyphen.

tip-off (n.), **tipped off** (v.)

titles Capitalize all formal titles before a name; lowercase them when they follow a name or stand alone. Some specifics:

1. Lowercase and spell out all titles not used with a name: The president issued a statement. The pope gave his blessing. The treasury secretary was present.

2. Lowercase and spell out all titles set off from a name by commas: The vice president, Al Gore, attended the ceremony. Paul VI, the current pope, does not plan to retire.

titles *continued*

3. Capitalize *Mr., Mrs., Miss, Ms.* See **courtesy titles**.
4. Capitalize formal titles with names: Pope Paul, President Washington, Vice Presidents John Garner and Nelson Rockefeller.
5. Lowercase titles that are primarily job descriptions: astronaut John Glenn, movie star Tom Hanks, peanut farmer Jimmy Carter. If in doubt about whether a title is formal or merely a job description, set it off by commas and use lowercase.
6. Capitalize *king, queen, shah,* etc., only when used directly before a name. See **nobility**.
7. Set long titles off with a comma and use lowercase: Charles Robinson, undersecretary for economic affairs. Or: the undersecretary for economic affairs, Charles Robinson.
8. If a title applies to only one person in an organization, insert *the:* John Jones, the deputy vice president, spoke.

See **abbreviations and acronyms, Cabinet titles, composition titles, honorary titles, legislative titles, military titles** and **religion**.

titleholder

TNT Preferred in all references for *trinitrotoluene.*

tobacco (s.), **tobaccos** (pl.) Tobacco is widely cultivated for its leaves. The mixture was a blend of fine tobaccos.

Tobago See **Trinidad and Tobago**.

(today) Use only in direct quotations and in phrases that do not refer to a specific day: Today's students may turn to the Internet for help with homework. Use the actual day of the week in all other cases. See **days** and **time**.

Tokyo The capital of Japan stands alone in datelines.

tollhouse, tollhouse cookies

Tommy Gun Trademark for a .45-caliber Thompson submachine gun. See **weapons**.

(tomorrow) Use only in direct quotations and in phrases that do not refer to a specific day: The sergeant said there would be no tomorrow if the mission failed. Use the actual day of the week in all other cases. See **days** and **time**.

ton There are three different types:
- A *short ton* is equal to 2,000 pounds.
- A *long ton,* also known as a *British ton,* is equal to 2,240 pounds.
- A *metric ton* is equal to 1,000 kilograms, or approximately 2,204.62 pounds.

Conversion equations:
- Short to long: Multiply by .89 (5 tons × .89 equals 4.45 long).
- Short to metric: Multiply by .9 (5 tons × .9 equals 4.5 metric).
- Long to short: Multiply by 1.12 (5 long tons × 1.12 equals 5.6 short).
- Long to metric: Multiply by 1.02 (5 long × 1.02 equals 5.1 metric).
- Metric to short: Multiply by 1.1 (5 metric × 1.1 equals 5.5 short).
- Metric to long: Multiply by .94 (5 metric × .94 equals 4.7 long).

(tonight) Use only in direct quotations. See **days** and **time**.

tornado A violent rotating air column that touches the ground. It usually starts as a funnel cloud and is accompanied by a loud roaring noise. On a local scale, it is the most destructive of all atmospheric phenomena. A *tornado warning* warns that a tornado exists or is suspected to exist. A *tornado watch* alerts of the possibility of a tornado.

Toronto The city in Canada stands alone in datelines.

topsy-turvy.

Tory (s.), **Tories** (pl.) Acceptable on second reference to the *Conservative Party* in Britain and its members.

total, totaled, totaling

toward Not *towards*.

town See **city**.

town council See **city council**.

town house

township Do not abbreviate. See **city**.

Toys "R" Us

trade-in (n., adj.), **trade in** (v.)

trade-off (n., adj.), **trade off** (v.)

trademark A trademark is a brand, symbol or word registered by a manufacturer or dealer and protected by law to prevent others from using it. Trademarks normally should be used only if they are essential to a story. But sometimes they will lend an air of reality to a story: The governor drove a Plymouth to the party may be preferable to the less specific *automobile*.

When a trademark is used, capitalize it.

Separate entries list common trademarks, followed by a generic term:

Styrofoam A trademark for a plastic foam.

In such an entry, *plastic foam* is the generic and preferred term.

trademark *continued*

If you have questions on other trademarks, or words you think might be trademarks, the U.S. Trademark Association is in New York.

traffic, trafficked, trafficking

trampoline Formerly a trademark, now a generic term.

trans- Hyphenate with a capitalized word: trans-Atlantic, trans-Pacific. Follow *Webster's New World College Dictionary,* hyphenating words not listed there.

transcripts See **texts, transcripts**.

transfer, transferred, transferring

Transportation Communications International Union *TCU* may be used on second reference. Headquarters is in Rockville, Md. Note: The union was once known as the *Brotherhood of Railway, Airline and Steamship Clerks, Freight Handlers, Express and Station Employees.*

transsexual

Trans World Airlines *TWA,* which had flown for more than 70 years, was merged into American Airlines in 2001.

travel, traveled, traveling, traveler

travelogue Not *travelog.*

treasurer Capitalize as a formal title before a name. Caution: The secretary of the U.S. Department of the Treasury (*secretary of the treasury* or *treasury secretary*) is not the same person as the U.S. treasurer.

treasury bill, treasury bond, treasury note See **loan terminology**.

trees See **plants**.

tri- Hyphenate with a capitalized word or to avoid a double *i:* tri-iode. Follow *Webster's New World College Dictionary,* hyphenating words not listed there.

tribes See **nationalities**.

trigger-happy

trimonthly Every three months.

TriMotor The proper name of a three-engine airplane once made by Ford Motor Co.

Trinidad and Tobago In datelines on stories from this island nation, use a city name followed by either Trinidad or Tobago — but not both — depending on where the city is located: *PORT-OF-SPAIN, Trinidad, Nov. 19 (UPI)* — .

(trio) Journalese for *a group of three.* Avoid it.

TriStar The name that Lockheed Aircraft Corp. used for L-1011 jetliners made between 1968 and the early 1980s. Note: Lockheed later merged with Martin Marietta Corp. to form *Lockheed Martin Corp.*

Trojan horse, Trojan War

troop An armored cavalry formation comparable to an infantry company, usually designated by letters. Capitalized with a lettered name: B Troop. Otherwise lowercase: the troop, troop commander. See **military units** and **squadron**.

troops Acceptable in all usage for *soldiers*. See **military titles**.

tropical storm, tropical depression Capitalize *tropical storm* as part of the name assigned to a storm: Tropical Storm Dolly. A tropical storm is a rotating wind system with a sustained surface speed from 39 to 73 mph (34 to 63 knots) inclusive. When a tropical storm loses wind speed below 39 mph, it becomes a *tropical depression*. See **hurricane**.

troublemaker, troublesome, trouble-shooter

troupe A group of theatrical performers. Not *troop*.

Truman, Harry S. With a period after the *S*.

trustee, trusty A *trustee* manages property for someone else; a *trusty* is a trustworthy person. Both are always lowercase.

tryout (n.), **try out** (v.)

(tsar) Use *czar* instead.

T-shirt Not *tee shirt*.

tuberculosis *TB* is acceptable on second reference.

Tucson The city in Arizona stands alone in datelines.

Tuesday See **days**.

tuneup (n., adj.), **tune up** (v.)

turboprop See **aircraft**.

turnpike Capitalize as part of a proper name: the Pennsylvania Turnpike. Lowercase standing alone. See **highways**.

TV Acceptable in any informal reference to *television* if it fits the occasion. Also: *a TV dinner, cable TV*. See **television**.

TVA Acceptable in all references for *Tennessee Valley Authority*.

Twelve Apostles Disciples of Jesus. Spell out *twelve*, an exception to the nine-and-under rule.

20th Century Fox, Twentieth Century Fund, Twenty-first Century Foundation Follow an organization's practice.

typhoon Capitalize as part of the name assigned to a storm: Typhoon Yutu. A typhoon is the same thing as a hurricane, except it develops west of the international date line. See **hurricane**.

U

U-boat German submarines of World War I and II vintage; no others. German subs of this era were designated by *U* numbers, *U-170, U-510,* etc. The *U* was an abbreviation for *unterseeboot.*

UFOs Acceptable in all references for *unidentified flying object(s).*

UHF Acceptable in all references for *ultrahigh frequency.*

Ukraine Not *the Ukraine.* In datelines: *KIEV, Ukraine, April 19 (UPI)* — .

Ukrainian Catholic Church See **Eastern Rite churches**.

Ulster An imprecise designation for *Northern Ireland.* Ulster properly encompasses six counties in Northern Ireland and three in the Irish Republic. Avoid it except in quotations. See **United Kingdom**.

ultra- Hyphenate with capitalized word: ultra-English, and to avoid a double *a:* ultra-ambitious. Elsewhere, follow *Webster's New World College Dictionary,* hyphenating words not listed there.

un- Hyphenate with a capitalized word: un-American. Elsewhere, follow *Webster's New World College Dictionary,* hyphenating words not listed there.

U.K. (with periods) Use it as an adjective, but not as a noun, for *United Kingdom.*

U.N. (with periods) Use it as an adjective, but not as a noun, for *United Nations.*

(Uncle Tom) A term of contempt applied to a black person, taken from the main character in Harriet Beecher Stowe's novel *Uncle Tom's Cabin.* It describes the practice of kowtowing to whites to curry favor.

Do not apply it to an individual. It carries potentially libelous connotations of having sold one's convictions for money, prestige or political influence.

undersecretary Always one word.

under way Usually two words: The project is under way. The naval maneuvers are under way. But it is one word as an adjective before a noun in a nautical sense: an underway flotilla.

unemployment rate In the United States, this estimate of the number of unemployed residents seeking work is compiled monthly by the Bureau of Labor Statistics, an agency of the Labor Department.

Each month the bureau selects a nationwide cross-section of the population and conducts interviews to determine the size of the *U.S. workforce,* defined as *the number of persons with jobs and the number looking for jobs.*

The unemployment rate is then expressed as a percentage figure. The essential calculation involves dividing the total workforce into the number of persons looking for jobs, followed by adjustments to reflect variable factors such as seasonal trends.

Note that the calculation of the unemployment rate is not based on the number of people receiving unemployment insurance.

UNESCO Acceptable on first reference for the *United Nations Educational, Scientific and Cultural Organization,* but provide the full name in the story. The organization was established in 1945. Headquarters is in Paris.

UNICEF Acceptable in all references for the *United Nations Children's Fund.* The words *International* and *Emergency,* originally part of the name, have been dropped. The organization was established in 1946. Headquarters is in New York.

Unification Church Acceptable in all references for *The Holy Spirit Association for the Unification of World Christianity.* The church was founded in Korea in 1954 by the Rev. Sun Myung Moon, who moved to the United States in 1971. Headquarters is in New York. Do not use the pejorative term *Moonies* in reference to church members.

Uniform Code of Military Justice The laws covering members of the U.S. armed forces.

uninterested See **disinterested, uninterested**.

union Capitalize as a proper name for the North during the Civil War: The Union defeated the Confederacy.

Union of American Hebrew Congregations See **Jewish congregations**.

Union of Needletrades, Industrial and Textile Employees *UNITE* is acceptable after the full name has been used. (Note: The union was

Union of Needletrades, Industrial and Textile Employees *continued*
formed in a 1995 merger of the *International Ladies Garment Workers Union* and the *Amalgamated Clothing and Textile Workers Union.*) Headquarters is in New York.

Union of Orthodox Jewish Congregations of America See **Jewish congregations.**

Union of Soviet Socialist Republics See **Russia, Soviet Union.**

unions See **local of a union** and separate entries for unions frequently in the news. See **closed shop** and **right-to-work.**

union shop, closed shop

Unipresser An employee of United Press International. See **Downhold Club.**

unique It means *one of a kind* and has no comparative form. Do not describe something as *rather unique* or *most unique.*

United Arab Emirates Do not abbreviate, even in datelines. Use *U.A.E.,* with periods, if in quoted matter.

United Auto Workers union Acceptable in all references for *United Automobile Aerospace and Agricultural Implement Workers of America. UAW* is acceptable on second reference. Headquarters is in Detroit.
Use *autoworkers* — one word, lowercase — when no specific reference to the union is intended.

United Church of Christ Do not confuse it with the Churches of Christ. See **Congregationalist churches.**

United Food and Commercial Workers International Union *Food and Commercial Workers union* is acceptable in all references. Headquarters is in Washington.

United Kingdom It encompasses Great Britain and Northern Ireland. Great Britain (or Britain) comprises England, Scotland and Wales. Ireland is independent of the United Kingdom. Spell out as a noun. Use *U.K.* (periods, no space) only as an adjective. See **datelines** and **Ireland.**

United Methodist Church See **Methodist churches.**

United Mine Workers union Acceptable in all references for *United Mine Workers of America. UMW* is acceptable on second reference. Headquarters is in Washington.
Use *mineworkers* — one word, lowercase — when no specific reference to the union is intended.

United Nations Spell out as a noun. Use *U.N.* (periods, no space) only as an adjective. In datelines: *UNITED NATIONS, Nov. 10 (UPI) —*

United Press International *UPI* is used in logotypes and is acceptable on second reference for the privately owned news agency formed in the May 16, 1958, merger of *United Press* and *International News Service*. Headquarters is in Washington.

United Service Organizations *USO* is acceptable on second reference.

United States Spell out as a noun. Use *U.S.* (periods, no space) only as an adjective.

United States Agency for International Development *USAID* is acceptable on second reference.

United States Department of Agriculture *USDA* is acceptable on second reference.

United Steelworkers union Acceptable in all references for *United Steelworkers of America*. Headquarters is in Pittsburgh.

United Synagogue of America The singular *synagogue* is correct. See **Jewish congregations**.

Unix Generic term (not an acronym) for a group of operating systems used on a wide variety of computers. *UNIX* (all caps) is a trademark for an industry consortium that defines *Unix* standards. See **Linux** and **operating system**.

(unless and until) Redundant. Avoid it.

(unveil) Journalese for *announce.*

-up Usually hyphenated in compounds: call-up, mix-up, mop-up, follow-up, but blowup, cleanup, coverup, buildup, smashup. See *Webster's New World College Dictionary.*

UPI Used in logotypes and acceptable on second reference for *United Press International.*

upload Send a file from your computer to another computer. See **download** and **FTP**.

uppercase (n., adj., v.) One word when referring to the use of capital letters.

URL (URLs) Acronym for *Uniform Resource Locator.* A standardized addressing scheme for Internet resources such as Web pages, text files, images. Every resource has a unique *URL.*

upstate Lowercase: upstate New York.

upward Not *upwards.*

U.S. (with periods)

usable Not *useable.*

USAID Acceptable on second reference for *United States Agency for International Development.*

US Airways Headquarters is in Arlington, Va. Note: The airline's former name was *USAir.*

U.S. Court of Appeals *A federal appeals court* or *a U.S. Court of Appeals* is acceptable in first reference.

Do not use *the* U.S. Court of Appeals or *the* U.S. Circuit Court of Appeals without designating which circuit.

The forms for the full name: the 8th U.S. Circuit Court of Appeals, the U.S. Court of Appeals for the 8th Circuit, the District of Columbia U.S. Circuit Court of Appeals, etc.

The jurists are called *judges,* not *justices.* See **judge**.

The court is divided into 12 circuits, as follows:

- District of Columbia Circuit: Based in Washington.
- 1st Circuit: Maine, Massachusetts, New Hampshire, Rhode Island, Puerto Rico. Sits in Boston.
- 2nd Circuit: Connecticut, New York, Vermont. Sits in New York.
- 3rd Circuit: Delaware, New Jersey, Pennsylvania, Virgin Islands. Sits in Philadelphia.
- 4th Circuit: Maryland, North Carolina, South Carolina, Virginia, West Virginia. Sits in Richmond, Va.
- 5th Circuit: Louisiana, Mississippi, Texas, Canal Zone. Sits in New Orleans.
- 6th Circuit: Kentucky, Michigan, Ohio, Tennessee. Sits in Cincinnati.
- 7th Circuit: Illinois, Indiana, Wisconsin. Sits in Chicago.
- 8th Circuit: Arkansas, Iowa, Minnesota, Missouri, Nebraska, North Dakota, South Dakota. Sits in St. Louis.
- 9th Circuit: Alaska, Arizona, California, Hawaii, Idaho, Montana, Nevada, Oregon, Washington, Guam. Sits in San Francisco.
- 10th Circuit: Colorado, Kansas, New Mexico, Oklahoma, Utah, Wyoming. Sits in Denver.
- 11th Circuit: Alabama, Florida, Georgia. Sits in Atlanta.

U.S. Court of Claims Sits in Washington. This court handles suits against the federal government.

U.S. Court of Customs and Patent Appeals Sits in Washington. This court handles appeals involving customs, patents and copyrights.

U.S. Court of Military Appeals This court, not part of the judicial branch as such, is a civilian body established by Congress to hear appeals from actions of the Defense Department.

U.S. Customs Court Sits in New York. This court handles disputes over customs duties that arise at any U.S. port of entry.

USDA Acceptable on second reference for *United States Department of Agriculture.*

U.S. District Court The federal trial courts. In shortened and subsequent references: District Court, the District Court at Richmond, Va., the court. See **judge**.

Usenet A worldwide computer-based system that supports tens of thousands of newsgroups. See **newsgroup**.

user-friendly Avoid using this term, unless it is a direct quotation.

> *Wrong:* A company official said the device is user-friendly.
> *Right:* A company official said the device is easy to use.

username

U.S. Information Agency *USIA* is acceptable on second reference.

U.S. Postal Service Directory of Post Offices The authority for the spelling of U.S. place names. See **geographic names.**

USS For *United States Ship, Steamer* or *Steamship,* before the name of a vessel: the USS Iowa. In datelines: *ABOARD THE USS IOWA, Nov. 10 (UPI) —*

U.S.S.R. The former Union of Soviet Socialist Republics. Avoid the initials unless they are in a direct quotation. Use *Soviet Union.* See **Commonwealth of Independent States, Russia** and **Soviet Union.**

U.S. Steel Acceptable in all references for *United States Steel Corp.,* which has headquarters in Pittsburgh. The company, founded in 1901, was known as *USX Corp.* for 15 years but got its original name back when USX was split up in 2001. See **Marathon Oil Corp.**

U.S. Supreme Court See **Supreme Court of the United States**.

U.S. Tax Court This is an administrative body within the U.S. Treasury Department rather than part of the judicial branch. It handles appeals in tax cases.

Utah Do not abbreviate. See **state(s)**.

UTC For *Coordinated Universal Time,* the modern equivalent of *GMT.* Because UTC is kept by atomic clocks and is more precise by fractions of seconds, it is used worldwide to coordinate technical and scientific data. UTC is also called *Zulu time, Universal Coordinated Time, Universal Time Coordinated, universal time, world time.* (The initials *UTC* were chosen as a compromise between English and French terms.) See **GMT** for conversion table.

U-turn

Uzi An unusually compact 9mm submachine gun designed by Maj. Uziel Gal of the Israeli army and used worldwide. See **weapons**.

V

VA Acceptable on second reference for the *Department of Veterans Affairs,* which adopted *VA* as its initials when it took over the old Veterans Administration.

vacuum One *c,* two *u*'s.

Valium A trademark for a tranquilizer.

valley Capitalize as part of a full name: the Mississippi Valley. Lowercase standing alone or in plural uses: the valley, the Missouri and Mississippi valleys.

Varig Brazilian Airlines *Varig* is acceptable in most references. Headquarters is in Rio de Janeiro.

Vaseline A trademark for a brand of petroleum jelly.

Vatican City Stands alone in datelines.

VCR Acceptable in all references for *video cassette recorder.*

VDT Acceptable on second reference for *video display terminal.*

V-E Day May 8, 1945, the day the surrender of Germany was announced, officially ending the European phase of World War II. The letters *V-E* stand for *Victory in Europe.*

V-8 The engine.

Velcro Trademark for a fabric fastener that can be easily pressed together and pulled apart.

venereal disease *VD* is acceptable on second reference.

verbal See **oral, verbal.**

verbs The splitting of compound verb forms, including infinitives, is not necessarily an error, but often is awkward.

An *infinitive* is a verb form containing the word *to:* to go. It is split when something separates the word *to* from its partner: to quickly go.

Avoid awkward constructions that would damage the rhythm or meaning of a sentence.

> *Awkward:* She was ordered *to immediately leave* on an assignment.
> *Better:* She was ordered *to leave immediately* on an assignment.

> *Awkward:* There stood the wagon that we *had* early last autumn *left* by the barn.
> *Better:* There stood the wagon that we *had left* by the barn early last autumn. (*Had left* is a verb form of *to leave.*)

But some constructions require that a compound verb be split. Examples:

> The budget *was* tentatively *approved.*

> I *will* not *concede* the election.

> How *has* your health *been?*

> He wanted *to* really *help* his mother.

Do not manufacture verbs from nouns.

> *Wrong:* She authored the book.
> *Right:* She wrote the book.

Verizon Communications Headquarters is in New York.
Vermont Abbreviation: *Vt.* See **state(s).**
verse See **poetry.**
versus Abbreviate as *vs.* in all uses.
very high frequency *VHF* is acceptable in all references.
Veterans Day Formerly *Armistice Day,* Nov. 11, the anniversary of the armistice that ended World War I in 1918. The federal legal holiday, observed on the fourth Monday in October during the mid-1970s, returned to Nov. 11 in 1978.
Veterans of Foreign Wars *VFW* is acceptable on second reference. Headquarters is in Kansas City, Mo.
veto (s.), **vetoes** (pl.), **vetoing**
VHF acceptable in all references for *very high frequency.*
via Means *by way of,* not *by means of.*

via *continued*

>*Wrong:* The president flew to Maine via Air Force One.
>*Right:* The president went to Cleveland via Pittsburgh.

vice- Two words in all uses:

vice admiral	vice consul	vice regent
vice chairman	vice president	vice secretary
vice chancellor	vice principal	a vice presidential candidate

Several are exceptions to *Webster's New World College Dictionary.*

vice president No hyphen. Capitalize as a formal title before a name. Vice President James Smith. Lowercase standing alone or set off by commas: the vice president, James Smith. Do not drop the first name when used with the title. Drop the title only on second reference. Also: *a vice presidential candidate.*

vice versa

Victrola Still a trademark for a brand of record player.

videodisk

video display terminal *VDT* is acceptable on second reference.

videotape (n., v.)

vie, vied, vying

Vienna The capital of Austria stands alone in datelines.

Vietnam Not *Viet Nam.* Also: *Vietnam War.* But: *The war in Vietnam.* The form in datelines: *HO CHI MINH CITY, Vietnam, Nov. 11 (UPI) —*

village See **city**.

VIP (s.), **VIPs** (pl.) Acceptable in all references for *very important person(s).*

Virginia Abbreviation: *Va.* Strictly speaking, it's a commonwealth, not a state. See **state(s)**.

Virgin Islands Do not abbreviate. In datelines: *CHARLOTTE AMALIE, Virgin Islands, Dec. 3 (UPI) —* . Specify an individual island in the text if needed. See **British Virgin Islands**.

virtual reality A computer-generated illusion of three-dimensional space.

virus A computer program that attaches itself to other programs and causes disruption or damage. See **worm**.

viscount, viscountess See **nobility**.

vienna coffee, vienna sausages See **food**.

vitamins Lowercase *vitamin:* vitamin A, vitamin B-12.

V-J Day The day of victory for the Allied forces over Japan in World War II. It is calculated both as Aug. 15, 1945, the day the fighting in Japan ended, and Sept. 2, 1945, the day Japan officially surrendered. The letters *V-J* stand for *Victory in Japan.*

V-neck

voice mail No hyphen. An electronic system that stores and delivers recorded telephone messages.

Voice of America *VOA* is acceptable on second reference.

Volkswagen of America Inc. The name of the U.S. subsidiary of the German company named Volkswagen A.G. Headquarters is in Auburn, Mich.

von See **foreign particles**.

voodoo

vote-getter

votes Use figures for the totals. Spell out below 10 in other related phrases related to voting: by a five-vote majority, with three abstentions, four votes short of the necessary two-thirds majority. For results that involve fewer than 1,000 votes on each side: The House voted 230-205, a 230-205 vote.

For totals that involve more than 1,000 votes on a side, separate the figures with *to* and avoid hyphenated adjectival constructions: The vote was 1,333 to 1,222. See **election returns** for examples.

VPN *Virtual Private Network.* A computer network supplied by common carriers (such as AT&T and MCI) that uses the Internet as its transmission medium.

vs. Use this abbreviation instead of *versus* in all uses.

V-STOL Acceptable on second reference for an aircraft capable of *vertical* or *short takeoff* or *landing.*

VTOL Acceptable on second reference for an aircraft capable of *vertical takeoff* or *landing.*

vulgarities See **obscenities**.

W

Wac, WAC *Wac* is no longer used by the military, but is acceptable in a reference to a woman who served in what used to be the *Women's Army Corps. WAC* is acceptable on second reference to the corps.

Waf, WAF *Waf* is no longer used by the military, but is acceptable in a reference to a woman who served in the Air Force. *WAF* is acceptable on second reference to the *Women's Air Force,* an unofficial organizational distinction formerly made by the Air Force but never authorized by Congress.

waiter (male), **waitress** (female)

Wales See **United Kingdom** and **datelines**.

walkup (n., adj.), **walk up** (v.)

Wall Street When the reference is to the entire complex of financial institutions in the area rather than the actual street itself, *the Street* is an acceptable short form.

Wal-Mart Headquarters is in Bentonville, Ark.

war Capitalize when used as part of the name for a specific conflict: the Civil War, the Cold War, the Korean War, the Vietnam War, the War of 1812, World War II, etc.

(War Between the States) The preferred term is *the Civil War.*

warden Capitalize as a formal title before a name.

wards See **political divisions**.

warfare, warhead, warlike, warlord, wartime, warplane, warship, but **war chest, war crime, war game, war horse**

Warner Bros. See TimeWarner.

Washington The nation's capital stands alone in datelines. If a distinction is needed, this is the preferred form: *Washington, D.C.* But if the context seems to require it: *the district.* Restrict *D.C.* alone to quoted matter.

Washington Abbreviation of the state: *Wash.* If a distinction is needed: *state of Washington* or *Washington state.* See **state(s).**

Washington's Birthday Capitalize *birthday* in references to the holiday. The date George Washington was born is computed as Feb. 22, 1732. (It was Feb. 11 under the calendar in use at the time.) The federal legal holiday is the third Monday in February.

wash 'n' wear

wash-up (n., adj.), **wash up** (v.)

Wave, WAVES *Wave* is no longer used by the military but is acceptable to refer to a woman who served in the Navy. *WAVES* is acceptable on second reference to the *Women's Auxiliary Volunteer Emergency Service,* an organizational distinction made for women in the Navy during World War II but subsequently discontinued.

wavelength

weak-kneed

weapons *Gun* is an acceptable term for all firearms.

Some frequently used terms:

artillery — Large-caliber cannons with rifled barrels, usually towed or mounted on ships, tanks, vehicles or airplanes. Calibers range from 20mm on airplanes to 16 inches on battleships. Short-barreled cannons for ground use are called *howitzers.* A cannon's projectile is commonly called a *shell.*

automatic — An *automatic* fires continuously as long as the trigger is pulled. A *semiautomatic* fires one shot each time the trigger is pulled. *Automatic,* however, is commonly used in referring to semiautomatic shotguns and pistols.

bore — The inside of a gun barrel; frequently used in adjective form: **smoothbore mortar, large-bore cannon.**

caliber — Measures the inside diameter of a gun barrel. Except for most shotguns, measurement ID is often dropped in popular usage with decimal fractions. The forms: **.22-caliber rifle, a .22 rifle, it is a .22, a 9mm pistol, a .357 Magnum, a Colt .45 automatic, a .38 special, an 81mm mortar, a 105mm howitzer, 16-inch naval gun.**

carbine — A short-barreled rifle.

cartridge — Ammunition for a gun. It comprises the *cartridge case, primer, powder* and *bullet.* Those for shotguns, cannons and

weapons *continued*

mortars are commonly called *shells.* All are frequently called *rounds.* (He fired 20 rounds from his M-16; the battleship fired 200 rounds at the beach fortifications.)

cartridge case — The brass shell that holds together the primer, powder and bullet. After a gun is fired, the empty *cartridge case* remains in the barrel or is ejected to one side.

gauge — Measures the inside diameter of most shotgun barrels. Shotguns come in 10, 12, 16, 20, 28 and .410 gauges. The higher the number, the smaller the *gauge.* The form: a 20-gauge shotgun. (Means 20 lead balls of that bore diameter weigh one pound.) Also: The shotgun is 12 gauge, a .410 shotgun (the .410 is really a *caliber,* but commonly is called a *gauge*).

grenade — A *hand grenade* is a small bomb that is thrown by hand. A *rifle grenade* is launched from a device that is attached to the muzzle of a rifle.

machine gun, submachine gun — Automatic weapons capable of continuous fire as long as the trigger is pulled. A *submachine gun* is hand-held and fires pistol ammunition. A *machine gun* is usually fixed to a mount and fires rifle ammunition.

Magnum — Nomenclature for cartridges that accept unusually large powder charges to give the bullet or shot charge higher velocity: *12-gauge Magnum shotgun, .44 Magnum pistol, .375 Magnum rifle.* All are trademarks owned by the various manufacturers.

mortar — A short-barreled cannon, usually with a smooth bore, used to fire finned shells in a highly curved trajectory. They can be disassembled and the components carried by individual soldiers.

pistol — A small weapon that may be fired with one hand. Also called a *handgun.* It may be a *semiautomatic* or a *revolver,* but the terms are not interchangeable. A *semiautomatic* carries its cartridges in a magazine and reloads itself after each shot is fired. A *revolver* carries its cartridges in a cylinder that must be manually revolved to align the next cartridge in a firing position. *Semiautomatic pistols* are commonly called *automatics.*

powder — The propellant that fills the cartridge case. Modern ammunition uses *smokeless powder,* which is more powerful than *black powder* used in antique and replica guns. Smokeless powder is not *Cordite,* a trademark for a peculiar cord-shaped propellant used by the British many years ago.

primer — The small cap inserted in the base of the cartridge case that ignites the power charge when struck by the firing pin.

rifle — A long-barreled weapon with a rifled bore fired from the shoulder.

rifling — Spiral grooves in the inside of a gun barrel that cause the bullet to spin in flight, thus causing it to travel point forward. Unnecessary in shotguns.

shot — Small lead or steel pellets fired in shotguns. A shotgun shell usually contains 1 to 2 ounces of shot. Small shot are called *pellets* or *birdshot;* large sizes are called *buckshot.*

shotgun — A long-barreled, shoulder-operated weapon with a smooth bore that fires pellets, buckshot and slugs.

slug — A solid lead projectile similar to a bullet that is fired by shotguns used in big game hunting; a slang term for any bullet.

small arms — A military term for weapons that can be fired by an individual soldier: *pistols, rifles, submachine guns* and *machine guns.*

Note: The *UPI Stylebook* includes many separate entries for weapons.

weather Widely used weather terms, based on definitions of the National Weather Service, are defined in separate, alphabetical entries.

(weather bureau) Don't use. Use *weather service* in references to the *National Weather Service.* **See National Weather Service.**

weatherman *Weather forecaster* is preferred.

Web, Web server, Web site, Web page, *but* **Web-based,** with a hyphen. The job title **webmaster** and **webcast** are solid and lowercase. See **World Wide Web, Internet.**

WebCrawler The formal name of one of many Internet search engines. See **search engine.**

Webster's New World College Dictionary The primary source for spelling and usage for questions not covered in this stylebook.

Webster's New World Computer Dictionary The main source for computer and Internet terms in this stylebook, and for others not covered in this book.

Webster's Third New International Dictionary The backup source for spelling and usage questions not covered in this stylebook or in *Webster's New World College Dictionary.*

Wedgwood Not *Wedgewood.* A trademark for pottery.

Wednesday See **days.**

weekday, weekend, weeklong, weeknight

Wehrmacht The German armed forces — army, air force and navy — of World War II.

weights Use numerals: the baby weighed 9 pounds, 7 ounces. She had a 9-pound, 7-ounce boy.

weird, weirdo Not *wierd.*

well- Follow *Webster's New World College Dictionary.* If a word is listed in the dictionary, follow that form, even after a noun: She is a well-known woman. The woman is well-known.

For combinations not listed in *Webster's New World College Dictionary,* hyphenate as a compound modifier before a noun; use no hyphen after it: She is a well-dressed woman. She is well dressed. See **good.**

well-to-do

West As defined by the U.S. Census Bureau, the 13-state region is broken into two divisions:

The eight *Mountain division* states are Arizona, Colorado, Idaho, Montana, Nevada, New Mexico, Utah and Wyoming.

The five *Pacific division* states are Alaska, California, Hawaii, Oregon and Washington.

See **North Central region, Northeast region,** and **South** for the bureau's other three regional breakdowns.

West Bank The form for datelines: *RAMALLAH, West Bank, Nov. 1. (UPI) —*

Western Europe *Western* and *Eastern Europe* are political, not geographic, divisions.

Western Hemisphere The continents of North and South America, and the islands near them.

West Germany Use instead of the *Federal Republic of Germany.* See **Germany.**

West Indies A large group of islands between North America and South America. It includes the Greater Antilles, Lesser Antilles and the Bahamas.

West Point Acceptable on second reference for the *U.S. Military Academy.* See **military academies.** In datelines: *WEST POINT, N.Y., Dec. 5 (UPI) —*

West Virginia Abbreviation: *W.Va.* (no space between *W.* and *Va.*). See **state(s).**

wheeler-dealer

whereabouts Use with a singular verb: His whereabouts is unknown.

which See **that, which.**

whip Capitalize as a formal title before a name. See **legislative titles**.

whiskey (s.), **whiskeys** (pl.) Not *whisky.*

white-collar (adj.)

White House Do not personify it with phrases such as the White House said. Instead, use phrases such as a White House official said. Do not use terms such as Florida White House or Western White House.

white paper Two words, lowercase, when used to refer to a special report.

who, whom Use *who* or *whom,* not *that* or *which,* to refer to humans or to animals with names.

  Whom is required in certain idiomatic expressions: to whom it may concern, for whom the bell tolls.

  Elsewhere, *who* is acceptable in all references: Who did you vote for? The man who came to dinner. He asked who I thought would be elected. Who shall I say is calling?

  Whom is also acceptable as the object of a verb or preposition, and many writers prefer to use it. But it often is awkward and can usually be eliminated.

> *Awkward:* The boy to whom I threw the ball cast it to the ground.
> *Better:* The boy I threw the ball to cast it to the ground.

whodunit A mystery story.

whole-wheat

who's, whose *Who's* is a contraction for *who is,* not a possessive: Who's there? *Whose* is the possessive: I do not know whose coat it is.

-wide No hyphen: citywide, continentwide, companywide, countrywide, industrywide, nationwide, statewide, worldwide.

(widow, widower) Because *widow* has been widely used and *widower* seldom used, *widow* has often taken sexist overtones. Avoid any sexist connotations. Use *wife* or *husband* instead. She was the wife of John Smith is just as clear as she is the widow of John Smith.

widths See **dimensions**.

(wierd) The correct spelling is *weird.*

Wilson's disease After Samuel A. Wilson, an English neurologist. A disease characterized by abnormal accumulation of copper in the brain, liver and other organs.

Windbreaker A trademark for a wind-resistant jacket.

wind chill index No hyphen. It expresses the combined effect of wind and low temperatures. A temperature of 15 degrees with a wind of 25

wind chill index *continued*

mph, for example, has the same chilling effect as a temperature of 22 below zero with no wind. Once wind speeds reach 40 mph they have little additional chilling effect.

Windows See **Microsoft.**

wine Lowercase geographic names in references to wines and other alcoholic beverages: bordeaux, bourbon, burgundy, calvados, champagne, cognac, scotch. But capitalize any reference to the region itself: The best burgundy comes from the Burgundy region of France. Capitalize brand names and trademarks.

wing A U.S. Air Force formation consisting of two or more groups. Capitalize a numbered unit: 34th Fighter-Bomber Wing. Otherwise, lowercase: the wing, the wing commander. See **military units** and **group (military)**.

winter, wintertime See **seasons.**

Wire Service Guild The nationwide local of *The Newspaper Guild* that represents news and other employees of UPI and AP. Headquarters is in New York. On second reference: *the Guild.* Subdivisions, corresponding to locals in other unions, are called *branches* and *chapters.*

wiretap, wiretapped, wiretapping, wiretapper Two *p*'s.

Wisconsin Abbreviation: *Wis.* See **state(s).**

witch hunt, witch hunting, witch hunter Hyphenate to convert these nouns to adjectives.

wise Use no hyphen if you mean *in the manner of* or *with regard to:* clockwise, lengthwise, otherwise, slantwise. Use no hyphen also in words coined and used for a single or particular occasion: moneywise, religionwise, etc. Such contrived words are usually best avoided.

Use a hyphen if you mean *skilled, smart* or *prudent:* penny-wise, street-wise.

For example, *weatherwise,* no hyphen, means *in regard to the weather:* Weatherwise, it may rain. *Weather-wise,* hyphenated, means *skilled in predicting the weather:* She is a weather-wise young woman.

WMD For *weapons of mass destruction.* Because use of the initials is so widespread, it is permissible to use them, but never on first reference. Try to confine them to quoted matter. Careful writers will find other ways to refer to the nuclear, chemical and biological weapons.

Woman's Christian Temperance Union *WCTU* is acceptable on second reference for the organization founded in 1874. (Note the singular *Woman's.*) Headquarters is in Evanston, Ill.

women Women should receive the same treatment as men in all areas of coverage. Physical descriptions, sexist references, demeaning stereotypes and condescending phrases should not be used.

To cite some examples, this means that:

- Copy should not assume maleness when both sexes are involved, as in: Jackson told newsmen.
- Copy should not express surprise that an attractive woman can also be professionally accomplished, as in: Mary Smith doesn't look the part, but she's an authority on placer mining.
- Copy should not gratuitously mention family relationships when there is no relevance to the subject, as in: Mary Jones, a doughty grandmother, spoke to the Senate.
- Use the same standards for men as for women in deciding whether to include specific mention of personal appearance or marital and family situation.

In other words, treatment of the sexes should be even-handed and free of assumptions and stereotypes. This does not mean that valid and acceptable words such as *mankind* or *humanity* cannot be used. They are proper. See **-persons**.

wondrous Not *wonderous*.

Woolworth Corp. Closed remaining F.W. Woolworth stores in 1997. Some were converted to *Champs Sports* and *Foot Locker* shoe stores under the *Venator Group*. Venator later changed its name to *Foot Locker Inc.* See **Foot Locker Inc.**

word processing, word processor No hyphen.

words as words Words occasionally are used as words rather than to convey the concept or thought they usually represent. Place such words, or groups of words, in quotation marks: "There" is never the subject of a sentence.

words commonly misspelled

accessibility	canceled	consensus
accommodate	categorically	consistency
adviser	changeable	curlicue
affect	coagulate	dietitian
affidavit	coconut	deity
all right	colossal	diphtheria
asinine	compatible	discernible
ballistic	competent	drought
calendar	conquer	drunkenness

words commonly misspelled *continued*

dumbbell	minuscule	resistance
dumfounded	mischievous	restaurateur
effect	misspelled	sacrilegious
embarrass	mold	salable
exorbitant	naphtha	sanatorium
eying	nicotine	sanitarium
flier	nonagenarian	sheik
gauge	occurred	siege
goodbye	occurrence	sizable
grammar	ophthalmologist	skier
grievance	parallel	skiing
harass	paraphernalia	skillful
hemorrhage	parishioner	sleuth
hygiene	parley	soluble
impostor	permissible	straitjacket
incalculable	picnicking	supersede
indispensable	plaque	surveillance
inflammation	Portuguese	temblor
innuendo	preventive	temperamental
inoculate	principal	tentacles
inseparable	principle	toward
insistence	propeller	transmitter
irreligious	protester	tying
irresistible	publicly	uncontrollable
judgment	questionnaire	under way
liaison	queue	usable
likable	rarefy	vacuum
marshal	rehearsal	weird
millennium	repetitious	

(The list of commonly misspelled words originally was compiled by Henry Minott, news editor of the United Press for many years in New England. Some words were added and a few changes made to reflect current usage.)

workbench, workbook, workday, workforce, workhorse, workhouse, workload, workout, workplace, workroom, workstation, workweek, *but* **work basket, work camp, work ethic, work farm, work sheet**

workers' compensation

-workers Generally two words. Exceptions: autoworkers, steelworkers, woodworkers.

working class (n.), **working-class** (adj.)

World Bank Acceptable in first reference for *International Bank of Reconstruction and Development,* but the body of the story should identify it as the shortened form of the name.

World Council of Churches This is the main international, interdenominational cooperative body of Anglican, Eastern Orthodox, Protestant and old or national Catholic churches. Roman Catholicism is not a member but cooperates with the council in various programs. Headquarters is in Geneva, Switzerland.

world court Lowercase to refer to the *International Court of Justice,* the principal judicial organ of the United Nations, formed at The Hague in 1945.

Use *World Court,* capitalized, only to refer to the *Permanent Court of International Justice,* which once operated as an arm of the League of Nations.

World Cup Competition every four years to determine the world soccer champion. On second reference: *the cup.*

World Health Organization *WHO* is acceptable on second reference. Headquarters is in Geneva, Switzerland.

World Series On second reference: *the series.*

World War I, World War II But: *the first world war, the second world war.*

worldwide

World Wide Web A global system of Internet sources that provide access to text, images and sound. *Web* is acceptable on second reference. Do not use *WWW.* Also *Web site, Web page.* See **Internet, Web**.

worm A malicious program that can infect a computer via e-mail and eat up resources by constantly replicating itself. Sometimes carries viruses. See **virus**.

worship, worshiped, worshiping, worshiper One *p.*

write-in (n., adj.), **write in** (v.)

write-off (n., adj.), **write off** (v.)

wrongdoing, wrongheaded

W3C For *World Wide Web Consortium,* an organization formed in 1994 to develop common standards for the Web.

Wyoming Abbreviated *Wyo.*

X

X The rating for *mature adults only.* See **movie ratings**.

Xerox A trademark for a brand of photocopy machine. Never use as a verb.

(Xmas) Never use this abbreviation, or any other, for *Christmas.*

XML *eXtensible Markup Language.* A document language that provides more flexibility on the Web than HTML. See **HTML**.

X-ray (n., adj., v.) Use for both the photographic process and the radiation particles themselves.

Y

Yahoo! An Internet search engine. The exclamation point is part of the name. See **search engine**.

yam Botanically, yams and sweet potatoes are not related, though several varieties of moist-fleshed sweet potatoes are popularly called *yams* in the United States.

yard Equal to 3 feet. In metric, it is about 0.91 meters. To convert to meters, multiply by .91 (5 yards × .91 equals 4.55 meters).

year-end, year-round, yearlong

yearling An animal one year old or in its second year. The birthday of all thoroughbred horses is arbitrarily set at Jan. 1. On that date, any foal born in the preceding year is regarded as 1 year old.

years Use figures: 1975. Use an *s* without an apostrophe to indicate spans of decades or centuries: the 1890s, the 1800s. Unlike most figures, a year may begin a sentence: 1976 was a very good year. See **dates** for punctuation guidelines.

yellow journalism The use of cheaply sensational methods to attract or influence readers. The term comes from the use of yellow ink in printing the "Yellow Kid," a comic strip, in the *New York World* in 1895.

(yesterday) Use only in direct quotations and in phrases that do not refer to a specific day: Yesterday we were young. Use the actual day of the week in all other cases. See **days** and **time**.

(yesteryear) See **time**.

yield The annual rate of return on an investment as paid in dividends or interest. It is expressed as a percentage obtained by dividing the

yield *continued*
current market price for a stock or bond into the dividend or interest paid in the preceding 12 months. See **profit terminology**.

Yom Kippur The Jewish Day of Atonement. Occurs in September or October.

Young Men's Christian Association *YMCA* is acceptable in all references. Headquarters is in Chicago.

Young Women's Christian Association *YWCA* is acceptable in all references. Headquarters is in New York.

youth Applicable to boys and girls from age 13 until the 18th birthday is reached. Use *man* and *woman* for individuals 18 and older. See **teenager**.

yo-yo Formerly a trademark, now a generic term.

Yugoslavia Former name of the country that became *Serbia* and *Montenegro*. See **Serbia-Montenegro**.

Yukon A territorial section of Canada. Do not abbreviate. See **Canada**. In datelines: *WHITEHORSE, Yukon, Feb. 25 (UPI)* —

yule, yuletide

Z

zero (s.), **zeros** (pl.) Not *zeroes.*

zigzag

Zionism The movement, formerly for re-establishing, now for support-ing, the biblical homeland, Israel, as the Jewish national state.

ZIP codes Use all-caps, *ZIP,* for *Zone Improvement Program,* but always lowercase the word *code.* Run the five digits together without a comma, and do not put a comma between the state name and the ZIP code: New York, NY 10017.

Zulu time See **UTC.**

Zuni A member of the language of a tribe of American Indians living in New Mexico. The plural is *Zunis.* The adjective is *Zunian.*

zzz Lowercase. Used to represent the sound of a person snoring.

PART 2

The UPI Guide to Newswriting

Writing for Print

*Reading maketh a full man; conference a ready man; and
writing an exact man.*   — *Francis Bacon*

If we expect our stuff to be read, we have to fork the hay down there where the cows can get at it. Too many reporters write like they talk in the bars where the press hangs out. Their stuff is too "inside."

The market-driven news report we need must be understandable to a large number of people, most of whom are busy. They also are smart, so there is no need to "write down" to them. Think of writing a news story as like briefing a busy person you like and respect. Present the facts quickly, succinctly. Good writers learn to do that in ways that entertain as well as enlighten.

One way is the deft use of quotes. This permits reporters to employ journalism's expert witnesses, such as the person at the scene who actually saw the plane crash, heard the explosion and inhaled the smoke. That kind of sight, sound and smell hooks readers.

Quotes can set up identification between people on different continents. For example, an Ethiopian woman telling in her own translated words of her despair at seeing her children starve is easily understood by a mother in Keokuk, Iowa. Such stories are effective because they emphasize reality over rhetoric. Good reporters treat people and their words with respect. This means that all words between quotation marks are precisely the way we heard them and wrote them in our notebooks.

Speaking of rhetoric, there is too much of it on our wires. Rhetoric is acquired easily from press releases, advance copies of speeches and over the telephone. Reality comes harder. Getting reality sometimes requires risk, and almost always shoe-leather reporting. The quality of news and feature stories is determined by the amount of work that goes into them.

There is a lot of technologically marvelous machinery around these days. It can deliver the stuff we type, but it cannot infuse it with the blood, sweat and tears that make people want to read it.

— **Leon Daniel**, former UPI special correspondent

> **1989**
> WASHINGTON (UPI) — When George and Barbara Bush move into the White House, don't expect their closest neighbor — homeless peace activist Concepcion Picciotto — to bake them a cake. Despite her eight-year residence in Lafayette Park just across the avenue from 1600 Pennsylvania, the tiny woman called Connie by her friends never even met outgoing tenants Ronald and Nancy Reagan. The Reagans, for that matter, never met their other homeless neighbors who sleep on nearby steam grates for warmth. The president explained recently that some homeless people actually prefer to sleep outdoors but he didn't say how he knew that.
> — Leon Daniel

BUILDING THE STORY

Reading good journalism is a pleasure. A tortured, turgid story is a sure way to end up on an editor's spike — or in the wastebasket.

To avoid the spike, it is essential to be clear on what you are going to write before you write it. The heart of a good story is the lead paragraph. Journalism students are often taught to put *who, what, when, where, why* and *how* in the first sentence. It often doesn't work that way.

You must include essential elements, but not all of them. You often cannot, and more often *should* not, try to cram the five *W*s and the *H* in that lead. Your lead should tease the readers, catch their interest, draw them further into the story and make them want to read more.

Newspapers often stress the *soft lead,* setting the scene first, introducing the characters, and then bringing in the lead somewhere down in the body of the story. Wire service journalism doesn't have that luxury. News stories must be shorter and to the point. Feature stories can start a bit slower, but features that run on and on can lose the reader.

One problem many journalists have is where to put the time element in a story. The obvious place is in the lead, but if the story is about events a few days earlier, it usually is better to put it in the second or third paragraph. On a story about something that happened today, certainly include it in the lead, but be careful where you place it: *The president sent a bill to Congress Monday; heavy snows Tuesday kept emergency crews busy,* etc. Don't ever let the day become the object of the verb: *The president sent Monday a bill to Congress.* And do not use "on" before the day or date unless it is necessary to avoid confusion: *The Supreme Court ruled Tuesday* (not *on Tuesday.*)

Once you have your lead crafted, it is time to begin adding the facts, the quotes, that make it whole, that make it interesting and lively. Lesser, non-essential details should come at the bottom, allowing client editors to cut to fit their space.

VIVID WRITING

Here are excerpts from a story written many years ago by a United Press correspondent. Note the impact of the story and study how the writer was able to paint such a vivid picture of what occurred.

1914
ON THE FIRING LINE NEAR WIRBALLEN, Russian Poland, Oct. 8 — Via The Hague and London — At sundown tonight after four days of constant fighting, the German army holds its strategic and strongly entrenched position east of Wirballen.

As I write this in the glare of a screened auto headlight, several hundred yards back from the German trenches, I can catch the occasional high notes of a soldier chorus. For four days the singers have lain cramped in those muddy ditches, unable to move or stretch except under cover of darkness. And still they sing. They believe they are on the eve of a great victory. . . .

Today I saw a wave of Russian flesh and blood dash against a wall of German steel. The wall stood. The wave broke — was shattered and hurled back. Rivulets of blood trickled back slowly in its wake. Broken bloody bodies, wreckage of the wave, strewed the breakers.

Tonight I know why correspondents are not wanted on any of the battle lines. Descriptions and details of battles fought in the year of our Lord 1914 don't make nice reading. . . .

In the morning sunlight, from the summit of the hill, I got my first view of the fighting that will go down in history as the battle of Wirballen. The line stretched off to the left as far as the field glasses would carry, in a great, irregular semi-circle, the irregularity being caused by the efforts of both armies to keep to high ground with their main lines.

As we watched, the entire fire of the Russian artillery seemed to be diverted to a village situated on a low plain about 2,000 yards to the northward of our position. The village — already deserted — was being literally flattened under a deluge of iron and steel.

The ruins were in flames. After half an hour the reason for shelling the deserted village became evident. A general advance against the German center was launched and the Russians were making certain that the village, directly in the line of advance, had not been occupied by the German machine guns during the night. . . .

Finally came the Russian order to advance. At the word hundreds of yards of the Russian fighting line leaped forward, deployed in open order and came on. One, two, three, and in some places four and five successive skirmish lines, separated by intervals of from 20 to 50 yards, swept forward. Some of them came into range of the German trench fire almost at once. These lines began to wilt and thin out. Others were able to make a considerable advance under cover. The smoke of the burning village gave a grateful protection to several regiments. . . .

As a spectacle the whole thing was maddening. I found my heart thumping like a hammer, and with no weapon more formidable than a pair of binoculars, I was mentally fighting as hard as the men with the guns. For the first time I sensed the intoxication of battle and learned the secret of the smiles on the faces of the battlefield's dead.

On came the Slav swarm — into the range of the German trenches, with wild yells and never a waver. Russian battle flags — the first I had ever seen — appeared in the front of the charging ranks. The advance line thinned and the second line moved up. Nearer and nearer they swept toward the German positions.

And then came a new sight. A few seconds later came a new sound. First I saw a sudden, almost grotesque, melting of the advancing lines. It was different from anything that had taken place before. The men literally went down like dominoes in a row. Those who kept their feet were hurled back as though by a terrible gust of wind. Almost in the second that I pondered, puzzled, the staccato rattle of machine guns reached us. My ear answered the query of my eye. . . .

The crucial period for the section of the charge on which I had riveted my attention probably lasted less than a minute. To my throbbing brain it seemed an hour.

Then, with the withering fire raking them, even as they faltered, the lines broke. Panic ensued. It was every man for himself. The entire Russian charge turned and went tearing back to cover and the shelter of the Russian trenches.

I swept the entire line of the Russian advance with my glasses — as far as it was visible from our position. The whole advance of the enemy was in retreat, making for its intrenched position.

After the assault had failed and the battle had resumed its normal trend, I swept the field with my glasses. The dead were everywhere. They were not piled up, but were strewn over acres.

More horrible than the sight of the dead, though, were the other pictures brought up by the glasses. Squirming, tossing, writhing figures everywhere! The wounded!

All who could stumble or crawl were working their way back toward their own lines or back to the friendly cover of hills or wooded spots.

But there appeared to be hundreds to whom was denied even this hope, hundreds doomed to lie there in the open, with wounds unwashed and undressed, suffering from thirst and hunger until the merciful shadows of darkness made possible their rescue by the Good Samaritans of the hospital corps, who are tonight gleaning that field of death for the third time since Sunday.

> — **Karl H. Von Wiegand,**
> United Press Staff Correspondent
> Copyright United Press International

Karl H. Von Wiegand was the Berlin correspondent of the United Press before war was declared. He was arrested in Berlin, suspected of being a spy, after hostilities opened. His credentials and the fact that he was of German birth speedily brought his release. Von Wiegand was the first man to send a story from Berlin after Germany's cable had been cut. He took his story to The Hague and cabled it to the United Press. He returned to Berlin, covering war news there, and finally went to the eastern front.

ACCURACY — SPEED

International News Service, which merged with United Press in 1958, had a slogan: *Get it first, but first get it right.*

Speed is fundamental for news agencies, but accuracy is more important. Never commit to a newswire any word about which there is any doubt. It is better to be late than to be wrong.

Because speed is so important, compromises are necessary. You may be able to rewrite a feature story a dozen times or until you are convinced it is the best you can produce. But you don't have such a luxury with breaking news stories. Some will have to move with rough edges and minus vital facts. But move them you must; refine them in subsequent leads or write-throughs.

CLARITY

Most people who read newspapers are in a hurry. They deserve clear writing in stories that get to the point in a straightforward way.

News writers should favor the active voice and use nouns and vivid verbs to punch positive images in the reader's mind. Avoid complex, mushy qualifiers and inverted clauses that lead the reader backward to the point. On the average, sentences should be short. If you write a long one, change pace and follow it with a short one.

Be exact. Use words in their precise meaning. Don't use *anticipate* when you mean *expect*. Don't use *convince* when you mean *persuade*. Use terms that get a reader's attention. *Chocolate-colored* gets more attention than *brown*. *Drunk* hits harder than *intoxicated*.

> **1911**
> NEW YORK, March 25 — I was walking through Washington Square when a puff of smoke issuing from the factory building caught my eye. I reached the building before the alarm was turned in. I saw every feature of the tragedy visible from outside the building. I learned a new sound — a more horrible sound than description can picture. It was the thud of a speeding, living body on a stone sidewalk.
>
> Thud-dead! Thud-dead! Thud-dead! Thud-dead!
>
> Sixty-two! The sound and the thought of death came to me, each time, at the same instant. There was plenty of chance to watch them as they came down; the height was 80 feet.
> — William Shepherd

WORD SELECTION

Write in standard English. In general, any word listed as standard in *Webster's New World College Dictionary* may be used unless this stylebook dictates otherwise. Words labeled *substandard, obsolete, old-*

fashioned, archaic, or *rare* should be used only in direct quotations or in cases where their character is pertinent.

Words listed as dialect should be avoided unless clearly relevant. Words listed as slang should be used with caution. Words listed as colloquial are simply informal and are acceptable if they fit the occasion. So are words labeled by a star (☆), which indicates they are Americanisms. Words in boldface italic type are foreign words that have not been fully accepted into the English language. If you use one, define it.

> **1917**
> PARIS, Oct. 18 (INS) — Mata Hari, which is Javanese for Eye-of-the-Morning, is dead. She was shot as a spy by a firing squad of Zouaves at the Vincennes Barracks. She died facing death literally, for she refused to be blindfolded.   — Henry G. Wales

HACKNEYED WORDS AND PHRASES

These are overused terms that should be assiduously avoided. They include common cliches, vogue words, officialese and legalese (gobbledygook), and journalese.

Officialese and legalese are those frequently absurd terms adopted by bureaucrats seeking an elegant ring to a common sound. *Prioritize* is a good example. *Interface* is another. Journalese is composed of the proprietary terms of journalism, many of which come to us from headline writers: *hike* for *increase, blast* for *denounce, huddled* for *met, behind closed doors* for *private.*

EUPHEMISMS, EUPHUISMS AND GENTEELISMS

These are weasel words that are certain to dull the edge of a sharp phrase: *underprivileged* for *poor, odor* for *stench, portly* for *fat, elderly* for *old, custodian* for *janitor, sanitation worker* for *garbage man, passed away* for *died, memorial garden* for *graveyard.*

Avoid pomposities. *Before* is better than *prior to; left* is better than *departed; helped* is better than *rendered assistance to; supports* is better than *supportive of.*

Don't coin words in serious writing *(minicontest),* and resist the tendency to convert nouns to verbs *(hosted).*

VOGUES

Vogue words are fads; they come and go. H.W. Fowler described them as "words owing their vogue to the joy of showing that one has acquired them." Wollcott Gibbs wrote, "They are detached from the language and inflated like little balloons." *Viable* is a good example. So is *targeted.*

Languages constantly change. New words are invented. Old ones fade away, take on new meanings or shades of new meanings. The language of newswriters must adapt to this evolution. But we should travel with the main body, not the advance guard.

> **1936 (APRIL 3)**
> TRENTON, N.J — The state of New Jersey, which spent $948,643.67 in convicting Bruno Richard Hauptmann of the kidnapping and murder of the Lindbergh baby, today killed him with 14 cents worth of electricity.
> — Harry Ferguson

Some current fads are certain to find a useful and permanent place in the American language, and as such they will become part of newswriting, indeed, of all writing. But we should let the neologisms become firmly fixed in the language before we accept them as our own.

This stylebook lays down many restrictions and some prohibitions, but it is not meant to fence in creative writers with confining formulas. Under certain circumstances, it's possible that any rule in the book could be violated and the story improved because of it.

But before you start tinkering with the offbeat, fooling around with the unusual, be aware you probably are not plowing new ground but merely duplicating what others might have tried and discarded as worthless.

As E.B. White wrote, "Writing good standard English is no cinch, and before you have managed it you will have encountered enough rough country to satisfy even the most adventurous spirit."

— **Robert McNeil,** former UPI Style Editor

NEWS, ANALYSIS AND COMMENTARY

News is the telling of facts that are interesting and important to the people hearing, watching or reading them.

News stories are written in a straightforward way — usually the classic pyramid format — with the basic information first: *who, what, when, where.* Details about the most important elements of the story come later, along with a look at the *why* and *how* of the story. The reporter presents the facts — including quotes from people directly involved as well as those whose viewpoints shed valuable light on the report — but the reporter keeps his or her personal opinions out of the story.

The story should be *balanced* — meaning comment is included from all relevant sides; *fair* — meaning it does not load up comment on one side at the expense of the other, and that, especially in a negative report about someone, includes comment from that person; and *accurate* — meaning the facts have been checked. The idea is to give readers a full range of information for them to draw their own conclusions.

News analysis is different from a straightforward telling of the facts. In news analysis, the writer works from the facts to explain the implications of a story — what it means, why it happened. The writer quotes people with expertise about the story — and the writer may include his or her own opinions about why a development occurred, what will be required for a particular outcome, and so on.

News commentary is different from analysis. In *analysis,* a writer is examining possible outcomes and explaining possibilities. In *commentary,* the writer is making an argument for why something is good or bad, right or wrong, wise or foolish, should be pursued or dropped. Good commentary is not a harangue, but a well-reasoned argument that relies on facts (and the facts should be attributed to their source, as with news reporting).

EDITING

A definition of a good editor that has stood the test of time: *"He breathes life into dull copy. He pulls frenetic writing down to earth. When a story needs it, he adds the professional touch. He respects good writing style and knows when to make changes and when not to."* (**Mert Akers,** United Press, 1950).

The trick in editing is to strike a balance between doing too little or too much. Editing is a fine-tuning process, shaving away verbiage, tightening the sentence and paragraph structure and spotlighting those special touches that reflect up-close reporting.

2001
WASHINGTON, March 19 (UPI) — When George W. Bush and Yoshiro Mori met Monday for talks at the White House, at least the lunch was good.

It was a bleak comment on the failure of both men so far to turn back the tides of economic woe threatening their great nations that this had to be rated an achievement. But at least the saffron pasta and the lobster and squid broth exceeded expectations.

Apparently nothing else did.
— Martin Sieff

Make sure the lead paragraph comes across clearly in one reading. It is the most important part of the story. If you do not understand it, neither will clients or their subscribers. Strike unfamiliar names, localisms and meaningless partial quotes.

Reshape leads cheapened by the crutch words *when, while, as* and *after.*

In addition to correcting errors of fact, grammar and spelling, be ever vigilant for libel.

> **1972**
> FLINT, Mich., March 7 — To make his plea for racial harmony heard, Paul L. Cabell Jr. put a shotgun to his head and pulled the trigger.

Do not try to second-guess the reporter. Before making substantive changes in a story, check with the writer. The only thing worse than a reporting error is an editing error.

Make sure whatever point being made in the lead is authoritatively backed up high in the story.

Go through the story sentence by sentence, clipping out unnecessary words, phrases and rambling quotes to keep the story at a manageable and readable length.

In stories with a lot of figures, make sure they all add up and do not conflict with each other. Too many figures overwhelm the reader. Strike those that are superfluous.

If you have to read a paragraph twice, the story is in trouble.

Use strong, vivid verbs in well-cast simple sentences to breathe life into dull copy. Verbs are the stars of any story. Adverbs, the "ly" words, should be used sparingly, if at all.

Look for interesting perspectives the writer may have missed.

Watch for subtleties in a story that may cast a person in an unfair light.

Identify elements of a story that will need development in subsequent leads, and tell the writer.

Make sure words precisely convey the proper meaning. Common mistakes include the use of *affect* when the writer means *effect, anticipate* instead of *expect, convince* instead of *persuade, emigrant* instead of *immigrant.*

Watch for localisms and other things that may be obvious to the writer but puzzling to the reader. People buy *hoagies* in some states. The same sandwich is known elsewhere by other names, including *hero, submarine* and *grinder.*

Eliminate unnecessary words, rambling quotes, meaningless partial quotes *(he said he was "excited" about the project)*.

Remove cliches such as *hammered out an agreement, huddled behind closed doors, claimed the life of, in the wake of, unveiled plans for,* etc. Good writers don't use them. Good editors won't allow them.

Be alert for words with editorial connotations, such as *claims, points out, notes;* for the ridiculous, such as *strangled to death, drowning death, two twins, totally enveloped, the first car was originally built;* and for *head-line words* that have no place in the body of a story, like *probed* and *urged.*

Watch for the correct usage of double-duty words that can be both verbs and nouns. There is much abuse on this score. Examples: *coverup* and *cover up, shutdown* and *shut down, turnover* and *turn over, cutoff* and *cut off,* in which the first is the noun or adjective form, the second the verb form.

Eliminate *currently, presently, respectively* and such transitional crutches as *at the same time* and *meanwhile.*

Watch for the *second comma* after states and dates (omitting it is a common sin): *They raced from Punxsutawney, Pa., to Liverpool, Ohio. He set the record on July 16, 1985, in a game against the Tigers.*

Alert the writer if a story clearly needs an opposing viewpoint.

In wire service copy (and often on the Web) each story has a brief

1945

NEW YORK, July 28 — A two-engine Billy Mitchell bomber rammed into the 79th story of the Empire State Building at 9:49 a.m. today, exploding in a cone of flames that turned the world's tallest skyscraper into a pillar of flame and brought death to at least 13 persons and injury to 25 more. It was the most spectacular disaster in the New York metropolitan area since the burning of the Zeppelin Hindenburg.

headline, just like a newspaper headline, but often with more constraints on length. The headline must be provocative, informative and never just a shortened version of the lead. A well-written story can be ruined by an uninspired headline, especially one that matches the lead, or a portion of it, word for word.

We are inundated with legalese, journalese, officialese, public relations claptrap and corporate jargon. Writers must sift through this garbage and write what it really means. And editors must crack down, insist that the news reports are free of these pomposities, and demand rewrites where necessary. We must write clearly.

Acknowledge excellent work. Compliment the writer. But don't get lazy with the copy of consistently smooth writers. Even the best need editing sometimes.

Study the stylebook. Violations of our own stylebook are embarrassing, inexcusable, and annoying to clients. A newspaper editor once told UPI, "The ugliest mistakes on your wire are violations of your own style."

> — Excerpts from texts by UPI Senior Editor **Bruce Cook** and former UPI Foreign Editor **Paul Varian**

2

Writing for Broadcast

Communication by the written word is a subtle and beautiful thing. But writing the spoken word — so that it will be listened to and understood — is an art that depends largely on simplicity. Readers decide what to read, when to read it, how fast to read it, how much to read and whether to reread for comprehension. A listener has only one option if the flow of words out of the radio or television speaker doesn't make sense immediately. The option is to tune out or turn off. Your finished product has to grab that listener's attention and hold it.

The broadcast writer is telling a friend about something that happened — not writing a story. In telling a story, you give your impression of what happened, not each and every detail. You tell different facts, one at a time. You sometimes repeat.

One reasonably sure way to interest the listener is to be interested in the story yourself — not just as a writer, but as a person. You must feel the urgency, the pathos, the excitement or the humor that makes an event newsworthy. And you must make the listener feel it, too.

Good broadcast writing is not necessarily tricky, offbeat leads. If a fancy lead doesn't fit, avoid it. Writing is good and listens well if it is tight, angled correctly and written in the active voice, not the passive. Make it active and make it move with your choice of verbs. Action verbs make the story jump without inflating it. Use words that trigger an image in the listener's mind — a smell, a sound, anything that involves the listener. If your words enable the listener to visualize the scene or background of the story, the item will hold the listener's attention.

A word of caution: The need to hold listeners does not give the writer license to sensationalize or distort. It does mean the writer must find the interest-compelling angle, pin the lead to it, then drive it home with pertinent detail.

> **1973**
> WASHINGTON — Sometime this week, Richard Nixon went to what must have been a private hell and came back with his loneliest decision.
> — John Milne

There is not necessarily a right or a wrong way to write something. The following suggestions result from years of trial and error — and can provide a platform from which to build your own approach:

1. Listen to broadcasts. Note items that give announcers difficulty. Remember, you are writing for announcers in small as well as large markets. The copy must be simple, clear, easy to read aloud and easy to understand when heard.

2. Listen to people talk. Notice the way quotations, attribution and numbers are handled in conversation. Broadcast news writing is still formal enough that we must avoid most of the slang, but it does not have to be stilted. Normal conversation isn't.

3. Read and understand your source copy, your story — not just the lead, but the whole story. Then put the source copy aside as you start to write. Don't paraphrase your source copy. Your job is to write, not to retype.

4. Write with attention to detail. Write so it is clear. Have someone else critique your copy.

5. Read what you have written out loud. If you have trouble with it, imagine what kind of trouble someone unfamiliar with the story is going to have — especially hitting it cold in front of an open microphone. When you type, talk to the keyboard like an old friend — hear and speak your copy. Project it, punch it; that's the only way you find the pauses, the inflections. A good pause is a speaker's way of underlining.

6. Tune in on every phase of what's going on. You're going to describe it, interpret it, evaluate it; so know it, feel it. Understand the politicians and professional thinkers, but also find out about "alternate lifestyles."

7. Mostly, be able to think, "This is a hell of a story." If you don't, no listener will.

SOME OTHER ADVICE

- Put the source of a story first: *The president said x x x,* not *x x x, the president said.*
- Put the location of the story in early. You can say: *Utah police,* or *Police in Provo, Utah,* but never say "here" or "there." They're meaningless.
- When quoting, use neutral verbs and make clear it's a quote: *"As Senator Kennedy said: "We must pass this bill."* Or, *"As he put it . . ."* or *"In Senator Kennedy's words . . ."*
- Avoid sibilants. The letter *S* is murder on announcers when it comes in rapid succession. So is *P* and even *B.* Whistling and speaking are distinct and separate arts and should remain so.
- Do not use abbreviations unless they are commonly known, such as *FBI, CIA, NAACP, U.N. OPEC, NATO.* But it's *Junior, Senior* after a name, and *Corporation, Company, Limited,* when dealing with businesses.

ACCURACY

The most important ingredient of any story you handle is accuracy. One of UPI's mottos is: *Get it first, but first get it right.* Never forget it.

Check and then recheck all facts, figures and names. In broadcasting, nine out of 10 corrections reach an entirely different audience. The time to make one is before the story goes out.

Any journalist has a personal commitment to tell the whole story. For the broadcast writer to tell a one-thousand-word print story in six lines is inherently impossible. So it becomes necessary to summarize.

Don't let extraneous details get in the way of a clearly told story. Get the facts right, but don't overload your story with them. On a complex story, it is better to summarize clearly than to add elements that cannot be expanded or backgrounded enough because of the medium's time limitation. For example, you have a story about a senator accusing a judge of financial misconduct. You write about this in four lines. Then you add two lines about the specific accusation that the judge received 120-thousand dollars from an outside source.

The story might be completely accurate in a technical sense. But if space limitations prevented you (and in this case they would) from adding the information that the money was paid over a 12-year period and all was spent on an educational project rather than on the judge's personal pleasure, you will have left the listener with a distorted view of the story. In this case, it would have been more accurate not to introduce the specific money charge. The rule is to write tightly, but always at sufficient length to prevent distortion. At the same time, there are realities of the medium, and your handling must bear these in mind.

IMMEDIACY

Broadcasting is the now medium. Broadcast writing must reflect the immediacy that only broadcasting can provide. Immediacy means telling the listener what the situation is right now. It does not mean having to put *today* — or any time element at all — in every lead.

It's better to say *President Bush and the Russian ambassador are holding a working dinner at the White House at this hour* than *President Bush and the Russian ambassador sat down to a working dinner at the White House tonight.*

Save that past-tense lead for later, when you can add information on what they said or accomplished: *President Bush and the Russian ambassador reportedly made progress on a nuclear weapons agreement during a working dinner at the White House tonight. Sources tell UPI they will hold more talks tomorrow.*

Often, news agency or newspaper writers must fashion an advance lead that will hold up after the event, such as: *The pope was scheduled to say Easter mass at the Vatican today.* But remember, nobody talks that way — and broadcast writing is contemporary spoken English with a now sound. Write it like this: *The pope will say Easter mass for thousands of pilgrims at the Vatican this morning* or *The pope says Easter mass for thousands of pilgrims at the Vatican this morning.*

A story may progress during the day or it may remain relatively static. The broadcaster must keep the story moving forward. Use different material — the eyewitness descriptions, the arrival of investigators or whatever may be happening now.

If there are no fresh developments, make the story sound different by highlighting different elements. Use the non-essential but intriguing aspects, in combination with the elements that made it a story in the first place, to give the piece a fresh sound.

HUMANIZATION

Remember, your listeners are real, live people. They're interested in other people. Tell your stories to these people in terms of people, not cold robot ciphers. Bureaucracy has eliminated the emotional elements from everything from unemployment statistics to tragic accidents. People have become dwellers, homeowners, illegal aliens, disadvantaged minorities, career professionals and dot-com workers.

Tell news stories in human terms. The big fire that levels a downtown block doesn't just cause millions of dollars in damage — it also displaces people. Statistics make news, but so do the reactions of people to those statistics.

You could say: *The latest government figures show the cost of living is up again, paced by a 16 percent increase in the cost of bread.* It might be better to say: *A loaf of bread is costing more these days. The government says a 16 percent rise in the cost of bread was the biggest factor in pushing the cost of living higher this month.*

A sure way to lose a listener is to overemphasize statistics, percentages and technical details. Unless they are essential to the meaning of the story, avoid them.

A note on casualties: Casualty figures often change as a story develops. That's why every casualty figure must be sourced until your figure is solid fact. Phrase the first death or injury figures to indicate they are preliminary and likely to change. Pin the figures on a source from the outset, and continue to source figures until they are solid. If the report of a plane crash or a mine disaster is just that — a report without a definite name as source — say that, too.

HUMOR

Humor is fragile stuff. It can be the icing on the cake, but any humorous story must tell itself.

There should be a continuous effort to lighten all the heavy news reports with a note of levity — preferably at the close of a package of items to offset the dark tales of crisis that have gone before. But attempts to be cute or to needle an unfunny story are deplorable.

Never make sport of infirmities, and never relate injury or death to humor. There's nothing funny in a man breaking his neck by tripping over a book of safety hints.

State the facts. If the facts are funny, somebody somewhere will smile.

PHONETICS (foh-neht'–ihks)

It's just as important for newscast copy to carry pronunciations of difficult words as it is for newspaper copy to be spelled correctly. Phoneticize (in parentheses) immediately after the word in question, usually proper or place names.

The Key to UPI Broadcast Pronunciation Style

Vowels

A   AY for long A (as in *mate*)
     A for short A (as in *cat*)
     AI for nasal A (as in *air*)
     AH for soft A (as in *father*)
     AW for broad A (as in *talk*)

E   EE for long E (as in *meat*)
     EH for short E (as in *get*)
     UH for hollow E (as in *the,* or French prefix *le*)
     AY for French long E with acute accent (as in *Pathe*)
     IH for middle E (as in *pretty*)
     EW for EW diphthong (as in *few*)

I   IGH for long I (as in *time*)
     EE for French long I (as in *machine*)
     IH for short I (as in *pity*)

O   OH for long O (as in *note* or "ough" as in *though*)
     AH for short O (as in *hot*)
     AW for broad O (as in *fought*)
     OO for double OO (as in *fool,* or "ough" as in *through*)
     UH for short OU (as in *touch*)
     OW for OW diphthong (as in *how,* or "ough" as in *plough*)
     UU for OO (as in *cook* or *wood*)

U   EW for long U (as in *mule*)
     OO for long U (as in *rule*)
     U for middle U (as in *put*)
     UH for short U (as in *shut*)

Consonants

     K for hard C (as in *cat*)
     S for soft C (as in *cease*)
     SH for soft CH (as in *machine*)
     CH for hard CH or TCH (as in *catch*)
     Z for hard S (as in *disease*)
     S for soft S (as in *sun*)

G for hard G (as in *gang*)

J for soft G (as in *general*)

ZH for soft J (as in French version of *Joliet*)

Some words defy a logical phoneticization. In such cases, use a rhyming technique: *Chairman Roger Blough (as in "now"*).

Writing for Television News

There are three words that sum up what's important, different and difficult about writing for television: *pictures, pictures, pictures.* Television is overwhelmingly a visual medium. The pictures must tell the story. The words play off the pictures, providing context and additional information. Juxtaposing words and pictures is the real skill of television newswriting. A television script that makes sense without the pictures is poorly written, because it's not properly using the most powerful element of any TV news report.

Many of the rules of writing for radio apply to TV — stories should be written conversationally. They must be simple, clear, easy to read aloud and easy to understand when heard. But TV writing also has its own rules. This section is intended as a brief introduction to some of them.

THE TELEVISION NEWS PACKAGE

The most basic element of TV news is the package. There are a number of other ways to present TV news, which will be touched on later, but the reporter package is the backbone of any TV bulletin.

There are four elements to any package.
- The intro, or cue, read by the anchor
- The pictures
- The links, the reporter's words read over the pictures
- The soundbites from the interviewees featured in the package

INTROS OR CUES — TELLING AND SELLING THE STORY

The intro should sum up the story, explain why it's important, and grab the viewer's attention. Usually, the intro should be no more than two or three sentences. It needs to conclude by introducing the reporter and the package.

Intros can be straightforward:

Fierce gun battles continued to rage in Macedonia, where ethnic Albanian rebels are holed up in the mountains near the border with Kosovo. The rebels have so far resisted attempts by the Macedonian army to force them back into Kosovo. There's growing concern that shelling by the Macedonian army may have killed dozens of civilians in a small village near Tetovo. From there, Peter Smith reports.

Sometimes intros have to be written like that because the package may be fed via satellite at the last minute and there's no way of knowing exactly what's in it. Where this isn't a factor, there's often an opportunity to say a little bit more about the issues the package addresses. If the package deals with a particular element or aspect of a story, the intro should make that clear:

Rolling blackouts hit California this morning, for the first time since March. With temperatures on the rise and no end in sight to the Golden State's power crisis, outages are expected to worsen. Peter Smith's in San Diego — finding out how businesses there are gearing up for a long, hot summer.

Where possible, an intro should be a road map of the package, outlining all the elements of the story the report will cover:

President Bush introduced his administration's long-awaited energy policy this afternoon. He warned there are no quick fixes for what he called America's looming energy crisis. But environmental groups said the president should do more to encourage conservation, and in Congress Democrats accused the administration of leaving power-strapped California in the lurch. Peter Smith reports.

This sets up a story with three soundbites: Bush, an environmentalist and a congressional Democrat. Because an intro like this lays out the elements of a story, it's often good discipline to write it first — as a plan for the whole package.

PICTURES: THE OPENING SHOT

The opening shot of a package is the most important thing about it. It's what the viewer is waiting for. The opening shot — and the accompanying script — should lay out the most important element of the story. Done right, it can leave an indelible image in the viewer's mind.

This also means that sometimes it is best to tell a story in a particular way — starting from a particular point — because it is the point where the best pictures are to be found. For instance, in a story about a missing girl the best pictures might be a moon-suited forensic scientist searching for clues at the edge of a wood — even if nothing was found there. Those could be the opening shots — if the story starts with the search rather than with the girl herself. Starting with the girl would mean starting on pictures — even if a still — of her.

Choose the pictures first. Write to them. Remember that vision is the primary sense and that the viewer will therefore register the pictures before they absorb your script. Sometimes silence is the best commentary. A short pause at a particularly dramatic or poignant moment emphasizes the power of the pictures.

LINKS: MOVING THE STORY ALONG

The links of a package are the elements of the story — the facts and the narrative in the reporter's own words. But they have two kinds of work to do in TV that they don't have in print. As well as imparting information, they have to move the story along, making clear the significance of any transitions — from today's pictures to yesterday's, or from one location to another:

> (*Over nighttime pictures of the fire.*) The flames roared through the historic seven-story building, which has stood here since Lincoln's time, and fire crews battled for hours to save the downtown landmark *(over pictures of the building's collapse)* . . . In vain . . . *(Over daytime footage of investigators)* Daylight brought questions . . . How did the fire start? . . . How did it spread so quickly?

"Daylight brought questions" moves the story along, both in time and in subject, smoothing the transition from nighttime to daytime pictures and turning neatly to the matter of the investigation.

But links also have to cue up the soundbites, introducing the speaker and, if possible, contextualizing their contribution:

> (*Over daytime footage of investigators.*) Daylight brought questions . . . How did the fire start? . . . How did it spread so

quickly? . . . Fire department investigators this afternoon had no word on what started the blaze, but said wood floors helped the flames engulf the building so fast. *[Steve Ericson, fire department investigator.]* "These old buildings, see, the joists and the boards get real dry over time and when the flames get a-hold, they just sweep right through . . . Terrible thing . . . it was a lovely place."

Typically, in a two-minute package, there will be two or perhaps three soundbites, each 15 or so seconds long, so each link can be at most half a minute long. That's just 90 or so words, so choose them with care.

SOUNDBITES: ADDING SOMETHING SPECIAL

Soundbites should be chosen with even greater care. In general, a reporter's script will be able to provide information more clearly and efficiently than an interviewee speaking off the cuff. From an interviewee, therefore, the reporter has to look for something more than just information: opinion perhaps, or emotion, or just a pungently expressed point of view.

Like every element of a package, the interview depends on pictures. Typically, reporters will use pictures of an interviewee to run over the introduction:

> Dave Barry, who runs a local campaign against the sales tax, says that the rate hike will hurt local businesses and the extra revenue will just be frittered away . . .

What pictures should be used to introduce Barry? The classic setup, the so-called walking shot — showing the subject, well, walking — almost never works well. It's usually better to film him doing something characteristic or relevant to the story — giving the script a chance to move the story along. In this example, pictures of Barry in his campaign headquarters — on the phone or photocopying fliers, perhaps — or distributing leaflets to the businesses he says will be hurt by the tax increase. In this last case, the script could point that out:

> Dave Barry, who runs a local campaign against the new sales tax, says the county will just fritter away any extra revenue and the rate hike will hurt local businesses like these . . .

THE CLOSER OR OUTCUE: THROWING THE STORY FORWARD

The last link needs to close up the story, or — if it is an open-ended one, as most are — look to the future. What will happen next? "Only time will tell" is a terrible cliche, but like most cliches, it became so because it does a useful job of work: reminding the audience that the story isn't over yet:

The investigation continues . . .

No one knows yet how the fire started . . .

A question that won't be answered until the vote on Thursday . . .

OTHER TV NEWS FORMATS

The Live Wrap

In a live wrap, the intro will end with a "throw" — the anchorman or anchorwoman introduces the reporter, typically asking a question that sets the stage for the reporter to introduce his own package:

> *Anchor:* And in Florida, police are continuing to search for a young couple suspected in a grisly series of murder-robberies that left 10 dead over the holiday weekend. Peter Smith is in Daytona Beach, the scene of the so-called Labor Day massacre. Peter, are the police any closer to catching these two?
>
> *Reporter:* Well, John, they say the net is tightening around the two, who they believe are laying low somewhere in the town, having abandoned their SUV and fled on foot — firing at police as they ran — after a high-speed car chase this morning.

This would nicely set up a package that opened with pictures of the abandoned vehicle, or helicopter or security camera footage of the chase.

When the anchorman ends with a throw, he or she needs to take care to leave the reporter something to say, otherwise he can be left lamely parroting the anchor:

> *Anchorman:* And in Florida, police are continuing to search for a young couple suspected in a grisly series of murder-robberies that left 10 dead over the holiday weekend. Peter Smith is in Daytona Beach, where a dramatic high-speed car chase this morning ended in a hail of bullets as the suspects got away on foot, firing at police as they went. Peter, are the police any closer to catching these two?
>
> *Reporter:* Well, John, they say the net is tightening around the two, who they believe are laying low somewhere in the town, having — as you said — abandoned their SUV and fled on foot a few hours ago.

The reporter will generally read the closer live, and then outcue with a throw back to the studio. If the story is important enough, or if there are late-breaking developments, the anchorman may ask another question.

The live wrap typically ends with a camera turn, where the host looks down at the desk, then up again at another camera before reading the next intro.

Wallpaper
When pictures are used as wallpaper, they are played over the words of the anchorman. This format is typically used either because there isn't time available in the bulletin for a reporter package, or because no package is available. It's a way of getting dramatic pictures on screen without allocating the resources or the airtime demanded by a complete package. It is a good way of handling very late breaking news that can't be packaged in time. Typically, an anchorman "read" under wallpaper will be 30–40 seconds or so — a little longer than a single link.

The UpSOF
An *UpSOF* (Up Sound Of Film) is a wallpaper read that ends with a soundbite. It is rarely used, partly because it requires very careful timing. Otherwise there will be either an awkward silence when the anchor finishes reading before the soundbite kicks in, or — worse — the anchor will "crash" (overlap with) the soundbite.

CONCLUSION
Movies like *Broadcast News* or HBO's *Live from Baghdad* may make TV journalism look glamorous and exciting, and for some it is. But the reality — for the vast majority of people who work in it — is very different. I'll never forget the time when I was part of the huge broadcast media pack outside the Kennedy compound in Hyannisport, Mass., after John Kennedy Jr.'s plane went missing. All the hotels for miles around were completely booked, so for the first three days the small BBC News team lived in the cars we'd hired at the airport. Not that we got any chance to sleep, since we were expected to be on the air every hour more or less round the clock. Never having been in the military, I didn't know what it was like not to be able to eat, sleep or change one's clothes for 48 hours, but it was an experience I could well have done without.

On the third day, I met a smartly turned out young man from ABC News. His main job, I discovered, was ferrying the clothes worn by the ABC anchors and correspondents to and from the dry cleaner's. He also had to ensure that the fridge in their air-conditioned dressing room trailer was always stocked with cold drinks and ice, and that there was fresh fruit and freshly cut sandwiches there, too. In his spare time he hung around the satellite uplink truck, trying to make himself useful to the harried producers there. He was, he explained, "trying to break into the business."

Not entirely glamorous. But at least he was with a network.

Like many broadcast journalists, I got my start in local news, trying desperately to make engaging, informative television out of the latest round of murders, road traffic incidents and zoning disputes. Sometimes I got so frustrated I could have cried.

Television is also an extraordinarily transient medium. They say in Britain where I come from that yesterday's newspapers wrap tomorrow's fish and chips. But at least you can do that with them. Yesterday's broadcast is gone and — more than likely — forgotten, probably forever, and sometimes it's for the best that way.

But you don't have to be covering the big issues to get a sense of satisfaction when you manage to do a good job against all the odds. Getting a really tricky and complex story on air in a clear and visually engaging way used to give me a great surge of delight every time I achieved it. And it still does.

Shaun Waterman is UPI's homeland and national security correspondent. He previously worked at the BBC, where he started as a trainee and worked as a producer for local TV and national radio. As a senior producer with BBC Radio News, he traveled to the Middle East, Bosnia and the United States, where he finally came to rest.

4

Covering the White House

The White House is the most dynamic news beat in the Western world and the most difficult. A wire service reporter assigned there may come to work at 9 a.m. and that same night be on a plane following the president of the United States to the Azores.

The U.S. president can govern from Air Force One at 35,000 feet in the air, agreeing to meet Russian President Vladimir Putin for tea in St. Petersburg in the afternoon and having breakfast with Italian President Silvio Berlusconi in Rome the next morning. He can attend a meeting of the National Security Council from a secure television hookup in a foreign capital and talk directly to the lead commander in the lead tank crossing the Iraqi desert to Baghdad. The modern system of communications and intelligence means that the president and White House staff can deal with hundreds of major or minor crises every single day.

From 1939 when World War II began to the present, the American president's role in the world has become increasingly more powerful. At the end of World War II, the United States was one of the two remaining world powers.

The Cold War from 1948 to 1989 saw the world divided in two, with a Russian empire, then called the Soviet Union, and to a lesser extent China being co-equal nuclear powers with the United States. By the mid-1960s both sides had nuclear arsenals mounted on intercontinental ballistic missiles so dangerous that they could destroy each other and the world with a single barrage.

U.S. foreign policy for those incredible four decades concentrated on containing Soviet and Chinese power and preventing nuclear destruction. No decision a president made, from entering the Vietnam War to responding to the seizing of a spy ship off the coast of Korea, could be taken without considering whether this could trigger a nuclear confrontation with the Soviet Union and the resulting Armageddon.

1945
WASHINGTON, April 12 — Harry S. Truman, one time $3 a-week "bottle duster" in a small-town Missouri drug store, was sworn in as the 32nd president of the United States, at 6:08 p.m. (E.W.T.) tonight, succeeding Franklin Delano Roosevelt, whose war and domestic policies he vowed to carry on. — Helen Ashby

In the same decades, the federal government's domestic power grew enormously. From President Franklin Roosevelt's New Deal to Lyndon Johnson's Great Society, the federal government began taking a greater and greater role in the lives of Americans.

This, of course, conditioned how Washington was covered by the news media, how White House reporters were chosen and how journalistic careers were shaped. Since so much was decided in Washington, news bureaus exploded in size, adding reporters on education, social services, labor, law and justice to the traditional Washington beats of Congress, the White House and national defense.

Prior to World War II a White House correspondent had most likely been a political reporter or a generalist who covered the president as a political entity. By the 1970s, a White House reporter had to understand the intricacies of missile throw weights, the impact of tax policy on the economy, national education trends and the medical and moral issues of late-term abortion.

The bigger news agencies, like UPI, tended to form teams to cover the White House. They couldn't provide experts on everything, but usually had one person deeply familiar with foreign issues, another a national political reporter and possibly a third person concentrating on economics or social issues.

At the same time that the world was changing and U.S. power was in the ascendancy, the reporting of news was undergoing two revolutions that directly affected how the president was covered by news organizations. One was, of course, television. By the 1980s, most Americans learned of breaking news from television. Readership of American newspapers declined and the print media's influence in politics and government dwindled.

The famous old newsreel scene of a bunch of reporters racing for a telephone after a chat with President Dwight Eisenhower's press secretary, Jim Hagerty, became an anachronism. Television's ability to send out an immediate image ended the newspaper's "extras," the newsboys' cries on late evening news, and most street sales of newspapers.

Though wire services still were the first alarm for television, radio and newspaper bureaus, slowly television assumed that function. Speed alone is no longer the top value. Print reporters must be able to analyze presidential actions and statements as they are made, find stories about what happens behind the scenes and break exclusives.

Over the past two decades, television cameras have turned most White House events, news conferences and even so-called background briefings into carefully choreographed verbal ballets, designed to put forth the president's "message," as President George W. Bush's White House calls it.

Beginning with Franklin Roosevelt, White House news secretaries, the famous names such as Hagerty, Ron Ziegler, Marlin Fitzwater, Jody Powell and Jim Brady, answered reporters' questions informally in regular daily briefings in which they tried to impart information as well as shape the coverage of the president. They could often stave off a political difficulty by giving a reporter "guidance" that would change the thrust of a story or cause the reporter to drop his idea altogether.

But a little over a decade ago, under pressure from the new 24-hour television news operations, the White House put the daily briefing on camera. It quickly made the reporters posers and actors and White House spokesmen shapers of editorial opinion.

The story was, in effect, published when the reporter asked the question, so they could not pursue a premise, follow up a tip or raise an unflattering matter about the president without creating a furor. Every question, for instance, about President Clinton's personal behavior became a story because of the televised news briefing, even if his news secretary, Joe Lockhart, could establish it was frivolous.

Political campaigns no longer ended when the president won election, but continued in every White House briefing as reporters brought questions from the president's political enemies and the White House batted them down using a few moments to put forth the president's political positions.

The second revolution that has shaped the White House reporting job — indeed reporting everywhere — is the computer. No longer does the dinging of wire service machine bells alert newsrooms to breaking news. But the change is much deeper and still not fully appreciated.

In some ways it has returned speed as a quality in newswire coverage. Computer Web pages have news content, which demand short, brisk, accurate and up-to-date news bulletins for millions of people working at their computers. Wireless telephones, hand-held PDAs and electronic communication devices are capable of providing immediate news bulletins displayed on their screens.

The e-mail system has broken down borders for news. A computer user in China, one of the world's most repressive societies, can now go on his computer and surf the Net and get information from hundreds of thousands of sources not previously available to him.

The White House now communicates by computer. It sends out every statement, every transcript, every official document to reporters by e-mail. Some of the announcements come almost instantaneously, and in theory a good deal of writing about White House activities could be accomplished without ever going there.

The flood of information that comes from the president every day perhaps presents the first hurdle for reporters. They must check it, balance it, sort it, choose what is important for readers to know, decide how to indicate what is valid, what isn't, and what is misleading or manufactured. In order to sift this great flow of information, covering the White House requires reporters to be aware, hour by hour, of the compelling public issues of the day.

Reading and more reading are key skills on the White House beat — three or four major papers a day, perhaps including the *Washington Post, Washington Times, New York Times, Wall Street Journal* and *Los Angeles Times.* All desks at the White House pressroom and in most Washington newsrooms have television sets that are constantly on, feeding in developments from 24-hour channels.

Washington is filled with so-called "think tanks," groups of academics or former government officials who are studying major issues, usually from one political perspective or another. They are publishing papers on issues — more reading — and act as sources for reporters trying to understand events.

The reporter has to understand the presidency, the U.S. political system and the history of this republic. Henry Hubbard, for a decade *Newsweek*'s White House correspondent, had read literally hundreds of books on the presidency and the presidents.

With the opening of the world after the collapse of communism, the number of things a reporter must know has exploded. He has to know the names and political views of foreign political parties, not just his own, and that some nations are supporting the United States not because they embrace our policies, but because they want our support in achieving their aims, like membership in NATO or the WTO. The White House correspondent should know the names of foreign leaders and where he can find a biography quickly. Much of this information will be supplied by the White House, but that too can be suspect.

Perhaps the most important challenge for a print reporter is establishing sources — people in the administration who will tell the reporter what is really going on. That is because the White House is going to say what it wants, and only what it wants, regardless of what questions reporters ask in briefings. In FDR's time he'd have a few reporters in for a chat, but in the ensuing decades the line of communication has become more structured, with a press secretary or two and dozens of aides between the press and the president.

For several decades now reporters have tried to improve their questioning of the president, at news conferences and the occasional photo op, and of press secretaries in order to elicit information. But presidents and press secretaries are now highly skilled at repeating their message and obfuscating when they see fit.

Therefore, to add any depth to White House pronouncements, a reporter must have sources. Often these sources are nurtured during a campaign, or through years of experience in Washington, attending ordinary events and policy conferences, writing myriad ordinary news stories and meeting all sorts of people in the nation's capital who someday may wind up in the top echelon of an administration.

Once sources are established, the information exchange can be either background, off-the record, or direct, quotable facts. Occasionally, White House figures, for their own personal or professional reasons, will seek out a White House reporter and "leak" a story. Often a reporter can capitalize on a policy disagreement between White House players trying to influence public opinion, or even the president's opinion.

And more than one good story has been written after obscenely large lobsters and large quantities of ridiculously expensive wine have been consumed at private salons in Georgetown or other trendy Washington neighborhoods.

Spouses — like Martha Mitchell, who was married to Richard Nixon's attorney general, John Mitchell — sometimes let a juicy story slip to a reporter. Often good information can be obtained even more indirectly, perhaps through a congressional aide or lobbyist who is a neighbor or friend of a White House staff member.

So what a White House reporter needs is a good sense of history, a grasp of numbers, a desire to work seemingly endless hours, a rich Rolodex, and more than a few well-placed friends, acquaintances, or even enemies, who will talk candidly about the issues of the day. It is all about who you know, and who will talk to you, like covering a city hall, Hollywood and Wall Street, all in one.

Nicholas M. Horrock, Chief White House Correspondent, is a veteran newsman with tours of duty with The New York Times *and* Chicago Sun-Times, *before joining UPI in 1999. He is also the author of Washington-based mystery novels.*

5

Covering Congress

F iling effective stories on Congress can be divided into two basic categories with overlapping strategies: *drumbeat news* and *breaking big stories*. The press gallery in the House or Senate will be the nerve center to develop both kinds of stories. The latter big story almost always grows out of curiosity formed while filing the former drumbeat news story.

During extremely busy weeks in Congress, a majority of the two to three stories filed each day will be drumbeat news — major political developments, committee hearings and floor votes, mostly. These are relatively easy to keep track of. All committee hearings and summaries of the days' likely major events are listed in two congressional "tip sheet" publications, *Congress Daily* and *CQ Daily Monitor*. Committee schedules are listed in *The Washington Post* and *Washington Times* as well.

The Senate and House galleries also have continuously updated lists of official press events occurring all over Capitol Hill displayed on television screens in both galleries. That list can also be sent to reporters via text pagers available through the Senate Radio and TV gallery.

During key votes, it can be fruitful to go into the seating gallery above the Senate or House floor and watch the votes. The body language and goings-on that take place in the House, but particularly in the smaller Senate, can be clues in themselves to events.

Paper copies of all amendments are available through the knowledgeable, friendly and helpful staffers who work in the two galleries. Reporters get to know these people well because they know what is going on much, much more than you might think. They can also take care of a whole list of things for the reporter, including saving seats at extremely packed hearings. It is best to be on their good side at all times.

Hand out business cards to every press person, particularly in leadership offices, and subscribe to their e-mail lists for press releases and statements. These will come in a deluge eventually, but will provide quotes and can even help avoid blind spots on a busy day.

One of the greatest things about working in Congress — for drumbeat news and breaking big news — is the access to the members of Congress. Stake out the Senate floor near the cloakroom before and after votes to talk to senators. All of the senators are also available following the Tuesday policy lunches, which take place on the second floor near the Senate cloakroom.

In both the House and the Senate, reporters can file a request to have a member called from the floor to talk. Sometimes representatives will do it, sometimes they won't. Ask press gallery staffers for help and advice on this. Also, of course, before and after official news conferences are good times to approach members for a confidential chat.

From there, drumbeat news is often improved by discussing developing stories with lobbyists, trade groups and former government officials. Rarely is the full, accurate picture available by sticking solely to sources in the building.

Breaking big news ahead of the drumbeat will almost always require serious phone work with lobbyists, staffers and other sources. Lunches and cocktails are also a good way to get them to talk.

1941

WASHINGTON, Dec. 8 — President Roosevelt today in person asked Congress to declare that "a state of war has existed between the United States and the Japanese Empire" as a result of Japan's "unprovoked and dastardly attack."

Members of Congress stood, waved and cheered wildly as the President declared, "We will win," and cheered again at the close of the speech.

— United Press

Mark Benjamin is an investigative reporter with six years experience covering Washington. Since 2001 Benjamin has been UPI's congressional bureau chief and has helped direct UPI's Washington coverage. Before that Benjamin was chief editor of Inside Washington Publishers' "Inside EPA" *weekly report on the Environmental Protection Agency. His investigative work has gotten him credit in* Vanity Fair, *and he has appeared on CBS's* 60 Minutes II.

Covering the Courts

When covering court action, reporters should be guided by the following mantra, repeated over and over again until it takes: *Use English.*

Once you become accustomed to the legalese used by lawyers and judges, it's tempting to use phrases such as "res judicata" or "collateral estoppel" just to show off. The only reason to use obscure legal terms in your copy is when the main point of your story is how a particular case is tied up in legal knots. Even then, even when the legal term is in general use, always immediately explain the term in conversational English.

An excellent online legal dictionary is available at dictionary.law.com.

Covering courts, whether at the state or federal level, can be one of the most interesting fields of journalism. Each case, each trial, can bring a change in life, whether for an individual, or for the nation as a whole.

HOW THE COURTS WORK

Generally, a legal case begins with a *complaint,* either civil or criminal, filed by a *plaintiff* in a particular trial court against a *defendant.*

A criminal complaint is sometimes followed by an *indictment,* but either one can stand independent of the other.

In other words, someone can be indicted without a formal criminal complaint, and someone can be held on a criminal complaint and tried without an indictment.

An indictment is returned by a grand jury, not a prosecutor. A *grand* jury, as opposed to a *petit* jury, is only used to hear information in secret and return a formal charge. An indictment simply means a majority of the grand jury agrees a crime has taken place; and, based on what the prosecutor has told them, it is likely that the target of the grand jury's deliberations has committed that crime. An example: "A federal grand jury Friday indicted John Smith on three counts of perjury." Each separate charge in an indictment is called a *count.*

Leaking grand jury information can be punished as contempt of court under the famous Rule 6e of the *Federal Rules of Criminal Procedure.* When seeking grand jury information from any official, remember the official is risking his or her freedom to convey that information to you.

> **1944**
>
> LONDON, June 3 — United States Flying Fortresses and Liberators twice hammered the Pas de Calais and Boulogne areas of the French invasion coast Saturday while at least 2,000 other Allied warplanes swept over Northern France and Belgium in the greatest Nazi hunt since the pre-invasion blitz opened nearly two months ago.   — Walter Cronkite

An *arraignment* is a formal presentation of charges against a defendant, and at an arraignment a defendant must be allowed to plead guilty or not guilty.

A *preliminary hearing* is a separate process that occurs when there is a criminal complaint but no indictment, and allows a judge or a magistrate to take the place of a grand jury to decide if there is enough evidence to charge the defendant with a crime.

All criminal defendants being held on a charge must appear before a magistrate or a judge within a short period of time. The historic right of *habeas corpus* — literally, "you have the body" — evolved as a defense against keeping prisoners in custody without some legal process reviewing that custody.

In the United States, habeas corpus is often understood as judicial review, state or federal, of a defendant's rights. In fact, once a convicted defendant exhausts state appeals, he or she has the right to ask for "habeas" review in federal courts. A 1996 federal law drastically shortens the number of times a death row inmate can tap into this "habeas" review. Some death row inmates had been delaying their executions for decades through the skillful use of the federal courts.

The Supreme Court declared this 1996 law constitutional only because the justices retained the right to issue "an original writ of habeas corpus" in individual cases. In other words, no matter what the federal law says, the Supreme Court can still swoop in and act if a majority of the justices feel that constitutional rights have been trampled.

BEFORE TRIAL

Trials, civil or criminal, are generally preceded by a number of hearings that may or may not include *motions* by lawyers on either side. Motions are simply requests from the lawyers for both sides asking the judge to do something. For instance, a defense attorney may file a motion asking for certain evidence to be suppressed because it was obtained unconstitutionally or would have an effect that would produce an unfair result. An example: "Smith's attorney asked the judge not to allow the jury to see slides of his ex-wife's body, saying the explicit photos. . . ."

A motion could also be made to dismiss the complaint: "Smith's attorney said the prosecution had not produced enough evidence to support a criminal charge against his client, and asked the judge to dismiss the case before it goes to trial."

A petit jury, or the jury that listens to witnesses and evaluates evidence at trial, is always simply called "the jury." Jury selection, or *voir dire,* is unimportant unless the trial is especially important. In other words, jury selection in most cases is not that big a deal. In the O.J. Simpson trial, it was a big deal and almost certainly determined the outcome. You just have to make a coverage decision on a case-by-case basis.

In selecting a jury, attorneys from either side are allowed a limited number of *peremptory strikes* — exclusion of a potential juror for no reason. Other potential jurors from a *panel* can be stricken for other reasons — for example, if they have already formed an opinion as to the guilt or innocence of a defendant. However, attorneys are not allowed to construct all-white or all-black juries, or juries of one gender.

Before a civil or criminal trial begins, attorneys must engage in what is called *discovery.* Generally, each side gets to look at the other's cards — what evidence the other side is hiding up its sleeve, what witnesses it intends to question and why they will be questioned.

In criminal cases, however, the defense gets to see the prosecution's cards, but the prosecution generally doesn't get to see the defense's cards. In other words, in most courts, discovery in criminal cases is one-sided. Motions from either side may be introduced while a trial proceeds.

Generally, from opening statements to closing arguments, the plaintiff goes first in presenting evidence and witnesses. Lawyers *examine* their own witnesses and *cross-examine* their opponents' witnesses.

Lawyers can *object* to any aspect of a trial while it is proceeding. The judge can *sustain,* or agree, with the objection, or *overrule* it. This sometimes dramatic gesture is not allowed outside the trial courts.

Crimes must be proved "beyond a reasonable doubt." Civil trials are decided by "a preponderance of the evidence."

If a judge does something an attorney doesn't like during a trial, the lawyer can sometimes ask a higher court to intervene before the trial concludes. This is called an *interlocutory appeal,* or sometimes just an *interlocutory.* Appeals courts generally frown on them. Avoid the use of "interlocutory" — just describe in general terms what's going on.

In most states, a jury returns a verdict in a civil or criminal trial, unless a defendant asks for a *bench trial* — when a judge alone hears the case and renders a verdict. If a judge has some conflict of interest in presiding over or deciding a case, he or she must *recuse* himself or herself. Avoid the use of "recuse." Just say, for example, "The judge withdrew from the case when it became apparent his third wife was involved."

AFTER THE TRIAL

All losing sides (and only losing sides; you have to have lost on at least some issue) have the right to *appeal,* but not all higher courts are *appellate* courts. Sometimes both sides feel they have come out the losers in a court case, and both appeal.

An appeal goes directly from a trial court to a higher court, and the higher court must decide whether to *reverse* or *affirm* — agree with — the trial court's judgment.

In the federal courts, trial court decisions are appealed to U.S. circuit court panels, consisting of three circuit judges, who have the power to *affirm* — agree with the lower court decision — or *reverse.*

Once the appeals court panel acts, the federal right to an appeal (on whatever issue is decided) is over. The losing side can ask the entire circuit, usually 12 circuit judges or more, to rehear the appeal *en banc,* but that request is usually refused. Either before or after the *en banc* refusal, the losing side can ask the Supreme Court for review. Petitions to the Supreme Court are not appeals. (See Supreme Court section below.)

In state courts, the losing side can appeal to some intermediate court, then ask the state's highest court for review. Not all state high courts are called "supreme" courts. The highest court in Alabama is the Alabama Supreme Court, but the highest court in New York is the New York Court of Appeals. The "Supreme Court of New York" is actually a trial court in that state. Simple, no?

Once a state's highest court has decided — or, more commonly, refused to decide — the issues in a case, the losing side can always ask the Supreme Court of the United States for review (notice the distinction once a state supreme court is introduced). When it is clear in a story that the "Supreme Court" is the Supreme Court of the United States, we use the shorter form. If not (usually when a state supreme court is also in the story), we use the longer form and refer to the U.S. Supreme Court on second reference.

> **1946**
> NUREMBERG, April 8 — Marshal Wilhelm Keitel, his voice quivering and his clenched fists pounding the witness box rail, testified today that he issued blanket orders for Nazi war crimes because he was under the malign domination of Adolf Hitler.

Theoretically, the U.S. Supreme Court has limited powers in reviewing state cases, unless there is some clear U.S. constitutional issue involved. In reality, the U.S. Supreme Court can and does review anything it wants to review, justifying its involvement in any way it sees fit. About 7,000 petitions come to the U.S. Supreme Court each year. The justices will rule *summarily* — without debate — in some of them, and will accept about 75 for argument and an eventual ruling.

PRECEDENT

In reality, all courts set "precedents." When a trial court rules a particular way for the first time, it sets an example for other courts; but that example may or may not be followed. Speaking strictly in legal terms, only appeals courts and higher set precedents, which must be followed within that court's jurisdiction. For example, a precedent set by Louisiana's highest court must be followed by the courts within that state. A precedent set by the U.S. Court of Appeals for the 11th Circuit must be followed by the federal courts (and sometimes the state courts, depending on the issue) within that geographic circuit — Alabama, Florida and Georgia.

THE FEDERAL COURTS

There are 12 geographic U.S. circuits, each with its own appeals court, in the United States and its territories and possessions — from the 1st Circuit (headquarters in Boston) to the 11th Circuit (headquarters in Atlanta). The U.S. Circuit for the District of Columbia is the 12th geographic circuit.

Each U.S. Supreme Court justice oversees at least one, and sometimes two or more, of the circuits. The chief justice — who, by the way, is chief justice of the United States, not the Supreme Court — oversees the 4th U.S. Circuit (headquarters in Richmond, Va.) as well as the D.C. Circuit.

The D.C. Circuit is probably the most important appeal court in the United States. Many cases dealing with federal law are decided here, even if they have roots in other parts of the country. For example, the Microsoft antitrust case was tried and the appeal was heard in the D.C. Circuit, even though Microsoft has headquarters in Redmond, Wash.

The chief justice also oversees the Federal Circuit, which is a separate entity dealing with intellectual property.

EMERGENCY APPEALS

All courts also receive emergency applications. For example, a condemned prisoner seeking to block his execution may ask a judge, an appeals court and then finally a state high court or a federal appeals court for help. The U.S. Supreme Court is the last stop for such emergency applications, whether they're from condemned prisoners or a couple seeking to stop the confiscation of their car. Emergency applications are granted only until the matter can be settled in some court. For instance, the U.S. Supreme Court may block an execution, but only until the death row inmate's case is reviewed in argument.

In the U.S. Supreme Court, any supervising justice can grant or deny an emergency application coming from within the U.S. circuit he supervises, even if the case below is in state rather than federal court. Or the supervising justice can refer the application to the full U.S. Supreme Court for a vote.

THE U.S. SUPREME COURT

When a case comes to the U.S. Supreme Court, justices can grant or deny *certiorari*. Reporters call it "accepting" or "rejecting" a case, or agreeing or refusing to hear argument in a case — all meaning the same thing and all referring to cases in which a state or federal appeals court has ruled. In rare instances, and usually when it is written into law, justices agree to hear an appeal that comes directly from a trial court.

When the justices reject a case, or refuse review, which is the same thing, we sometimes say they "let stand" the lower court ruling. This is not a precedent, has no force of law outside the jurisdiction of the lower court, and does not mean that the justices will reject a similar case when it reaches the court the following week. It is not considered a *decision* by the court when they simply reject a case.

Once the justices accept a case, or grant an appeal, they have a variety of options. In the case of a decision handed down after argument, they can affirm or reverse the lower court ruling that led to the decision. If they think more court time is needed, they can affirm or reverse and remand, meaning the case is sent back to the lower court for a new hearing based on the decision.

They can also *vacate,* or throw out, a lower court ruling, and either *remand* — send back — for a new hearing based on a new or old Supreme Court decision, or *vacate* and dismiss when the case is *moot.* Whenever the justices vacate a lower court ruling, we say they "throw out" the ruling, which is essentially what they do. They're not ruling for one side or the other as in a reversal or affirmation.

They can also do all these things without hearing argument, but then they reverse, affirm or vacate in reference to an earlier Supreme Court decision in what is usually a *per curiam* — meaning unsigned — decision by the whole court, though individual justices can write separately to support or dissent from the per curiam decision.

COVERING THE SUPREME COURT

Covering the U.S. Supreme Court is something like entering a monastery. You pretty much work in isolation and silence. The high court acts like no other government agency in Washington.

The justices do not issue press releases, hold news conferences or try to manage the news. They conduct business in the courtroom and issue decisions.

This means a Supreme Court reporter must look at all of the incoming cases, at least the paid ones, and decide for himself or herself which are of importance.

Many are important, even if the justices reject them. For instance, if the justices reject a petition asking for reversal of the U.S. Court of Appeals for the District of Columbia Circuit, then the lower court ruling stands and applies to the entire country.

Other cases are important because they deal with a high-profile issue or person, and should be "backgrounded" — the facts and issues in a case should be written in story form — so that a story can be quickly filed to the wire if and when the Supreme Court acts on it.

Many cases are of such importance that it's obvious even before the justices accept a case that the Supreme Court will consider them for argument — such as *Bush vs. Gore.* Other cases are challenges to contro-

317

versial federal laws, and sometimes Congress includes a provision in the law itself that says the final challenge must be heard by the high court; the Bipartisan Campaign Act includes such a provision, that the U.S. Supreme Court must hear any challenge on direct appeal.

Supreme Court reporters spend a great deal of time in the pressroom of the Supreme Court building reading cases as they come in — or at least they should. Many reporters rely on the news wires to tell them which cases should be read.

Under court tradition, UPI and AP receive copies of all paid cases that come to the high court. Both wire service bureaus maintain libraries of Supreme Court cases, and at least look at every case.

A Supreme Court reporter covers all the significant arguments heard by the justices. This usually works out to about a dozen a year.

Arguments are important, but not for the usual reasons. Lawyers can argue a case brilliantly before the justices but still lose the case. While attending an argument, a Supreme Court reporter looks for comments from the bench and does a head count — who's for and who's against — to get a reasonable idea of how a case is going to be decided.

After a case is argued, lawyers will sometimes go to a stakeout on the Supreme Court plaza and review how they did. Wire reporters rarely get to attend the stakeouts, because they're hurrying to get their stories on the wire.

The Supreme Court public information officer (PIO) determines who gets to sit in the courtroom for arguments. The seating plans take three forms:

1. Open seating, when anyone can sit in the media section of the courtroom, which is to the right of the bench — two pews at a 90-degree angle to the bench.
2. "Plan B," only reporters credentialed by the Supreme Court may sit in the media pews; other reporters are assigned seats under the pillars or in the hall adjacent to the court — you may or may not hear what is going on, but you won't see much, if anything. If you don't know the sound of a justice's voice, you might not know who's speaking.
3. Reserved seating, senior Supreme Court reporters in assigned seats fill the two pews inside the courtroom; others are assigned seats under the pillars or in the hall.

Whether the seating is Plan B or reserved, UPI always takes seat 1B — it's in the courtroom, closest to the bench, but handy to get out of in case a reporter must leave to file. If a justice jumps up in the middle of an

argument, clutches his chest and falls over the bench, God help whoever's between the UPI reporter and the exit.

Typical sources for Supreme Court stories are the parties involved —
rarely — the lawyers who are arguing the case (their office phone numbers are on the briefs) and outside commentators, usually law professors.

Finally, covering the Supreme Court takes experience. The toughest
thing to do is receive an opinion in an important case — the PIO hands
them out in an office next to the pressroom — glance over it and write a
correct story within minutes. Opinions may seem to be saying one thing
but are actually saying something quite different. You must have background. You can't be just an occasional visitor to the court and expect to
understand an opinion that quickly. You have to put in the time.

This lack of experience was apparent in *Bush vs. Gore.* Many network
correspondents covering the case were at the Supreme Court for the first
time in their lives. That's why they stumbled for an hour or so on Dec. 12,
2000, trying to figure out if the presidential election was finally over.

---

*Mike Kirkland is UPI's senior legal affairs correspondent and has covered the
Supreme Court, appeals courts, independent counsels' investigations and the various
elements of the Justice Department since 1993. Before that he was managing editor
for* Army Times, *covering military activities from Panama to the Soviet Union.*

Pamela Hess

7

Covering the Pentagon
and the Military

The Pentagon, the heart of the U.S. military, is a great place for reporters — 25,000 potential sources at your fingertips. The hardest part is getting a lead on a story before it breaks. Seek out sources in the various branches of the armed services who work in the Pentagon and among the industries that provide the military with their hardware. Remember, however, the latter will be totally motivated by what benefits their company, so they are often willing to provide documents critical of other companies and weapons systems, not their own. Cultivating sources in the House and Senate committees that oversee the military is also a great way to get tips on stories before they become public.

SOME BASICS

1. The Pentagon has a briefing at least twice a week, on Tuesdays and Thursdays, usually at 1:30 p.m. There are more briefings when there's a major conflict in progress. Usually, any subject is game. The media desk in the public affairs office can confirm the time of the briefing.

2. Keep track of the competition by checking their reports often. This can be through the Internet from such resources as the *Drudge Report.* The Pentagon is a huge beat, and other reporters invariably will turn up great material that you can confirm if you call the right people.

3. Find the right people. You can always start with the public affairs office, but don't rely on them. Each of the services also has its own public affairs operations, which also deserve a call. But often they don't want the information to get out and may not be any help. They will invariably say, "I'll get back to you." Don't hold your breath. If they call back, it will probably be after your deadline. So stay in touch with them, but hunt down other avenues of information.

4. Reporters can go pretty much wherever they want in the Pentagon, and hanging out in the halls will allow you to grab officials for quick conversations.

5. Keep in mind that no one but spokesmen are supposed to talk to you. Others can get fired or be transferred if they have a big mouth, so protect your sources.

6. Majors and lieutenant colonels are great sources of information. They know everything. Colonels are cagier, smarter, older and desperate to be promoted to general. You have to cultivate them carefully. Generals are sometimes treasure troves of information, and sometimes useless — too political, too senior, too wary. Try to get them on the record. They are high enough in the chain to put their names on information. However, those found to be willing to provide useful information should be kept on background so they feel comfortable and don't stop talking.

7. The Pentagon phone book is your best friend, although it seems kind of impenetrable. Familiarize yourself with it. It is great for getting names and numbers of officials who are not supposed to talk to you.

HOW TO GET THROUGH TO OFFICIALS
WHO ARE NOT SUPPOSED TO TALK TO YOU

Civilian officials' military assistants are probably your best source for information to begin with. Secretaries or military assistants answer phones, and they are instructed to send all reporters to public affairs, so don't identify yourself as a reporter.

Here is advice I gave to our State Department reporter who wanted to get Department of Defense information from a particular official (he had leverage because he had State Department information to share, which DOD had a hard time getting otherwise):

Call and ask for Lieutenant Colonel Dennis Dugan or Colonel Yaggi. I think it's pronounced "Yaw-gee." If a secretary tells you he no longer works there, feign surprise and ask who replaced him, then ask to speak with that person. To get past secretaries, here is the general rule: Ask to speak to whoever you want, then fill in immediately with information about why you are calling — trying to avoid mentioning your affiliation. This generally fries their circuits and they forget to ask who you represent and they put you through to the people you want, to whom you may then identify yourself. The secretaries are actually required to patch you through to public affairs, which you don't want to happen, so you want to break their chain of asking "Who, what organization, what subject?"

Once in a while you'll get a secretary who will rat you out to public affairs, but this tactic works 90 percent of the time. The conversation will probably go like this:

> *You:* "May I speak with Lieutenant Colonel Dugan please?"
> *Secretary:* "He no longer works here. May I ask who's calling?"
> *You:* "This is Joseph Doe. Who replaced Dugan?"
> *Secretary:* "Bob Jones."
> *You:* "May I speak with Mr. Jones please? It's about the North Korea talks in Kuala Lumpur."

At this point she is trying to process your subject and usually will forget to find out if you are a reporter. Good luck.

When you talk to the people you are trying to reach, tell them who you work for (try to avoid using the word "reporter," which raises emotional red flags), and say you are just asking for a reality check on what people at State are telling you about the Kuala Lumpur meeting.

Don't talk about *on the record* or *on background* until after your conversation. Offer to go on background by saying you don't want to get them in trouble — you are just trying to figure out if the State Department is being straight with you.

If they still seem reluctant, say you'd just like to tell them first what you're hearing and that if any of it is flat wrong, maybe they could just point that out to you. You are just afraid you are "being taken for a little ride; I don't know if I can trust these people." There's a backhanded compliment in this for them — that you believe you can trust them. That's what the military people think of themselves — honest brokers.

The way to find out anything at the Pentagon is to determine who, if the rumor you are hearing is true, is most threatened/angered/upset about it. They have an axe to grind and are much more likely to want to talk. People who like the new idea are probably feeling defensive so are more likely to turn you down.

Remember, people in the military are early risers. The earlier you call in the day (before 8 a.m., for instance), the more likely you will get them on the phone. Secretaries roll in after that, so often the higher-ups (a general maybe) answer their own phones.

> 1972
> TORRINGTON, Wyo., Oct. 31 (UPI) — The boys in the bar, a little wiser from the bourbon, decided that Sen. George McGovern couldn't beat President Nixon with a stick — not on election day and not in a million years.
> — Peter M. Kelly

If you get voice mail, don't leave much info: just your name, number and the subject, and try to sound friendly and curious and as if you and the person you are calling have known each other for a long time. They will call back, if only because they are worried they should remember you but don't.

WRITING THE STORY

For a developing story for a wire service, you want to get the story out within the hour of the close of the event, such as a court-martial, court of inquiry or some sort of ceremony.

It's difficult to organize a lot of material in that short amount of time, but one way to do it (the way I do on stories that develop throughout the day) is to pre-write a nut graph or two explaining that this is the first (or second or whatever) day of the Naval inquiry, or whatever it is. Then give a sentence about what that proceeding is and a two-sentence summary of the accident or the issue in court. Provide the basic background. Keep these paragraphs for stories every day and you won't have to rewrite (although you'll be able to tighten them as the days wear on).

Then whenever something interesting happens or is said, write a paragraph and a quote that can sit on top of those nut graphs. As the day goes on, just keep adding paragraphs on top. Then when it is time to file (or if an editor or desk calls you desperate for some info), you can send what you have. Before you send off your final story, reorganize the graphs, putting the most interesting, vital stuff at the top. Rewrite the lead to reflect the reorganized story, put the nut graphs in the top third of your article and you should be good to go. Doing it this way protects you if you find you can't read earlier notes, or forget some detail.

If you are filing successive stories on an event, it helps to keep a copy of your earlier stories. Often you can just update each successive version throughout and it will keep you from having to re-create a story out of whole cloth.

As in all good journalism, make sure you lead your stories with the most important and interesting information. I sometimes personally have a problem with backing into stories, wanting to tell them chronologically, as I experienced them. But remember, this is why you have a job. You sit here and listen chronologically so someone else doesn't have to spend the time to do it, and then you spit out the stuff from the most important to least important so they don't have to wade through a transcript to get the whole story. Try to think about telling the story to your grandmother — grab her at the beginning with the newest hottest stuff, backfill some detail so she knows what you are talking about, then plow through what happened and explain why it is important and why she should care.

Pamela Hess, who was named the Pentagon correspondent for United Press International in March 1999, has also covered the White House, and spent a month in Afghanistan covering the formation of a new government. At the Pentagon she has broken numerous national and international news stories, including Singapore's secret arrest of 15 terrorists plotting to attack U.S. and western government targets. She was an award-winning chief editor of two independent investigative news weeklies, Inside the Air Force and Defense Information and Electronics Report. Before that she was a feature writer for George magazine and a contributor to the Washington Post.

Eli J. Lake

8

State of the State Department

The State Department is one of the choice beats for any reporter in Washington. It is where the U.S. government's current international policies are transmitted and explained to other governments around the world.

Almost every day the State Department spokesman gives a briefing between noon and 2 p.m. These briefings are largely reactive, in that they provide a U.S. position on the events of the day. The background portion of the briefing comes after the main briefing. The spokesman is usually empowered to give more information in this session.

It's important to prepare for this briefing by reading up on the international stories of the day, thinking of stories that need updating with a U.S. quote. In addition to domestic media, reading the international papers — such as the *Jordan Times* for a Middle East story, or *Xinhua* for China, or the major English, French and German newspapers — is helpful.

But the State Department beat is hardly just the briefing. When State wants to announce a new policy, the secretary will usually hold a news conference or arrange a briefing with appropriate senior officials. Sometimes these are on background, but nonetheless they are very useful.

Many stories generate from people who come in and out of the C Street entrance to the building — diplomats, opposition groups, lobbyists and various federal government officials. These people are usually approachable when they leave.

The secretary's schedule is public record and is previewed on background every Friday for what is called "the week ahead" after the main Friday briefing. This is invaluable for planning purposes. For example, if you know that the Indian foreign minister is coming on Wednesday, call the embassy on Monday to find out what he's going to talk about.

> **1948**
>
> TEL AVIV, May I — The new Jewish state of Israel was proclaimed in Palestine today as Britain's 30-year rule of the Holy Land ended. The Jewish dream of nearly 2000 years — a state of their own — came true at 4 p.m. (10 a.m. EDT) as the provisional government broadcast to the world that a new Jewish republic called Israel had been born and would be defended against all enemies.   — Eliav Simon

When in Washington the secretary sometimes will have a joint news conference with a visiting dignitary. But usually reporters will be briefed on any bilateral discussions on background.

It's important to know the code of "diplospeak" in these situations. "Frank exchange of views" means they disagreed. "Warm and friendly conversation" means there is little news. Often the spokesman will say only what topics were broached and won't categorize what the other side said. If the story is worth it, the reporter should try to get someone from the visitor's embassy to give the other side of the story.

When the secretary is traveling, the press operation tries to control the reporters' schedule. This has its benefits and drawbacks. On the one hand, there is access to senior officials who can be turned into sources back in Washington. On the other, it's hard to get the opposite side of the issue, because you are constantly being shuttled from photo opportunities into motorcades and back again. If you are covering an international conference or negotiation, try to hang out where other foreign journalists are to get their take on the story of the day. For example, when I covered the Sharm el-Sheik peace summit, I regularly went to the hotel where the Israeli and Palestinian delegations were staying just to pick up their spin.

Another avenue for tracking news outside the State Department building is congressional testimony. Often, under questioning from a senator or House member, an assistant secretary will be forced into publicly stating a position the department's official spokesman would otherwise have left unsaid. For this reason, it's also very important to become friends with the staffs of the Senate Foreign Relations Committee and

House International Relations Committee. These people are State's watchdogs.

Senate and House Select Intelligence Committee sources are also good to have. Many times, representatives of the State Department and the National Security Council will brief these committees on policy before it's released to the press. Having a source connected with these committees can give a reporter foreign policy scoops.

State Department heads have their own way of doing things. Madeline Albright liked to make decisions through her own staff and often ignored the individual bureaus. Colin Powell was the opposite. He empowered the bureaus to make policy. An assistant secretary for a given region can either be a good source of information or just another bureaucrat, depending on the secretary. Regardless, it's good to get to know their staffs, particularly the person who vets the assistant secretary's appointments.

The State Department has numerous bureaus that keep an eye on various parts of the world or on specific issues. It is extremely important to establish friendly relationships with the regional bureau's press operations. Press officers for a given region work for the bureau, not for the department spokesman. Many of these people can be very valuable. They can confirm events in the region: Was there a coup today in Mauritius? And they can explain U.S. positions with more clarity. On breaking news, these people are often more accessible than the spokesman. The bureau press officers are almost always on background.

It's nearly impossible to get bureaucrats not authorized to talk to the press to return your phone calls, because there are severe penalties for chatting. However, there are always a few people with an agenda. You can find them on smoke breaks outside the C Street entrance, at diplomatic receptions and in the cafeteria. A good piece of advice for a State Department reporter is to develop a smoking habit, or at least pretend. Since State, like all federal buildings, is smoke-free, many State Department employees use that entrance to take smoking breaks, and that's a good time to get them to talk.

Get to know people in the embassies. Ambassadors, deputy chiefs of missions and charges d'affaires almost always like to talk.

Finally, make sure to read a calendar of events and get to know analysts at the think tanks. Foreign officials will often give speeches at think tanks before they go to the State Department, and this can be used in the subsequent story. Also think tanks are chock-full of former State Department officials who can say how a policy or approach to an issue has changed in a new administration.

Eli J. Lake covered the State Department for United Press International. His work has appeared in the National Review, *the* New Republic, *the* Weekly Standard, *the* Los Angeles Times, *the* Washington Times *and the* Washington Post. He has appeared on NPR, BBC, MSNBC, Fox News, Al-Jazeera, C-Span's Washington Journal *and the Pacifica Radio Network. He lives in Washington, D.C.*

Mike Rabun

Sportswriting Has Changed a Lot

For years, sportswriters were drawn to their jobs because they enjoyed the competition and being around the stars. That is no longer enough. Sports has long since stopped being just about the games. A broad covering of sports now requires knowledge of sociology, economics, labor law, substance abuse and even the world of entertainment as sports personalities become celebrities.

In fact, the term "sportswriter" no longer applies. Nor is it an exclusively male domain. Women have been walking into locker rooms for years now for those post-game interviews. Those covering sports are journalists in the true sense. They must ask the right questions and withstand the kind of pressure a big-time sports organization can bring to bear. Sportswriting is not a lark. A love for games doesn't hurt. But it is only a start.

For those covering a team or organization full time, it is vital to get to know the players and club officials to at least a slight degree. The more substantial the relationship, the better. It is good to get to know them as people rather than just as a linebacker, third baseman or general manager. Do not hold them in awe just because they make huge salaries or are household names.

Once the player or official recognizes and gets to know the reporter, it makes it easier for that reporter to get the one-on-one time needed to avoid the pack journalism that exists in the 21st century. Once a relationship is established, it helps the reporter ask the difficult questions when

1939

NEW YORK, July 5 — "Iron Horse" Lou Gehrig broke down and wept Tuesday during ceremonies in his honor at Yankee stadium, witnessed by more than 60,000 fans. He stood there in the bright sun, chin down on his chest and tears trickling down his cheeks, just after a spokesman for the New York Giants of the National league had presented him with a fruit bowl and two candlesticks and had called Lou "the greatest first baseman of all time."

they must be asked. And, as in any profession, courtesy can carry you a long way.

REPORTING AND WRITING SPORTS

Often a sports story is treated as an opportunity to be cute. That urge should be suppressed. The very best stories, whether they deal with the games themselves or off-the-field activities, are those that both inform and entertain. The emphasis, however, should be on informing.

Various editors have their own desires about how copy in their publication should be treated, but one can never go wrong by telling the reader what happened as quickly as possible. Too often, stories appear in newspapers with a cute or corny first paragraph followed by some history involving the participants that led up to whatever happened on this particular occasion. Forget all that. Just say what happened. It can be done in an entertaining or clever manner, but the significant facts — who won or lost and why and how — are paramount.

In the broad scope, set yourself up as an expert and deliver. Put things in perspective. In many instances, it is not only important to relate what happened and why it happened, but what impact those happenings will have.

Use the active voice. Shun the passive voice. And be wary of adjectives that have no meaning. Just what is an "incredible" catch? If the catch is so incredible, explain it in detail — whether it was juggled twice as the receiver was falling to the ground or whatever it might have been. Give the reader as clear a picture as possible of the unusual happenings, and let the reader decide if he wants to call it incredible.

Sportswriting is, in the end, no different than any other form of

1907 (NOV. 23)

Appollonio was downed within six inches of the line. The Yale stands went wild. Old men threw their hats in the air, and women cried hysterically.

— Excerpt from United Press story on 12–0 Yale victory over Harvard

journalism. Study the subject, gather the facts and use basic words to describe the event — just as one would with a severe thunderstorm, a sharp drop in the stock market or a city council meeting.

Reference material is vital and there can never be enough of it. It has long been said that it is not so important to know everything about a subject, but it IS important to know where you can find the information you need. Sports organizations issue record books annually, and these are a valuable source of information about the teams' histories, their coaches, their facilities and their players. And as a career progresses, a collection of sources and phone numbers should grow and grow. Never throw away a phone number. You never know when it might come in handy.

> **1994**
> LILLEHAMMER, Norway (UPI) — Against a dazzling natural backdrop created by Norway's deepest snowfall on record, the 17th Winter Olympics began Saturday in a quaint mountain village seemingly built just for the occasion.   — Mike Rabun

---

Veteran UPI sports correspondent-editor **Mike Rabun** *began working for UPI in 1962 compiling high school football scores. He also helped cover the assassination of President Kennedy and was eyewitness to Jack Ruby's slaying of Lee Harvey Oswald. He has also covered space and medical stories. In 1972 he switched to sports full time and since then has covered 14 Super Bowls, 10 Olympics (seven summer, three winter), about 30 major golf tournaments, five Final Four basketball tournaments and several thousand other sporting events.*

10

Science Writing

Science and technology reporting is one of the most rewarding and potentially influential types of journalism there is. Decisions about the future of reproduction or stem-cell research can affect more people than a declaration of war. A story about a new medical discovery or an environmental problem may directly affect people's lives.

Whether you write about computer snooping, the discovery of water on Mars or problems with a cancer treatment, what you write can make a difference.

There are many kinds of science and technology reporting. Although some people think science reporters write only about the latest journal article, many of today's front-page stories need a specialist's insight. It takes a science-savvy reporter, for example, to accurately weigh claims over human cloning. Investigative stories into drug side effects or whether cell phones might cause cancer require digging through medical data and tracking down reliable sources. You need knowledge of computers and software to determine if new eavesdropping technology is performing as law enforcement promised. The best information on what to do during a "dirty bomb" or bioterror attack comes from reporters who can talk to the scientists devising countermeasures.

All of these stories have one thing in common: To really get at the truth, a reporter must be able to understand and interpret the technology being used or the science being argued.

There also are stories to be written about political fights over science-based issues such as climate change and cloning. This type of story represents a particular challenge, as the line between science and politics has now become profoundly blurred. Opposing camps line up glib experts, with seemingly solid credentials, who may cloud issues intentionally with pages of mind-numbing jargon. Some reporters just back down because they cannot sort through the conflicting claims.

Don't be intimidated — and don't let some fast-talker with a lot of letters after his or her name snow you. Any conscientious and determined journalist can cut

1999

SAN FRANCISCO, Dec. 10 (UPI) — The steadfast silence of the Mars Polar Lander is causing an uproar on Planet Earth, 158 million miles away.
— Lidia Wasowicz

through the details and get to the big picture. Do your own research. Read the reports — actually read them. Talk to people on both sides and listen carefully. With a bit of practice, you will soon become adept at sorting through the flak.

HELPFUL TIPS

1. *Give yourself time.* Beyond working your personal sources for exclusive stories (always the best approach), there are news feeds such as Eurekalert, from the American Association for the Advancement of Science, that will clue you in to upcoming stories on an embargoed basis. Many science stories can be identified days — even weeks — in advance. This gives you time to get the study and locate the experts.

2. *Read the studies you are writing about.* Although it is tempting to rely on a press release or somebody else's summary of research, it is important to read the scientist's own report on what was found. You will want to know how big the study sample was, for example, and who funded it. You will want to look at the statistics and all the exceptions the researcher points out.

3. *Use at least two solid and unrelated sources.* It is necessary to get comment from at least one independent source for nearly any story to give it depth, validity and perspective. You can find experts by tapping into professional societies and universities. An Internet search is usually all you need to find the right person. The researcher who wrote the original study often will be a good source of names of organizations.

Keep in mind, however, that not all sources are created equal. There is a temptation, especially with politically sensitive stories, to just get someone from each side. But as a responsible reporter you will need to find qualified people who can speak authoritatively and honestly to the scientific aspects of your story. A doctor who has never worked in a particular field might have an opinion on a research finding, but it will not be as well-informed as one who actually has conducted research in the area.

Always describe the qualifications of the people you are quoting in your story. If you are using a less-qualified source, perhaps to encompass all the perspectives, you should be gracious but clear about the background of the person being quoted. Do not put a scientist who has never done work in a field side by side with that discipline's most recent Nobel Prize winner as if they were equally qualified to comment.

4. *Get pictures.* Nothing makes a story as interesting as a picture to go with it. For some pieces, such as those about deep-space discoveries, the picture is the story. Most organizations will have pictures you can use if you just remember to ask for them. Ask when you set up your interview in case they need a little time to send the images to you.

5. *Tell the human side of a discovery.* The best science stories are the ones that provide drama as well as information. Most new discoveries are either the result of years of painstaking work — including lots of dead ends and dashed hopes — or sudden, unpredictable surprises. If you can give readers a sense of how these factors played a role in the discovery, you will draw them in and keep them reading.

6. *Think critically about statistics.* Remember the old saying, "There are lies, damn lies and statistics." Dealing with statistics can be particularly burdensome, especially if the press release has overstated the importance of a discovery.

For example, it might be true that a particular type of pollution doubles the risk of cancer, but if that means that two people out of 400,000 are likely to get that type of cancer instead of one, the risk is still quite small. Ask yourself what the numbers are really saying. Be careful not to scare your readers when there is little to be scared about.

7. *Be gracious with your sources.* Many scientists are inexperienced in dealing with reporters and might be unfamiliar with standard terms such as "off the record." Your job is to find out and explain

in an unbiased way to your readers what is going on — not to play a game of "gotcha." Make sure your sources know you will be quoting them by name. If they balk, you might have to find someone else. Or if what they tell you is valuable, ask to use the quote without naming them. If they insist on no quote and no name, either honor their request or drop them from the story.

Generally, it is best to resolve all this before your interview. If you sense confusion at what you are proposing, pause for a second to clarify what your terms mean. In all cases, you will get much better stories if you approach sources in an open and fair way — and you will preserve your reputation and UPI's if you demonstrate your integrity.

DEALING WITH JARGON

Jargon is unwelcome in a UPI science story. If you cannot explain the research in plain language, you probably have not worked hard enough to understand the material. Use technical terms only when they are essential — and even then make sure you provide a clear definition.

Find ways to explain things with familiar comparisons. Use analogies to help readers visualize and understand. For example, UPI once had a story describing a mathematical formula that predicted the way wildfires spread. The likely movement of a fire was determined by using actual field tests, probabilities and a two-dimensional matrix. For the readers, that process was described by using a checkerboard to show how scientists went to an old fire site and measured risk by seeing how the fire jumped from one particular "square" to another.

Some of the best resources for understanding jargon are the scientists themselves. They are almost always happy to talk about their work and will go the extra mile to make sure you understand their research. This can be enormously helpful, especially if you are covering an area of science with which you are totally unfamiliar.

> **1969**
>
> SPACE CENTER (UPI) — Neil Armstrong and Edwin Aldrin Jr. safely blasted off from the moon's surface Monday to begin their voyage home from man's first conquest of an alien world.
>
> "Eagle is in safe orbit," Armstrong reported 7½ minutes after their moonship boiled the lunar dust with its rocket engine and roared off from the Sea of Tranquility.

VERIFYING FACTS, NAMES AND PLACES

The Internet is a great source of specialty dictionaries and other references. They are easily located through a general search, which can help you find out what terms mean.

Always check unfamiliar terms as you find them while reading a report — doing so will help you remember them and make your interview later go much more smoothly.

> **1927**
> ROOSEVELT FIELD, New York,
> May 20 — Charles E. Lindbergh, alone
> and without ceremony sailed off into
> the gray of this foggy morning in his
> Ryan monoplane, shouting to his friends
> that tomorrow he will be in Paris. He
> started at 6.51½ a.m., eastern standard
> time.

The Internet also is a great way to check such items as spellings, locations and titles. Rule of thumb: If you cannot find a person or a place on the Web, chances are something is wrong with the name.

For example, a UPI science stringer once filed a story from a medical conference. When the science editor checked the name of the principal researcher on the Internet, the check turned up no references. The editor called the stringer, who had used the conference program for the name. Just then, the researcher walked into the newsroom, wearing a nametag with his name spelled the same way as in the program. When the reporter asked the researcher about the spelling of his name, he replied it was misspelled both in the program and on the tag. When the correct spelling was searched on the Internet, up popped 300-plus references.

MORE THINGS TO REMEMBER

1. *Is the research peer-reviewed?* This means a group of the researcher's peers examined the study to determine the research has been conducted properly and the conclusions appear solid. Non-peer-reviewed research needs to be handled much more carefully.

2. *Who funded the study? Is there a vested interest backing the research?* If so, that interest might have used its financial clout to influence the results. That should make you view the results more skeptically and require you to obtain absolutely first-rate independent comment. Some study results are too suspect to publish.

3. *Are these preliminary results?* Some studies report findings from tests done in a petri dish or among a dozen laboratory rats. The research might still be worth reporting, but do so cautiously and disclose the limitations.

4. *Was this reported already?* Some studies are done to validate earlier research. It might still be worth a story, but be sure to put it into context. There also will be cases where the same research is being published in different places, perhaps under the name of another member of the same research team. Always do a quick Web search before taking on an assignment. You might find it is a repeat study and you will save yourself from spending time on a story that is not worth the effort.

COVERING MEDICAL JOURNALS

Covering medical research requires special care. There are dozens of reputable scientific journals, each publishing hundreds of studies per year. Sometimes it is difficult to sort through and find the most relevant stories. When plowing through the studies, ask yourself the following:

- How many people will the results affect — just a few or hundreds of thousands?
- How important is the research? Does the research show a new drug is a couple of percentage points better at performing its task than standard medications? Or is it a possible major breakthrough in treatment? If it is the former, it probably is best left to the technical community, not a general readership.
- How far along is the research? Generally speaking, studies involving large numbers of people over long periods of time are preferred over short, small studies. A 10-year drug study will account for more possible side effects than a one-year study.
- Is the study well designed? Did the researchers take into account pertinent factors such as income level, age and gender? Is the study double-blind, meaning neither the patients nor the administrators of the medication know what is being given? Some studies analyze the results of a large number of related studies. This approach can be very revealing; but remember, the new study is also subject to the original limitations of the data being summarized.

THE REALLY GOOD STUFF

Covering science and technology is personally enriching. Many reporters say it's like getting paid to go to graduate school and having the best teachers in the world at your personal disposal.

Also, it can be a lot of fun. Depending on your beat, you can test-drive the latest robots, peer through telescopes, or check out an electronic tongue depressor that sends images to your brain. Let's face it — this is the beat with the best toys!

On a more serious note, what you do is important not only because it provides news to the public about scientific discoveries and technological advances, but also because it tells deeply human stories of determination and effort. As Carl Sagan, the late astronomer, author and advocate of science, once wrote:

> Scientists and technicians work for years — against long odds, often for low salaries, and never with a guarantee of success. They have many motivations, but one of them is the hope of helping others, of curing diseases, of staving off death. When too much cynicism threatens to engulf us, it is buoying to remember how pervasive goodness is.

Most reporters who cover science do so because they love it. If you share that love, you will never be bored and your passion and enthusiasm will shine through to your readers.

Dee Ann Divis, UPI's Health and Science editor, has a broad background in space and aerospace reporting with Aviation Week, Geospatial Solutions *and* GPS World *magazine, where she was Washington editor. She has also done investigative reporting on post-9/11 security initiatives and bioterrorism.*

Deputy Science & Technology Editor **Phil Berardelli** *has been a journalist, editor and teacher for more than 30 years. His work has appeared in the* Washington Post, Los Angeles Times, Pittsburgh Post-Gazette *and many other publications. He is the author of two books.*

Business Journalism

Through most of the '70s and '80s, business journalism was narrowly focused on meeting the needs of financial professionals. Though this is still a primary goal, more people who are first-time, small investors are trying to turn their savings into steady retirement income and are interested in business news.

As this goal has changed, so has the overall definition for business journalism. It was with the oil embargoes of the early '70s that international business and economics began to become a topic that was of relevance and interest to the average reader. Business — in this case, the oil business — had become a "pocketbook" issue, not just of interest to professional investors.

Slowly, interest in the multifaceted world of business began to grow. Along with this was greater understanding of how the global linkages of business affected the average reader. With the stock market boom of the dot-com era in the mid and late '90s, suddenly everyone was reading the business and financial pages of their daily newspaper, watching business reports on TV and browsing financial Web sites.

It became the task of the business news professional to simplify complex corporate and financial market behavior; explain financial products such as stocks, bonds and mutual funds; act as watchdog; put economic globalization into a local perspective and often fit local business action into a global perspective.

For business and financial journalists today, the areas of relevant coverage can range from the U.S. federal agencies or governmental watchdogs, such as the Securities and Exchange Commission, to businesses around the world, central banks of various nations and Wall Street and other major financial exchanges such as Japan's Nikkei, the Paris Bourse and the London Stock Exchange.

There are more than 15,000 corporations publicly traded on the U.S. markets. Thousands more are traded on major international stock exchanges, influencing the ups and downs of the FTSE 100 in London, the Xetra Dax in Germany, the Hang Seng in Hong Kong and the Nikkei 225 in Tokyo. The industry sectors covered in business journalism can include anything from biotechnology, heavy machinery or silicon chips to Famous Amos cookies.

> **1973**
> ISRAELI BASE X, Golan Heights — The cease-fire zero hour is 75 minutes away and there are no heroes at this command post four miles from the front. No one wants to be the last to die.
> — Thomas Cheatham

An average daily routine for a business journalist or editor may begin with a story on the Asian markets, followed by the opening of the U.S. financial markets, a congressional hearing into business fraud, an interview with a major CEO or an analysis on the business prospect for a big corporation such as Microsoft or General Motors. He or she might look at how a recent election in any of the 180-plus countries around the world will affect business, or write about earnings reports from corporations large and small.

A business journalist can have topical specialties that might range from investment banking, pension fund management or derivatives to high technology, the auto industry or commercial aviation.

It is a given that in business and economic journalism a correspondent or editor will overlap all the other areas of journalism, including politics, international conflicts, features and even sports. So a business journalist must be conversant in all areas of news.

EARNINGS

In the era when teletype machines and tickers lined the walls of newsrooms, and the only noise you heard was that of the machines, the ripping of the paper and the chatter of typewriters, young reporters were trained in necessary cynicism. They were instructed to read the full text of any press release from a company before they read the headlines, because the headlines in business news were written by the company that put out the release. They were told to look toward the bottom, where the bad news, if any, was usually stashed. Today, things have not changed. Most, if not all, business news is supplied though the PR Newswire and the Business Wire. Their copy is not edited and is released for a service fee to the world exactly as the company wants it.

Since the Enron and WorldCom accounting imbroglios, corporate America has made reading releases a little more difficult. But veteran reporters examining quarterly earnings releases know to ignore the glowing reports in the text and go to the tables on the bottom. There they begin with the *net income* (before special charges) and the *per share net income.* They look at corporate sales, or *revenues,* to get a snapshot of how a company really performed. They then look at the bottom of the text for information the company needs to report but doesn't want to make too public. It may include sales of assets or layoffs.

The *annual report* from a company is a very complex publication that is issued yearly by all publicly held corporations and freely available to all shareholders and to the public. It reveals the company's assets, liabilities, revenues, expenses and earnings for the past year, along with other financial data. This is often accompanied by a glossy presentation of the company's achievements and philosophy. But it is the accounting information that is required by law that allows investors to gauge the financial health of the company.

A company may also issue an annual *balance sheet,* or a condensed *financial statement,* showing the nature and amount of a company's assets, liabilities and capital on a given date. In dollar amounts the balance sheet shows what the company owned, what it owed and the ownership interest in the company of its stockholders.

This company information is of interest to many people who have invested some of their hard-earned cash into the markets. With the decline in company-offered pensions, people who used to think putting their money in a savings account was a wise move have been investing in stocks and bonds, trying to build a comfortable cushion for retirement. Often that is through a mutual fund.

MUTUAL FUNDS

A *mutual fund* is the king of 401(k)s. It's a portfolio of stocks, bonds or other securities administered by a team of one or more managers from an investment company who make buy and sell decisions.

Capital is contributed by smaller investors who buy shares in the mutual fund rather than the individual stocks and bonds in its portfolio.

The return on the fund's holdings is distributed back to its contributors, or *shareholders,* minus various fees and commissions. This system allows small investors to participate in the reduced risk of a large and diverse portfolio that they could not otherwise build themselves. They also have professional managers, who have the time and expertise to analyze and pick securities, overseeing their money.

There are two types of mutual funds, *open-* and *closed-end.* Shares in closed-end funds, some of which are listed on the New York Stock Exchange, are readily transferable in the open market and are bought and sold like other stock. These funds do not accept new contributions from investors, but only reinvest the return on the existing portfolio.

Open-end funds sell their own new shares to investors, stand ready to buy back their old shares and are not listed on exchanges. Open-end funds are so called because their capitalization is not fixed; they issue more shares as people want them. Many open-end funds allow contributors extra perks, such as the ability to write checks with their portion.

FINANCIAL MARKETS

The stocks in these funds are traded on various *financial markets,* including the New York Stock Exchange, the American Stock Exchange and the Nasdaq, which is the over-the-counter market. In addition there are electronic clearinghouses used by day traders, people who sell and buy on their own via computers.

News from the New York Stock Exchange is always hot. The NYSE marketplace blends public pricing with assigned dealer responsibilities. Aided by advanced technology, public orders meet and interact on the trading floor with a minimum of dealer interference. The NYSE is linked with other markets trading listed securities through the Intermarket Trading System (ITS).

Most trading is conducted by *brokers* acting on behalf of customers rather than by dealers trading on their own account. For this reason, the NYSE is often described as an *agency auction market.* The interaction of natural buyers and sellers determines the price of a NYSE-listed stock.

Investors also look for *stock splits,* or when a company increases the number of shares outstanding by splitting existing shares. A *2-for-1 split* means each stockholder gets two new shares for each one he or she owns, and a *3-for-2 split* means they get three shares for every two they own. The price of an individual share falls, but stockholders do not lose money, because they are being given the equivalent number of new shares.

TICKER SYMBOLS

Corporate America rarely changes its *ticker symbol,* the three- or four-letter abbreviation used to identify a security, whether on the floor, a TV screen or a newspaper page. Ticker symbols are part of the lore of Wall Street. They were originally developed in the 1800s by telegraph operators to save bandwidth. One-letter symbols were therefore assigned to the most active stocks.

Railroads were the dominant issues at the time, so they retain a majority of the one-letter designations. Ticker symbols today are assigned on a first-come, first-served basis. Each marketplace — the NYSE, the American Stock Exchange and others — allocates symbols for companies within its purview, working closely to avoid duplication. A symbol used for one company cannot be used for any other, even in a different marketplace.

BONDS

And then there are *U.S. treasuries,* or debt obligations of the U.S. government. Treasuries are among the safest investments, since the full faith and credit of the government secures them.

The interest of treasuries is exempt from state and local taxes but is subject to federal income tax. There are three types of treasuries: *treasury bills,* with maturities of one year or less; *treasury notes,* with maturities ranging from one to 10 years; and *treasury bonds,* long-term instruments with maturities of 10 years or more.

But do not confuse treasuries with *bonds.* Bonds are promissory notes or IOUs issued by a corporation or local government to its lenders. They are usually issued in multiples of $1,000 or $5,000, although $100 and $500 denominations are available. A bond is evidence of a debt on which the issuing party usually promises to pay the bondholder a specified amount of interest at intervals over a specified length of time and to repay the original loan on the expiration date. A bond represents debt; therefore its holder is a creditor of the corporation and not a part owner as the stockholder is.

BULLS, BEARS AND MARKET FLUCTUATIONS

For generations, bulls and bears on Wall Street have referred to two decidedly different types of investors — the *bulls* being those who expect stock prices to rise, the *bears* being those who believe prices are about to decline.

A crash is something that occurs with a car, *not* in the markets. In response to the market breaks in October 1987 and October 1989, the

343

New York Stock Exchange instituted several circuit breakers to reduce market volatility and promote investor confidence.

CURRENCIES

Unlike stocks, *currencies* are not traded on any specific exchange market. The buying and selling of dollars, euros, yen, and other major currencies are conducted by banks, based on demand. That demand can be driven by necessity. For instance, a U.S. company that manufactures pharmaceuticals in Germany will have to repatriate its profits from Germany, which would be earned in euros, back to the United States and converted into dollars.

Currency trading is also done for sheer speculation, as traders bet the money of one country going up against another and sell off what they believe will be the losing currency. The volume of demand in currency trading across the globe means that foreign exchange markets are open 24 hours a day, seven days a week centered around New York, London and Tokyo. Given that currency traders buy the money of one country by selling the money of another, they must be particularly attuned to the political as well as the economic developments of the countries they are trading on. As a result, the currency market is seen to be more global than the stock market and more susceptible to the hazards of geopolitical risks.

And if you think that doesn't interest you, just wait until you go abroad and try to find the best way to exchange your currency for the local currency. Bureaus of exchange and banks make more money on these transactions by charging you fees for the privilege of spending their money.

All of this falls in the field of the business journalist, who must not only be able to write quickly, clearly and interestingly, but also must be familiar with the world outside the financial markets and able to talk intelligently about them at all levels, from boardroom to barroom.

Frank Schnaue was a veteran financial writer for United Press International based in New York.

Timothy K. Maloy is UPI's senior business writer, covering major corporate action, U.S financial markets, Capitol Hill, the major federal agencies. He specializes in coverage of the high-tech and biotechnology industry business sectors. He is also an adjunct professor at American University in Washington and author of two books on writing and researching on the Internet.

12

Photography and Photojournalism

Every year many young men and women are drawn to photography and to photojournalism because they perceive it to be a glamorous profession, putting them close to the big stars, the big events and the big names in the news. It does that, but getting there means a lot of non-glamorous hard work and attention to details of the craft, with outlays for equipment reaching into the thousands of dollars.

If one's interest lies in capturing the best and worst of humanity, photojournalism can be a rewarding career. It's a highly competitive field, packed with pressure to get the best shot, the telling image. Whether they are covering a small-town parade with the band leading the way or on the sidelines of the Super Bowl, photojournalists are on the front lines of history with the difficult job of documenting events for all who can't be there.

Photography has many faces. There is studio photography, where the shoots are setups of models, or formal portraits of families or promotional shots of personalities. There is commercial photography, where the subjects might be anything from buildings, storefronts and trains to hamburgers and milkshakes. There is fashion photography, a subset that focuses on that industry.

And there is photojournalism, where the types of photography skills needed vary and the topics are of world events big and small — whether it is a presidential news conference, the local football game, famine in Africa, a portrait in a studio or war in whatever part of the world is currently chaotic. Photojournalists have to wear the many hats of photography. They are required to use the photographic skills from every spectrum and must continuously keep up with a constantly changing environment in which to work, as well as the massive leaps in photographic technology.

Photojournalism can be routine, it can be dangerous, it can be fun, and it's always hard work. Unlike news reporters who can grab a pencil and notebook and perhaps a small tape recorder and are on their way, photojournalists have to carry cameras, lenses, ladders, filters, sometimes their own lighting in case there's not enough and in recent years laptop computers and telephones.

Often news reporters can watch an important event on television, or find a transcript of what's been said, in order to write their story. Sometimes they can even participate in a telephone news conference and ask questions. But photographers have to be there on the front lines, their lens pointed at the subject and their finger on the shutter.

Even before they get to that point, they have had to make sure they are properly accredited for the event, that they have a good position from which to get the best picture, that they and their equipment won't be marred by driving rain or blinding sun, a blizzard, a sandstorm or the darkness of night. They have to understand the light type and choose the right lenses for the particular situation. They make the correct camera settings so their shots are clear, focused, properly exposed and, most of all, tell the story.

When they put their eye to the camera, they have to shift their focus to composition and balance and capture the split-second moment so the picture tells a meaningful story. It all has to be done quickly and under pressure. News reporters don't need to do that. They can tape-record the event and make notes and then later decide which points they want to emphasize. Not photographers. Once the event is over, there is no going back, and they have to live with what they have.

1956

MONACO, Apr. 18 — Grace Kelly, the queen of Hollywood, today became the princess of Monaco. Her prince was so shy he gave her his kingdom without a kiss. — Elizabeth Toomey

Not only that. They must also gather information about the assignment, where they are, and particulars of the event so they can write a caption to go with the pictures. And if photojournalists are alone on assignment, they must collect enough information to produce full text as well as pictures.

DIGITAL PHOTOGRAPHY

After the assignment, a photojournalist must get images into the hands of editors quickly and professionally. With the recent advances in digital technology, the majority of photojournalists are shooting their work digitally. With this technology, photographers can have a picture of an event a world away into the hands of editors or circulated around the globe within minutes.

If deadlines are not the main focus, some photojournalists may opt to shoot film for a variety of reasons. Some may shoot slide film for quality magazines while others may need high film speeds for low light situations. Others may still use film due to the high initial cost of going digital, where a camera body capable of the high quality needed can cost $4,000 to $8,000, not counting lenses. Those who do use film may have to ship it off to a lab they trust for processing, or they may bring mobile darkrooms and scanners to locations where they will be working.

> **1980**
> HOLLYWOOD (UPI) — Sir Alfred Hitchcock, the pear-shaped, fat-jowled master of macabre suspense whose 54 movies successfully blended murder, laughter and gore, died peacefully at his Bel-Air home. He was 80.
> —Vernon Scott

Even using digital photography, the picture must be put into a usable form and that means using a computer, usually a laptop when in the field or a desktop where available.

Then, using photography enhancement programs the picture can be toned or color adjusted, cropped, have a caption attached embedded with information about the image, then transmitted remotely via phone or the Internet or sent to editors directly to be published.

Chris Corder was UPI Senior Photographer, covering the White House and the Iraqi War.

CAPTIONS

The information required to go with a photograph is called a *caption*. In writing captions the photographer is required to follow appropriate grammatical style. All captions should be read carefully by an editor before being published. Reading captions aloud will help avoid typos and other mistakes.

- Accuracy in captions is paramount. Keep in mind the words: "When in doubt, leave it out."
- Captions should include all essential information in complete but brief sentences in the active voice. A caption should rarely exceed five single-spaced typewritten lines, or about 75-100 words.
- Libel laws apply to photo captions as well as news stories. Read every caption carefully before you send it out. When an important statement or opinion is made and included in a caption, it must not be made to read as if UPI is making the pronouncement. Always attribute such statements to the source.
- If a picture might be in poor taste because of what it shows, consult with the photo chief or senior news editors on duty.
- Photographers should be familiar with UPI style and follow the rules. If there is uncertainty about a word or term and it is not in the stylebook, use a dictionary. UPI uses *Webster's New World College Dictionary.*

UPI'S FIELD TRANSMISSION GUIDELINES

The *UPI Standard Image* is 3,000 pixels (long side) at 300 dpi, which will produce a 10 x 8 image document.

The *UPI Base Image* is 2,000 at 300 dpi.

Both should be saved as jpeg files in high quality in Photoshop. Use "9" for Photoshop 5.5 & higher.

To get this type of quality image, Nikon and Canon digital cameras should be set to "fine" quality setting. This will produce a jpeg that is compressed at approximately 4 to 1.

Although the *UPI Standard Image* is the goal, some early generation digital cameras are not capable of this resolution. Furthermore, extreme crops cannot be resized properly. In these cases, please use the *UPI Base Image* requirements.

In Adobe Photoshop, the *"Image Size"* dialogue box needs to be filled in like this:

UPI Standard Image:

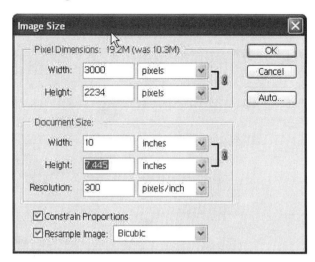

UPI Base Image:

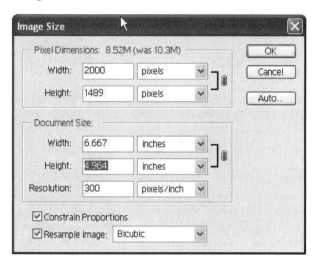

All picture files should be sent by **FTP** to *photos.upi.com*. The user-name is **photos** and password is **pixs.**

You may need to set your FTP software to Passive Mode (PASV). Send the image as a "binary" file and not "Mac-binary." When using Adobe Photoshop, remember that less is better. Do not overtone the image.

349

It is important that the IPTC header is filled in properly, using off-the-shelf software or Adobe Photoshop "file info." A typical IPTC header from Multipic looks like this:

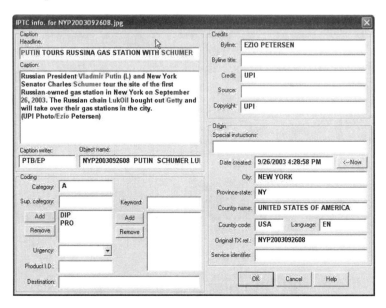

Adobe Photoshop "file info" samples follow this note. Please observe the following guidelines:

Caption — The *slugline* is no longer necessary. However, you must put the date of the picture and where it was taken in the body of the caption. All captions should have complete information and answer the "who, what, why, where, when" questions.

Example:

> *Russian President Vladmir Putin (L) and New York Sen. Charles Schumer tour the site of the first Russian-owned gas station in New York on Sept. 26, 2003. The Russian chain LukOil bought out Getty and will take over its gas stations in the city. (UPI Photo/Ezio Petersen)*

If it is not a major city like New York, you must put the state in the caption: *Richmond, Va.* Use the UPI stylebook for UPI state abbreviations in the caption, p. 234, but use the postal abbreviation, p. 235, in the state IPTC field.

Object Name (**Title** in Photoshop) — This may change slightly in the future, but for now use the picture number plus two or three descriptive words. Please note that all fields are in all capital letters except for the caption. Example: *NYP2003092608 PUTIN SCHUMER LUKOIL*

Byline (**Author** in Photoshop) — The photographer's name in capital letters.

Caption Writer — Initials of the caption writer. If the image is edited in any way, then use a second set of initials. Example: *EP;* if edited, *PTB/EP.*

Category — Put a one-letter code in this field. Example: *"A"* means picture made in the United States, *"I"* means made outside the United States, *"S"* means any sports picture, *"E"* means entertainment.

Supplemental Category — Please see the complete list of supplemental category codes.

Major ones are *SPO* (Sports), *ENT* (Entertainment), *FAS* (Fashion), *PRO* (People), *DIP* (International Relations), *DIS* (Disasters, Accidents), *POL* (Domestic Politics), *REL* (Religion), *SCI* (Science), *VIO* (Civil Conflict, War)

Date Created — Date the picture was made, not when it was transmitted.

City — City where the picture was made.

State — Use the postal abbreviations: *NY* and not *New York.*

Country Name — Full name of the country. Example: *United States of America*

Country Code — Please see the complete list of three-letter codes. They are available at: http://ftp.ics.uci.edu/pub/ietf/http/related/iso3166.txt. Use the list under A3.

Credit — Credit is *UPI*

Source — If this is a pickup, the name of the newspaper, law enforcement agency, branch of government or other source.

Headline Field — A short descriptive phrase of less than 50 characters. Example: *PUTIN TOURS RUSSIAN GAS STATION WITH SCHUMER*

Original Transmission Reference (OTR) — This is the picture number. The first three letters are a transmission reference, based on the city where the picture was taken. That is followed by the year, then month, day and finally the number of the picture that day from that location. Example: *NYP2003092608* is the eighth picture transmitted on Sept. 26, 2003, from New York Pictures.

In Photoshop, the IPTC data is entered into three of the four "File Info" dialogue boxes. For the above example, it will look like this:

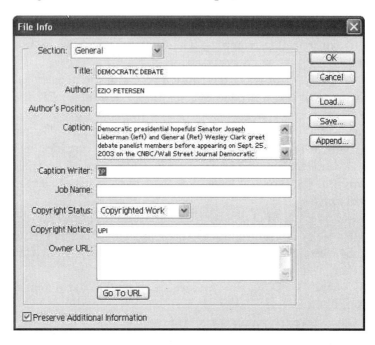

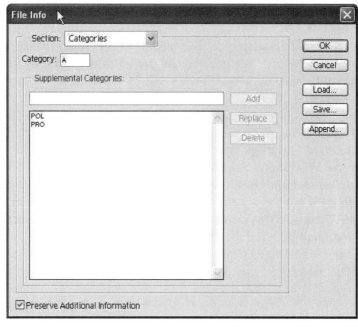

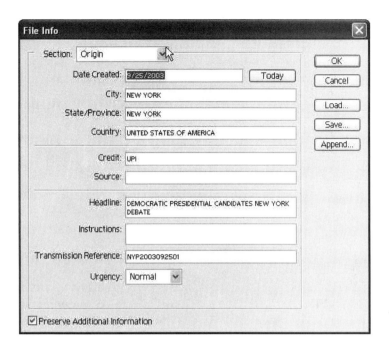

SUPPLEMENTAL CATEGORIES

AIR	Airlines Transport	BNK	Banking
ARC	Archery	BOX	Boxing
AUT	Automobile	CAN	Canoe
BAD	Badminton	CAR	Auto, Motorcycle Racing
BBA	American League Baseball	CHESS	World Chess Championships
BBN	National League Baseball	CORA	Corporate Actions
		CRIM	Crime/Law Enforcement
BBO	Baseball (other)	CVN	US Political Convention
BBO	Baseball	CYC	Cycling
BEV	Beverages Tobacco	DEF	Defence
BKC	College Basketball (Men's)	DIP	International Relations
		DIS	Disasters/Accidents/ Natural Catastrophes
BKN	NBA Basketball		
BKO	Men's Basketball	DIV	Diving
BKO	Basketball (other)	EDU	Education
BKW	Women's Basketball	ELC	Electrical Electronics
BKW	College Basketball (Women's)	ELN	Election
		ENR	Energy Resources

ENT	Arts/Culture/Entertainment	REA	Real Estate
		REL	Religion
ENV	Environment/Natural World	RES	Company Results
		RET	Merchandising
EQU	Equestrian	ROW	Rowing
FAS	Fashion	RUN	Track and Field
FBC	College Football	RUN	Athletics
FBN	NFL Football	SCI	Science/Technology
FBO	CFL Football	SHO	Shooting
FEN	Fencing	SKI	Skiing
FRX	Forex Markets	SOC	Soccer
GLF	Golf	SOF	Softball
GYM	Gymnastics	SPO	Sports
HAN	Handball	STX	Stock Market Reports
HEA	Health/Medicines	SWM	Swimming
HKN	NHL Hockey	SYN	Synchro Swimming
HKY	Field Hockey	TEL	Telecommunications
INT	Interest Rates	TEN	Tennis
IOL	Travel Tourism	TEX	Textiles Apparel
JOB	Labor Employment Strikes	TOUR	Travel/Tourism
		TTN	Table Tennis
JOB	Labor Issues	VBB	Beach Volleyball
JUD	Judo	VBL	Volleyball
LEI	Leisure Tourism	VIO	Civil Conflict/War/Riots/Demonstrations
MGR	Mergers		
OBIT	Obituaries	VOTE	Elections
ODD	Human Interest	WEA	Weather
OLY	Olympics	WELF	Welfare/Social Services
PEN	Modern Pentathlon	WRE	Wrestling
POL	Domestic Politics	WTL	Weight Lifting
PRO	People	WTP	Water Polo
PUB	Broadcasting and Publishing	YAH	Yachting
		ZCC	Closing Ceremonies
RAC	Horse Racing	ZOC	Opening Ceremonies

13

The Foreign Correspondent

Few job titles in journalism light up the imagination of reporter and public alike as that of *foreign correspondent.* Images immediately spring to mind of exotic locales, trench coats, tuxedos and battle fatigues.

Fair enough. The overseas reporter and his or her derring-do has long been the stuff of Hollywood and print fiction, either in star billing or in supporting cast. But what's the reality?

A foreign correspondent is little different from colleagues back home, except he or she may be a bit more adventurous, a bit more of a round-peg-in-a-square-hole sort of person at home, and a bit of a maverick. Many ex-wives or ex-husbands of foreign correspondents have a different perspective, especially on those who thrive in what was once called the Third World. These foreign correspondents, they often opine, are incorrigible teenagers who refuse to grow up — in their thinking, anyway.

Yeah, so what's their point?

The foreign correspondent must cover the news. A picky point to be sure, but company accountants do demand reporters actually earn their paychecks and justify their expense accounts. That means keeping abreast of events and people and uncovering all sorts of news stories — from political happenings, to social upheavals, to curious little experiences that tell something about the people among whom you are living. For example, what could be particularly interesting about people going to church? Not much to many. But when that church service is performed outdoors with Masai tribespeople, when the priest is a gregarious, garrulous Irish missionary, and when partakers of after-service tea and biscuits have to swipe away flies as they sit outside dung-made homes in the Masai Mara, it can be a story. Even a good one. Or at least one that will bring a smile to your editors. Mine did. It happened to coincide with Pope John Paul II's first trip to Africa.

As at home, a foreign correspondent establishes sources wherever he or she can, checks the facts as much as possible and transmits the copy home. But added to the basics is the constant need to put the information into context for people thousands of miles away and more than likely uninformed about the geopolitical and cultural world in which the events take place.

> **1971**
> STRABANE, Northern Ireland, Aug. 20 — Eamonn McDevitt was deaf and dumb. He died kneeling on the street because he could not hear a British soldier order him to stand.
> — Lucinda L. Franks

That means finding and presenting the import and pathos quickly.

It also means being pithy, clever, poignant or all three to pique and then maintain interest. This is where the reporter, as a person, and instincts come in. It's not only what you managed to learn in the classroom, it's the breadth of your interests, your curiosity about people and what makes them tick; it's the experience you gained dealing with all types of people in all types of circumstances. It's the sum experience of your life and personality.

Foreign language proficiency? Sure, it's important, and a great help, but not absolutely necessary. It's amazing how much you pick up just living among the people of another country. Thirsty? Very thirsty? You'll learn the local lingo for *gin and tonic* pretty quick!

Translators can be had for a price, of course, and many people speak English. Finding the right interpreter is just part of your work routine. Will that interpreter relate what you have been doing or who you have been talking to back to authorities in the more authoritarian countries? More than likely. Good foreign correspondents would automatically assume so, learn to deal with it and factor it into their behavior and thinking.

So what other qualities are necessary? Chutzpah — never take *no* for the definitive answer; always try another angle, play the dumb, silly foreigner if caught out!

During the Angolan civil war, getting to the front was next to impossible, but you could get close with a bit of ingenuity. Many a correspondent in Luanda, the Angolan capital, found that the colored paper top of a milk bottle and a bit of ribbon on "orders" you'd had written by your hotel's concierge worked wonders at military roadblocks. The assumption that many of the troops — fresh out of the countryside — couldn't read proved true, thankfully, when they "read" the ersatz orders upside down and let you pass (minus a few cigarettes).

Leave home when you leave home. And leave whatever arrogance you may have behind. Forget DVDs and Starbucks' latte. Your new world, if you're to be happy and productive in it, is the one you've set up shop in. They only have one hour of TV a night? So what? Do what they do, go out and socialize. Learn to live by their customs — or at least learn to respect their adherence to them — and you won't go wrong. Don't let whatever ideas you may have of cultural or political superiority get in the way of appreciating others. This doesn't mean you lose your moral compass or cultural roots; it just means you learn to understand others more, and as such will be able to convey what you learn to the folks back home.

Keep a sense of humor, especially a self-effacing one, even if the laugh is known only to you. A correspondent named Norman used to do this all the time in Thailand, where the people are particularly proud of their heritage and culture. If a *farang* (foreigner) spoke their language too fluently in the countryside, the locals sometimes would become less than helpful. Now Norman was fluent, very fluent — he went to high school in Bangkok and married a Thai lady — yet he always made it a point to be less than grammatical when outside the capital. The result — jokes about Norman's terrible accent but also a lot of cooperation and help in getting what he wanted and needed.

Be inventive (or just outrageous). Picture this scene: As a correspondent in Bangkok, you are late for an interview with a Lao prince who has information of crash sites of U.S. planes during the Vietnam War.

2001
AMMAN, Jordan, March 29 (UPI) — Small buses wind through multiple checkpoints where armed soldiers in khaki board and scan faces and check bright yellow press badges. It's part of the daily trip for journalists to a large press center ... journalists from around the world in long, flowing robes, crumpled suits and spike heels dash from press conference to interviews ... No one wants the men and women who cover the world blown up or mowed down — that would be very bad public relations.
— Laura E. Chatfield, excerpts from a commentary during the Arab summit in Jordan

You're a couple of miles away from the hotel, but streets are flooded from monsoon rains, auto traffic is jammed and not moving. What to do? Why, stop the first motorcyclist, of course. Point in the direction you want to go, repeat the name of the hotel destination and shove 40 baht ($1) into the cyclist's hand as you climb on to his bike uninvited.

1973

DALLAS — The last sale Gustavo Cuello made in his La Chica grocery was a ham sandwich and it cost 52 cents. He sold it to a killer.

— Donald Myers

Be prepared to go with the flow. Picture it: You're in the disco of a hotel in Blackpool, England, at the end of a Conservative Party congress. It has been a long day. You're tired, you're disheveled. Suddenly, Prime Minister Margaret Thatcher appears and takes to the dance floor, party faithfuls sharing a few steps with her as she makes her way around the floor. Now she is in front of you, waiting for you to take her hand. What do you do? Boogie like a demon, of course. No hesitation, no possible affront.

Know when to keep your mouth shut. In Iran, at the height of the revolution to oust Shah Mohammed Reza Palavi, a group of angry demonstrators surrounded my driver. After a few minutes of gesticulated conversation, they backed off and watched sullenly as the driver approached me.

"What was that about?" I asked.

"Oh, they thought you were Israeli because of the way you look," he said. "I told them you were really Canadian."

"Canadian? I'm American," I said.

"I know," said the driver. "And now you're still alive."

Richard Tomkins was a foreign correspondent for 17 years in Africa, Asia and the Middle East, covering wars and revolutions and breaking bread with dictators and saints alike in pursuit of the news — and a few good times.

Robert D. Lystad

14

The Law of Libel

I n reporting the news, journalists should strive for one goal above and
beyond all others: accuracy. And yet, getting the facts right will not
insulate journalists from facing the typically unpleasant experience
of being sued. Indeed, lawsuits for libel often are brought not because a
newspaper or television or radio station misstated the facts, but because
the subjects of those reports feel they were not treated fairly.

The law does not purport to serve as a useful guide on fairness —
that's better left to the ethics experts. But the law does provide an extensive guide to determine whether you can be held liable for reporting
false statements of fact. This brief synopsis describes the fundamental
elements of a libel lawsuit, the defenses to such claims, and some practical suggestions for avoiding trouble altogether.

ELEMENTS OF A LIBEL CLAIM

Generally speaking, *libel* is based on the printed word; *slander,* on the
spoken word. In virtually every jurisdiction, libel and slander are treated
the same. To simplify matters, then, only the term *libel* will be used. The
general definition of libel is: *A false statement of fact about another that
tends to harm his or her reputation in the eyes of the community.* An inquiry
into any libel lawsuit starts with the "elements," that is, what a plaintiff
must prove to a judge or jury to make out a legal claim for libel. These
elements are as follows:

Publication

A plaintiff must show that a statement was "published" to a third person. In the media context, this typically is easy to prove, because the plaintiff can wave a copy of a newspaper article or a tape of a TV or radio broadcast to show that others have read, watched or heard what was being said about them. But publication is not limited to just these forms of expression. For instance, a letter sent to a third person, a scribbled note to a news source, or even verbal statements or questions that you ask a source over a telephone all can constitute "publication," even though the statements were not disseminated to a wide audience.

False Statement of Fact

The readers or viewers of the publication, radio or TV station must reasonably believe that the statement made by one person about another falsely stated a fact as opposed to expressing an opinion. A more detailed explanation of the fact/opinion dichotomy is described later.

Of and Concerning Another

The statement must reasonably be read or viewed as pertaining to a specific individual or company (whether or not they are named), not an observation about an unidentifiable person or large group of individuals.

Defamatory Meaning

The statement must diminish an individual's (or company's) reputation in the community — for example, by exposing that individual (or company) to public scorn, ridicule, hatred or contempt.

Fault

The maker of the statement must have been at fault in making the statement, either by being negligent or acting with "actual malice." These standards are discussed in more detail below.

Damage

The statement must cause a provable "injury" in the form of specific monetary harm, such as lost wages, or more nebulous harm, such as impairment of reputation and standing in the community, personal humiliation or mental anguish.

DEFENSES TO A LIBEL CLAIM

As in all tort actions, there are certain defenses that shield a reporter from liability. The defenses to a libel claim are as follows:

Substantial Truth

Libel lawsuits often begin and end with the concept of falsity. A libel plaintiff must prove that a challenged statement is false. The law of libel provides protection so long as the statement published or broadcast is "substantially true," that is, if the gist or sting of what is written is true.

Opinion

A common refrain to an allegation of libel is "but that was just my opinion!" Unfortunately, it's not that easy. It is true that pure statements of opinion cannot form the basis for libel liability. Thus, a statement that "the county council is not doing enough to improve our schools" is just too nebulous to subject the speaker of the statement to liability. Statements that amount to rhetorical hyperbole (e.g., "Candidate Alfred Jordan is full of malarkey") likewise do not reasonably assert a statement of fact.

But many statements fall into a gray zone. The legal test to determine whether a statement is one of fact or one of opinion is to assess whether the challenged statement can reasonably be verified as being true or false. If a statement can be verified as true or false, then it is considered a fact and thus may be actionable. In making this assessment, one must consider the context in which the statement is published. If a statement reflects a subjective evaluation by an author, then it likely will be considered opinion and hence not actionable.

Thus, saying in a sports column that a baseball player is a "sloppy" fielder is the writer's subjective assessment of the player's abilities and would not be actionable. Such a statement is not subject to objective verification, and the context in which it is published — a sports column — alerts the reader to expect the writer's opinion. But saying in a news article that a businessman "has illegally shielded millions of dollars in assets to avoid tax liability" could be proved true or false and thus could subject the maker of the statement to liability. When expressing an opinion, it is advisable to state the facts upon which that opinion is based.

Fair Report Privilege

A "privileged" communication is one that would be libelous under normal circumstances, but the occasion on which it is made allows the statement to be made without liability. The privilege is granted on the theory that the interest of the individual being libeled is outweighed by the public interest in the proceeding or report in which the statement is made.

The privilege to report about government activities may be the strongest defense to any libel action, because it can shield one from liability even if a statement is false and even if the false statement injured someone's reputation. This privilege, commonly known as the "fair report privilege," provides that a news outlet or its employees cannot be held liable for the publication of defamatory statements if the published statements are a fair and accurate account of what occurred during an official proceeding or were made in an official report.

The privilege applies to reports about judicial, legislative and other official government proceedings. And the privilege applies even if the underlying statements being reported upon are not true. Thus, one may report the content of police logs and city council minutes without fear of liability, provided that the account is fair, accurate and impartial.

THE FAULT STANDARDS: NEGLIGENCE AND ACTUAL MALICE

There are three categories of plaintiffs: public officials, public figures and private figures. Both public officials and public figures must prove that a media defendant published a false statement of fact with "actual malice." Unfortunately, the term "actual malice" is confusing and often misunderstood. The term does *not* mean that a reporter acted against a news subject with spite or ill will. Rather, the term "actual malice" means that a publisher or broadcaster entertained serious doubts as to a statement's truth or falsity, or consciously disregarded the truth, for instance, by ignoring a reliable source's statement that what was about to be published was false.

Private individuals, on the other hand, merely have to prove "negligence," that is, proving that the print or broadcast media failed to exercise ordinary care expected of competent journalists prior to publishing or broadcasting a false and defamatory statement about the individual. This is a lower, much easier standard for a plaintiff to meet than the "actual malice" required of public officials and public figures.

So, who then is "public" and who is "private"?

Public officials include elected government officials, city managers, public school superintendents and other "high level" government workers. Other government officials — such as public high school teachers and mid-level "bureaucrats" — may similarly be treated as public officials in some states if the stories relate to their official duties. But lower-level government workers without managerial responsibilities will, in most cases, be considered private individuals for libel purposes.

Public figures — as opposed to public officials — are a separate category that is further broken up into two parts. First are "general purpose" public figures. These are famous people who are constantly in the public eye, such as celebrities, high-profile company executives and professional athletes.

The more common public figure in libel cases is the "limited purpose" public figure, an individual who otherwise may be fairly private — or unknown to the community at large — except for the limited purpose of getting deeply involved in some type of controversy that becomes worthy of media attention. If, for instance, the county council is considering a proposal to build a new highway extension through a neighborhood, and one resident leads the opposition among local activists, then that resident probably would be considered a limited purpose public figure in a lawsuit challenging the accuracy of statements made about her in a newspaper account about the highway controversy.

SOME PRACTICAL TIPS
Prepublication Review
The best prepublication review comes from the reporter first and the editor second. On sensitive stories, having a lawyer pore over copy prior to publication may not necessarily make a story libel-proof, but it can help. Good First Amendment lawyers are trained to spot discrepancies in a reporter's newsgathering efforts and can refine language to present the intended meaning of a phrase or sentence without running a risk of liability for libel.

Legal review of stories typically is limited to lengthy investigative pieces, and yet these types of stories do not generate most libel lawsuits. Rather, lawsuits more often stem from everyday, routine stories, especially stories about crime, children, and professionals (such as teachers, doctors and lawyers who trade on their reputation). And the cause of most errant reporting is just plain sloppiness, such as when a headline or photographic caption does not match a story, or when rewrites or summaries are prepared by those who are removed from the fact-gathering process.

The following should be standard procedure for all stories:
- Facts of a story should be verified as far as practicable.
- News stories should be objective and, if practicable, present differing views on a particular topic.

363

- Care should be given to quotations, since quoting someone accurately is not a defense to a libel claim if the quoted statement contains false and defamatory information about another.

Handling Retractions

Most media outlets have a straightforward rule: If you publish or broadcast an error and subsequently learn of your mistake, you correct it. This is a sound journalistic policy, though it is not a complete defense to a libel claim. Generally speaking, publishing a retraction will only mitigate damages. Importantly, retractions should be drafted carefully, especially where the original false report has damaged someone's reputation. To the extent possible, a publisher should try to avoid repeating the libelous statement and just set the record straight. A well-meaning correction may inadvertently compound the damage to a plaintiff or, worse, admit that the publisher or broadcaster was negligent in making the statement at issue, when in fact a reporter had sound justification for the original story. It is advisable to consult with an attorney when preparing such corrections.

NEWSGATHERING ACCESS ISSUES

Even if the content of news reports is fair and accurate, journalists' newsgathering methods can land them in legal trouble. Obviously, a journalist, like every citizen, must not violate criminal laws to obtain information, but the line between criminal and non-criminal behavior is not always distinct. Even the total avoidance of criminal behavior in newsgathering might not immunize a journalist from legal challenge and, occasionally, defeat in trespass or invasion of privacy lawsuits.

While the law does not set clear boundaries between permissible and impermissible newsgathering practices, it does provide general guidelines to help steer reporters clear of most legal problems without sacrificing the assertiveness necessary for strong reporting. The extent to which a journalist may permissibly engage in reporting or surveillance largely depends on the venue. Generally, restrictions on newsgathering in private homes and private places are stricter than those for public lands or traditionally public areas. One of the first steps a reporter should take if denied access by government officials or owners of private property is to assess the forum. The best way to avoid any trouble, of course, is to obtain consent to enter and gather news in any place where access is restricted in one way or another.

Public Places

A journalist is essentially free to gather news on public streets and in public parks, and anything that can be seen (and photographed) or heard on or from a public street is fair game. However, the paparazzi-esque pursuit of particular subjects, even on public streets, has landed a few journalists in legal trouble, especially where the newsgathering implicates the privacy of children. The right to engage in newsgathering on public streets has usually been extended to other places where the public is traditionally welcome — such as airport terminals, flea market booths, and professional sporting events — but this right sometimes has not applied to private parties held in otherwise "public" places.

Crime and Disaster Scenes

The freedom to gather news in public places has extended to crime and disaster scenes in most cases. For example, a journalist may permissibly record an arrest on a public street, or in a courthouse or police station. This freedom may be limited if a law enforcement investigation or other official activity is still in progress.

Even the express consent of law enforcement officials to gathering news in non-public places (such as on police "ride-alongs") is no guarantee that a journalist will escape legal trouble. Some journalists have been held liable for damages when they enter a private home without the consent of the owners, even if their presence was permitted by law enforcement officials.

Private Homes

Gathering news in a private home without consent of the owner is an extremely risky proposition. Courts have found the media liable for invasion of privacy, trespass and intentional infliction of emotional distress both where the journalist used surreptitious means to enter a home and where a journalist gathered news in plain view but without the consent of the homeowner.

Restaurants and Bars

Bars and restaurants are, of course, open to the public, and journalists are traditionally granted the same freedom as ordinary citizens to enter the public areas of such businesses. However, this freedom does not mean journalists may do as they please in the name of newsgathering. If a journalist ignores a patron's objection to the newsgathering, that journalist may be subjected to liability just as if he or she had entered a private home. In addition, reporters have not been immune when gathering news in the private parts of otherwise public businesses (such as a restaurant kitchen).

Other Private Businesses

The public areas of other private businesses are generally considered open to the media as well. In private parts of private businesses, the media's liability for newsgathering may vary depending on the means by which the journalist gained access, the methods used to gather news, the sensitivity of the material obtained, or countless other factors. Generally, journalists using either hidden cameras or ambush tactics risk trespass and possibly fraud lawsuits, and if the material obtained and published is highly personal or offensive, the journalist flirts with liability for invasion of privacy. Such tactics should be used only if more traditional news-gathering techniques are unavailable or impractical.

Robert D. Lystad is a partner in the Washington, D.C., office of Baker & Hostetler LLP. A graduate of the Medill School of Journalism at Northwestern University and the University of Chicago School of Law, Lystad serves as co-chairman of the ABA First Amendment and Media Litigation Subcommittee on Libel, Rights of Privacy and Publicity, and Emerging Torts, and as co-vice chairman of the Libel Defense Resource Center Committee on Federal Legislation. Prior to law school, Lystad was a reporter for States News Service, where he served as a Washington correspondent for the Florida newspapers owned by The New York Times Co.

15

Codes of Ethics

Nearly every organization and professional society has developed a code of ethics to guide members in doing their jobs. The news industry is no exception. Some newspapers and broadcast operations have loosely defined codes passed by word of mouth to new staffers. Others are in printed form and are included in employee handbooks.

The Center for the Study of Ethics in the Professions at the Illinois Institute of Technology has more than 850 codes of ethics online, including more than three dozen from the news media. Some are explicit about what a journalist can and cannot do, such as accepting gifts, travel and the like. Others are limited to the rights of those being reported, and issues of fairness and respect for individuals and the environment.

The following codes of ethics broadly cover the profession of journalism and of news broadcasting, both radio and television. UPI's Editorial Guidelines are also listed.

SOCIETY OF PROFESSIONAL JOURNALISTS
CODE OF ETHICS
Preamble
Members of the Society of Professional Journalists believe that public enlightenment is the forerunner of justice and the foundation of democracy. The duty of the journalist is to further those ends by seeking truth and providing a fair and comprehensive account of events and issues.

Conscientious journalists from all media and specialties strive to serve the public with thoroughness and honesty. Professional integrity is the cornerstone of a journalist's credibility. Members of the Society share a dedication to ethical behavior and adopt this code to declare the Society's principles and standards of practice.

Seek Truth and Report It

Journalists should be honest, fair and courageous in gathering, reporting and interpreting information.

Journalists should:

- Test the accuracy of information from all sources and exercise care to avoid inadvertent error. Deliberate distortion is never permissible.
- Diligently seek out subjects of news stories to give them the opportunity to respond to allegations of wrongdoing.
- Identify sources whenever feasible. The public is entitled to as much information as possible on sources' reliability.
- Always question sources' motives before promising anonymity. Clarify conditions attached to any promise made in exchange for information. Keep promises.
- Make certain that headlines, news teases and promotional material, photos, video, audio, graphics, sound bites and quotations do not misrepresent. They should not oversimplify or highlight incidents out of context.
- Never distort the content of news photos or video. Image enhancement for technical clarity is always permissible. Label montages and photo illustrations.
- Avoid misleading re-enactments or staged news events. If re-enactment is necessary to tell a story, label it.
- Avoid undercover or other surreptitious methods of gathering information except when traditional open methods will not yield information vital to the public. Use of such methods should be explained as part of the story.
- Never plagiarize.
- Tell the story of the diversity and magnitude of the human experience boldly, even when it is unpopular to do so.
- Examine their own cultural values and avoid imposing those values on others.

- Avoid stereotyping by race, gender, age, religion, ethnicity, geography, sexual orientation, disability, physical appearance or social status.
- Support the open exchange of views, even views they find repugnant.
- Give voice to the voiceless; official and unofficial sources of information can be equally valid.
- Distinguish between advocacy and news reporting. Analysis and commentary should be labeled and not misrepresent fact or context.
- Distinguish news from advertising and shun hybrids that blur the lines between the two.
- Recognize a special obligation to ensure that the public's business is conducted in the open and that government records are open to inspection.

Minimize Harm

Ethical journalists treat sources, subjects and colleagues as human beings deserving of respect.

Journalists should:
- Show compassion for those who may be affected adversely by news coverage. Use special sensitivity when dealing with children and inexperienced sources or subjects.
- Be sensitive when seeking or using interviews or photographs of those affected by tragedy or grief.
- Recognize that gathering and reporting information may cause harm or discomfort. Pursuit of the news is not a license for arrogance.
- Recognize that private people have a greater right to control information about themselves than do public officials and others who seek power, influence or attention. Only an overriding public need can justify intrusion into anyone's privacy.
- Show good taste. Avoid pandering to lurid curiosity.
- Be cautious about identifying juvenile suspects or victims of sex crimes.
- Be judicious about naming criminal suspects before the formal filing of charges.
- Balance a criminal suspect's fair trial rights with the public's right to be informed.

Act Independently

Journalists should be free of obligation to any interest other than the public's right to know.

Journalists should:

- Avoid conflicts of interest, real or perceived.
- Remain free of associations and activities that may compromise integrity or damage credibility.
- Refuse gifts, favors, fees, free travel and special treatment, and shun secondary employment, political involvement, public office and service in community organizations if they compromise journalistic integrity.
- Disclose unavoidable conflicts.
- Be vigilant and courageous about holding those with power accountable.
- Deny favored treatment to advertisers and special interests and resist their pressure to influence news coverage.
- Be wary of sources offering information for favors or money; avoid bidding for news.

Be Accountable

Journalists are accountable to their readers, listeners, viewers and each other.

Journalists should:

- Clarify and explain news coverage and invite dialogue with the public over journalistic conduct.
- Encourage the public to voice grievances against the news media.
- Admit mistakes and correct them promptly.
- Expose unethical practices of journalists and the news media.
- Abide by the same high standards to which they hold others.

The SPJ Code of Ethics is voluntarily embraced by thousands of writers, editors and other news professionals. The present version of the code was adopted by the 1996 SPJ National Convention, after months of study and debate among the Society's members.

Sigma Delta Chi's first Code of Ethics was borrowed from the American Society of Newspaper Editors in 1926. In 1973, Sigma Delta Chi wrote its own code, which was revised in 1984, 1987 and 1996.

THE RADIO-TELEVISION NEWS DIRECTORS ASSOCIATION CODE OF ETHICS AND PROFESSIONAL CONDUCT

The Radio-Television News Directors Association, wishing to foster the highest professional standards of electronic journalism, promote public understanding of and confidence in electronic journalism and strengthen principles of journalistic freedom to gather and disseminate information, establishes this Code of Ethics and Professional Conduct.

Preamble

Professional electronic journalists should operate as trustees of the public, seek the truth, report it fairly and with integrity and independence, and stand accountable for their actions.

Public Trust

Professional electronic journalists should recognize that their first obligation is to the public.

Professional electronic journalists should:

- Understand that any commitment other than service to the public undermines trust and credibility.
- Recognize that service in the public interest creates an obligation to reflect the diversity of the community and guard against oversimplification of issues or events.
- Provide a full range of information to enable the public to make enlightened decisions.
- Fight to ensure that the public's business is conducted in public.

Truth

Professional electronic journalists should pursue truth aggressively and present the news accurately, in context and as completely as possible.

Professional electronic journalists should:

- Continuously seek the truth.
- Resist distortions that obscure the importance of events.
- Clearly disclose the origin of information and label all material provided by outsiders.

Professional electronic journalists should not:

- Report anything known to be false.
- Manipulate images or sounds in any way that is misleading.
- Plagiarize.
- Present images or sounds that are reenacted without informing the public.

Fairness

Professional electronic journalists should present the news fairly and impartially, placing primary value on significance and relevance.

Professional electronic journalists should:

- Treat all subjects of news coverage with respect and dignity, showing particular compassion to victims of crime or tragedy.
- Exercise special care when children are involved in a story and give children greater privacy protection than adults.
- Seek to understand the diversity of their community and inform the public without bias or stereotype.
- Present a diversity of expressions, opinions, and ideas in context.
- Present analytical reporting based on professional perspective, not personal bias.
- Respect the right to a fair trial.

Integrity

Professional electronic journalists should present the news with integrity and decency, avoiding real or perceived conflicts of interest and respect the dignity and intelligence of the audience as well as the subjects of news.

Professional electronic journalists should:

- Identify sources whenever possible. Confidential sources should be used only when it is clearly in the public interest to gather or convey important information or when a person providing information might be harmed. Journalists should keep all commitments to protect a confidential source.
- Clearly label opinion and commentary.
- Guard against extended coverage of events or individuals that fails to significantly advance a story, place the event in context, or add to the public knowledge.
- Refrain from contacting participants in violent situations while the situation is in progress.
- Use technological tools with skill and thoughtfulness, avoiding techniques that skew facts, distort reality, or sensationalize events.
- Use surreptitious newsgathering techniques, including hidden cameras or microphones, only if there is no other way to obtain stories of significant public importance and only if the technique is explained to the audience.
- Disseminate the private transmissions of other news organizations only with permission.

Professional electronic journalists should not:
- Pay news sources who have a vested interest in a story.
- Accept gifts, favors, or compensation from those who might seek to influence coverage.
- Engage in activities that may compromise their integrity or independence.

Independence

Professional electronic journalists should defend the independence of all journalists from those seeking influence or control over news content.

Professional electronic journalists should:
- Gather and report news without fear or favor, and vigorously resist undue influence from any outside forces, including advertisers, sources, story subjects, powerful individuals and special interest groups.
- Resist those who would seek to buy or politically influence news content or who would seek to intimidate those who gather and disseminate the news.
- Determine news content solely through editorial judgment and not as the result of outside influence.
- Resist any self-interest or peer pressure that might erode journalistic duty and service to the public.
- Recognize that sponsorship of the news will not be used in any way to determine, restrict, or manipulate content.
- Refuse to allow the interests of ownership or management to influence news judgment and content inappropriately.
- Defend the rights of the free press for all journalists, recognizing that any professional or government licensing of journalists is a violation of that freedom.

Accountability

Professional electronic journalists should recognize that they are accountable for their actions to the public, the profession, and themselves.

Professional electronic journalists should:
- Actively encourage adherence to these standards by all journalists and their employers.
- Respond to public concerns. Investigate complaints and correct errors promptly and with as much prominence as the original report.

- Explain journalistic processes to the public, especially when practices spark questions or controversy.
- Recognize that professional electronic journalists are duty-bound to conduct themselves ethically.
- Refrain from ordering or encouraging courses of action that would force employees to commit an unethical act.
- Carefully listen to employees who raise ethical objections and create environments in which such objections and discussions are encouraged.
- Seek support for and provide opportunities to train employees in ethical decision-making.

In meeting its responsibility to the profession of electronic journalism, RTNDA has created this code to identify important issues, to serve as a guide for its members, to facilitate self-scrutiny, and to shape future debate.

— *Adopted at RTNDA2000 in Minneapolis September 14, 2000.*

UPI EDITORIAL GUIDELINES

1. UPI's policy is to provide accurate, fair, objective and balanced news coverage, analysis and commentary.
2. News reports must include context and comment from all relevant sides. Correspondents and editors should test the accuracy of information from all sources and be careful to avoid error. Deliberate distortion is never permissible.
3. Information must be attributed to its source and sources must be clearly identified.
4. Avoid unnamed sources unless there is a compelling reason. A reporter must provide the identities of the sources to a senior editor upon request.
5. Avoid conflicts of interest, and fully disclose associations when relevant. Where the writer has had a significant association with the subject of the article being written, particularly an employment relationship, that association must be disclosed to the writer's editor and should be mentioned in a reader's note attached to the bottom of the article.
6. News analysis represents the best independent judgment of our analysts about why something is happening, its implications and expected outcome. Our analysts have no hidden agendas, the only

agenda is to interpret and explain the news. Analyses should include independent reporting. Material from outside experts must be attributed.

7. News commentaries take positions on issues, offering the writer's opinion whether something is good or bad, right or wrong, likely to succeed or fail, and so on. UPI's objective is to provide a full range of comment, to illuminate all sides of important developments and issues to enhance understanding, but in furtherance of no particular agenda, political or otherwise.

AFTERWORD

Accuracy in reporting news is of paramount importance. Your story may affect industry, the stock market, may lose a man his job, may cause a bankruptcy, may lead to a divorce, a suicide or a murder. The slightest error is a glaring one to those who know. Every news story affects someone; if not, it's not news.

Excitement is a luxury that you cannot afford when writing a story. If you are excited, you are not master of your story. On a battlefield an hysterical soldier is shot or put under arrest. This simple solution is impractical in a news room, so you have to be your own policeman.

Write no story you do not understand. If you do not understand it, editors and readers cannot be assumed to be able to understand it.

"Culture" is a new watchword in America. Scientific news, religious news and news of the arts command ever-increasing attention. Keep pace.

The quickest way to an editor's heart is a short first sentence that tells the story. If it isn't and doesn't, rewrite it.

The coolest man on the hottest story makes the fastest time. One stumble may cost the race. When you start to lose your head, slow up; you're about to stumble.

A reader can do his own "emoting." It is unnecessary to say an incident is tragic, dramatic, pathetic or the like.

If you handle your story in an original manner, the telegraph editor will remember it twice as long. You won't make an impression by handling your story just as the other fellow has patterned his.

Get the name of the person in the story right. Nothing so irritates anyone as to see his name misspelled.

The United Press is an impartial news service. It never takes sides in any controversy. When covering a story developing around a controversy, United Press has but one policy, and that is to present all sides and carry the news.

The United Press keeps the corners of its mouth up.

— *Reprinted from the United Press Manual, Copyright 1929*

BIBLIOGRAPHY

Agnes, Michael E. *Webster's New World College Dictionary,* 4th ed., New York: Webster's New World, 1999.

Banks, Arthur S., ed., *Political Handbook of the World, 1976.* New York: McGraw Hill, 1976.

Banks, Arthur S., et al., eds. *Political Handbook of the World, 1995-1996: Governments and Intergovernmental Organizations As of September 1, 1995 (Serial).* CSa, 1996.

Banks, Arthur S., & Muller, Thomas C., eds. *Political Handbook of the World, 2000-2002: Governments and Intergovernmental Organizations As of March 1, 2000, or Later, With Major Political Developments Noted Through June 1, 2002 (Political Handbook of the World, 2000 2002).* CSa, forthcoming.

Bernstein, Theodore M. *The Careful Writer: A Modern Guide to English Usage,* 2nd ed. New York: Free Press.

Cohen, Saul. *Columbia Gazetteer of the World Online* [www.columbia-gazetteer.org]. Columbia University Press, 2003

Copperud, Roy H. *American Usage and Style, the Consensus.* New York: Van Nostrand Reinhold, 1980.

Editors of the American Heritage Dictionary, eds. *Roget's II The New Thesaurus,* 3rd ed. Boston: Houghton Mifflin Co., 2003.

Editors of the American Heritage Series, eds. *American Heritage Book of English Usage: A Practical and Authoritative Guide to Contemporary English,* Boston-New York: Houghton Mifflin, 1996

Elster, Charles H., & Kipfer, Barbara Ann. *Sisson's Word and Expression Locater.* Englewood Cliffs, N.J.: Prentice Hall, 1997.

Flesch, Rudolf. *Art of Plain Talk.* New York: MacMillan, 1985.

Follet, Wilson, & Wensberg, Erik. *Modern American Usage: A Guide,* rev. ed. New York: Hill & Wang, 1998.

Freedman, Alan, Glossbrenner, Alfred, & Glossbrenner, Emily. *The Internet Glossary and Quick Reference Guide.* New York: AMACOM, a division of American Management Association, 1998.

Gove, Philip Babcock, & Merriam-Webster, eds. *Webster's Third New International Dictionary, Unabridged.* Merriam-Webster, Inc., 2002.

Jane's Information Group, various titles (information on defense, geopolitics, transport, military topics). www.janes.com.

Kennedy, P.J., & National Register Publishing, eds. *The Official Catholic Directory 2001,* New York: P.J. Kennedy & Sons, 2001

Lindner, Eileen W., ed. *Yearbook of American and Canadian Churches.* New York: The National Council of Churches, 2003. (A new edition is published each year.).

Lloyd's Register. *Lloyd's Register of Shipping.* London: Lloyd's Register. www.lr.org

New York Public Library. *New York Public Library Desk Reference,* 4th ed. New York: Hyperion, 2002.

Official Railway Guide — Freight Service. New York: Official Railway Guide.

Official Railway Guide — Passenger Travel Edition. New York: Official Railway Guide.

Pfaffenberger, Bryan. *Webster's New World Computer Dictionary, 10th ed.* New York. Webster's New World, 2003

Shaw, Harry. *Dictionary of Problem Words and Expressions,* rev. ed. New York: Mcgraw-Hill

Skillin, Marjorie, et al., *Words Into Type,* 3rd ed. Pearson PTP, 1974.

Standard & Poor's Register of Corporations, Directors and Executives: 2004 (Standard & Poor's Register of Corporations, Directors and Executives). New York: Standard & Poors, 2004

Strunk, William Jr., & White, E. B. *The Elements of Style, 4th ed.* Needham, Mass.: Allyn & Bacon, 2000.

U. S. Government Printing Office. *Congressional Directory.* Washington: U.S. Government Printing Office. [www.gpoaccess.gov/cdirectory/index.html]

U. S. Government Printing Office. *Style Manual.* Washington, D.C.: U.S. Government Printing Office, 2000.

U. S. Postal Service. *National Five-Digit ZIP Code & Post Office Directory.* Washington, D.C.: U.S. Postal Service, 2001.

University of Chicago Press. *The Chicago Manual of Style,* 15th ed., Chicago: University of Chicago Press, 2003.

Wright, John W., ed. *The New York Times Almanac 2004.* New York; Penguin, 2004. (A new edition is published each year.)